Library of
Davidson College

An Introduction to Algebraic and Combinatorial Coding Theory

An Introduction to Algebraic and Combinatorial Coding Theory

IAN F. BLAKE

Department of Electrical Engineering
University of Waterloo
Waterloo, Ontario, Canada

RONALD C. MULLIN

Department of Combinatorics and Optimization
University of Waterloo
Waterloo, Ontario, Canada

ACADEMIC PRESS   New York   San Francisco   London
A Subsidiary of Harcourt Brace Jovanovich, Publishers

To our parents

COPYRIGHT © 1976, BY ACADEMIC PRESS, INC.
ALL RIGHTS RESERVED.
NO PART OF THIS PUBLICATION MAY BE REPRODUCED OR
TRANSMITTED IN ANY FORM OR BY ANY MEANS, ELECTRONIC
OR MECHANICAL, INCLUDING PHOTOCOPY, RECORDING, OR ANY
INFORMATION STORAGE AND RETRIEVAL SYSTEM, WITHOUT
PERMISSION IN WRITING FROM THE PUBLISHER.

ACADEMIC PRESS, INC.
111 Fifth Avenue, New York, New York 10003

United Kingdom Edition published by
ACADEMIC PRESS, INC. (LONDON) LTD.
24/28 Oval Road, London NW1

ISBN 0–12–103560–3

PRINTED IN THE UNITED STATES OF AMERICA

Contents

PREFACE		vii
PREFACE TO THE ORIGINAL EDITION		ix
ACKNOWLEDGMENTS		xi

1. Finite Fields and Coding Theory

1.1	Introduction	1
1.2	Fields, Extensions, and Polynomials	2
1.3	Fundamental Properties of Finite Fields	7
1.4	Vector Spaces over Finite Fields	10
1.5	Linear Codes	15
1.6	Polynomials over Finite Fields	29
1.7	Cyclic Codes	40
1.8	Linear Transformations of Vector Spaces over Finite Fields	58
1.9	Code Invariance under Permutation Groups	63
1.10	The Polynomial Approach to Coding	66
1.11	Bounds on Code Dictionaries	83
1.12	Comments	89
	Exercises	90

2. Combinatorial Constructions and Coding

2.1	Introduction	95
2.2	Finite Geometries: Their Collineation Groups and Codes	95
2.3	Balanced Incomplete Block Designs and Codes	119
2.4	Latin Squares and Steiner Triple Systems	132
2.5	Quadratic Residues and Codes	139

2.6	Hadamard Matrices, Difference Sets, and Their Codes	144
2.7	Self-Dual and Quasicyclic Codes	152
2.8	Perfect Codes	161
2.9	Comments	165
	Exercises	166

3. Coding and Combinatorics

3.1	Introduction	170
3.2	General t Designs	170
3.3	Matroids	173
3.4	Chains and Chain Groups	175
3.5	Dual Chain Groups	178
3.6	Matroids, Graphs, and Coding	179
3.7	Perfect Codes and t Designs	183
3.8	Nearly Perfect Codes and t Designs	186
3.9	Balanced Codes and t Designs	189
3.10	Equidistant Codes	192
3.11	Comments	201
	Exercises	201

Appendix A. The Möbius Inversion Formula 205

Appendix B. Lucas's Theorem 206

Appendix C. The Mathieu Groups 207

References 215

INDEX 223

Preface

This volume arose out of the book "The Mathematical Theory of Coding" by the same authors. Several instructors mentioned that the first three chapters of the original volume provided a convenient introduction to algebraic coding theory for the mathematically oriented student. The last three chapters dealt with the structure of semisimple algebras, group representations, and their application to constructing codes for the Gaussian channel. A theme of that book was that Chapter 4 on semisimple algebras provided a bridge between the coding theories for discrete and continuous channels.

The first three chapters were essentially independent of the remainder. The publishers accordingly felt that this soft cover version of these chapters would be appropriate. All reference to the last three chapters has been erased, and this monograph is entirely self-contained. The preface of the original has been retained to give a more detailed outline of that book and hence, perhaps, some indication of why the present volume was possible.

The authors would like to thank the publishers for their excellent cooperation and encouragement with this project. They would also like to thank the many students and colleagues who kindly pointed out in the original errors that have been corrected here.

Preface to the Original Edition

The subject of coding theory, for both discrete and continuous channels, has developed rapidly over the past twenty-five years with the application of more and more diverse algebraic and combinatoric methods. The aim of this book is to present a unified treatment of these mathematical ideas and their use in the construction of codes. It is not at all concerned with the practical matters of code implementation, and the subject of decoding is considered only insofar as it relates to the mathematical ideas involved. In many instances we have purposely chosen for a problem an approach that is mathematically more advanced than required in order to expose the reader to as wide a scope of concepts as possible, within the context of coding. Such an approach is not designed to achieve a given result with maximum efficiency.

In many ways this book complements the currently available texts on algebraic coding theory. It is assumed that the reader has an introductory knowledge of modern algebra since it would otherwise have been impossible to cover the contents in a single volume. Many readers will want to skip sections containing familiar mathematical ideas, and the book has been written with this in mind.

The first three chapters deal with coding for the discrete channel, i.e., algebraic coding theory, while the last two deal with codes obtainable from group representations for the continuous channel. Chapter 4 contains algebraic material that is common to both discrete and continuous coding. In the rather lengthy first chapter we have presented an exposition on finite fields together with properties of polynomials over finite fields, the linear groups of transformations of a vector space over a finite field, and elementary geometric properties of such vector spaces. These ideas are applied to the analysis and construction of several classes of linear and cyclic codes. Codes that are best studied from a combinatorial point of view are given in Chapters 2 and 3. Thus, for example, the finite geometry codes, while they can be considered as a subclass of cyclic codes or extensions of cyclic codes and their duals, are in our opinion best considered from the geometrical point of view, where their essential geometric flavor is retained and the importance of their geometric structure is demonstrated. The results of Chapter 3 are all stated and proven with the use of matroids. This was not necessary but was in keeping with our aim of providing maximum exposure to mathematical concepts that either have proved useful or have the potential of being so. In Chapter 4, the structure of semisimple rings is explored. This material is common to coding for both discrete and continuous channels. For the discrete case, of course, it is not necessary to have a knowledge of semisimple rings. However, study of the manifestations of this assumption and the resulting structure of the codes, viewed as ideals in the appropriate algebra, is a rewarding exercise.

Elements of the theory of group representations are contained in Chapter 5. A modern approach to this subject would use module-theoretic arguments. The structure of semisimple rings plays a vital role in such an approach. Initially it was our intention to build on the structure theorems of Chapter 4 to give this approach. This was abandoned, however, since it would have required a considerably expanded fourth chapter. Thus our presentation on group representations is from the matrix point of view and the two approaches are reconciled in Section 5.8.

The final chapter utilizes group representations to construct codes for the Gaussian channel. While this theory is still in its infancy, there are sufficiently interesting results available to warrant inclusion. Indeed, it would be rewarding to the authors if the account of group representations and their codes given here encouraged further consideration of this problem.

Reference to a section within the same chapter is given by the section number only. Reference to a section in another chapter includes the chapter number. The same is true for theorems, the theorem numbering beginning anew for each section. At the end of each chapter are sections for comments and problems. An attempt is made in the comment section to cite sources that for one reason or another were not given in the text. The problems are used both to provide exercises and to indicate results that were not considered in the chapter. Several problems in this last category are quite difficult and for these references are quoted.

Acknowledgments

The authors are indebted to many individuals for their assistance in the preparation of this book. The most significant contribution was provided by Dr. Phillipe Delsarte of MBLE in Belgium, who painstakingly read a rough draft and provided us with many constructive suggestions. In many cases he saved us from making false or inconclusive statements, and we gratefully acknowledge his assistance. The authors are also grateful to Professor W. Tutte for his permission to make such liberal use of his lucid treatment of matroid theory in Chapter 3. Thanks are also due Mrs. Janet Schell for her patient and skillful typing and retyping of the manuscript. Finally, we cannot omit mention of our wives for their understanding and forbearance throughout the project. Their support was greatly appreciated.

An Introduction to Algebraic and Combinatorial Coding Theory

1 Finite Fields and Coding Theory

1.1 Introduction

Many introductory books on algebra contain a section on finite fields and prove some of their basic properties. Often their interest is to discuss Wedderburn's theorem on finite division rings or to consider the structure of groups of transformations of vector spaces over fields. For these ends only the elementary properties of finite fields are needed. In this chapter we attempt to give a more detailed account of the theory of finite fields, including material on polynomials over finite fields and linear transformations of vector spaces over finite fields. For this purpose it is convenient to assume of the reader an introductory course of algebra. This allows an efficient development of the properties of finite fields and places them in their proper algebraic perspective as particular and interesting examples of a more general theory. The next section reviews some of the theory of fields, extensions of fields, and polynomials over fields. No proofs are given in this section since these are readily available elsewhere.

The remainder of the chapter is concerned with the use of finite field theory in the construction and analysis of codes. Many of the important classes of codes and approaches to coding are included. Those that either arise from combinatorial constructions or else are best treated from a combinatorial point of view are considered in the next chapter, along with the required combinatorial background.

1.2 Fields, Extensions, and Polynomials

We shall denote fields by italic capitals, usually E and F or K, L, M, etc. Let L be a field containing a subset K, which is itself a field under the operations inherited from L. Then L is called an extension of K, and K a subfield of L. Every field has a smallest subfield, called the prime subfield, which is isomorphic to either the rationals Q, in which case we say it has characteristic zero, or to the integers mod p, p a prime, in which case we say it has characteristic p. We shall denote the characteristic of an arbitrary field K by char K. For elements of an arbitrary field we shall use lowercase Greek letters, α, β, etc. If $\alpha \in L \supset K$ and $\alpha \notin K$, then the smallest field containing both K and α will be denoted by $K(\alpha)$. Similarly, the smallest field containing K and the elements $\alpha_1, \ldots, \alpha_n$, $\alpha_i \in L \supset K$ will be written $K(\alpha_1, \ldots, \alpha_n)$. Any extension field L of K can be viewed as a vector space over K and the dimension of this vector space is called the degree of L over K and is denoted by $[L:K]$. If L is a finite-dimensional extension of K and M a finite extension of L, then $[M:K] = [M:L][L:K]$.

Denote by $K[x]$ the ring of polynomials over K in the variable x. Then $K[x]$ is a principal ideal domain. A polynomial in $K[x]$ is said to be monic if the coefficient of the highest power in x is unity. It is irreducible if it is not the product of two nonscalar polynomials in $K[x]$. If $f(x)$ is an irreducible polynomial in $K[x]$, then there exists a smallest extension field L of K, which contains a zero of $f(x)$. Furthermore, L is isomorphic to the quotient field $K[x]/\langle f(x) \rangle$, where $\langle f(x) \rangle$ denotes the ideal in $K[x]$ generated by $f(x)$. If the irreducible polynomial $f(x)$ is of degree n, then $[L:K] = n$. If a is the zero of $f(x)$ in question, then $L = K(a)$ and the elements $1, a, \ldots, a^{n-1}$ form a basis of L over K.

It is often of interest to construct fields containing all the roots of a given polynomial and we introduce the following definition.

Definition Let $f(x) \in K[x]$. The smallest field containing K and all the zeros of $f(x)$ is called the *splitting field* of $f(x)$ over K.

The following theorem justifies our calling it "the" splitting field.

Theorem 2.1 Let $f(x)$ be an irreducible polynomial in $K[x]$. Then a splitting field for $f(x)$ over K exists and any two such splitting fields are isomorphic.

If $f(x)$ is a polynomial in $K[x]$ of degree n, then its splitting field over K is at most of degree $n!$ and this bound may or may not be obtained, depending on the polynomial and the field. We now consider some elementary properties of polynomials over a field. If $f(x) \in K[x]$ is given by

$$f(x) = \beta_n x^n + \beta_{n-1} x^{n-1} + \cdots + \beta_1 x + \beta_0, \qquad \beta_i \in K$$

1.2 Fields, Extensions, and Polynomials

then by the derivative of $f(x)$, denoted by $f'(x)$, will be meant the polynomial

$$f'(x) = n\beta_n x^{n-1} + (n-1)\beta_{n-1} x^{n-2} + \cdots + \beta_1$$

which is a polynomial of degree at most $n - 1$. Notice that the derivative of a polynomial may be zero even though the polynomial is not a constant. Thus, for example, over the field of two elements the polynomial $f(x) = x^2 + 1$ has a zero derivative. A polynomial $f(x) \in K[x]$ is said to have a zero α of multiplicity m in some extension field F of K if m is the largest positive integer for which

$$(x - \alpha)^m | f(x)$$

in $F[x]$, where the vertical bar indicates $(x - \alpha)^m$ divides $f(x)$. The zeros of an irreducible polynomial $f(x) \in K[x]$ in the splitting field for $f(x)$ are called conjugates. Let $f(x), g(x) \in K[x]$ be two polynomials such that $\deg f > \deg g$, where $\deg f$ denotes the degree of $f(x)$. By the Euclidean algorithm there exist two polynomials $q(x)$ and $r(x)$ such that

$$f(x) = q(x)g(x) + r(x), \qquad \deg r < \deg g$$

By repeated application of the algorithm the greatest common divisor (hereafter denoted gcd) $d(x)$ of $f(x)$ and $g(x)$ can be expressed as

$$d(x) = (f(x), g(x)) = a(x)f(x) + b(x)g(x), \qquad a(x), b(x) \in K[x]$$

For further reference we collect some elementary properties of polynomials in the following theorem.

Theorem 2.2 Let $f(x), g(x) \in K[x]$ and let L be any extension of K. Then:

(i) If $(f(x), g(x)) = d(x)$ in $K[x]$, then $(f(x), g(x)) = d(x)$ in $L[x]$.
(ii) $f(x)|g(x)$ in $K[x]$ iff $f(x)|g(x)$ in $L[x]$.
(iii) $f(x)$ has a multiple zero iff $(f(x), f'(x)) \neq 1$.

It is significant that two polynomials have a common root in some extension field if they have a common divisor over the original field.

The question of multiplicities of roots of irreducible polynomials can be settled precisely. If $f(x) \in K[x]$, char $K = 0$, and $f(x)$ is irreducible, then $f(x)$ cannot have multiple zeros. If char $K = p$, then an irreducible polynomial $f(x)$ having multiple zeros must be of the form $f(x) = g(x^p)$ for some polynomial $g(x) \in K[x]$. In this case each zero of $f(x)$ has the same multiplicity. We will show in Section 1.6 that if $f(x)$ is an irreducible polynomial over a finite field, then it has only simple (multiplicity one) zeros. Thus the only fields over which an irreducible polynomial may have a multiple zero are infinite fields with characteristic p. Moreover, irreducible polynomials with multiple roots over such fields do exist [e.g., Herstein (1964, p. 193)]. Recall also the following important and basic theorem.

Theorem 2.3 A polynomial $f(x) \in K[x]$ of degree n has at most n zeros in any extension of K.

We consider now the problem of classifying the various types of extensions of a field and give the basic properties of such extensions. In later sections we will only be interested in finite extensions of finite fields, but the present material will place the problem in better perspective.

An element $\alpha \in L \supset K$ is said to be algebraic of degree n over K if it satisfies an irreducible polynomial of degree n over K. That monic polynomial $m(x)$ in $K[x]$ of lowest degree of which α is a zero is called the minimal polynomial of α over K. The other zeros of $m(x)$ are the conjugates of α, the terminology coming from the more usual concept of the roots of an irreducible quadratic over the reals. If every element is algebraic over K, then L is called an algebraic extension of K. It follows easily that if $\alpha \in L$ is algebraic over K and if $[K(\alpha):K] = n$, then the degree of the minimal polynomial of α over K is n. It can be shown that any finite extension of a field is an algebraic extension. An extension that is not algebraic is called transcendental.

An extension L of K is called simple if there exists an element $\alpha \in L\setminus K = \langle \beta \in L \,|\, \beta \notin K \rangle$ such that $L = K(\alpha)$. If K has characteristic zero, then any finite extension is both algebraic and simple. Also, if K is a finite field and L a finite extension of K, then L is again both simple and algebraic.

By a normal extension L of K we mean a finite extension which has the property that any irreducible polynomial $f(x) \in K[x]$ that has one zero in L will have all its zeros in L. It can be shown that if K has characteristic zero, then L is a normal extension of K iff it is the splitting field of some polynomial over K. We will shortly tie the concept of normal extensions to that of normal subgroups of a certain group of automorphisms.

An element $\alpha \in L \supset K$ is separable over K if it satisfies an irreducible polynomial with simple zeros. If every element in L is separable, it is called a separable extension. Every finite-dimensional, separable extension of a field K is a simple extension. We have already noted that if char $K = 0$, then an extension is normal if it is a splitting field for some polynomial. The same is true if K is a finite field. If K is an infinite field with char $K = p$, then an extension of K is normal iff it is separable and a splitting field for some polynomial. The separability condition eliminates the possibility of an irreducible polynomial having multiple zeros.

A field K is perfect if all its finite-dimensional extensions are separable. Any field with characteristic zero is perfect, and it will follow from later work that every finite field is perfect. A field K is said to be algebraically closed iff every $f(x) \in K[x]$ factors into linear factors in $K[x]$. This is equivalent to the statement that K possesses no proper algebraic extensions. Every field possesses an extension that is algebraically closed.

1.2 Fields, Extensions, and Polynomials

We consider now the concept of field isomorphism, which will be useful in the investigation of finite fields. An isomorphism of the field K_1 onto the field K_2 is a one-to-one onto map that preserves both field operations, i.e.,

$$\tau(\alpha + \beta) = \tau(\alpha) + \tau(\beta), \qquad \tau(\alpha\beta) = \tau(\alpha)\tau(\beta), \qquad \alpha, \beta \in K_1$$

An automorphism of K is an isomorphism of K onto itself. The set of all automorphisms of a field forms a group under composition. If $\tau_1, \ldots, \tau_n$ are distinct isomorphisms of K_1 onto K_2, then these isomorphisms are linearly independent over K_2 in the sense that if

$$\sum_{i=1}^{n} a_i \tau_i(b) = 0, \qquad a_i \in K_2$$

for all $b \in K_1$, then $a_i = 0$, $i = 1, \ldots, n$. In particular, distinct automorphisms of a field are linearly independent.

A field automorphism clearly leaves elements of the prime subfield fixed. The automorphism may leave a larger subfield fixed. More generally, if

$$K' = \{a \in K \mid \tau_i(a) = a, i = 1, \ldots, n\}$$

then K' is a subfield of K, called the fixed field of K with respect to the distinct automorphisms τ_i. It can be shown that $[K: K'] \geq n$. We will be interested in subgroups of the group of all automorphisms that fix certain subfields. We shall denote the group of all automorphisms of a field L by $G(L)$ and the subgroup of $G(L)$ that fixes all elements of the subfield $K \subseteq L$ by $G(L/K)$. It is important to note that the fixed field of $G(L/K)$ may properly contain K. It is easily shown that $G(L/K)$ is a subgroup of $G(L)$. Conversely, if H is a subgroup of $G(L)$, then the set of elements of L fixed by H is a subfield of L. This correspondence between subfields and subgroups is fundamental to Galois theory.

We call $G(L/K)$ the Galois group of L over K. If $G(L/K)$ is a finite subgroup of $G(L)$, then $[L: K] \geq |G(L/K)| = $ the order of $G(L/K)$. The inequality arises essentially from the fact that we have already noted, namely, that $G(L/K)$ may fix a larger field than K. If K is the largest subfield fixed by $G(L/K)$, then it can be shown that $[L: K] = |G(L/K)|$. If L is a normal extension of K, however, then K is always the fixed field of $G(L/K)$. Indeed an alternative way of defining a normal extension is to say that L is a normal extension of K if, for any element of $L \backslash K$, there exists an automorphism of $G(L/K)$ moving it.

The original Galois theory was concerned with the solvability by radicals of polynomials and we briefly point out the connection between this problem and the foregoing material. Let $f(x)$ be an irreducible polynomial of degree n in $K[x]$ and L a splitting field for $f(x)$. If the zeros of $f(x)$ are denoted $\alpha_1, \ldots, \alpha_n$, then there exist elements $\tau_i \in G(L/K)$ such that $\alpha_i = \tau_i(\alpha_1)$, $i = 1, \ldots, n$. Of course for any $\tau \in G(L/K)$, $\tau(\alpha_1)$ is a zero of $f(x)$ since $f(\tau(\alpha_1)) = \tau(f(\alpha_1))$

= 0. It follows that elements of $G(L/K)$ permute the roots of $f(x)$, and hence $G(L/K)$ is isomorphic to a permutation group on n letters. Since every normal extension is a splitting field for some polynomial, the same statement may be made for any normal extension L of K.

The Galois group of a polynomial $f(x) \in K[x]$ is $G(L/K)$, where L is the splitting field for $f(x)$. The term "solvable group" originates from the famous theorem of Galois stating that a polynomial is solvable by radicals iff its Galois group is solvable (in the group-theoretic sense of the word). The concept of a normal subgroup is connected with normal extensions in the following way. Let L be the splitting field for a polynomial $f(x) \in K[x]$ and let K' be an intermediate field, $K \subset K' \subset L$. Then K' is a normal extension of K iff $G(L/K')$ is a normal subgroup of $G(L/K)$. The extension L of K is cyclic, Abelian, solvable, etc., if $G(L/K)$ is cyclic, Abelian, solvable, etc.

We conclude this section with a brief discussion of the norm and trace of an element. Let L be a normal extension of finite degree n over a subfield K. It follows that there are precisely n distinct elements $\tau_1, \tau_2, \ldots, \tau_n$ of $G(L/K)$. We define the functions on L

$$N(\alpha) = \prod_{i=1}^{n} \tau_i(\alpha), \qquad T(\alpha) = \sum_{i=1}^{n} \tau_i(\alpha)$$

called the norm and trace of α, respectively. The dependence of these functions on the fields L and K is understood. If we view L as a vector space over K, then by a linear functional we mean a K-linear map of L into K. The set of all such maps is called the dual of L over K, denoted by L^*, and it is itself a vector space over K. The trace function is easily seen to be a linear functional by showing that for any element $\alpha \in L$, $T(\alpha) \in K$. Notice that the trace function is additive and the norm function is multiplicative. Suppose the minimum polynomial $m(x)$ of $\alpha \in L \backslash K$ is of degree n. If τ is an arbitrary element of $G(L/K)$, then $m(\tau(\alpha)) = \tau(m(\alpha)) = 0$ and hence $\tau_i(\alpha)$ are all roots of the minimum polynomial. Thus the minimum polynomial can be written as

$$m(x) = \prod_{i=1}^{n} [x - \tau_i(\alpha)] = x^n - \left[\sum_{i=1}^{n} \tau_i(\alpha)\right] x^{n-1} + \cdots + (-1)^n \prod_{i=1}^{n} \tau_i(\alpha)$$

and the second and last coefficients with appropriate sign changes are the trace and norm, respectively. It is a simple calculation to observe that the coefficients of this polynomial are left invariant by elements of $G(L/K)$ and thus lie in K. We shall have some use for these functions in the investigation of finite fields.

From the foregoing we conclude that a finite extension of a finite field is always separable, normal, simple, algebraic, and perfect. It is indeed a well-behaved structure.

1.3 Fundamental Properties of Finite Fields

Much of the material in the previous section was given to simplify some of the proofs presented here and in later sections and to establish the proper algebraic setting in which to discuss finite fields. Many of the theorems discussed can be proved by more elementary methods. However, such a treatment tends to be less satisfying.

Theorem 3.1 Any finite field L with characteristic p has p^n elements for some positive integer n.

Proof Denote by K the prime subfield of L. The vector space of L over K is of some finite dimension, say n, and there exists a basis $\alpha_1, \ldots, \alpha_n$ of L over K. Since every element of L can be expressed as a linear combination of the α_i over K, i.e.,

$$\gamma = \sum_{i=1}^{n} \beta_i \alpha_i, \qquad \beta_i \in K$$

and since K has p elements, L must have p^n elements. □

The uniqueness and existence can be deduced from the following theorem.

Theorem 3.2 Let L be a field with characteristic p and prime subfield K. Then L is the splitting field for $f(x) = x^{p^n} - x$ iff L has p^n elements.

Proof Suppose L is the splitting field for $f(x) = x^{p^n} - x$ over K. Since $(f(x), f'(x)) = 1$, the roots of $f(x)$ are distinct and L has at least p^n elements. Consider the subset $E = \{\alpha \in L \mid \alpha^{p^n} = \alpha\}$ of L. Clearly E contains p^n elements since it consists of the roots of $f(x)$. Suppose $\alpha, \beta \in E$; then $(\alpha\beta)^{p^n} = \alpha^{p^n}\beta^{p^n} = \alpha\beta$ and hence $\alpha\beta \in E$. Also,

$$(\alpha + \beta)^{p^n} = \sum_i \binom{p^n}{i} \alpha^i \beta^{p^n - i} = \alpha^{p^n} + \beta^{p^n} = \alpha + \beta$$

since $p \mid \binom{p^n}{i}$ for $0 < i < p^n$, and hence $(\alpha + \beta) \in E$. The existence of additive and multiplicative inverses in E is trivial and hence E is a subfield of L and also a splitting field for $f(x)$. Thus $E = L$ and L contains p^n elements.

Suppose now that L contains p^n elements. The multiplicative group of L, for which we shall adopt the notation L^*, forms a group of order $p^n - 1$ and hence the order of any element in L^* divides $p^n - 1$. Thus $\alpha^{p^n} = \alpha$ for all $\alpha \in L^*$ and the relation is trivially true for $\alpha = 0$. Thus $f(x)$ splits in L. Notice that

$$f(x) = \prod_{\alpha \in L} (x - \alpha) \quad □$$

Some important corollaries follow immediately from this theorem.

Corollary 1 Any two finite fields with p^n elements are isomorphic.

Proof Since $f(x) = x^{p^n} - x$ splits over any field with p^n elements and splitting fields are isomorphic (from Theorem 2.1), the result follows. □

We shall denote a field with p^n elements by $GF(p^n)$, the Galois field of order p^n. Where the prime p and integer n play no essential role or are understood, we shall often use the notation $GF(q)$.

Corollary 2 $GF(p^n)$ is the splitting field for $f(x) = x^{p^n} - x$ over $GF(p)$.

Proof This is a restatement of Theorem 3.2 and Corollary 1. □

Corollary 3 For any prime p and integer n, $GF(p^n)$ exists.

Proof By Theorem 2.1 the splitting field of $x^{p^n} - x$ over $GF(p)$ exists and by Corollary 2 it is $GF(p^n)$. □

The following important theorem will be used to establish, among other things, the subfield structure of $GF(p^n)$.

Theorem 3.3 $GF(p^n)^*$ is cyclic.

Proof The multiplicative group $GF(p^n)^*$ is, by definition, Abelian and of order $p^n - 1$. If $p^n - 1 = p_1^{e_1} \cdots p_k^{e_k}$, then, factoring $GF(p^n)^*$ into a direct product of its Sylow subgroups, we have

$$GF(p^n)^* = S(p_1) \times \cdots \times S(p_k)$$

where $S(p_i)$ is the Sylow subgroup of order $p_i^{e_i}$. The order of every element in $S(p_i)$ is a power of p_i and let $a_i \in S(p_i)$ have the maximal order, say $p_i^{e_i'}$, $e_i' \leqslant e_i$, for $i = 1, \ldots, k$. Since $(p_i, p_j) = 1$, $i \neq j$, the element $a = a_1 a_2 \cdots a_k$ has maximal order $m = p^{e_1'} \cdots p_k^{e_k'}$ in $GF(p^n)^*$. Furthermore, every element of $GF(p^n)^*$ satisfies the polynomial $x^m - 1$, implying that $m \geqslant p^n - 1$. Since $a \in GF(p^n)^*$ has order m, m divides $p^n - 1$ and hence $m = p^n - 1$. The element a, by construction, is a generator of $GF(p^n)^*$. □

To consider the subfield structure of $GF(p^n)$, it is convenient to have the following theorem and a few definitions.

Theorem 3.4 Over any field K, $(x^m - 1) | (x^n - 1)$ iff $m | n$.

1.3 Fundamental Properties of Finite Fields

Proof If $n = qm + r$, $r < m$, then by direct computation

$$x^n - 1 = x^r(\sum_i x^{im})(x^m - 1) + (x^r - 1)$$

It follows that $(x^m - 1)|(x^n - 1)$ iff $x^r - 1 = 0$, i.e., $r = 0$. □

Corollary For any prime integer p, $(p^m - 1)|(p^n - 1)$ iff $m|n$.

Proof The proof parallels that of Theorem 3.4 and is omitted. □

In any group G, if $g \in G$ is of order n, then g^k is of order $n/(n, k)$, a consequence of the fact that $kn/(k, n)$ is the least common multiple of k and n.

Definition The Euler totient function $\varphi(n)$ denotes the number of integers less than n and relatively prime to n.

Definition A primitive element of $GF(p^n)$ is a generator of $GF(p^n)^*$.

It follows from these two definitions that the number of primitive elements of $GF(p^n)$ is simply $\varphi(p^n - 1)$. The basic subfield structure of finite fields is contained in the following theorem.

Theorem 3.5 $GF(p^m) \subset GF(p^n)$ iff $m|n$.

Proof Suppose $GF(p^m) \subset GF(p^n)$; then $GF(p^n)$ may be interpreted as a vector space over $GF(p^m)$ with dimension, say, k. Hence $p^n = p^{km}$ and $m|n$. Now suppose $m|n$, which, from the previous theorem and its corollary, implies that $(x^{p^m-1} - 1)|(x^{p^n-1} - 1)$. Thus every zero of $x^{p^m} - x$ that is in $GF(p^m)$ is also a zero of $x^{p^n} - x$ and hence in $GF(p^n)$. It follows that $GF(p^m) \subset GF(p^n)$. Notice that there is precisely one subfield of $GF(p^n)$ of order p^m, since otherwise $x^{p^m} - x$ would have more than p^m roots. □

Example As an example of this theorem, the inclusion relationships of $GF(2^{12})$ can be demonstrated as shown in Fig. 1.

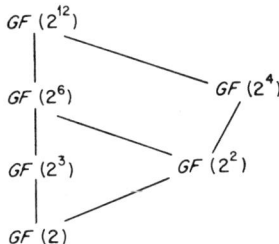

FIG. 1

When considering an arbitrary finite field, we shall often denote it by $GF(q)$, where $q = p^n$ for some prime p and integer n. An extension field of dimension k over $GF(q)$ will then be denoted $GF(q^k)$. It follows from the proof of the previous theorem that the elements of $GF(q^k)$ that are also in $GF(q)$ are precisely those that satisfy the equation $x^q = x$. This is often a useful characterization of a subfield.

Let us now examine the group of automorphisms of $GF(q^n)$ that fix $GF(q)$, i.e., the Galois group of the extension $GF(q^n)$ over $GF(q)$, $G(GF(q^n)/GF(q))$, which we shall denote by $G(q^n/q)$ for convenience.

Theorem 3.6 $G(q^n/q)$ is cyclic.

Proof Since any finite extension of $GF(q)$ is normal, it follows that $|G(q^n/q)| = n$. Consider the map $\tau: \alpha \to \alpha^q$ which takes $GF(q^n)$ into itself. It is readily checked that τ is an automorphism of $GF(q^n)$ that fixes $GF(q)$. The map τ^n must be the identity map i since $x^{q^n} = x$ for all $x \in GF(q^n)$. Furthermore, if $\tau^k = i$, for $k < n$, then $x^{q^k} = x$ for all $x \in GF(q^n)$, which is clearly impossible. Hence $G(q^n/q)$ is the set of maps $\{\tau^j, j = 1, \ldots, n\}$ and is cyclic. □

Most of the fundamental properties of finite fields have been established. These will be used extensively in the rest of this chapter.

1.4 Vector Spaces over Finite Fields

Perhaps one of the first problems that should be considered in any discussion of vector spaces is the existence of certain types of bases, and once again the particular nature of finite fields provides some interesting examples of the more general theory.

The problem of proving the existence of an orthogonal basis, with respect to some form that is yet to be defined, does not depend on the finiteness of the field so much as on the characteristic of the field. A field of characteristic two must be treated separately. In light of this we give only an informal discussion of the problem and for the present will consider the general case of a vector space V over an arbitrary field K. If V is of dimension n over K, we shall sometimes refer to it as $V_n(K)$.

Definition A bilinear form f on V is a mapping from $V \times V$ to K such that

$$f(\alpha x + \beta y, z) = \alpha f(x, z) + \beta f(y, z)$$
$$f(x, \alpha y + \beta z) = \alpha f(x, y) + \beta f(x, z)$$

1.4 Vector Spaces over Finite Fields

for all $x, y, z \in V$ and $\alpha, \beta \in K$. If, in addition,

$$f(x, y) = f(y, x)$$

for all $x, y \in V$, then f is said to be symmetric.

The particular symmetric bilinear form of interest to us will be the usual inner product obtained by fixing a basis in V. Thus if $v_1, v_2, \ldots, v_n$ is a basis of V and

$$x = \sum \alpha_i v_i, \qquad y = \sum \beta_i v_i, \qquad \alpha_i, \beta_i \in K$$

then

$$f(x, y) = \sum \alpha_i \beta_i$$

If $v_1, v_2, \ldots, v_n$ is a fixed basis of V, then the matrix $F = (f(v_i, v_j))$ is called the matrix of the form f with respect to the basis $v_1, v_2, \ldots, v_n$. A change of basis will yield a matrix that is congruent to F. Thus the following definition is consistent.

Definition The bilinear form f is said to be degenerate if the rank of the matrix of f is less then n, the dimension of V. If the rank is n, f is said to be nondegenerate.

Two vectors $x, y \in V$ are said to be orthogonal with respect to f if $f(x,y) = 0$. If V_1 is a subspace of V, we define the subset $V_1^\perp$ to be

$$V_1^\perp = \{x \in V | f(x, y) = 0 \text{ for all } y \in V_1\}$$

It is easily seen to be a subspace. It is also not difficult to show that a symmetric bilinear form f on V is nondegenerate iff $V^\perp = \{0\}$.

For the case of $V = V_n(\mathbb{R})$, $\mathbb{R}$ the reals, if f is the usual inner product, we have that

$$n = \dim V = \dim V_1 + \dim V_1^\perp$$

where V_1 is any subspace of V. For such a vector space it is also true that

$$V = V_1 \oplus V_1^\perp$$

i.e., V is the direct sum of V_1 and $V_1^\perp$ and each element $v \in V$ can be written uniquely as $v = v_1 + v_2$, $v_1 \in V_1$, $v_2 \in V_1^\perp$. For the general case, if f is a nondegenerate bilinear form on V, then, again,

$$\dim V = \dim V_1 + \dim V_1^\perp$$

If f is a nondegenerate form on V, then its restriction to a subspace V_1 may or may not be degenerate. In order for V to be the direct sum of a subspace V_1 and $V_1^\perp$, it is sufficient that the symmetric bilinear form f be nondegenerate on both V and V_1.

As a simple example of these ideas, let V be the space of 5-tuples over $GF(2)$ and let f be the usual inner product. If V_1 is the subspace generated by the vectors $(1, 0, 0, 0, 0)$ and $(0, 1, 0, 0, 0)$, then f is nondegenerate on both V and V_1 and $V_1^\perp$ is spanned by $(0, 0, 1, 0, 0)$, $(0, 0, 0, 1, 0)$, and $(0, 0, 0, 0, 1)$ and $V = V_1 \oplus V_1^\perp$. If V_2 is the subspace spanned by $(1, 1, 0, 0, 0)$ and $(0, 0, 1, 1, 0)$, then $V_2^\perp$ is spanned by $(1, 1, 0, 0, 0)$, $(0, 0, 1, 1, 0)$, and $(0, 0, 0, 0, 1)$ and $V_2 \subset V_2^\perp$. The form f on the subspace V_2 is degenerate and, although $\dim V = \dim V_2 + \dim V_2^\perp$, it is not true that $V = V_2 \oplus V_2^\perp$.

If the bilinear form f on V is such that $f(x, x) = 0$ for all $x \in V$, we call f an alternating form. If V is over a field K such that char $K \neq 2$, then f is alternating iff it is skew symmetric, i.e.,

$$f(x + y, x + y) = f(x, x) + f(y, y) + f(x, y) + f(y, x)$$

and hence

$$f(x, y) = -f(y, x)$$

for any $x, y \in V$. On the other hand, if f is skew symmetric, then $f(x, y) = -f(y, x)$ for any $x, y \in V$. In particular if $x = y$, we have $2f(x, x) = 0$, which implies $f(x, x) = 0$ for any $x \in V$. Thus the case of char $K = 2$ is special and is usually treated separately. However, the result that we want, which we state without proof, is valid for either case.

Theorem 4.1 Let V be a nondegenerate vector space with respect to the symmetric, bilinear, nonalternating form f. Then V possesses an orthogonal basis.

If $v_1, v_2, \ldots, v_n$ is an orthogonal basis for $V_n(K)$, then the matrix of the form f is diagonal. The existence of an orthonormal basis then depends on whether or not the elements on the diagonal are squares in K. Thus for vector spaces over finite fields we are always assured of an orthogonal basis if not an orthonormal one.

For some purposes bases other than orthogonal may be of interest. One such basis has already been used, namely, the basis $1, \alpha, \alpha^2, \ldots, \alpha^{n-1}$ for $GF(q^n)$ over $GF(q)$, where $\alpha \in GF(q^n)$ has a minimal polynomial of degree n. For the remainder of the section we confine our attention to the vector space of $GF(q^n)$ over $GF(q)$.

Recall from Theorem 3.6 that the Galois group of $GF(q^n)$ over $GF(q)$, $G(q^n/q)$, is cyclic and is generated by the map $\tau: x \mapsto x^q$. If there exists an element $u \in GF(q^n)$ such that

$$u, \tau(u), \tau^2(u), \ldots, \tau^{n-1}(u), \qquad \tau^i(u) = u^{q^i}$$

1.4 Vector Spaces over Finite Fields

is a basis for $GF(q^n)$ over $GF(q)$, then it is said to be a normal basis. We now show that a normal basis always exists for $GF(q^n)$ over $GF(q)$. The automorphisms τ^i, $i = 0, 1, \ldots, n-1$ are linearly independent, i.e., if $\sum_{i=0}^{n-1} \alpha_i \tau^i(\beta) = 0$ for all $\beta \in GF(q^n)$, then $\alpha_i = 0$ for all i. However $\tau^n = i$, the identity map, implying that the minimal polynomial of τ as a linear transformation of $GF(q^n)$ is $x^n - 1$. However, since the characteristic polynomial of any linear transformation of $GF(q^n)$ over $GF(q)$ is of degree n, we must have that the characteristic polynomial of τ is also $x^n - 1$. Thus τ can have only the one nontrivial similarity invariant and its rational canonical form must be the companion matrix of $x^n - 1$, or

$$\begin{bmatrix} 0 & 1 & 0 & 0 & \cdots & 0 \\ 0 & 0 & 1 & 0 & \cdots & 0 \\ \vdots & \vdots & \vdots & \vdots & & \vdots \\ 0 & 0 & 0 & 0 & \cdots & 1 \\ 1 & 0 & 0 & 0 & \cdots & 0 \end{bmatrix}$$

implying that there exists a basis of $GF(q^n)$ over $GF(q)$ for which τ is represented by this matrix. Suppose $v_1, v_2, \ldots, v_n$ is the given basis; then the action of τ on this basis is $\tau(v_i) = v_{i+1}$, $i = 1, \ldots, n-1$, and $\tau(v_n) = v_1$. Thus $v_i = \tau^i(v_1)$, $i = 0, 1, \ldots, n-1$, and v_1 is the desired element which gives the desired normal basis. Note that the basis can also be written as $v_1, v_1^q, \ldots, v_1^{q^{n-1}}$. It has been shown that for $GF(p^n)$ over $GF(p)$ there are at least $(p-1)^n$ elements u of $GF(p^n)$ such that $u, u^p, \ldots, u^{p^{n-1}}$ is a normal basis. Futhermore, the element u may always be taken to be primitive, in which case we call it a primitive normal basis. It should be mentioned that the notion of a normal basis of an extension field over a given field arises for normal extensions of infinite fields also.

We shall have need of another type of basis, called a dual basis, which is related to any given basis, say $v_1, \ldots, v_n$ of $GF(q^n)$ over $GF(q)$. We first consider the trace function more carefully and recall that the trace of any element $\alpha \in GF(q^n)$ over $GF(q)$ is

$$\text{tr } \alpha = \alpha + \alpha^q + \alpha^{q^2} + \cdots + \alpha^{q^{n-1}}$$

This function may be viewed as a linear map from $GF(q^n)$ to $GF(q)$, i.e., a linear functional, since it is clear that

$$\text{tr}(\alpha + \beta) = \text{tr } \alpha + \text{tr } \beta, \qquad \alpha, \beta \in GF(q^n)$$
$$\text{tr}(\gamma \alpha) = \gamma \text{ tr } \alpha, \qquad \gamma \in GF(q), \quad \alpha \in GF(q^n)$$

and that $\text{tr } \alpha \in GF(q)$ for any $\alpha \in GF(q^n)$. But now a linear functional from $GF(q^n)$ to $GF(q)$ is completely determined by its action on a basis of $GF(q^n)$ over $GF(q)$. Since there are n basis elements and each element may be mapped into any of the q elements of $GF(q)$, there are preciseley q^n distinct linear functions of $GF(q^n)$ into $GF(q)$. Now choose a fixed element $\eta \in GF(q^n)$ and consider the linear function that takes $\alpha \in GF(q^n)$ to $\mathrm{tr}(\eta\alpha) \in GF(q)$ for any $\alpha \in GF(q^n)$. This is clearly a linear function. Moreover, if $\mathrm{tr}(\eta\alpha) = \mathrm{tr}(\delta\alpha)$, $\delta \in GF(q^n)$, for all $\alpha \in GF(q^n)$, then $\mathrm{tr}[(\eta - \delta)\alpha] = 0$, which implies that $\eta - \delta = 0$ and hence the q^n trace functions are distinct. We conclude that any linear map of $GF(q^n)$ into $GF(q)$ can be taken as a trace function.

Now let $\alpha_1, \alpha_2, \ldots, \alpha_n$ be n elements of $GF(q^n)$. Suppose these elements are linearly dependent over $GF(q)$. Then the subspace spanned by them, say V_1, is a proper subspace. This implies that we can construct a nontrivial linear map f such that $f(\alpha_i) = 0$, $i = 1, \ldots, n$, but that there exist elements $\alpha \in V \setminus V_1$ such that $f(\alpha) \neq 0$, i.e., there exists an $\eta \in GF(q^n)$ such that $\eta \neq 0$ and $f(\alpha) = \mathrm{tr}(\eta\alpha)$ such that $\mathrm{tr}(\eta\alpha_i) = 0$, $i = 1, \ldots, n$. Conversely, suppose that $\mathrm{tr}(\eta\alpha_i) = 0$, $i = 1, \ldots, n$. Then $\mathrm{tr}(\eta\alpha) = 0$ for $\alpha \in V_1$, V_1 the subspace spanned by α_i, $i = 1, \ldots, n$. Since the map $\mathrm{tr}(\eta \cdot)$ is assumed nontrivial, the subspace V_1 is proper and thus the α_i are dependent.

Expanding the trace function, this condition yields the set of equations

$$\sum_{j=0}^{n-1} (\eta\alpha_i)^{q^j} = 0$$

which has a solution for the vector $(\eta, \eta^q, \ldots, \eta^{q^{n-1}})$ and hence for η iff the matrix

$$\begin{bmatrix} \alpha_1 & \alpha_1^q & \cdots & \alpha_1^{q^{n-1}} \\ \alpha_2 & \alpha_2^q & \cdots & \alpha_2^{q^{n-1}} \\ \vdots & \vdots & & \vdots \\ \alpha_n & \alpha_n^q & \cdots & \alpha_n^{q^{n-1}} \end{bmatrix}$$

is singular. This is perhaps the more familiar condition.

We return now to the problem of constructing a dual basis for the given basis $\alpha_1, \ldots, \alpha_n$, a concept that we have yet to define. If ε is an arbitrary element of $GF(q^n)$, then

$$\varepsilon = \sum_{i=1}^{n} a_i \alpha_i, \qquad a_i \in GF(q)$$

and the map or projection

$$f(\varepsilon) = a_i$$

for some fixed i is a linear function from $GF(q^n)$ to $GF(q)$. Thus there exist elements $\beta_1, \beta_2, \ldots, \beta_n \in GF(q^n)$ such that

$$a_i = \mathrm{tr}(\beta_i \varepsilon), \qquad i = 1, \ldots, n$$

1.5 Linear Codes

In particular, choosing $\varepsilon = \alpha_j$, we have that

$$\delta_{ij} = \text{tr}(\beta_i \alpha_j)$$

where δ_{ij} is the Kronecker delta function. Expressing this equation in matrix form gives

$$\begin{bmatrix} \beta_1 & \beta_1^q & \cdots & \beta_1^{q^{n-1}} \\ \beta_2 & \beta_2^q & \cdots & \beta_2^{q^{n-1}} \\ \vdots & \vdots & & \vdots \\ \beta_n & \beta_n^q & \cdots & \beta_n^{q^{n-1}} \end{bmatrix} \begin{bmatrix} \alpha_1 & \alpha_2 & \cdots & \alpha_n \\ \alpha_1^q & \alpha_2^q & \cdots & \alpha_n^q \\ \vdots & \vdots & & \vdots \\ \alpha_1^{q^{n-1}} & \alpha_2^{q^{n-1}} & \cdots & \alpha_n^{q^{n-1}} \end{bmatrix} = \begin{bmatrix} 1 & & & \\ & 1 & & 0 \\ & & \ddots & \\ & 0 & & \\ & & & 1 \end{bmatrix}$$

Thus the β matrix is nonsingular, and the elements $\beta_1, \beta_2, \ldots, \beta_n$ are independent and form the dual basis of $\alpha_1, \alpha_2, \ldots, \alpha_n$. From the form of the trace function and the fact that $\alpha^{q^n} = \alpha$ for any $\alpha \in GF(q^n)$ it is readily seen that if $\alpha_1, \alpha_2, \ldots, \alpha_n$ is a normal basis, i.e., $\alpha_i = \alpha_1^{q^{i-1}}$, then $\beta_1, \beta_2, \ldots, \beta_n$ is also a normal basis, i.e., $\beta_i = \beta_1^{q^{i-1}}$.

We consider briefly the problem of computations in a finite field. Essentially the problem is to determine a suitable representation for the elements of a finite field, so that addition and multiplication are as simple as possible. If x is a primitive element in $GF(q^n)$, then, if any two nonzero elements are expressed as powers of x, say x^i and x^j, multiplication becomes trivial. On the other hand, for addition we have $x^i + x^j = x^i(1 + x^{j-i})$ and we require a tabulation of the elements $1 + x^k$. If one represents the elements of $GF(q^n)$ as n-tuples over $GF(q)$ with respect to some basis, then addition is quite trivial, while multiplication tends to be cumbersome.

Suppose we define a function $z(i)$ on the integers i, $0 \leqslant i \leqslant q^n - 2$, such that if x is a primitive element of $GF(q^n)$,

$$x^j + 1 = x^{z(j)}$$

With the aid of this function, all arithmetic operations in $GF(q^n)$ become simple. Similar functions can be defined for the vector approach.

1.5 Linear Codes

As in Section 1.4, we denote by $V_n(q)$ a vector space of dimension n over $GF(q)$. We fix a basis in $V_n(q)$ and identify an element of $V_n(q)$ by the n-tuple of its components in the basis.

Definition A linear block code over $GF(q)$ of block length n and dimension k is a k-dimensional subspace of $V_n(q)$. It will be denoted as an (n, k) code.

The term block code refers to the fact that all codewords have the same length, i.e., are n-tuples. The word linear follows since the codewords form a subspace. Very often these codes are referred to as group codes since a subspace forms an Abelian subgroup. This notation is less than desirable, however, since over a nonprime field we can have a collection of vectors that forms an additive subgroup but that does not form a subspace, e.g., if $z \in GF(3^2)\backslash GF(3)$, then the set of vectors $\{(0, 0), (z, 1), (2z, 2)\}$ forms a cyclic additive Abelian group but not a subspace.

Definition The Hamming distance $d(u, v)$ between two n-tuples u and v in $V_n(q)$ will be the number of coordinate places in which they differ. The Hamming weight $\omega(u)$ of the n-tuple $u \in V_n(q)$ is the number of nonzero coordinates of u.

Most work in coding theory is concerned with the Hamming metric and we confine our attention exclusively to this case. Another metric for which some results are available is the Lee metric. The Lee weight of a codeword $u = (x_1, \ldots, x_n)$ is defined as the rational sum of the Lee weights $\omega_L(x_i)$ of its components and

$$\omega_L(x_i) = |x_i|$$

and

$$|x_i| = \begin{cases} x_i & \text{if } 0 \leq x_i \leq \tfrac{1}{2}p \\ -x_i \pmod{p} & \text{if } \tfrac{1}{2}p < x_i \leq p - 1 \end{cases}$$

where the components are interpreted as integers mod p, where p is a prime. It is not hard to verify that this weight function can be used to define a metric. Although in certain physical applications the Lee metric may be a more natural one to use, we shall not mention it further.

In the transmission of a codeword over some medium, errors may occur, where by an error we mean any change in a coordinate of the transmitted n-tuple. The point of coding is that under certain conditions these errors can be corrected. We examine the situation further.

Definition By a sphere $S_r(x)$ of radius r about $x \in V_n(q)$, where r is some nonnegative integer, is meant the set of vectors of $V_n(q)$ of distance r or less from x, i.e.,

$$S_r(x) = \{y \in V_n(q): d(x, y) \leq r\}$$

In a decoding operation we can elect either to correct or detect errors, where detection implies that we are aware that an error has been made in transmission but that we cannot correct it. When we say that a code is capable

1.5 Linear Codes

of correcting t errors and detecting $t + s$, $s > 0$, errors, we mean that when t or fewer errors are made in transmission, the structure of the code is such that it will permit the correction of these errors, while if $t + j$, $0 < j \leqslant s$, errors occur, we will be able to detect this fact without being able to correct it.

Definition The minimum distance d of a block code $\mathscr{C}$ is

$$d = \min_{\substack{u, v \in \mathscr{C} \\ u \neq v}} d(u, v)$$

Perhaps the single most important reason for considering linear codes is that the minimum distance of such codes is the weight of the minimum weight codeword, which follows since

$$d(u, v) = d(u - v, 0) = \omega(u - v)$$

and, from linearity, $u - v$ is in the code if u and v are in the code. As a matter of notation, when we want to exhibit the minimum distance (or simply distance) of an (n, k) code explicitly we will refer to it as an (n, k, d) code. The field over which the code is defined will be understood. If the code happens to be nonlinear and has M codewords, we refer to it as an (n, M, d) code, where now d is the minimum distance between any two distinct codewords. If M is written as an integer, then it will be clear from the context whether it refers to a dimension or the actual number of codewords. In order to decode a transmitted codeword, suppose we adopt the rule to choose that codeword closest to the received word as the transmitted codeword. For a large class of channels this results in what is called a maximum likelihood decoder, which minimizes the probability of error if each codeword is equally likely to be transmitted. We can now show the following theorem.

Theorem 5.1 A block code with distance d is capable of correcting all patterns of t or fewer errors and detecting all patterns of $t + j$, $0 < j \leqslant s$, errors if $2t + s < d$.

Proof Assume the block code is a subset (not necessarily a subspace) of vectors from $V_n(q)$. We use the "closest codeword" (also called nearest neighbor) decoding rule described earlier and notice that any received codeword with t or fewer errors will lie in the sphere of radius t about the transmitted codeword. Thus, in order to correct t errors, we merely have to verify that the spheres of radius t about the codewords are disjoint. Suppose that they are not and that $u \in V_n(q)$ lies in $S_t(x_1)$ and $S_t(x_2)$, where x_1 and x_2 are codewords. Then

$$d(x_1, x_2) \leqslant d(x_1, u) + d(u, x_2) \leqslant 2t$$

the first inequality due to the triangle inequality of metrics. This contradicts the fact that the code dictionary was assumed to have distance $d > 2t + s$, $s > 0$. In order to detect $t + j$ errors, $0 < j \leq s$, it is sufficient to show we can detect $t + s$ errors. To achieve this, we show that a received word with $t + s$ errors will not lie in any sphere of radius t about a codeword and hence be corrected in error. By the same argument as before, this cannot happen if $d > 2t + s$. □

It is possible to have a situation where the vectors lying within and on spheres of radius t about the codewords of a linear (n, k) code account for all vectors in $V_n(q)$. Such a code is called a perfect t-error-correcting code. It has recently been established (Tietäväinen, 1971, 1973) that all perfect codes are known. All of these will be encountered in later sections and the next chapter.

Since an (n, k) code, which at times it is convenient to denote by a script letter, say $\mathscr{C}$, is a vector subspace of $V_n(q)$, we can choose a set of basis vectors $v_1, v_2, \ldots, v_k$ and any linear combination

$$\sum_{i=1}^{k} \alpha_i v_i, \qquad \alpha_i \in GF(q)$$

will be a code vector. It is thus convenient to think of the code as the row space of a generator matrix G whose rows are the basis $v_1, v_2, \ldots, v_k$. Since elementary row operations leave the code space invariant, we may also choose a basis of the subspace, such that the corresponding generator matrix G' is of the form

$$G' = [I_k \vdots A]$$

where I_k is the $k \times k$ identity matrix and A is some $k \times (n - k)$ matrix over $GF(q)$. The matrix G' is just the row reduced form of G. Choosing this basis for the code is attractive since it leads to the following encoding situation. If $\alpha = (\alpha_1, \alpha_2, \ldots, \alpha_k)$ is a row vector of k information symbols, then we can identify the codeword $\alpha G'$ with α. In other words, we map the information sequence α into the codeword $\alpha G'$. However, the first k symbols of $\alpha G'$ are the information symbols, and the remaining $n - k$ symbols are certain $GF(q)$ sums on the first k symbols determined by the matrix A. Such a code is called a systematic code.

The orthogonal complement of the (n, k) code $\mathscr{C}$ is of dimension $n - k$, as discussed in Section 1.4, and is spanned by the vectors $u_1, u_2, \ldots, u_{n-k}$, say, where every vector of the code $\mathscr{C}$ is orthogonal to each u_i, $i = 1, \ldots, n - k$. As a subspace of $V_n(q)$, the orthogonal complement, denoted by $\mathscr{C}^\perp$, is also a code and is called the dual code of $\mathscr{C}$. It is clearly an $(n, n - k)$ code and its generating matrix H can always be written in the form

$$H' = [B \vdots I_{n-k}]$$

1.5 Linear Codes

where B is an $(n - k) \times k$ matrix over $GF(q)$. The orthogonality of the codes $\mathscr{C}$ and $\mathscr{C}^\perp$ can be expressed by the fact that if G is any generating matrix of $\mathscr{C}$ and H any generating matrix of $\mathscr{C}^\perp$, then

$$GH^T = 0$$

Thus, for the two particular forms G' and H' it follows that the matrices A and B must satisfy the relationship $B = -A^T$. It will be convenient at times to think of the original (n, k) code $\mathscr{C}$ as the null space of a matrix H^T, i.e., an element $x \in V_n(q)$ is in $\mathscr{C}$ iff

$$xH^T = 0$$

A code defined in this manner is often referred to as a parity check code.

Example Let $\mathscr{C}$ be a binary linear (n, k) code. To show that either the weight of every codeword is even, or else half of them have even weight and the other half odd weight, consider adding a row of all ones to the parity check matrix H of $\mathscr{C}$, giving

$$H' = \begin{bmatrix} H \\ 1 \quad 1 \quad \cdots \quad 1 \end{bmatrix}$$

If the last row is linearly independent of the first $n - k$ rows, then the null space of H', say $\mathscr{C}'$, consists of the codewords of even weight in $\mathscr{C}$ and the dimension of $\mathscr{C}'$ is $k - 1$, i.e., half the codewords of $\mathscr{C}$ have even weight. If the last row is linearly dependent on the first $n - k$ rows, then every word of $\mathscr{C}$ has even weight.

We shall call two codes $\mathscr{C}_1$ and $\mathscr{C}_2$ equivalent if the words of $\mathscr{C}_1$ can be obtained from the words of $\mathscr{C}_2$ by applying a fixed permutation to the coordinate places of all words in $\mathscr{C}_2$. If $\mathscr{C}_1$ and $\mathscr{C}_2$ are (n, k) codes over $GF(q)$, and D_1 and D_2 are $q^k \times n$ matrices formed by using the q^k codewords of $\mathscr{C}_1$ and $\mathscr{C}_2$ as rows, then $\mathscr{C}_1$ and $\mathscr{C}_2$ are equivalent codes if and only if D_1 can be obtained from D_2 by appropriate permutation of rows and columns of D_2. It is clear in a physical sense that this concept can be expanded upon. Suppose D is the matrix of codewords of an (n, k) code $\mathscr{C}$. Then apart from permuting the columns of D, we can multiply any column of D by a nonzero field element and even interchange the nonzero field elements by some permutation of them, and we will not affect the error-correcting capabilities of the code. Now suppose that G_1 and G_2 are the generator matrices of the two codes $\mathscr{C}_1$ and $\mathscr{C}_2$. Then (MacWilliams, 1961) we can call $\mathscr{C}_1$ and $\mathscr{C}_2$ equivalent iff

$$G_2 = A\phi(G_1)\Pi\Lambda$$

where (i) A is a $k \times k$ nonsingular matrix (which preserves the subspace); (ii) ϕ is an automorphism of the field $GF(q)$ and $G_1 = (g'_{ij})$; then $\phi(G_1) = (\phi(g'_{ij}))$; (iii) Π is an $n \times n$ permutation matrix (permutes the columns); (iv) Λ is an $n \times n$ nonsingular diagonal matrix (multiplies columns by nonzero field elements).

Although this definition of the equivalence of codes is natural, we will, in general, reserve equivalence to mean a permutation of coordinate places unless specified otherwise. It is clear that equivalent codes have precisely the same distance structure, but codes that have the same distance structure may not be equivalent. The matrix H is the parity check matrix of the code $\mathscr{C}$ and the generator matrix of the code $\mathscr{C}^\perp$. It is a simple matter to show that for every linear code there is an equivalent parity check code and conversely, and also that the classes of linear systematic and parity check codes coincide. It is, of course, possible to have systematic nonlinear codes.

The equation

$$xH^\mathrm{T} = 0$$

defines a set of parity check equations for the code $\mathscr{C}$. It has been assumed that both x and the rows of H are n-tuples of $V_n(q)$. However, the columns of the $(n-k) \times n$ matrix H are $(n-k)$-tuples over $GF(q)$ and hence we can identify a column of H with an element of $GF(q^{n-k})$ to obtain a $1 \times n$ matrix H' over $GF(q^{n-k})$. The solutions in $V_n(q)$ to

$$xH'^\mathrm{T} = 0$$

are again the code $\mathscr{C}$. Similarly, if s is a divisor of $n-k$, then we can identify a column of H with an $[(n-k)/s]$-tuple over $GF(q^s)$. This formulation of the parity check matrix is sometimes useful and convenient.

Let $\mathscr{C}$ be a given (n, k) code in $V_n(q)$, which we treat as a vector subspace. The factor space $V_n(q)/\mathscr{C} = \{x_i + \mathscr{C}\}$, where the x_i are coset representatives, has significance in decoding. We list the n-tuples of cosets in rows of an array, which Slepian (1956) calls the standard array, and which we denote by $S = (s_{ij})$, where each s_{ij} is an n-tuple over $GF(q)$. The first row of S contains the elements of $\mathscr{C}$ and for standardization we assume that s_{11} is the zero vector. The elements of the first column of S are a set of coset representatives and we assume that each representative is a minimal weight vector of its coset. These are, of course, not in general unique. In coding theory such a set of vectors is termed a set of coset leaders. We denote a set of coset leaders by $\{x_1 = 0, x_2, \ldots, x_m\}$ with $m = q^{n-k}$ and the code vectors by $\{c_1 = 0, c_2, \ldots, c_{q^k}\}$. Thus the element s_{ij} of the standard array is given by $s_{ij} = x_i + c_j$. A simple decoding rule that is maximum likelihood for a large class of channels would be to assume that if a received word x is $x_i + c_j$, then the transmitted codeword was c_j. It is easy to see that if all possible error patterns with t or fewer nonzero coordinate places over $GF(q)$ occur as coset leaders, then this decoding method will correct all patterns of t or fewer errors. If more than t errors occur, then errors may occur in the decoding. Essentially the coset leaders represent correctable error patterns. Clearly, if the minimal weight n-tuple in a coset is not unique and is of weight t, then the code cannot correct all error patterns with t errors. If x is the received vector, we call the quantity xH^T the syndrome of x. Two elements have the same syndrome if and only if they belong to the same coset. If the syndromes of the coset leaders are known, then the table lookup method of decoding may be simplified as follows. For the received word x, calculate the syndrome S. Find the coset leader x_i with the same syndrome. Then $x - x_i$ is the codeword assumed to have been transmitted. It is easily shown that this standard array decoding is just minimum distance decoding.

From the foregoing discussion it is clear that the concept of a perfect t-error-correcting code introduced earlier can be interpreted as one for which the coset leaders are unique and contain exactly all those vectors of weight t or less. Since there are few classes of such codes, the weaker concept of a quasiperfect code is sometimes of interest. Peterson (1961) defines this as a code that, for some t, has all vectors of weight t or less appearing as coset leaders, some vectors of weight $t + 1$ appearing as coset leaders, and no vectors of weight greater than $t + 1$ appearing as coset leaders.

If we are given an (n, k) linear code over $GF(q)$ with parity check matrix H and generator matrix G, there are many ways G and H can be modified to yield other codes. We will mention only two such methods, which will be of use to us. Suppose that to H we add a row of all ones to form H_1. This has the effect of demanding that all codewords in the new code have coordinates that sum to zero. Thus if the all-ones row is linearly dependent on the other rows of H_1, then this will leave the code unchanged. If it is independent, however, then only those codewords in the original code whose coordinates sum to zero will be in the new code. Any process that removes codewords from a code will be referred to as expurgation.

The only other process of modifying a code that we will be interested in is that of adding an overall parity check, i.e., to each codeword in the (n, k) code $\mathscr{C}$ over $GF(q)$ we add an $(n + 1)$th coordinate, which is the negative of the sum of the first n coordinates. This yields an $(n + 1, k)$ code, often called the extended code of $\mathscr{C}$, whose parity check matrix H' can be obtained from H by first adding a column of zeros to H and then a row of all ones. This gives an $(n - k + 1) \times (n + 1)$ matrix if H is defined over $GF(q)$ and is of rank $n - k + 1$. Many other operations of adding or deleting information or check bits may be carried out, but we prefer to avoid a discussion of these since it is very difficult to say much of a general nature on these operations.

Suppose now that we are given two codes, $\mathscr{C}_1$, an (n_1, k_1) code over $GF(q)$ with generator matrix G_1, and $\mathscr{C}_2$, an (n_2, k_2) code also over $GF(q)$ with generator matrix G_2. There are various ways of constructing a third code from these two given codes. For example, one could form a generator matrix $G = G_1 \oplus G_2$, the direct sum of G_1 and G_2, to give an $(n_1 + n_2, k_1 + k_2)$ code with minimum distance equal to the minimum of the minimum distances of codes $\mathscr{C}_1$ and $\mathscr{C}_2$. A more interesting construction is to form the Kronecker or direct product $G' = G_1 \otimes G_2$ of G_1 and G_2, which is readily seen to give an $(n_1 n_2, k_1 k_2)$ code $\mathscr{C} = \mathscr{C}_1 \otimes \mathscr{C}_2$ with minimum distance equal to the product of the minimum distances of codes $\mathscr{C}_1$ and $\mathscr{C}_2$. An equivalent formulation of a Kronecker product code $\mathscr{C} = \mathscr{C}_1 \otimes \mathscr{C}_2$ is to describe each codeword as an $n_1 \times n_2$ matrix such that each column is a codeword of $\mathscr{C}_1$ and each row is a codeword of $\mathscr{C}_2$. The set of all such matrices is the code $\mathscr{C}$.

The parity check matrix method of defining a linear code allows the basic problem of coding theory to be posed in a slightly different manner. Specifically, let H be an $r \times n$ matrix over $GF(q^s)$ and define the code $\mathscr{C}$ to be

$$\mathscr{C} = \{x \in V_n(q) | xH^T = 0\}$$

If W is the null space of H over $GF(q^s)$, then $\mathscr{C} = W \cap V_n(q)$. For a given code distance d we want $|\mathscr{C}|$ to be as large as possible or, conversely, for a given $|\mathscr{C}|$ we want d to be as large as possible. In general, because of the method of specifying H and the different fields being used, it is very difficult to obtain exact expressions for either d or $|\mathscr{C}|$. This situation will become clear when we consider the class of BCH codes in Section 1.7. The problem of coding then may be stated as determining a method of specifying H [over $GF(q^s)$] for general parameters r, n, q, s such that the dimension of the null space of H in $V_n(q)$ and the code distance can be bounded below. The code distance corresponds to the minimum number of columns of H that are linearly dependent over $GF(q)$.

Until recently, by far the most successful solution to this problem was in the construction of BCH codes (Section 1.7). However, a recent discovery of Goppa (1971) has led to the following approach. We consider only the binary codes, although the approach is easily extended to arbitrary $GF(q)$. Let $L = \{\alpha_1, \ldots, \alpha_n\}$ be a set of elements from $GF(2^m)$ and for convenience we assume the elements are distinct. If $x = (a_1, \ldots, a_n) \in V_n(2)$, then we define the rational function over $GF(2^m)$

$$R_x(z) = \sum_{i=1}^n \frac{a_i}{z - \alpha_i}$$

Let $g(z)$ be a polynomial over $GF(2^m)$ and assume that it does not have roots in L.

1.5 Linear Codes

Definition The (L, g) Goppa code is the set

$$\mathscr{C} = \{x \in V_n(2) \mid R_x(z) \equiv 0 \ (\text{mod } g(z))\}$$

We call $g(z)$ the generating polynomial of the code, although this term will be used in quite a different sense when we come to cyclic codes. Let the vector $x \in V_n(2)$ have nonzero elements only in positions $i_1, i_2, \ldots, i_k$ and, corresponding to x, define the polynomial

$$f(z) = \prod_{j=1}^{k} (z - \alpha_{i_j})$$

It follows that we have $R_x(z) = f'(z)/f(z)$, where the prime indicates the formal derivative operation, and all arithmetic is in the algebra $GF(2^m)[z]/(g(z))$. Clearly we have that $f'(z) \equiv 0 \bmod g(z)$. If $f(z) = \sum_i f_i z^i$, then $f'(z) = \sum_i i f_i z^{i-1}$ and $if_i = 0$ if i is even. Thus no odd powers of z are present in $f'(z)$, implying that it is a perfect square. We conclude that $f'(z) \equiv 0 \bmod g^2(z)$. Since the degree of $f(z)$ is the number of nonzero components of the corresponding code vector, the code distance d is such that $d \geqslant 2 \deg(g) + 1$.

To find the parity check matrix of this code, recall that $x = (a_1, a_2, \ldots, a_n) \in V_n(2)$ is a code vector iff

$$R_x(z) = \sum_{i=1}^{n} \frac{a_i}{z - \alpha_i} \equiv 0 \bmod g(z)$$

In $GF(2^m)[z]/(g(z))$ the inverse element of $z - \alpha_i$ is, by direct calculation,

$$(z - \alpha_i)^{-1} \equiv \frac{g(z) - g(\alpha_i)}{z - \alpha_i} g^{-1}(\alpha_i) \bmod g(z)$$

$$\equiv g(\alpha_i)^{-1} b_r z^{r-1} + g(\alpha_i)^{-1}(b_{r-1} + \alpha_i b_r) z^{r-2}$$
$$+ g(\alpha_i)^{-1}(b_{r-2} + \alpha_i b_{r-1} + \alpha_i^2 b_r) z^{r-3}$$
$$+ \cdots + g(\alpha_i)^{-1}(b_1 + \cdots + \alpha_i^{r-1} b_r) \quad (5.1)$$

where $g(z) = \sum_{i=0}^{r} b_i z^i$. Thus $x \in V_n(2)$ is a code vector iff $xH^T = 0$, where

$$H = ((z - \alpha_1)^{-1}, (z - \alpha_2)^{-1}, \ldots, (z - \alpha_n)^{-1})$$

where, again, inverses are in the algebra of polynomials mod $g(z)$. Replacing the inverse elements by the polynomial, in Eq. (5.1) and considering like powers of z, we have $x \in \mathscr{C}$ iff $xH^T = 0$, where

$$H = \begin{bmatrix} b_r g(\alpha_1)^{-1} & \cdots & b_r g(\alpha_n)^{-1} \\ (b_{r-1} + b_r \alpha_1) g(\alpha_1)^{-1} & \cdots & (b_{r-1} + b_r \alpha_n) g(\alpha_n)^{-1} \\ \vdots & & \vdots \\ (b_1 + b_2 \alpha_1 + \cdots + b_r \alpha_1^{r-1}) g(\alpha_1)^{-1} & \cdots & (b_1 + \cdots + b_r \alpha_n^{r-1}) g(\alpha_n)^{-1} \end{bmatrix}$$

The rows of this matrix span the same space as the rows of the matrix

$$H' = \begin{bmatrix} g^{-1}(\alpha_1) & \cdots & g^{-1}(\alpha_n) \\ \alpha_1 g^{-1}(\alpha_1) & \cdots & \alpha_n g^{-1}(\alpha_n) \\ \vdots & & \vdots \\ \alpha_1^{r-1} g^{-1}(\alpha_1) & \cdots & \alpha_n^{r-1} g^{-1}(\alpha_n) \end{bmatrix}$$

$$= \begin{bmatrix} 1 & \cdots & 1 \\ \alpha_1 & \cdots & \alpha_n \\ \vdots & & \vdots \\ \alpha_1^{r-1} & \cdots & \alpha_n^{r-1} \end{bmatrix} \begin{bmatrix} g^{-1}(\alpha_1) & \cdots & & 0 \\ & \ddots & & \\ \vdots & & \ddots & \vdots \\ 0 & & \cdots & g^{-1}(\alpha_n) \end{bmatrix} \quad (5.2)$$

Since $\alpha_i, g^{-1}(\alpha_i) \in GF(2^m)$, we can expand these elements into binary m-tuples and observe that the dimension of the null space of H, i.e., the dimension of the code, is $n - mr = n - m \deg g(z)$. Thus an (L, g) code has length $|L|$, dimension $\geq [n - m \deg g(z)]$, and distance $d \geq 2 \deg g(z) + 1$ if $g(z)$ has distinct roots. There will doubtless be much investigation of these codes.

The minimum distance of a linear code is the weight of the minimum weight codeword, and this is a critical parameter in the evaluation of a code. However, in many practical instances it is important to know the number of codewords of each weight, and this determination is labeled the weight enumeration problem. Although for certain classes of codes a complete weight enumeration is known, in general only very incomplete results are known. In this section we develop the results of MacWilliams and Pless relating the weight structure of a code to that of its dual. The results are important since, if, in an (n, k) code over $GF(q)$, k is greater than $n/2$, then it may be easier to determine the weight structure of the dual code, which contains fewer vectors.

We turn now to the formulas of MacWilliams and Pless. We define the weight enumerator of a code to be

$$A(z) = \sum_{i=0}^{n} A_i z^i$$

if the code contains A_i codewords of weight i. Following the notation of MacWilliams (1962), we will denote the weight enumerator of a given code $\mathscr{C}$ by $A(z)$ and that of its dual $\mathscr{C}^\perp$ by $B(z)$.

Theorem 5.2 (*MacWilliams*) Let $\mathscr{C}$ be a linear (n, k) code over $GF(q)$ with weight enumerator $A(z)$ and $\mathscr{C}^\perp$ the dual code with weight enumerator $B(z)$. Then

$$\sum_{i=0}^{n} A_i [1 + (q-1)z]^{n-i} (1-z)^i = q^k \sum_{i=0}^{n} B_i z^i$$

1.5 Linear Codes

or, stated another way,

$$[1 + (q - 1)z]^n A\left(\frac{1 - z}{1 + (q - 1)z}\right) = q^k B(z)$$

Proof Let V be any u-dimensional subspace and $V^\perp$ its dual. Then we claim that

$$|V \cap \mathscr{C}| = q^{k-(n-u)} |\mathscr{C}^\perp \cap V^\perp|$$

We first note that the dual of $V \cap \mathscr{C}$ is the smallest subspace containing both $V^\perp$ and $\mathscr{C}^\perp$, which we denote by $V^\perp \cup \mathscr{C}^\perp$. Since

$$\dim(V \cap \mathscr{C}) + \dim(V^\perp \cup \mathscr{C}^\perp) = n$$

we have

$$|V^\perp \cup \mathscr{C}^\perp| \cdot |V \cap \mathscr{C}| = q^n$$

Since, from the previous section,

$$\dim(V^\perp \cup \mathscr{C}^\perp) = \dim V^\perp + \dim \mathscr{C}^\perp - \dim(V^\perp \cap \mathscr{C}^\perp)$$

we have

$$|V^\perp \cup \mathscr{C}^\perp| = \frac{q^{n-u} q^{n-k}}{|V^\perp \cap \mathscr{C}^\perp|}$$

It follows that

$$|V \cap \mathscr{C}| = \frac{q^n}{|V^\perp \cup \mathscr{C}^\perp|} = \frac{q^n}{q^{n-u} q^{n-k}} |V^\perp \cap \mathscr{C}^\perp|$$

For a particular basis of $V_n(q)$ take the set of vectors v_i, $i = 1, \ldots, n$, where v_i has all components zero except the ith, which is the unit element. We choose for the subspace V the subspace generated by $\{v_i, i \in t\}$, where $t = \{i_1, i_2, \ldots, i_{n-u}\}$ is a collection of $n - u$ integers from the first n positive integers. To be more specific, we denote this subspace by V_t, and it has dimension $n - u$. We denote by V_s the dual of V_t, and V_s is generated by the set $\{v_i, i \in s\}$, where s is the complement set of integers to t.

The number of code vectors in V_t is $|V_t \cap \mathscr{C}|$, and it is the number of code vectors orthogonal to V_s. Now suppose $x \in \mathscr{C}$ is a codeword of weight i; then it is orthogonal to precisely $n - i$ of the basis vectors v_i, $i = 1, \ldots, n$. We can choose u vectors from a set of $n - i$ such vectors in $\binom{n-i}{u}$ ways. For each choice of u vectors, the subscripts of which form a set s and the vectors generate V_s, the complement set of vectors generates V_t. Thus the number of code vectors orthogonal to a V_t as the set s varies over all sets of u subscripts must be

$$\sum_{i=0}^{n} A_i \binom{n-i}{u}$$

where, as usual, $\binom{n-i}{u} = 0$ if $u > n - i$. If $\sum_s$ denotes summation over all possible sets of subscripts of cardinality u, and $\sum_t$ a summation over all possible complement subsets of cardinality $n - u$, then the foregoing statement can be expressed as

$$\sum_t |\mathscr{C} \cap V_t| = \sum_{i=0}^{n} A_i \binom{n-i}{u}$$

The above argument is symmetric in that it can as well be applied to $\mathscr{C}^\perp$ and $V_t^\perp = V_s$ to give

$$\sum_s |\mathscr{C}^\perp \cap V_s| = \sum_{i=0}^{n} B_i \binom{n-i}{n-u}$$

However, for any fixed set s and t we have already seen that

$$|\mathscr{C} \cap V_t| = q^{-n+k+(n-u)} |V_t^\perp \cap \mathscr{C}^\perp| = q^{k-u} |V_t^\perp \cap \mathscr{C}^\perp| = q^{k-u} |V_s \cap \mathscr{C}^\perp|$$

where u is the cardinality of the set s and V_t is of dimension $n - u$. Summing over all sets of indices s of cardinality u and their complements, we have

$$\sum_t |\mathscr{C} \cap V_t| = q^{k-u} \sum_s |V_s \cap \mathscr{C}^\perp|$$

or, using previous equations,

$$\sum_{i=0}^{n} A_i \binom{n-i}{u} = q^{k-u} \sum_{i=0}^{n} B_i \binom{n-i}{n-u}$$

To obtain the desired identities, we multiply both sides of this equation by z^u, where z is indeterminate, and sum over allowable values of u, i.e., from zero to n, to give

$$\sum_{u=0}^{n} \left[\sum_{i=0}^{n} A_i \binom{n-i}{u} \right] z^u = \sum_{u=0}^{n} q^{k-u} \left[\sum_{i=0}^{n} B_i \binom{n-i}{n-u} \right] z^u$$

Interchanging the order of summation on both sides and using the familiar binomial expansion for $(1 + x)^\alpha$, we obtain

$$\sum_{i=0}^{n} A_i (1+z)^{n-i} = q^k \left(\frac{z}{q}\right)^n \sum_{i=0}^{n} B_i (1 + qz^{-1})^{n-i}$$

Cancelling a factor of $(1 + z)^n$ and setting $z_0 = 1/(1 + z)$ then gives

$$\sum_{i=0}^{n} A_i z_0^i = \frac{q^k}{q^n} [1 + (q-1)z_0]^n \sum_{i=0}^{n} B_i \left(\frac{1-z_0}{1+(q-1)z_0}\right)^i$$

or

$$A(z_0) = \frac{q^k}{q^n} [1 + (q-1)z_0]^n B\left(\frac{1-z_0}{1+(q-1)z_0}\right)$$

1.5 Linear Codes

The formula is symmetric in the sense that if we let

$$z_1 = \frac{1-z_0}{1+(q-1)z_0}$$

then this last equation can be written

$$[1+(q-1)z_1]^n A\left(\frac{1-z_1}{1+(q-1)z_1}\right) = q^k B(z_1)$$

which is the result of the theorem. □

A very elegant proof of this theorem using character theory is given by van Lint (1971) and also in the original paper by MacWilliams (1962). Two generalizations of the MacWilliams identities have recently appeared. The first, due to MacWilliams *et al.* (1972) shows that if one defines the dual of an arbitrary (i.e., linear or nonlinear) code in a certain way, then the identities are still valid. Delsarte (1973a) investigates codes over Abelian groups. Again, with the proper definition of a dual code, the MacWilliams identities still hold. There are also interesting relationships between Krawtchouk polynomials and weight enumeration [see MacWilliams *et al.* (1972c) and Delsarte (1973a)] and some of these are mentioned in Exercise 22.

If the weight enumerator $B(z)$ of $\mathscr{C}^\perp$ is known, then the above theorem gives a set of $n+1$ linear equations in the $n+1$ unknowns A_i, $i = 0, \ldots, n$. In a practical situation it is possible that not all of the coefficients of $B(z)$ may be known and in this case the so-called power moment identities of Pless (1963) may be important.

Theorem 5.3 (*Pless*) Let $\mathscr{C}$ be a linear (n, k) code over $GF(q)$ with weight enumerator $A(z)$ and $\mathscr{C}^\perp$ the dual code with weight enumerator $B(z)$. Then

$$\sum_{j=0}^{n}(n-j)^r A_j = \sum_{j=0}^{n} B_j \left[\sum_{l=0}^{r} l!\, S(r,l) q^{k-l} \binom{n-j}{n-l}\right]$$

where $S(r, l)$ is a Stirling number of the second kind, which satisfies the equation

$$(n-j)^r = \sum_{l=0}^{r} l!\,\binom{n-j}{l} S(r,l)$$

Proof By direct calculation

$$\sum_{j=0}^{n}(n-j)^r A_j = \sum_{j=0}^{n}\left[\sum_{l=0}^{r} l!\binom{n-j}{l} S(r,l)\right] A_j$$

$$= \sum_{l=0}^{r} l!\, S(r,l) \left[\sum_{j=0}^{n} \binom{n-j}{l} A_j\right]$$

Using the result of MacWilliams for the expression in brackets, this gives

$$\sum_{j=0}^{n} (n-j)^r A_j = \sum_{l=0}^{r} l!\, S(r,l) \left[q^{k-l} \sum_{j=0}^{n} \binom{n-j}{n-l} B_j \right]$$

$$= \sum_{j=0}^{n} B_j \left[\sum_{l=0}^{r} l!\, S(r,l) q^{k-l} \binom{n-j}{n-l} \right]$$

which is the result of the theorem. □

As in the case of the MacWilliams identities, we can derive a second relationship, which is

$$\sum_{i=0}^{n} j^r A_j = \sum_{j=0}^{n} (-1)^j B_j \left[\sum_{l=0}^{r} l!\, S(r,l) q^{k-l}(q-1)^{l-j} \binom{n-j}{n-l} \right]$$

For $r = 0$ this last equation reduces to, for $q = 2$,

$$\sum_{j=0}^{n} A_j = 2^k$$

For $r = 1$ it yields

$$\sum_{j=0}^{n} j A_j = 2^{k-1} n - 2^{k-1} B_1$$

and for $r = 2$ it yields

$$\sum_{j=0}^{n} j^2 A_j = 2^{k-2} n(n+1) - 2!\, 2^{k-2} n B_1 + 2!\, 2^{k-2} B_2$$

and so on. In general the identities express the first r moments of $A_0, A_1, \ldots, A_n$ in terms of $B_0, B_1, \ldots, B_r$. Now suppose only r of the A_i are unknown and $B_0, B_1, \ldots, B_{r-1}$ are known. In matrix form the equations would read

$$\begin{bmatrix} 1 & 1 & 1 & \cdots & 1 \\ 0 & 1 & 2 & \cdots & n \\ 0 & 1 & 2^2 & \cdots & n^2 \\ \vdots & \vdots & \vdots & \cdots & \vdots \\ 0 & 1 & 2^{r-1} & \cdots & n^{r-1} \end{bmatrix} \begin{bmatrix} A_0 \\ A_1 \\ \vdots \\ A_n \end{bmatrix} = \begin{bmatrix} f_0 \\ f_1 \\ \vdots \\ f_{r-1} \end{bmatrix}$$

where f_i is a known function of $B_0, B_1, \ldots, B_i$. Transposing to the right-hand side all terms in the matrix product that are known leaves a matrix equation in the unknowns $A_{i_1}, \ldots, A_{i_r}$:

$$\begin{bmatrix} 1 & 1 & \cdots & 1 \\ i_1 & i_2 & \cdots & i_r \\ i_1^2 & i_2^2 & \cdots & i_r^2 \\ \vdots & \vdots & & \vdots \\ i_1^{r-1} & i_2^{r-1} & \cdots & i_r^{r-1} \end{bmatrix} \begin{bmatrix} A_{i_1} \\ A_{i_2} \\ \vdots \\ A_{i_r} \end{bmatrix} = \begin{bmatrix} \gamma_1 \\ \gamma_2 \\ \vdots \\ \gamma_r \end{bmatrix}$$

where the right-hand side is known. Since the matrix is invertible, we can solve for the unknowns.

The MacWilliams and the Pless identities have been used in many ways to resolve problems in weight enumeration. However, there is much yet to be learned on the subject.

1.6 Polynomials over Finite Fields

It was observed in Section 1.2 that finite extensions of finite fields provide some interesting examples of the general theory. The same is true for polynomials over finite fields the elementary properties of which we consider in this section.

Theorem 6.1 Let $f(x)$ be an irreducible polynomial of degree k over $GF(q)$. Then the splitting field for $f(x)$ is $GF(q^k)$.

Proof Let α be a root of $f(x)$ and consider the extension $GF(q)(\alpha)$. If $f(x) = \sum_{i=0}^{k} a_i x^i$, then

$$f(\alpha^{q^j}) = \sum_{i=0}^{k} a_i \alpha^{iq^j} = \left(\sum_{i=0}^{k} a_i \alpha^i \right)^{q^j} = [f(\alpha)]^{q^j} = 0$$

since it was previously observed that $(a+b)^p = a^p + b^p$ over a field of characteristic p. We conclude that α^{q^j} is also a root of $f(x)$ for any integer j. Suppose l is the smallest positive integer such that $\alpha^{q^l} = \alpha$. Consider the polynomial $g(x)$ defined as

$$g(x) = \prod_{i=0}^{l-1} (x - \alpha^{q^i})$$

Now

$$[g(x)]^q = \prod_{i=0}^{l-1} (x - \alpha^{q^i})^q = \prod_{i=0}^{l-1} (x^q - \alpha^{q^{i+1}}) = \prod_{i=0}^{l-1} (x^q - \alpha^{q^i}) = g(x^q)$$

and this implies that, if $g(x) = \sum_{i=0}^{l} b_i x^i$, then

$$[g(x)]^q = \sum_{i=0}^{l} b_i^q x^{iq} = g(x^q) = \sum_{i=0}^{l} b_i x^{iq}$$

whence $b_i^q = b_i$ and $g(x) \in GF(q)[x]$. Since $g(x) | f(x)$ in the splitting field for $f(x)$, then $g(x) | f(x)$ in $GF(q)[x]$ and hence $g(x) = f(x)$. It follows that $k = l$. Notice that the elements $1, \alpha, \alpha^2, \ldots, \alpha^{k-1}$ form a basis of $GF(q)(\alpha)$ over $GF(q)$ since, if a linear relationship over $GF(q)$ of these elements existed, α would be a root of a polynomial of degree less than k, which is not possible. Thus the splitting field of $f(x)$ is $GF(q^k)$. □

Theorem 6.2 Let $f(x)$ be an irreducible polynomial over $GF(q)$ of degree k. Then $f(x)|(x^{q^n} - x)$ iff $k|n$.

Proof Suppose $f(x)|(x^{q^n} - x)$ in $GF(q)[x]$. Then the splitting field for $f(x)$, $GF(q^k)$, must be contained in $GF(q^n)$ since $f(x)$ has its roots in $GF(q^n)$. From Theorem 3.5 we have that $k|n$. Conversely, suppose that $k|n$, which implies that $GF(q^k) \subset GF(q^n)$. Since both $f(x)$ and $x^{q^n} - x$ split in $GF(q^n)$, this implies $f(x)|(x^{q^n} - x)$ over $GF(q^n)$ and, by Theorem 2.2, over $GF(q)$. □

These last two theorems provide some information that we should note. From Theorem 6.2, since $x^{q^n} - x$ has only simple zeros, it follows that any irreducible polynomial over a finite field has simple zeros. Also, if α is a zero of an irreducible polynomial of degree k over $GF(q)$, then the other zeros are $\alpha^q, \alpha^{q^2}, \ldots, \alpha^{q^{k-1}}$. This fact will be important in the following.

Theorem 6.3 The polynomial $x^{q^n} - x$ equals the product of all distinct, monic, irreducible polynomials over $GF(q)$ whose degrees divide n.

Proof If $f(x)$ and $g(x)$ are two distinct, monic, irreducible polynomials whose degrees divide n, since distinct, irreducible polynomials are relatively prime, $f(x)g(x)|(x^{q^n} - x)$. The theorem then follows from Theorem 6.2, and the fact that $x^{q^n} - x$ has simple zeros and can be factored into distinct, irreducible, monic polynomials. □

We now digress slightly to consider in some detail the above factorization and to give some notation that will be useful later. Recall the following definition.

Definition The minimal polynomial of an element $\alpha \in GF(q^n)$ over $GF(q)$ is the monic polynomial that is irreducible in $GF(q)[x]$ and has α as a zero.

Notice from Theorem 6.2 that any element α in $GF(q^n)$ satisfies an irreducible polynomial over $GF(q)$ of degree at most n. Let $\alpha \in GF(q^n)$ be an arbitrary element and denote its minimal polynomial over $GF(q)$ by $m_\alpha(x)$. From the proof of Theorem 6.1, the roots of $m_\alpha(x)$ are $\alpha, \alpha^q, \alpha^{q^2}, \ldots, \alpha^{q^{k-1}}$, where $\deg m_\alpha(x) = k$ and $k|n$. The polynomial $m_\alpha(x)$ is also the minimal polynomial of the other roots. The factorization of $x^{q^n} - x$ of Theorem 6.3 may then be considered as the product of all distinct minimal polynomials of elements of $GF(q^n)$ over $GF(q)$. Let z be a primitive element of $GF(q^n)$, i.e., nonzero elements of $GF(q^n)$ can be expressed by z^i, $i = 0, 1, \ldots, q^n - 2$. It is sometimes convenient to introduce the symbol ∞ to denote $z^\infty = 0$, and we shall use this occasionally. Now form sets of elements of $GF(q^n)$ such that each set is a collection of roots of a minimal polynomial, i.e., each set is of the form $\{z^i, z^{iq}, z^{iq^2}, \ldots, z^{iq^{k-1}}\}$, which corresponds to the minimal polynomial of z^i

1.6 Polynomials over Finite Fields

(or x^{iq^j}). Notice that for each set $k | n$. This process partitions elements into disjoint subsets. Elements of $GF(q)$ are in sets of cardinality one. All other elements are in sets with more than one element. This partition of elements of $GF(q^n)$ induces a partition of the integers $0, 1, \ldots, q^n - 2$ where each set of integers comprises the exponents of the elements in a set in the partition of $GF(q^n)$. Conversely, let i be an integer, $0 \leqslant i \leqslant q^n - 2$, and define the mapping

$$\sigma_{(q^n-1)}(i) = iq \bmod (q^n - 1)$$

This mapping partitions the integers into disjoint sets which we shall denote by s_i and, again, the cardinality of each such set is a divisor of n. Each set s_i is of the form $s_i = \{j, jq, jq^2, \ldots, jq^{k-1}\}$, where the integers are taken $\bmod(q^n - 1)$ and such a set corresponds to an irreducible polynomial $m_{x^j}(x)$, the minimal polynomial of x^j, where x may be taken as any primitive element of $GF(q^n)$. We shall denote the collection of the sets s_i by $\Sigma_q(q^n - 1)$ and the number of sets in $\Sigma_q(q^n - 1)$ by $\sigma_q(q^n - 1)$. The element $x^\infty = 0$ corresponds to the polynomial x and is neglected in these considerations. A set $s_i \in \Sigma_q(q^n - 1)$ will be called a q chain of $q^n - 1$.

A problem that is closely related to the foregoing, and one that we shall require for cyclic codes, is the factorization of $x^n - 1$ over $GF(q)$. Let $GF(q^m)$ be a splitting field for $x^n - 1$ and let η be a primitive nth root of unity in $GF(q^m)$. Then if $(n, q) = 1$, $x^n - 1$ factors into the product of distinct minimal polynomials of the elements η^i, $i = 0, 1, \ldots, n - 1$. Thus the zeros of the minimal polynomial of η^i are $\eta^{iq}, \eta^{iq^2}, \ldots, \eta^{iq^{k-1}}$, where k is the least positive integer such that $\eta^{iq^k} = \eta^i$ and the exponents are taken $\bmod n$. By precisely the same argument as before we can partition the elements η^i into sets, each set corresponding to an irreducible factor of $x^n - 1$. Equivalently, we can partition the integers $0, 1, \ldots, n - 1$ into sets s_i where each set is invariant under the mapping

$$\sigma_{(n)}(i) = iq \bmod n$$

To each set $s_i = \{j, jq, \ldots, jq^{k-1}\}$, integers mod n, there corresponds an irreducible polynomial with zeros $\eta^j, \eta^{jp}, \ldots, \eta^{jq^{k-1}}$, exponents mod n. The collection of these sets will be denoted by $\Sigma_q(n)$ and the cardinality of this set $\sigma_q(n)$. A set $s_i \in \Sigma_q(n)$ will be called a q chain of n or a q chain mod n. Finally, notice that if S is a union of sets $s_i \in \Sigma_q(n)$, then the polynomial

$$f(x) = \prod_{i \in S} (x - \eta^i)$$

is a polynomial over $GF(q)$ and is a factor of $x^n - 1$. Furthermore, any factor of $x^n - 1$ is formed in this manner.

Notice that if $(n, q) \neq 1$, then $x^n - 1$ can be expressed as a power of $x^{n_1} - 1$, $n_1 < n$, $n_1 | n$, and $(n_1, q) = 1$. Thus every irreducible factor of $x^{n_1} - 1$ has the same multiplicity in the factorization of $x^n - 1$.

Let α be an arbitrary nonzero element of $GF(q^n)$. If the order of α is m, then $m|(q^n - 1)$ since $\alpha^{q^n-1} = 1$ for any $\alpha \in GF(q^n)$. As noted previously, the order of α^q is $m/(m, q)$. But $(m, q) = 1$ since a common divisor of m and q would be a common divisor of $q^n - 1$ and q, which are relatively prime. Thus α and α^q have the same order and all zeros of an irreducible polynomial have the same order. If $f(x)$ is an irreducible polynomial over $GF(q)$ whose zeros have order m, then $f(x)|(x^m - 1)$ since $x^m - 1$ has as zeros all elements of order m in its splitting field of order m. Also $f(x) \nmid (x^k - 1)$, $k < m$.

Definition Let $f(x)$ be an arbitrary polynomial in $GF(q)[x]$ not divisible by x. The exponent of $f(x)$ is the least positive integer e such that $f(x)|(x^e - 1)$.

For an irreducible polynomial the exponent is the order of its zeros. For an arbitrary polynomial $f(x)$ the exponent can be found in terms of the exponents of its irreducible factors, but we do not pursue the matter here [see Berlekamp (1968, Theorem 6.21)].

Definition A primitive polynomial of degree k over $GF(q)$ is a monic, irreducible polynomial whose zeros are primitive elements of $GF(q^k)$.

Alternatively, a primitive polynomial of degree k over $GF(q)$ has exponent $q^k - 1$. We have already seen that there are $\varphi(q^k - 1)$ primitive elements in $GF(q^k)$. If x is any primitive element of $GF(q^k)$, then, by definition, $x^{q^k} = x$ and $x^i \neq x$ for $i < q^k$. Thus the minimal polynomial of any primitive element is of degree k and there are precisely $\varphi(q^k - 1)/k$ primitive polynomials. It is clear that there may exist minimal polynomials of nonprimitive elements that are also of degree k over $GF(q)$. These correspond to elements α of order less than $q^k - 1$ but for which $\alpha, \alpha^q, \ldots, \alpha^{q^{k-1}}$ are distinct.

There are $\varphi(q^k - 1)$ primitive elements in $GF(q^k)$. If $d|(q^k - 1)$, how many elements of order d are there? Denote by $N_{q^k}(d)$ the number of elements of order exactly d in $GF(q^k)$. Then we have

$$\sum_{s|d} N_{q^k}(s) = d$$

To solve this equation, we use the Möbius inversion formula (see Appendix A) to give

$$N_{q^k}(d) = \sum_{s|d} \mu(s) \frac{d}{s}$$

where $\mu(s)$ is the Möbius function (also defined in Appendix A). In particular,

$$\varphi(q^k - 1) = N_{q^k}(q^k - 1) = \sum_{s|q^k-1} \mu(s) \frac{q^k - 1}{s}$$

1.6 Polynomials over Finite Fields

By a similar argument we can find the number of monic, irreducible polynomials of degree k over $GF(q)$, a quantity that we shall denote by $I_q(k)$.

Theorem 6.4 The number of monic, irreducible polynomials of degree k over $GF(q)$ is given by

$$I_q(k) = \frac{1}{k} \sum_{d|k} \mu\left(\frac{k}{d}\right) q^d$$

where the summation ranges over all divisors of k.

Proof The degree of the product of all distinct, monic, irreducible polynomials over $GF(q)$ whose degrees divide k is given by

$$\sum_{d|k} d I_q(d) = q^k$$

where the equality follows from Theorem 6.3. By the Möbius inversion formula, the result of the theorem follows. □

We should observe that $I_q(k) \geq 1$ for any prime power q and positive integer k. This is easily deduced from the fact that a primitive element always exists in $GF(q^k)$ and its minimal polynomial is of degree k. Alternatively we can argue from the above formula. Suppose $I_q(k) = 0$ for some q, k and let d' be the smallest value of d for which $\mu(k/d) \neq 0$. Factor out $q^{d'}$ and notice that we have expressed 1 as a sum of powers of q. Since by the construction this sum is divisible by q, while 1 is not, we have a contradiction.

This information suggests a method for constructing a representation of $GF(q^k)$ given an irreducible polynomial of degree k over $GF(q)$. Suppose $f(x) = \sum_{i=0}^{k} a_i x^i$ is such a polynomial and denote a zero of $f(x)$ by α. Then in a splitting field for $f(x)$ the elements $1, \alpha, \alpha^2, \ldots, \alpha^{k-1}$ would be independent. The set of all linear combinations of these elements over $GF(q)$ forms the elements of $GF(q^k)$. Addition follows from the addition in $GF(q)$ and since higher powers of α than $k-1$ can be expressed as a linear combination of the basis elements, using the fact that $f(\alpha) = 0$, it can be shown that multiplication is also well defined. Since $I_q(k) \geq 1$, up to isomorphism any finite field can be constructed in this manner.

Example The ideas of the foregoing theory will be illustrated in the following example. Let α be a zero of the primitive polynomial $x^6 + x + 1$ over $GF(2)$. The minimal polynomials and their corresponding zeros and their orders are shown in Table I. It follows that

$$x^{2^6} - x = \prod_{i=1}^{14} f_i(x)$$

TABLE I

1	$\alpha, \alpha^2, \alpha^4, \alpha^8, \alpha^{16}, \alpha^{32}$	$f_1(x) = x^6 + x + 1$	Primitive
2	$\alpha^3, \alpha^6, \alpha^{12}, \alpha^{24}, \alpha^{48}, \alpha^{33}$	$f_2(x) = x^6 + x^4 + x^2 + x + 1$	Roots order 21
3	$\alpha^5, \alpha^{10}, \alpha^{20}, \alpha^{40}, \alpha^{17}, \alpha^{34}$	$f_3(x) = x^6 + x^5 + x^2 + x + 1$	Primitive
4	$\alpha^7, \alpha^{14}, \alpha^{28}, \alpha^{56}, \alpha^{49}, \alpha^{35}$	$f_4(x) = x^6 + x^3 + 1$	Roots order 9
5	$\alpha^9, \alpha^{18}, \alpha^{36}$	$f_5(x) = x^3 + x^2 + 1$	Roots order 7
6	$\alpha^{11}, \alpha^{22}, \alpha^{44}, \alpha^{25}, \alpha^{50}, \alpha^{37}$	$f_6(x) = x^6 + x^5 + x^3 + x^2 + 1$	Primitive
7	$\alpha^{13}, \alpha^{26}, \alpha^{52}, \alpha^{41}, \alpha^{19}, \alpha^{38}$	$f_7(x) = x^6 + x^4 + x^3 + x + 1$	Primitive
8	$\alpha^{15}, \alpha^{30}, \alpha^{60}, \alpha^{57}, \alpha^{51}, \alpha^{39}$	$f_8(x) = x^6 + x^5 + x^4 + x^2 + 1$	Roots order 21
9	α^{21}, α^{42}	$f_9(x) = x^2 + x + 1$	Roots order 3
10	$\alpha^{23}, \alpha^{46}, \alpha^{29}, \alpha^{58}, \alpha^{53}, \alpha^{43}$	$f_{10}(x) = x^6 + x^5 + x^4 + x + 1$	Primitive
11	$\alpha^{36}, \alpha^{54}, \alpha^{45}$	$f_{11}(x) = x^3 + x + 1$	Roots order 7
12	$\alpha^{31}, \alpha^{62}, \alpha^{61}, \alpha^{59}, \alpha^{55}, \alpha^{47}$	$f_{12}(x) = x^6 + x^5 + 1$	Primitive
13	$\alpha^{63} = 1$	$f_{13}(x) = x + 1$	
14	0	$f_{14}(x) = x$	

In this representation the subfields $GF(2) \subset GF(2^2) \subset GF(2^3) \subset GF(2^6)$ are given by

$$GF(2) = \{0, 1\}$$
$$GF(2^2) = \{0, 1, \alpha^{21}, \alpha^{42}\}$$
$$GF(2^3) = \{0, 1, \alpha^9, \alpha^{18}, \alpha^{27}, \alpha^{36}, \alpha^{45}, \alpha^{54}\}$$

The minimal polynomials and the corresponding zeros of $GF(2^6)$ over $GF(2^2)$ are given in Table II, where $\gamma = \alpha^{42}$ and $\varepsilon = \alpha^{21}$. These computations were carried out with the aid of Table III.

We introduce the interpolation problem for polynomials in order to consider the Van der Monde matrix and determinant. We want a polynomial $f(x) = \sum_{i=0}^{n} a_i x^i, a_i \in GF(q)$ that takes on the values $\beta_1, \beta_2, \ldots, \beta_n, \beta_i \in GF(q)$ at the distinct points $\alpha_1, \alpha_2, \ldots, \alpha_n$ of $GF(q)$. Denoting by **a** and **β** the row vectors of the a_i and β_i, respectively, a solution to the problem is a solution to the set of linear equations

$$\mathbf{a}V = \boldsymbol{\beta}$$

where V is the Van der Monde matrix of the elements $\alpha_1, \ldots, \alpha_n$ given by

$$V = \begin{bmatrix} 1 & 1 & \cdots & 1 \\ \alpha_1 & \alpha_2 & \cdots & \alpha_n \\ \alpha_1^2 & \alpha_2^2 & \cdots & \alpha_n^2 \\ \vdots & \vdots & & \vdots \\ \alpha_1^{n-1} & \alpha_2^{n-1} & \cdots & \alpha_n^{n-1} \end{bmatrix}$$

1.6 Polynomials over Finite Fields

TABLE II

1	$\alpha, \alpha^4, \alpha^{16}$	$g_1(x) = x^3 + x^2 + \gamma x + \varepsilon$
2	$\alpha^2, \alpha^8, \alpha^{32}$	$g_2(x) = x^3 + x^2 + \varepsilon x + \gamma$
3	$\alpha^3, \alpha^{12}, \alpha^{48}$	$g_3(x) = x^3 + \gamma x + 1$
4	$\alpha^6, \alpha^{24}, \alpha^{33}$	$g_4(x) = x^3 + \varepsilon x + 1$
5	$\alpha^5, \alpha^{20}, \alpha^{17}$	$g_5(x) = x^3 + \gamma x^2 + \varepsilon x + \gamma$
6	$\alpha^{10}, \alpha^{40}, \alpha^{34}$	$g_6(x) = x^3 + \varepsilon x^2 + \gamma x + \varepsilon$
7	$\alpha^7, \alpha^{28}, \alpha^{49}$	$g_7(x) = x^3 + \varepsilon$
8	$\alpha^{14}, \alpha^{56}, \alpha^{35}$	$g_8(x) = x^3 + \gamma$
9	$\alpha^9, \alpha^{36}, \alpha^{18}$	$g_9(x) = x^3 + x^2 + 1$
10	$\alpha^{11}, \alpha^{44}, \alpha^{50}$	$g_{10}(x) = x^3 + \gamma x^2 + \gamma x + \gamma$
11	$\alpha^{22}, \alpha^{25}, \alpha^{37}$	$g_{11}(x) = x^3 + \varepsilon x^2 + \varepsilon x + \varepsilon$
12	$\alpha^{13}, \alpha^{52}, \alpha^{19}$	$g_{12}(x) = x^3 + x^2 + x + \varepsilon$
13	$\alpha^{26}, \alpha^{41}, \alpha^{38}$	$g_{13}(x) = x^3 + x^2 + x + \gamma$
14	$\alpha^{15}, \alpha^{60}, \alpha^{51}$	$g_{14}(x) = x^3 + \gamma x^2 + 1$
15	$\alpha^{30}, \alpha^{57}, \alpha^{39}$	$g_{15}(x) = x^3 + \varepsilon x^2 + 1$
16	α^{21}	$g_{16}(x) = x + \varepsilon$
17	α^{42}	$g_{17}(x) = x + \gamma$
18	$\alpha^{23}, \alpha^{29}, \alpha^{53}$	$g_{18}(x) = x^3 + \varepsilon x^2 + x + \gamma$
19	$\alpha^{46}, \alpha^{58}, \alpha^{43}$	$g_{19}(x) = x^3 + \gamma x^2 + x + \varepsilon$
20	$\alpha^{27}, \alpha^{54}, \alpha^{45}$	$g_{20}(x) = x^3 + x + 1$
21	$\alpha^{31}, \alpha^{61}, \alpha^{55}$	$g_{21}(x) = x^3 + \gamma x^2 + \varepsilon x + \varepsilon$
22	$\alpha^{62}, \alpha^{59}, \alpha^{47}$	$g_{22}(x) = x^3 + \varepsilon x^2 + \gamma x + \gamma$
23	$\alpha^{63} = 1$	$g_{23}(x) = x + 1$
24	0	$g_{24}(x) = x$

TABLE III

$1 + \alpha = \alpha^6$	$1 + \alpha^{14} = \alpha^{52}$	$1 + \alpha^{27} = \alpha^{18}$	$1 + \alpha^{40} = \alpha^{55}$	$1 + \alpha^{53} = \alpha^{51}$
$1 + \alpha^2 = \alpha^{12}$	$1 + \alpha^{15} = \alpha^{23}$	$1 + \alpha^{28} = \alpha^{41}$	$1 + \alpha^{41} = \alpha^{28}$	$1 + \alpha^{54} = \alpha^{36}$
$1 + \alpha^3 = \alpha^{32}$	$1 + \alpha^{16} = \alpha^{33}$	$1 + \alpha^{29} = \alpha^{60}$	$1 + \alpha^{42} = \alpha^{21}$	$1 + \alpha^{55} = \alpha^{40}$
$1 + \alpha^4 = \alpha^{24}$	$1 + \alpha^{17} = \alpha^{47}$	$1 + \alpha^{30} + \alpha^{46}$	$1 + \alpha^{43} = \alpha^{39}$	$1 + \alpha^{56} = \alpha^{19}$
$1 + \alpha^5 = \alpha^{62}$	$1 + \alpha^{18} = \alpha^{27}$	$1 + \alpha^{31} = \alpha^{34}$	$1 + \alpha^{44} = \alpha^{37}$	$1 + \alpha^{57} = \alpha^{58}$
$1 + \alpha^6 = \alpha$	$1 + \alpha^{19} = \alpha^{56}$	$1 + \alpha^{32} = \alpha^3$	$1 + \alpha^{45} = \alpha^9$	$1 + \alpha^{58} = \alpha^{57}$
$1 + \alpha^7 = \alpha^{26}$	$1 + \alpha^{20} = \alpha^{59}$	$1 + \alpha^{33} = \alpha^{16}$	$1 + \alpha^{46} = \alpha^{30}$	$1 + \alpha^{59} = \alpha^{20}$
$1 + \alpha^8 = \alpha^{48}$	$1 + \alpha^{21} = \alpha^{42}$	$1 + \alpha^{34} = \alpha^{31}$	$1 + \alpha^{47} = \alpha^{17}$	$1 + \alpha^{60} = \alpha^{29}$
$1 + \alpha^9 = \alpha^{45}$	$1 + \alpha^{22} = \alpha^{50}$	$1 + \alpha^{35} = \alpha^{13}$	$1 + \alpha^{48} = \alpha^8$	$1 + \alpha^{61} = \alpha^{10}$
$1 + \alpha^{10} = \alpha^{61}$	$1 + \alpha^{23} = \alpha^{15}$	$1 + \alpha^{26} = \alpha^{54}$	$1 + \alpha^{49} = \alpha^{38}$	$1 + \alpha^{62} = \alpha^5$
$1 + \alpha^{11} = \alpha^{25}$	$1 + \alpha^{24} = \alpha^4$	$1 + \alpha^{37} = \alpha^{44}$	$1 + \alpha^{50} = \alpha^{22}$	$1 + \alpha^{63} = 0$
$1 + \alpha^{12} = \alpha^2$	$1 + \alpha^{25} = \alpha^{11}$	$1 + \alpha^{38} = \alpha^{49}$	$1 + \alpha^{51} = \alpha^{53}$	
$1 + \alpha^{13} = \alpha^{35}$	$1 + \alpha^{26} = \alpha^7$	$1 + \alpha^{39} = \alpha^{43}$	$1 + \alpha^{52} = \alpha^{14}$	

The determinant of V is zero if $\alpha_i = \alpha_j$ for $i \neq j$ and hence $\Pi_{i>j}(\alpha_i - \alpha_j) | |V|$. Since the coefficient of the term $1\alpha_2\alpha_3^2 \cdots \alpha_n^{n-1}$ is unity in both $|V|$ and $\Pi_{i>j}(\alpha_i - \alpha_j)$ and since they are polynomials of the same degrees in the α's, we must have that

$$|V| = \prod_{i>j}(\alpha_i - \alpha_j)$$

For certain cases an explicit form for V^{-1} may be exhibited if $|V| \neq 0$. Of course, $|V| \neq 0$ iff $\alpha_i \neq \alpha_j$; $i \neq j$, a fact that has been used previously in this chapter.

Any two polynomials of degree less than or equal to n whose values coincide at $n + 1$ points must be equal since the difference of the polynomials, which is of degree at most n, has $n + 1$ roots. Suppose then that $\beta_i = f(\alpha_i)$, $i = 0, 1, \ldots, n$, at the $n + 1$ points $\alpha_0, \alpha_1, \ldots, \alpha_n$. The polynomial

$$f(x) = \sum \beta_i \left(\prod_{\substack{j=0 \\ j \neq i}}^{n} \frac{x - \alpha_j}{\alpha_i - \alpha_j} \right)$$

satisfies these conditions and since it is of degree n or less, it is the unique polynomial of this degree that does so. The above formula is the Lagrange interpolation formula.

Let the monic polynomial $f(x) = \sum_{i=0}^{m} a_{m-i} x^i$ over $GF(q)$ split in $GF(q^n)$ and let its roots be $\alpha_1, \ldots, \alpha_m$, i.e.,

$$f(x) = \sum_{i=0}^{m} a_{m-i} x^i = \prod_{i=1}^{m}(x - \alpha_i), \qquad a_0 = 1$$

Define the functions of the zeros

$$\beta_1 = \alpha_1 + \alpha_2 + \cdots + \alpha_m$$
$$\beta_2 = \alpha_1\alpha_2 + \alpha_1\alpha_3 + \cdots + \alpha_2\alpha_3 + \alpha_2\alpha_4 + \cdots + \alpha_{m-1}\alpha_m$$
$$\vdots$$
$$\beta_m = \alpha_1\alpha_2 \cdots \alpha_m$$

where $\beta_i = (-1)^i a_i$. We can regard these functions as functions of m variables $\alpha_1, \alpha_2, \ldots, \alpha_m$. A function of m variables that is unchanged by a permutation of the variables is called a symmetric function. The functions β_i play a central role in the theory of such functions and are called the elementary symmetric functions. Notice that since $f(x)$ is a polynomial over $GF(q)$ the elementary symmetric functions are invariant under any automorphism of $G(q^n/q)$. If $f(x)$ is irreducible over $GF(q)$, then it splits in $GF(q^m)$ and $\alpha_i = \alpha_1^{q^{i-1}}$, $i = 1, \ldots, m$. Thus the function β_1 is the trace of any of the roots of $f(x)$ over $GF(q)$ and β_m is the norm function.

1.6 Polynomials over Finite Fields

Let P_i denote the sum of the ith powers of the roots of the arbitrary monic polynomial $f(x)$ of degree m over $GF(q)$. By direct computation the following recursive relationships can be derived:

$$0 = P_1 + a_1$$
$$0 = P_2 + a_1 P_1 + 2a_2$$
$$\vdots$$
$$0 = P_{m-1} + a_1 P_{m-2} + a_2 P_{m-3} + \cdots + (m-1)a_{m-1}$$

To these equations we can add the following:

$$0 = P_m + a_1 P_{m-1} + a_2 P_{m-2} + \cdots + ma_m$$
$$0 = P_{m+1} + a_1 P_m + a_2 P_{m-1} + \cdots + a_m P_1$$

and in general, for $l > m$,

$$0 = P_l + a_1 P_{l-1} + a_2 P_{l-2} + \cdots + a_m P_{l-m}.$$

These equations are easily found by equating the quantities $\sum_{i=1}^{m} \alpha_i^k f(\alpha_i)$ to zero. Together with the previous equations they are called the Newton identities.

Apply these equations and the previous ones to the polynomial

$$f(x) = x^q - x$$

which, of course, splits over $GF(q)$ and has all the elements of $GF(q)$ as zeros. Since $a_i = 0$, $i \neq q-1$, and $a_{q-1} = -1$, we conclude that $P_i = 0$ for $0 < i < q-1$ and $P_{q-1} = q-1$. Since, in $GF(q)$, $\alpha^q = \alpha$, we can reduce exponents $(q-1)$ for nonzero elements and state the following:

Theorem 6.5 Let θ_i, $i > 0$, denote the sum of the ith powers of the elements of $GF(q)$. Then

$$\theta_i = \begin{cases} q - 1 & \text{if } (q-1) | i \\ 0 & \text{otherwise} \end{cases}$$

There is a fascinating literature on the study of polynomials over a finite field but it would be inappropriate to review it here. The work tends to be on factorizing polynomials and determining irreducible polynomials. The books by Dickson (1958) and Albert (1956) contain much information on these problems. We have relegated to the exercises some of these interesting results. On the factorization of polynomials, the algorithm by Berlekamp is very efficient and is described in Chapter 6 of his book (Berlekamp, 1968). The problem has also been considered by Swan (1962) and McEliece (1969). The irreducibility of trinomials, polynomials of the form $x^n + x^k + 1$ has also received a great deal of attention. The problem is of importance in the generation of shift register sequences with specified properties. Swan (1962) gives some important results on the problem and much of the work is described by Berlekamp (1968). Zierler and Brillhart (1968) give a listing of all binary irreducible trinomials of degree <1000 as well as indicating which ones are primitive and the exponents of those that are not. Zierler (1970) lists all irreducible trinomials of the form $x^n + x + 1$, $n < 30,000$, together with their exponent. We conclude this section with a discussion of two problems, the irreducibility of $x^{k-1} + x^{k-2} + \cdots + x + 1$ and the cyclotomic factorization of $x^n - 1$. Since these problems illustrate much of the foregoing material, we present them as examples.

Example. Cyclotomic Polynomials In the factorization of $x^{q^m} - x$ over $GF(q)$ one approach is to sort out roots of unity according to their order. This approach has already been considered in another context. Consider the equation $x^n - 1 = 0$ in the field of complex numbers, which contains n roots of unity. There are $\varphi(n)$ primitive nth roots of unity.

Definition The polynomial

$$\Phi_n(x) = \prod_{(i,n)=1} (x - \beta^i)$$

where β is a primitive nth root of unity, is called the nth cyclotomic polynomial. It is of degree $\varphi(n)$.

If $n = kd$, then β^k is of order d and is a primitive dth root of unity. We can write the dth cyclotomic polynomial as

$$\Phi_d(x) = \prod_{(i,d)=1} (x - \beta^{ik})$$

Clearly each nth root of unity will be a primitive dth root of unity for precisely one d and this leads to a sorting of the n roots. The sorting leads to the factorization of $x^n - 1$:

$$x^n - 1 = \prod_{\substack{1 \leq d \leq n \\ d|n}} \Phi_d(x)$$

which is referred to as the cyclotomic factorization of $x^n - 1$. Applying the Möbius inversion formula to this equation gives

$$\Phi_n(x) = \prod_{d|n} (x^d - 1)^{\mu(n/d)} = \prod_{d|n} (x^{n/d} - 1)^{\mu(d)}.$$

The first three cyclotomic polynomials are

$$\Phi_1(x) = x - 1, \quad \Phi_2(x) = x + 1, \quad \Phi_3(x) = x^2 + x + 1$$

It is readily established, either by induction or by inspection of the formula for $\Phi_n(x)$, that all cyclotomic polynomials have integer coefficients. In fact, the first 104 cylotomic polynomials have coefficients that are either

1.6 Polynomials over Finite Fields

$+1$, 0, or -1. The 105th has a coefficient that is $+2$. It is also true that we can always find an n, for a given integer N, such that $\Phi_n(x)$ has a coefficient larger then N. The cyclotomic polynomials are irreducible over the rationals.

As an example of this situation that will also point out the relevance of factoring $x^n - 1$ over a finite field, consider the cyclotomic factorization of $x^{15} - 1$ over the complex numbers. We have that

$$x^{15} - 1 = \Phi_{15}(x)\Phi_5(x)\Phi_3(x)\Phi_1(x)$$

where

$$\Phi_1(x) = x - 1, \qquad \Phi_3(x) = x^2 + x + 1$$

$$\Phi_5(x) = \frac{(x^5 - 1)}{(x - 1)} = x^4 + x^3 + x^2 + x + 1$$

and

$$\Phi_{15}(x) = \frac{(x^{15} - 1)(x - 1)}{(x^5 - 1)(x^3 - 1)} = x^8 - x^7 + x^5 - x^4 + x^3 - x + 1$$

Although this factorization was over the complex numbers, it could equally well have been performed over any field containing primitive nth roots of unity. In particular, in $GF(p^n)$

$$x^{p^n - 1} - 1 = \prod_{d | p^n - 1} \Phi_d(x)$$

where, of course, the coefficients of $\Phi_d(x)$ are field integers. The $\Phi_d(x)$ are not, in general, irreducible over a subfield of $GF(p^n)$, but the foregoing is at least a partial factorization of $x^{p^n - 1} - 1$. Notice that $\Phi_d(x)$ has as roots all elements in $GF(p^n)$ of order d. An element of order d in an extension field of $GF(q)$ has a minimal polynomial of degree k over $GF(q)$ where k is the smallest integer such that $d | q^k - 1$. There are $\varphi(d)$ elements of order d and hence there are $\varphi(d)/k$ irreducible polynomials of degree k over $GF(q)$ of exponent d. Their product is equal to $\Phi_d(x)$, where the coefficients are taken as field integers.

From our previous factorization of $x^{15} - 1$ over $\mathbb{C}$, we consider the factorization over $GF(2)$. Since $15 | (2^4 - 1)$ and $\Phi_{15}(x)$ is a polynomial of degree eight, it must factor into two irreducible polynomials of degree four over $GF(2)$. In fact we have

$$\Phi_{15}(x) = x^8 + x^7 + x^5 + x^4 + x^3 + x + 1 \qquad [\text{over} \quad GF(2)]$$
$$= (x^4 + x + 1)(x^4 + x^3 + 1)$$

where the two polynomials in brackets are irreducible over $GF(2)$. The polynomials $\Phi_1(x)$ [$= x + 1$ over $GF(2)$], $\Phi_3(x)$, and $\Phi_5(x)$ are irreducible over $GF(2)$. Thus the problem of factorizing $x^n - 1$ over a finite field, which, as we will see later, has importance in coding theory, may be assisted by considering first the cyclotomic factorization over $\mathbb{C}$ and determining the number of irreducible polynomials of the same degree contained in the factorization of each cyclotomic polynomial.

Example. Irreducibility of Certain Polynomials Consider first the number of irreducible polynomials of degree m over $GF(q)$ of exponent e. Since the smallest extension field of $GF(q)$ containing the roots of an irreducible polynomial of degree m over $GF(q)$ is $GF(q^m)$, then $e|(q^m - 1)$ and $e \nmid (q^k - 1)$ $k < m$. Since $e|(q^m - 1)$, we have that $(x^e - 1) | (x^{q^m-1} - 1)$ and $GF(q^m)$ contains all the eth roots of unity in this case. Thus it contains $\varphi(e)$ primitive eth roots of unity, of which we suppose β is one. From the previous consideration the elements $\beta, \beta^q, \beta^{q^2}, \ldots, \beta^{q^{m-1}}$ are distinct, and thus the minimal polynomial of any primitive eth root of unity is of degree m. We conclude that there are precisely $\varphi(e)/m$ irreducible polynomials of exponent e and note that the only dependence of q is through the condition that $e|(q^m - 1)$ and $e \nmid (q^k - 1)$, $k < m$.

We now ask the question, when is

$$f(x) = \frac{x^e - 1}{x - 1} = x^{e-1} + x^{e-2} + \cdots + x^2 + x + 1$$

irreducible over $GF(q)$? We must have only a single irreducible polynomial of exponent e, which implies that $m = e - 1$ and $\varphi(e)/(e-1) = 1$, which implies that e is a prime number. Furthermore, it must be true that $e|(q^{e-1} - 1)$ but $e \nmid (q^k - 1)$, $k < e - 1$, i.e., q is a primitive $(e-1)$th root of unity mod e. Thus $f(x)$ is irreducible over $GF(q)$ iff these conditions are satisfied.

In a similar vein it is possible to show that the polynomial $\varepsilon^p x^p - \varepsilon x - \gamma$, $\varepsilon \neq 0$, ε, γ in $GF(q), q = p^n$, is irreducible over $GF(q)$ iff the trace of γ in $GF(q)$ over $GF(p)$ is nonzero. First observe that $\varepsilon^p x^p - \varepsilon x - \gamma$ is reducible over $GF(q)$ iff it has a root in $GF(q)$. Notice that if $x^p - x = \gamma$, then $\gamma + \gamma^p + \cdots + \gamma^{p^{n-1}} = x^{p^n} - x$. Thus if x is any element of $GF(q)$, then $x^q - x = 0$ and it follows that tr $\gamma = 0$. Conversely, if tr $\gamma \neq 0$, then there can be no solution in $GF(q)$. There are many other constructions of irreducible polynomials and the reader is referred to the books by Dickson (1958, pp. 19–44) and Albert (1956, pp. 132–155). A few of the more interesting theorems have been included as exercises at the end of this chapter.

1.7 Cyclic Codes

The class of linear codes is unfortunately still too general for us to say much on the problem of constructing codes with good distance properties. We therefore add another restriction.

1.7 Cyclic Codes

Definition A code is cyclic if it is linear and if every cyclic shift of the coordinates of a codeword is a codeword.

Thus if $c = (\alpha_0, \alpha_1, \ldots, \alpha_{n-1})$ is a codeword, then $(\alpha_{n-1}, \alpha_0, \alpha_1, \ldots, \alpha_{n-2})$ is also a codeword. It is convenient to identify a codeword with a codeword polynomial. The codeword polynomial for the codeword c is

$$c(x) = \sum_{i=0}^{n-1} \alpha_i x^i$$

A cyclic shift of this codeword c is equivalent to multiplication by x and reducing exponents mod n. However, reducing exponents mod n is equivalent to reducing the polynomial mod $(x^n - 1)$.

Let $GF(q)[x]$ denote the set of all polynomials over $GF(q)$ in the variable x. This is a principal ideal domain and there is a natural isomorphism between the quotient ring $GF(q)[x]/(x^n - 1)$, where $(x^n - 1)$ is the ideal generated by the polynomial $x^n - 1$, and the ring of polynomials of degree less than n with multiplication defined mod $(x^n - 1)$. We shall denote the ring $GF(q)[x]/(x^n - 1)$ by A_n. It is also an algebra over $GF(q)$. The ideal consisting of all multiples of the element $a(x)$ will be denoted $(a(x))$. We mention again that a codeword, which is an n-tuple over $GF(q)$, is identified with an element of A_n. The algebra A_n is, of course, a commutative ring with identity and a principal ideal domain, so that every ideal has a single generator. In Chapter 4 we will consider the structure of A_n from the purely algebraic point of view. The algebra A_n is isomorphic to the group algebra $GF(q)C_n$, C_n the cyclic group of order n, and in this formulation it leads to an interesting generalization. The following theorem is of a fundamental nature.

Theorem 7.1 An (n, k) linear code $\mathscr{C}$ over $GF(q)$ is cyclic iff it is an ideal of A_n.

Proof Let $\mathscr{C}$ be an ideal in A_n. It is clearly a linear subspace of A_n as a vector space and it remains to check that it is a cyclic subspace. But since $\mathscr{C}$ is an ideal, it is closed under multiplication by x and hence cyclic.

Conversely, suppose $\mathscr{C}$ is a cyclic subspace. It is closed under addition and multiplication by x and hence closed under multiplication by any element of A_n. Thus $\mathscr{C}$ is an ideal. □

The polynomial $x^n - 1$ plays a key role in the theory of cyclic codes and we have considered its factorization in the previous section. In general, it is desirable that it should not have any factors of multiplicity greater than 1. From the previous section, a necessary and sufficient condition that $x^n - 1$ not have any factors of multiplicity greater than 1 over $GF(q)$ is that $(n, q) = 1$. We now investigate the ideals or codes A_n.

Theory 7.2 The unique monic polynomial $g(x)$ of minimal degree in any ideal A of A_n is a generator of A and divides $x^n - 1$. The dimension of A is $n - \deg g(x)$. Conversely, a divisor of $x^n - 1$ is a generator of an ideal in A_n.

Proof Note that by a generator $g(x)$ of an ideal A we mean that every element of A may be writen $a(x)g(x)$ for some $a(x) \in A_n$. Let $g(x)$ be that unique monic polynomial of minimal degree in A and $c(x)$ any other element in the ideal. By the division algorithm

$$c(x) = q(x)g(x) + r(x), \qquad \deg r < \deg g$$

Since A is an ideal, $(c(x) - q(x)g(x)) \in A$ and hence $r(x) \in A$, contradicting the fact that $g(x)$ was of minimal degree. Thus $r(x) = 0$ and $g(x)$ divides every element in the ideal.

We can apply exactly the same argument to the polynomial $x^n - 1$, i.e.,

$$x^n - 1 = q_1(x)g(x) + r_1(x), \quad \deg r_1 < \deg g$$

whence $-r_1(x) \in A$, which again gives a contradiction and implies that $g(x) | (x^n - 1)$.

Suppose $g(x)$ is of degree $n - k$. Then the elements $g(x), xg(x), x^2 g(x), \ldots, x^{k-1} g(x)$ are linearly independent in A. Since any element in the ideal is of the form $a(x)g(x)$, $\deg a < k$, then these elements span the ideal. Thus A has dimension k. Notice that if $g(x) = \sum_{i=0}^{n-k} g_i x^i$, then the generator matrix of the code has the convenient form

$$G = \begin{bmatrix} g_0 & g_1 & g_2 & \cdots & g_{n-k-1} & 1 & 0 & \cdots & 0 & 0 \\ 0 & g_0 & g_1 & \cdots & g_{n-k-2} & g_{n-k-1} & 1 & \cdots & 0 & 0 \\ \vdots & & & & & & & & & \vdots \\ 0 & 0 & 0 & \cdots & 0 & g_0 & g_1 & \cdots & g_{n-k-1} & 1 \end{bmatrix}$$

Now, conversely, suppose that $g(x)$ is any monic polynomial that divides $x^n - 1$ and consider the ideal $(g(x)) = A_n g(x)$. Suppose $c(x) \in (g(x))$; then

$$c(x) = a(x)g(x) \bmod (x^n - 1)$$
$$= a(x)g(x) + b(x)(x^n - 1)$$

and since $g(x) | (x^n - 1)$, $g(x) | c(x)$. That $g(x)$ is the monic polynomial of minimum degree then follows readily, which completes the theorem. □

If $f(x)$ is any polynomial of degree t, then the reciprocal polynomial, which we shall denote by $f^*(x)$, is given by $f^*(x) = x^t f(1/x)$.

Theorem 7.3 Let $\mathscr{C}$ be a cyclic (n, k) code with generator polynomial $g(x)$. Then the dual code $\mathscr{C}^\perp$ is a cyclic $(n, n - k)$ code with generator polynomial $\alpha h^*(x)$, where $h(x) = (x^n - 1)/g(x)$, and α is chosen to make $\alpha h^*(x)$ monic.

1.7 Cyclic Codes

Proof Since $x^n - 1$ is the zero polynomial in $GF(q)C_n$, if $g(x) = \sum_{i=0}^{n-k} g_i x^i$ and $h(x) = \sum_{i=0}^{k} h_i x^i$, then

$$g(x)h(x) \equiv 0 = \sum_{i=0}^{n-1} \left(\sum_{j=0}^{n-1} g_j h_{i-j} \right) x^i$$

implies that

$$\sum_{j=0}^{n-1} g_j h_{i-j} = 0 \quad \text{for} \quad i = 0, 1, \ldots, n-1$$

where $h_i = 0$ if $i < 0$ or $i > k$. However, this equation implies that the vector $(g_0, g_1, \ldots, g_{n-k}, 0, 0, \ldots, 0)$ is orthogonal to the vector $(h_k, h_{k-1}, \ldots, h_1, h_0, 0, \ldots, 0)$ and all cyclic shifts of it. Thus a parity check matrix for $\mathscr{C}$ can be written as

$$H = \begin{bmatrix} h_k & h_{k-1} & \cdots & h_1 & h_0 & 0 & \cdots & 0 & 0 \\ 0 & h_k & \cdots & & h_1 & h_0 & \cdots & 0 & 0 \\ \vdots & & & & & & & & \vdots \\ 0 & \cdots & 0 & 0 & h_k & h_{k-1} & \cdots & h_1 & h_0 \end{bmatrix}$$

which is of rank $n - k$ and hence this is the generator matrix of $\mathscr{C}^\perp$, a cyclic $(n, n-k)$ code with generator polynomial $h^*(x)$, up to a scalar multiple. $\square$

Let A_1 and A_2 be ideals in A_n. The intersection of A_1 and A_2, $A_1 \cap A_2$, is again an ideal. The union (set-theoretic) of A_1 and A_2 is not, in general, an ideal and so we define $A_1 \cup A_2$ (sometimes written as $A_1 + A_2$) as the smallest ideal in $GF(q)C_n$ containing A_1 and A_2. Finally, we define a product ideal $A_1 A_2$ to be the set of finite sums of the form $\sum_i a_{i_1} a_{i_2}$, $a_{i_1} \in A_1$, $a_{i_2} \in A_2$. It is readily checked that this is an ideal.

Theorem 7.4 Let A_1 and A_2 be two ideals in the cyclic group algebra $GF(q)C_n$ with generators $g_1(x)$ and $g_2(x)$, respectively. Then

(i) $A_1 \cup A_2$ is generated by $(g_1(x), g_2(x))$.
(ii) $A_1 \cap A_2$ is generated by $[g_1(x), g_2(x)]$.
(iii) $A_1 A_2$ is generated by $(g_1(x)g_2(x), x^n - 1)$.

Proof Every element of $A_1 \cup A_2$ is of the form $a_1(x)g_1(x) + a_2(x)g_2(x)$. Let $d(x) = (g_1(x), g_2(x))$; then clearly $d(x)$ divides each element of $A_1 \cup A_2$ and $A_1 \cup A_2 \subseteq (d(x))$. On the other hand, since there exist two polynomials $b_1(x)$ and $b_2(x)$ such that $b_1(x)g_1(x) + b_2(x)g_2(x) = d(x)$, then $d(x) \in A_1 \cup A_2$ and $(d(x)) \subseteq A_1 \cup A_2$ and $(d(x)) = A_1 \cup A_2$.

Every element of $A_1 \cap A_2$ is a multiple of $e(x) = [g_1(x), g_2(x)]$, the least common multiple of $g_1(x)$ and $g_2(x)$, since it is divisible by both $g_1(x)$ and $g_2(x)$. Since $e(x)$ is in both A_1 and A_2, $e(x) \in A_1 \cap A_2$ and $A_1 \cap A_2 = (e(x))$.

For two-sided ideals, $A_1 \cdot A_2 \subseteq A_1 \cap A_2$. But $A_1 A_2 = (g_1(x)g_2(x))$ and as a consequence of Theorem 7.2, the generator of $A_1 A_2$ is $(x^n - 1, g_1(x)g_2(x))$. This can also be seen as follows: Let

$$d_1(x) = a(x)g_1(x)g_2(x) + b(x)(x^n - 1) = (x^n - 1, g_1(x)g_2(x))$$

Then $d_1(x) = a(x)g_1(x)g_2(x) \bmod(x^n - 1)$ and $d_1(x) \in A_1 A_2$. Since $d_1(x)$ divides every element of the form $c(x)g_1(x)g_2(x)$, it follows that $A_1 A_2 = (d_1(x))$.

Notice that in general $A_1 A_2 \neq A_1 \cap A_2$. In the case when $(n, q) = 1$, however, $A_1 A_2 = A_1 \cap A_2$. This follows from the fact that in this case $x^n - 1$ has no repeated factors. Thus

$$(g_1(x)g_2(x), x^n - 1) = [g_1(x), g_2(x)]$$

since $g_1(x)$, $g_2(x)$, and $x^n - 1$ are all products of distinct irreducible factors of multiplicity one. □

Now suppose $g(x)$ is a generator of a cyclic (n, k) code $\mathscr{C}$, which is of exponent less than n, say e, so that $g(x) | (x^e - 1)$. Then, if $(x^e - 1) = a(x)g(x)$, the codeword $(x^e - 1)$ is in $\mathscr{C}$ and is a word of weight two. Thus the minimum distance of the code is at most two and the code can only detect one error and correct none. Clearly we are only interested in polynomial generators of exponent n for (n, k) cyclic codes. In a similar vein we note that if $(n, q) \neq 1$, then $x^n - 1 = (x^{n_1} - 1)^{k_1}$ for some n_1 and k_1. If $g(x)$ is a generator of a cyclic (n, k) code, then $g(x)$ may divide $x^{n_1} - 1$, leading to a code with minimum distance two. To eliminate these problems from consideration, we will often assume $(n, q) = 1$. It should be mentioned that the case $(n, q) \neq 1$ is not uninteresting and in fact some interesting and important codes arise in this manner. Assmus and Mattson (1969) describe one such class of optimal codes, which are of length p and have generator polynomials $(x - 1)^i$, $i = 1, \ldots, p - 1$, over $GF(p)$. We will consider this class of codes later. For the remainder of this chapter, however, we will assume that $(n, q) = 1$ unless explicitly mentioned otherwise and that the generator polynomial has exponent n. We will also assume that all codes do not have an all zero coordinate position.

A cyclic (n, k) code over $GF(q)$ corresponds to an ideal in A_n that is generated by $g(x)$, a divisor of $x^n - 1$. From the previous section there are $\sigma_q(n)$ irreducible factors of $x^n - 1$ over $GF(q)$ and hence there are $2^{\sigma_q(n)}$ cyclic codes of length n over $GF(q)$, $(n, q) = 1$. These include the trivial codes consisting of the null code and the whole algebra.

Also, some of these codes may be equivalent and perhaps we should consider this problem before proceeding. First note that if $\mathscr{C}$ is a cyclic (n, k) code generated by $g(x)$ with roots $\{\eta^i, i \in k\}$, where η is a primitive nth root of unity and k is a set of q chains mod n in $\sum_q(n)$, then $c(x)$ is a codeword if and only if $g(x) | c(x)$, which is equivalent to saying that $c(x)$ is a codeword if and only if $c(\eta^i) = 0$, $\forall i \in k$.

1.7 Cyclic Codes

Theorem 7.5 Let η and μ be any two primitive nth roots of unity in a suitable extension field of $GF(q)$. Then if k is a union of q chains mod n, the polynomials

$$g_\eta(x) = \prod_{i \in k}(x - \eta^i), \qquad g_\mu(x) = \prod_{i \in k}(x - \mu^i)$$

generate equivalent codes.

Proof Notice that there are $\varphi(n)$ primitive nth roots of unity and that if η is a given primitive root, the others are η^j, where $(j, n) = 1$. Let η and $\mu = \eta^j$ be two primitive roots and suppose $c(x) = \sum_{i=0}^{n-1} c_i x^i$ is a codeword in $(g_\eta(x))$. Then $\sum_{i=0}^{n-1} c_i(\eta^l)^i = 0$ for all $l \in k$. Define the permutation mapping on the integers $0, 1, \ldots, n-1$ by

$$\tau_j(i) = ij \bmod n$$

Then this polynomial can be written as

$$\sum_{i=0}^{n-1} c_{\tau_j(i)}(\eta^l)^{\tau_j(i)} = 0 = \sum_{i=0}^{n-1} c_{\tau_j(i)}((\eta^j)^l)^i$$

$$= \sum_{i=0}^{n-1} c_{\tau_j(i)}(\mu^l)^i, \qquad l \in k$$

which implies that $(c_{\tau_j(0)}, c_{\tau_j(1)}, \ldots, c_{\tau_j(n-1)})$ is a codeword in $(g_\mu(x))$ and establishes the equivalence of the codes $(g_\eta(x))$ and $(g_\mu(x))$. □

Consider now the minimal ideals of A_n. Assume that over $GF(q)$, $x^n - 1$ factors into the irreducible factors $g_1(x)g_2(x) \cdots g_t(x)$, where $t = \sigma_q(n)$. Then the ideal $(g_i(x))$ for any i, $1 \leq i \leq t$, clearly corresponds to a maximal ideal since if A is an ideal such that $(g_i(x)) \subset A \subset A_n$, then A is generated by some polynomial $f(x)$ such that $f(x) | g_i(x)$ and $f(x) | (x^n - 1)$, which is impossible unless $f(x) = 1$ or $f(x) = g_i(x)$. Similarly, the polynomial $(x^n - 1)/g_i(x)$ generates a minimal ideal that we shall denote by M_i. These minimal ideals are disjoint and hence $M_i \cap M_j = 0$ and

$$M_i \cup M_j = M_i \oplus M_j = \{m_i + m_j, m_i \in M_i, M_j \in M_j\}$$

and this direct sum has a generator polynomial, from Theorem 7.4(i), of

$$\left(\frac{x^n - 1}{g_i(x)}, \frac{x^n - 1}{g_j(x)}\right) = \frac{x^n - 1}{g_i(x)g_j(x)}$$

Thus for any ideal $A = (g(x))$, where $g(x) = g_{i_1}(x)g_{i_2}(x) \cdots g_{i_s}(x)$, then

$$\frac{x^n - 1}{g_{j_1}(x) \cdots g_{j_r}(x)} = g_{i_1}(x)g_{i_2}(x) \cdots g_{i_s}(x)$$

and A is the direct sum of the minimal ideals $M_{j_1}, M_{j_2}, \ldots, M_{j_r}$.

For the remainder of the section we consider some well-known classes of cyclic codes, beginning with those of Hamming (1950), although in his original formulation the cyclic nature of the codes was not considered. The original codes of Hamming were restricted to the binary case and we shall treat these first before generalizing them. Define the $m \times (2^m - 1)$ parity check matrix H for these codes as the set of all nonzero, binary m-tuples. Since the addition of any column to another cannot be zero, and since it is easy to find three linearly dependent columns, this defines a code with distance three. The rank of H is clearly m and hence we have a $(2^m - 1, 2^m - m - 1, 3)$ code over $GF(2)$. In this formulation the ordering of the columns of H was irrelevant. A little thought will show that if we let α be a primitive element of $GF(2^m)$, then we can as well express H as the $1 \times (2^m - 1)$ matrix

$$H = [1 \; \alpha \; \alpha^2 \; \cdots \; \alpha^{2^m - 2}]$$

where it is understood that a code vector is one whose corresponding polynomial has α as a zero. In this formulation the code is cyclic. From Section 1.6, if $h(x)$ is the primitive polynomial with root α, then the generator polynomial of the code is $h(x)$.

There are many ways of generalizing Hamming codes but we shall only discuss two of them. Define the parity check matrix H of a code over $GF(q)$ as the $m \times [(q^m - 1)/(q - 1)]$ matrix with the property that no two of its columns are scalar multiples of one another. The matrix has rank m and by definition has distance three. The result is a $((q^m - 1)/(q - 1), (q^m - 1)/(q - 1) - m, 3)$ code over $GF(q)$. When $(n, q - 1) = 1$, $n = (q^m - 1)/(q - 1)$, a cyclic version of this code can be described as follows. Let α be a primitive element in $GF(q^m)$. Then $\beta = \alpha^{q-1}$ is a primitive nth root of unity, where

$$n = \frac{q^m - 1}{q - 1}$$

and α^n is a primitive element of $GF(q)$. Define a parity check matrix by

$$H = [1 \; \beta \; \beta^2 \; \cdots \; \beta^{n-1}]$$

and suppose two of these columns are linearly dependent over $GF(q)$, which implies

$$\beta^i = \alpha^{jn} \beta^k, \quad i \neq k, \quad i, k \leq n - 1, \quad j < q - 1$$

or

$$\alpha^{(q-1)(i-k)} = \alpha^{jn}$$

which implies that

$$(q - 1)(i - k) = jn$$

1.7 Cyclic Codes

Since $j < q - 1$, this equation will have no solutions if $(n, q - 1) = 1$, and in this case the powers of β will be linearly independent over $GF(q)$, as required. Notice that for $q = 2$ the parameters of this code reduce to those of the binary code and the arguments remain valid and give the same code as in the binary case.

That the above codes are perfect follows from the direct calculation

$$q^n = q^{(q^m-1)/(q-1)} = \left[\binom{n}{1}(q-1) + 1\right] q^{[(q^m-1)/(q-1)]-m}$$

which is readily verified.

By a straightforward argument, the weight enumerator polynomial for these codes can be obtained. As previously, we denote the number of words in the code of weight i by A_i and the weight enumerator polynomial by

$$A(z) = \sum_{i=0}^{n} A_i z^i$$

where n is the length of the code. We will consider linear combinations of columns of the parity check matrix H that correspond to codewords, i.e., we are interested in linear dependence relations among the columns. There are precisely A_j of these relationships with j terms. The number of linear combinations of $j - 1$ columns with the property that a scalar multiple of one more term may be added to give a linearly dependent relationship is jA_j since for each code n-tuple of weight j there are j ways to choose the column to be added. From the construction of the matrix H a linear sum of any $j - 1$ columns of H is a scalar multiple of some column of H. This column may or may not be in the original set of $j - 1$ columns. There are a total of

$$\binom{n}{j-1}(q-1)^{j-1}$$

linear combinations of $j - 1$ columns, of which

$$\binom{n}{j-1}(q-1)^{j-1} - A_{j-1}$$

yield nonzero answers. If our linear sum of $j - 1$ columns can be written as a linear sum of $j - 2$ columns which add to zero (which corresponds to a codeword of weight $j - 2$) plus a scalar multiple of one other column, then the number of ways this can be done is

$$[n - (j-2)](q-1)A_{j-2}$$

since there are $n - (j - 2)$ ways of choosing the $(j-1)$th column. There is also the possibility that the $j - 1$ terms in the linear sum add to a scalar multiple of a column already included in the sum. If the scalar multiple were the negative of the coefficient of that column in the sum, it would cancel and we would be reduced to the above case. Thus we assume this does not happen and conclude that there are

$$(j-1)(q-2)A_{j-1}$$

ways in which this situation arises. Collecting the pieces, we have the recursion relationship

$$jA_j = \binom{n}{j-1}(q-1)^{j-1} - A_{j-1} - (j-1)(q-2)A_{j-1}$$
$$- [n(-j-2)](q-1)A_{j-2} \qquad (7.1)$$

To obtain an explicit relationship, we multiply this equation by z^{j-1} and sum from $j = 0$ to $j = n + 2$ to obtain

$$A'(z) = [1 + (q-1)z]^n - A(z) - (q-2)zA'(z)$$
$$- n(q-1)zA(z) + (q-1)z^2 A'(z)$$

This is a first-order differential equation with the initial condition $A(0) = 1$. Its solution is

$$A(z) = \frac{1}{n(q-1)+1}$$
$$\times \{[1 + (q-1)z]^n + n(q-1)[1 + (q-1)z]^{(n-1)/q}(1-z)^{[n(q-1)+1]/q}\}$$

which is the required weight enumerator for the $((q^m - 1)/(q - 1), [(q^m - 1)/(q - 1)] - m, 3)$ Hamming codes over $GF(q)$.

We define a maximum length (n, k) code to be one whose null space is generated by a primitive polynomial of degree k over $GF(q)$ for which $n = q^k - 1$. Suppose $a(x)$ is the primitive polynomial and $b(x) = (x^n - 1)/a(x)$; then $b(x)$ is the generator of an equivalent code. Consider a permutation of the codeword $b(x)$, say $x^l b(x)$, and suppose $x^l b(x) = b(x)$ mod $(x^n - 1)$. This implies that $a(x)|(x^l - 1)$, which, since $a(x)$ is primitive, implies $l \geq q^k - 1$, which in turn implies that $b(x)$ is distinct from its $q^k - 1$ permutations. Since the code only contains $q^k - 1$ nonzero codewords, we conclude that every nonzero codeword is a cyclic permutation of every other nonzero codeword. Since the code is constrained to be linear, any code with this property must have length $q^k - 1$ for some integer k. If the length of the code exceeded $q^k - 1$ and all permutations of a single codeword were distinct, then it would have more then q^k codewords, contradicting the fact that it is an (n, k) code. Thus the name maximal length is appropriate.

If the distance of the code is d, then it is clear that the weight enumerator polynomial is

$$A(z) = 1 + (q^k - 1)z^d$$

1.7 Cyclic Codes

To determine the code distance, we argue as follows. Denote the code space by V and consider the set of codewords that have a zero in some fixed coordinate position which, without loss of generality, we may take as the first. This set forms a subspace of V, say V_1, and consider the decomposition $V = V_1 \cup V_2 \cup \cdots \cup V_m$ of V into cosets of V_1, where the V_i are cosets. In any one coset the first coordinate position contains the same element. Since V is a subspace, all elements appear in the first position in the code and $m = q$. Since V_1 is also a subspace, it contains q^l vectors for some positive integer l and from the foregoing equation we must have that $q \cdot q^l = q^k$ or $l = k - 1$. It follows readily that each element of $GF(q)$ appears in the jth coordinate position exactly q^{k-1} times in any linear (n, k) code over $GF(q)$, unless the coordinate is identically zero, a case we have already excluded. To determine the distance d of the maximum length code, we simply count the number of nonzero elements appearing in all coordinate positions of each codeword. Since each nonzero codeword has weight d, this gives $(q^k - 1)d$. On the other hand, each coordinate position contains $(q - 1)q^{k-1}$ nonzero elements and there are $q^k - 1$ coordinate positions, giving

$$(q^k - 1)d = (q - 1)q^{k-1}(q^k - 1)$$

or

$$d = (q - 1)q^{k-1}$$

The maximum length codes have the parameters $(q^k - 1, k, (q - 1)q^{k-1})$, and weight enumerator polynomial

$$A(z) = 1 + (q^k - 1)z^{(q-1)q^{k-1}}$$

Since a primitive polynomial of degree k exists for any positive integer k, maximum length codes with these parameters always exist. It can also be shown that these codes are optimum in the sense that no other $(q^k - 1, k)$ code can have a larger distance, which follows from the fact that the d attained with maximum length codes satisfies the Plotkin bound (see Section 1.11). For linear codes this bound states that an (n, k, d) code cannot exist unless

$$d \leq \frac{q^k(q-1)}{(q^k-1)q} n$$

and a maximum length code satisfies this bound with equality.

The relationship between maximum length and Hamming codes is clarified by the following discussion. Let G be a $k \times (q^k - 1)$ matrix over $GF(q)$ which is a generator matrix of a maximum length code. The columns of G comprise all the nonzero k-tuples over $GF(q)$ since, if two columns were identical, it would imply that two distinct permutations of the same word are identical, contrary to the assumption that the code is maximum length. Label the nonzero elements of $GF(q)$ by α^i, $i = 1, \ldots, q - 1$, α a primitive element, and partition the matrix G into

$$G = [H \mid \alpha H \mid \alpha^2 H \mid \cdots \mid \alpha^{q-2} H]$$

where H is a $k \times l$ matrix over $GF(q)$, $l = (q^k - 1)/(q - 1)$, whose columns are pairwise independent over $GF(q)$. Clearly H is a parity check matrix of a Hamming code with appropriate parameters. If H is considered as the generator matrix of a code $\mathscr{C}$, then we claim that every nonzero codeword in $\mathscr{C}$ has weight q^{k-1}. To see this, let $\mathbf{X}$ be a nonzero word in $\mathscr{C}$ and $\mathbf{y} = (\mathbf{X}, \alpha\mathbf{X}, \alpha^2\mathbf{X}, \ldots, \alpha^{q-2}\mathbf{X})$ the corresponding word in the maximum length code. If w is the weight of $\mathbf{X}$ then $(q - 1)w = (q - 1)q^{k-1}$, from which the result follows. Thus the weight enumerator of the code is

$$A(z) = \sum_{i=0}^{l} A_i z^i = 1 + (q^k - 1)z^{q^{k-1}}$$

Using the MacWilliams identity

$$B(z) = \sum_{i=0}^{l} B_i z^i = \frac{1}{q^k} \sum_{i=0}^{l} [1 + (q - 1)z]^{l-i}(1 - z)^i$$

it readily follows that

$$B(z) = \frac{1}{q^k} \{[1 + (q - 1)z]^l + (q^k - 1)[1 + (q - 1)z]^{l-q^{k-1}}(1 - z)^{q^{k-1}}\}$$

from which the coefficients B_i can be obtained.

Certainly one of the most interesting, and general, classes of random error-correcting codes is given by the so-called BCH codes which were found independently by Bose and Ray-Chaudhuri (1960a,b) and Hocquenghem (1959). This original work was restricted to binary codes of length $2^m - 1$ for some integer m and was later extended by Gorenstein and Zierler (1961) to the nonbinary case, ie., $GF(q)$ and any length prime to q. We give the code construction for the general case of an (n, k) code over $GF(q)$. Let γ be an nth root of unity in $GF(q^m)$ and let $f(x) \in GF(q)[x]$ be the minimal polynomial of the set of elements

$$\gamma^{m_0}, \gamma^{m_0+1}, \gamma^{m_0+2}, \ldots, \gamma^{m_0+d-2}$$

where m_0 is an arbitrary positive integer less than n. Since the order of γ^{m_0+i} divides n, n is a common multiple of the orders of these roots, and $f(x) \mid (x^n - 1)$. Hence we may take $f(x)$ to be the generator of an (n, k) code where

1.7 Cyclic Codes

k is the code dimension. We can express the parity check matrix of such a code as

$$H = \begin{bmatrix} 1 & \gamma^{m_0} & (\gamma^{m_0})^2 & \cdots & (\gamma^{m_0})^{n-1} \\ 1 & \gamma^{m_0+1} & (\gamma^{m_0+1})^2 & \cdots & (\gamma^{m_0+1})^{n-1} \\ \vdots & \vdots & \vdots & & \vdots \\ 1 & \gamma^{m_0+d-2} & (\gamma^{m_0+d-2})^2 & \cdots & (\gamma^{m_0+d-2})^{n-1} \end{bmatrix}$$

and the code is the null space of this matrix over $GF(q)$. We now show that any set of $d-1$ columns of H cannot be linearly dependent, a fact that will imply the code has distance at least d. Choose an arbitrary set of $d-1$ columns whose first entries are, say, $(\gamma^{m_0})^{i_1}, (\gamma^{m_0})^{i_2}, \ldots, (\gamma^{m_0})^{i_{d-1}}$. This set of $d-1$ columns forms a $(d-1) \times (d-1)$ determinant from which we can factor out $(\gamma^{m_0})^{i_j}, j = 1, \ldots, d-1$, to give

$$\gamma^{m_0 i_1 + m_0 i_2 + \cdots + m_0 i_{d-1}} \begin{vmatrix} 1 & 1 & \cdots & 1 \\ \gamma^{i_1} & \gamma^{i_2} & & \gamma^{i_{d-1}} \\ \gamma^{2i_1} & \gamma^{2i_2} & & \gamma^{2i_{d-1}} \\ \vdots & \vdots & & \vdots \\ \gamma^{(d-2)i_1} & \gamma^{(d-2)i_2} & \cdots & \gamma^{(d-2)i_{d-1}} \end{vmatrix}$$

Since the powers of γ in the second row are distinct and this is a Van der Monde matrix, its determinant is nonzero and hence any set of $d-1$ columns is linearly independent.

There are two slight problems with this construction. In general, it is very difficult to say much about the code dimension k and the distance d, the "designed distance," is only a lower bound on the actual distance of the code. At times this bound will be useful for codes that were not initially constructed as BCH codes, i.e., if we are given a cyclic code and can show that its generator polynomial has a sequence of roots of length $d-1$ that are successive powers of a given root, then the code has distance at least d. This bound is commonly referred to as the BCH bound regardless of the type of code under consideration. Stiffler (1971, p. 405) shows that the dimension k of a BCH code over $GF(q)$ with design distance d may be bounded below by the quantity $n - v$, where v is given for $m_0 = 0$ and $m_0 = 1$ by

$$v = \begin{cases} \left[\dfrac{q-1}{q}(d-1)\right]m + 1, & m_0 = 0 \\ \left[\dfrac{q-1}{q}d\right]m, & m_0 = 1 \end{cases}$$

A BCH code of length $q^m - 1$ for some positive integer m is termed a primitive BCH code. Otherwise, we call it a nonprimitive BCH code. This terminology will carry over to other codes as well. Binary BCH codes have received a considerable amount of attention and a great deal more is known about specific cases than the foregoing outline would indicate. The reader is referred to Peterson and Weldon (1972) and Berlekamp (1968).

Let us examine the relationship between these BCH codes and the (L, g) Goppa codes introduced in Section 1.5. From Equation (5.2) of that section the (L, g) code is defined as the null space of the matrix

$$H = \begin{bmatrix} 1 & \cdots & 1 \\ \alpha_1 & \cdots & \alpha_n \\ \vdots & & \vdots \\ \alpha_1^{r-1} & \cdots & \alpha_n^{r-1} \end{bmatrix} \begin{bmatrix} g^{-1}(\alpha_1) & & & 0 \\ & \ddots & & \\ & & \ddots & \\ 0 & & & g^{-1}(\alpha_n) \end{bmatrix}$$

If we choose the set $L = \{\alpha_1, \ldots, \alpha_n\}$ to be the set of all nonzero elements of $GF(2^m)$ and $g(z) = z^{2r}$, then

$$H = \begin{bmatrix} 1 & 1 & \cdots & 1 \\ 1 & \alpha & \cdots & \alpha^{n-1} \\ \vdots & \vdots & & \vdots \\ 1 & \alpha^{2r-1} & \cdots & \alpha^{(2r-1)(n-1)} \end{bmatrix} \begin{bmatrix} 1 & & & & 0 \\ & \alpha^{-2r} & & & \\ & & \alpha^{-4r} & & \\ & & & \alpha^{-6r} & \\ & & & & \ddots \\ 0 & & & & \alpha^{-2r(n-1)} \end{bmatrix}$$

$$= \begin{bmatrix} 1 & \alpha^{-2r} & \alpha^{-4r} & \cdots & \alpha^{-2r(n-1)} \\ 1 & & & & \\ \vdots & \vdots & \vdots & & \vdots \\ 1 & \alpha^{-1} & \alpha^{-2} & \cdots & \alpha^{-(n-1)} \end{bmatrix}$$

where $n = 2^m - 1$. Notice that although the roots of $g(z)$ are not contained in L, they are repeated and hence we have only the bound $d \geq 2r + 1$, the usual BCH bound. Thus, Goppa codes contain the class of primitive BCH codes. In order to compare the relative performance of BCH and Goppa codes, we list the roughly comparable double-error-correcting codes in Table IV.

A particular and interesting subclass of BCH codes are the Reed–Solomon or RS codes (Reed and Solomon, 1960), whose appearance actually antedated the BCH codes. If in the construction of BCH codes we choose $m = m_0 = 1$ then the generating polynomial is

$$f(x) = \prod_{i=1}^{d-1} (x - \gamma^i)$$

1.7 Cyclic Codes

TABLE IV

A COMPARISON OF (n, k) GOPPA AND BCH CODES

Redundancy	(L, g) code	BCH code
8	(14,6)	(15,7)
10	(30,20)	(31,21)
12	(62,50)	(63,51)
14	(126,112)	(127,113)
16	(254,238)	(255,239)

and we obtain an $(n, n - d + 1)$ code with minimum distance at least d. However, it is not difficult to show that for any (n, k, d) linear code it is always true that

$$d \leqslant n - k + 1$$

To establish this, we notice that an (n, k) code over $GF(q)$ with distance d will have an $(n - k) \times n$ parity check matrix H of rank $n - k$. It follows that every set of $n - k + 1$ columns of H will be a linearly dependent set, implying

$$d \leqslant n - k + 1$$

which is called the Singleton bound. The relationship between this bound and the Plotkin bound quoted for maximum length codes is made clear upon noting that a RS code over $GF(q)$ may not have length greater than $q - 1$ (we assumed length equal to $q - 1$ in our discussion). For a maximum length code over $GF(q)$ of length $q - 1$ we have $k = 1$. When $k = 1$ both the Plotkin and the Singleton bounds are identical. For $n \leqslant q - 1$, the Singleton bound is stronger than the Plotkin bound since it can always be achieved in this case.

Theorem 7.6 Let a (not necessarily linear) code have q^k codewords of block length n over an alphabet of q letters. If the minimum distance between any two codewords is d, then we have

$$d \leqslant n - k + 1$$

Proof Choosing any k coordinate positions, it is clear that we have at most q^k distinct k-tuples appearing in these positions among the q^k codewords. If any two of these k-tuples are the same, then $d \leqslant n - k$. If no two of these k-tuples agree in all k-places, then since there are q^k words, at least two must agree in $k - 1$ positions, which implies $d \leqslant n - k + 1$. □

Corollary If $d = n - k + 1$, then all q^k k-tuples appear in any k coordinate positions.

Any code satisfying the bound in Theorem 7.6 with equality will be called a maximum-distance-separable code. We avoid the term optimal, which some authors use, since its meaning tends to vary with the application.

We restrict our attention now to linear (n, k) codes over $GF(q)$ whose distance satisfies with equality the above bound. It turns out that we can completely determine the weight enumerator of this code. The following line of reasoning is due to Goethals (1969).

Theorem 7.7 Every k columns of a generator matrix of an (n, k) maximum-distance-separable code over $GF(q)$ are linearly independent.

Proof Suppose there exist k dependent columns of the $k \times n$ generator matrix G of rank k. This would imply that the k-tuples appearing in the rows corresponding to these k columns are also dependent. Thus there exists a nontrivial dependency relation among the k rows of G, yielding a nonzero codeword with zeros in the k-dependent columns. This is impossible since it would imply $d \leqslant n - k$. □

Corollary The dual of a maximum-distance-separable code is also a maximum-distance-separable code.

Proof If we let the matrix G of Theorem 7.7 be the parity check matrix of the dual code, it is clear that no codeword of the dual has weight less than $k + 1$ and that there trivially exist codewords of this weight. Thus the dual code is an (n, k', d') code, $k' = n - k$, $d' = k + 1$, and $d' = k + 1 = n - k' + 1 = n - (n - k) + 1$. □

Theorem 7.8 Let $\mathscr{C}$ be a maximum-distance-separable (n, k) code and $\mathscr{C}'$ be the subcode of $\mathscr{C}$ consisting of all those codewords with zeros in j fixed positions, $j \leqslant k - 1$, and with these j positions deleted. Then $\mathscr{C}'$ is a maximum-distance-separable $(n - j, k - j)$ code.

Proof Without loss of generality assume the j fixed positions to be the first j positions. Transforming the generator matrix into systematic form, it is evident that the last $n - j$ positions of the lower $k - j$ rows span an $(n - j, k - j)$ code with a distance of $n - k + 1$ inherited from the original code, i.e., a maximum-distance-separable code. □

With these facts we proceed to find the weight distribution of any linear (n, k) maximum-distance-separable code over $GF(q)$. Recall the MacWilliams weight enumeration identities:

$$\sum_{i=0}^{n-r} A_i \binom{n-i}{r} = q^{k-r} \sum_{j=0}^{r} \binom{n-j}{n-r} B_j$$

1.7 Cyclic Codes

where $A(z) = \sum_i A_i z^i$ and $B(z) = \sum_i B_i z^i$ are the weight enumerations of a linear code $\mathscr{C}$ and its dual $\mathscr{C}^\perp$, respectively. Since for a maximum-distance-separable code we have $A_0 = 1$ and $A_1 = A_2 = \cdots = A_{n-k} = 0$ and $B_0 = 1$ and $B_1 = B_2 = \cdots = B_k = 0$, then

$$\sum_{i=0}^{n-r} A_i \binom{n-i}{r} = q^{k-r}\binom{n}{r}, \qquad r = 0, 1, \ldots, k-1$$

Solving this set of equations, recursively or otherwise, yields the following result.

Theorem 7.9 The number of vectors of weight $n - i$ in a maximum-distance-separable linear (n, k) code over $GF(q)$ is given by

$$A_{n-i} = \sum_{j=i}^{k-1} (-1)^{j-i} \binom{j}{i}\binom{n}{j}(q^{k-j} - 1), \qquad i = 0, 1, \ldots, k-1$$

Thus the number of codewords of minimum (nonzero) weight in such a code is given by

$$A_{n-k+1} = \binom{n}{k-1}(q - 1)$$

while the number of codewords of the next highest weight is given by

$$A_{n-k+2} = \binom{n}{k-2}(q^2 - 1) - \binom{k-1}{k-2}\binom{n}{k-1}(q - 1)$$

$$= (q - 1)\binom{n}{k-2}[(q + 1) - (n - k + 2)]$$

Since this quantity must be positive, we have that

$$q + 1 \geqslant n - k + 2 \qquad \text{or} \qquad q - 1 \geqslant n - k$$

Applying the same argument to the dual code gives the following theorem.

Theorem 7.10 If a linear (n, k) code over $GF(q)$ is maximum distance separable, $2 \leqslant k \leqslant n - 2$, then

$$q - 1 \geqslant \max(k, n - k)$$

This theorem is, of course, not sufficient to yield a maximum-distance-separable code. For example, we could consider a given non-maximum-distance-separable code over $GF(q)$ as a code over an extension field chosen sufficiently large to satisfy the inequality.

For $q = 2$ and $k = 1$ the binary repetition code is maximum distance separable, while for $q = 2$ and $k = n - 1$ the set of all 2^{n-1} binary n-tuples with an overall parity check added (i.e., $d = 2$) is a maximum-distance-separable code. The Reed–Solomon codes of length $q - 1$ are also maximum distance separable. It can be shown in fact (Goethals, 1969) that if $k < n \leqslant q$, then there always exists a maximum-distance-separable code over $GF(q)$. The case when $k = 2$ has been completely solved (Singleton, 1964) in the sense that any maximum-distance-separable code with q^2 codewords over an alphabet of q letters is equivalent to a set of $n - 1$ pairwise orthogonal Latin squares. We will prove this in the next chapter and indicate how other interesting codes can be obtained from Latin squares. For $3 \leqslant k \leqslant n - 3$ the problem of existence of maximum-distance-separable codes is only partially solved. The following two classes of codes, both due to Assmus and Mattson, are examples of maximum-distance-separable codes that do not seem to fall into any of the particular classes of codes discussed so far.

Class 1   Consider the prime p and cyclic codes of length p over $GF(p)$. We should immediately remark that, by and large, cyclic codes whose length is not relatively prime to the field characteristic have not received much attention. There is one obvious reason for this situation, as shown previously. For example, let $2 | n$ and consider a cyclic code over $GF(2)$ generated by $g(x)$. Since $x^n + 1 = (x^{n/2} + 1)^2$, if $g(x) | (x^{n/2} + 1)$, then the code will have a word of weight two. If $g(x) \nmid (x^{n/2} + 1)$, it is possible to obtain interesting codes. A less obvious reason, as we will show in Chapter 4, is that when the characteristic of $GF(q)$ and code length n are not relatively prime then the algebra $GF(q)[x]/(x^n - 1)$ is nonsemisimple and, in general, has a considerably more complex structure than when $(n, q) = 1$. Returning to the codes at hand, we first observe that $x^p - 1 = (x - 1)^p$ over $GF(p)$ and since any ideal of $GF[x]/(x^p - 1)$ is generated by a divisor of $(x^p - 1)$, we have that all of the ideals, say A_i, have generator polynomials $(x - 1)^i$, $i = 0, \ldots, p$, and these account for all the ideals, including the two trivial ideals. Clearly, these ideals satisfy the strict inclusion relation

$$GF(p)[x]/(x^p - 1) = A_0 \supset A_1 \supset A_2 \supset \cdots \supset A_p = (0)$$

Since the inclusions are strict, the dimension of A_i is $p - i$. To determine the minimum weight of A_i, let $f(x)$ be a minimum weight code polynomial permuted so as to have a nonzero constant term. Since $(x - 1)^i | f(x)$, $f(x) = a(x)(x - 1)^i$, it follows that the formal derivative of $f(x)$, $f'(x) = a'(x)(x - 1)^i + a(x)i(x - 1)^{i-1}$, is a codeword polynomial of A_{i-1}. Its weight is, at most, one less than the minimum weight of A_i. Thus the minimum weight of A_i, d_i, is a strictly increasing function of i. Since $d_0 = 1$ and $d_{p-1} = p - 1$, we conclude that $d_i = i + 1$ and the codes are maximum distance separable.

Actually, Assmus and Mattson (1969), were able to prove a far stronger result contained in the following theorem:

1.7 Cyclic Codes

Theorem 7.11 Let p be any prime. Then for all but a finite number of primes p', each cyclic code of length p over $GF(p'^i)$ is maximum distance separable for all i.

Class 2 Let α be a primitive nth root of unity that we consider in some extension field of $GF(q)$, where q is assumed to be equal to $-1 \bmod n$. The polynomial $(x - \alpha)(x - \alpha^{-1}) = x^2 - (\alpha + \alpha^{-1})x + 1$ is irreducible over $GF(q)$ since, if $q + 1 = kn$, then

$$(\alpha + \alpha^{-1})^q = \alpha^q + \alpha^{-q} = \alpha^{-1+kn} + \alpha^{-(-1+kn)} = (\alpha + \alpha^{-1})$$

and hence $(\alpha + \alpha^{-1}) \in GF(q)$. When n is odd these irreducible polynomials, as α runs through half of the nth roots of unity, together with $x - 1$, form all the irreducible factors of $x^n - 1$. When n is even there is the additional factor $x + 1$.

Theorem 7.12 For $q \equiv -1 \bmod n$ there exists a cyclic (n, k) maximum-distance-separable code over $GF(q)$ for every dimension k if n is odd. If n is even, we can construct two such codes if k is odd.

Proof When n is odd we choose a generator polynomial with roots

$$\alpha^{-m}, \alpha^{-m+1}, \ldots, \alpha^{-1}, 1, \alpha, \ldots, \alpha^m$$

where $k = n - (2m + 1)$ and, as before, α is a primitive nth root of unity. From the BCH distance bound the resulting cyclic $(n, n - 2m - 1)$ code has distance $2m + 2$. For an odd dimension k we choose the generator polynomial roots to be the $2m$ consecutive powers

$$\alpha^{\frac{1}{2}(n-1)-(m-1)}, \alpha^{\frac{1}{2}(n-1)-(m-2)}, \ldots, \alpha^{\frac{1}{2}(n-1)}, \alpha^{\frac{1}{2}(n+1)}, \alpha^{\frac{1}{2}(n+1)+1},$$
$$\ldots, \alpha^{\frac{1}{2}(n+1)+(m-1)}$$

When n is even we can construct two different generating polynomials containing as roots $2m + 1$ consecutive powers of α, namely,

$$\alpha^{-m}, \ldots, \alpha^{-1}, 1, \alpha, \ldots, \alpha^m \quad \text{and} \quad -\alpha^{-m}, \ldots, -\alpha^{-1}, -1, -\alpha, \ldots, -\alpha^m$$

both of which yield $(n, n - 2m - 1)$ codes of distance $d = 2m + 2$. Notice that the dual of a code in this class is also in this class. □

We briefly discuss some elementary properties of primitive root (PR) codes discovered by Anderson (1968). As in his paper, we restrict our attention to codes over $GF(p)$, p a prime, and consider codes of length $p^m - 1$. Let $p_1(x), p_2(x), \ldots, p_l(x)$ be the primitive polynomials of degree m over $GF(p)$ and note that $l = \varphi(p^m - 1)/m$.

Definition A PR code of length $p^m - 1$ over $GF(p)$ is a code with a generator polynomial of the form

$$g(x) = (x^{p^m - 1} - 1)/p_{i_1}(x)p_{i_2}(x) \cdots p_{i_r}(x)$$

where the $p_{i_j}(x)$ are distinct primitive polynomials of degree m over $GF(p)$.

Alternatively, a PR code may be described as one whose codewords contain all the nonprimitive elements of $GF(p^m)$ as roots. Since the degree of $g(x)$ is $p^m - 1 - rm$, a PR code has the parameters $(p^m - 1, rm)$. A simple bound on the minimum distance of the code is contained in the following theorem.

Theorem 7.13 A PR code of length $p^m - 1$ over $GF(p)$ with generator polynomial

$$g(x) = (x^{p^m - 1} - 1)/p_{i_1}(x)p_{i_2}(x) \cdots p_{i_r}(x)$$

is the intersection of at most rm BCH codes, and at least one of these codes has a minimum distance at least $[(p^m - 1)/rm] + 1$.

Proof Let α be any primitive element of $GF(p^m)$. Then the roots of the generator polynomial $g(x)$ are all those powers of α that are not one of the rm roots of $p_{i_1}(x) \cdots p_{i_r}(x)$. This implies that in the sequence of powers of α that are roots of $g(x)$ there are at most rm subsequences of successive powers, and each subsequence of consecutive powers generates a BCH code. Thus the code generated by $g(x)$ is, from the previous section, an intersection of at most rm BCH codes. Among the at most rm subsequences of consecutive powers there must be at least one of length at least $(p^m - 1)/rm$ and hence the corresponding BCH code will have distance at least $[(p^m - 1)/rm] + 1$, which is thus also a lower bound on the minimum distance of the PR code. □

A more detailed discussion of these codes is given by Anderson (1968). We will encounter many more classes of codes in later sections.

1.8 Linear Transformations of Vector Spaces over Finite Fields

Perhaps one of the more important applications of finite fields in mathematics is the study of groups of linear transformations over finite fields. Many important group-theoretic notions arise in this manner. It can be shown that the group of automorphisms of a finite field, regarded as a vector space over its prime subfield, is isomorphic to the group of automorphisms of the finite field regarded as an additive Abelian p group. We consider certain subgroups of these automorphism groups in this section.

1.8 Linear Transformations of Vector Spaces over Finite Fields

As before, we denote the vector space of $GF(q^n)$ over $GF(q)$ by $V_n(q)$ and a k-dimensional subspace of it by $V_n^k(q)$. Before considering groups of automorphisms we deal with certain counting problems that will arise. The number of ways of choosing a basis for $V_n(q)$ is clearly equal to

$$(q^n - 1)(q^n - q)(q^n - q^2) \cdots (q^n - q^{n-1})$$

where the basis is ordered and there are $q^n - 1$ ways of choosing the first basis element, $q^n - q$ ways of choosing the second, since we delete all linear combinations of the first, etc. A more convenient way of writing this is

$$q^{(n-1)n/2} \prod_{i=1}^{n} (q^i - 1)$$

To find the number of distinct subspaces of dimension k of $V_n(q)$, we note that there are

$$(q^n - 1)(q^n - q) \cdots (q^n - q^{k-1})$$

ways of choosing k linearly independent vectors. Each such set of vectors generates a k-dimensional subspace $V_n^k(q)$ and each such subspace can be generated in

$$(q^k - 1)(q^k - q) \cdots (q^k - q^{k-1})$$

ways. Thus if we denote by $\begin{bmatrix} n \\ k \end{bmatrix}$ the number of distinct subspaces of dimension k in $V_n(q)$, then

$$\begin{bmatrix} n \\ k \end{bmatrix} = \frac{(q^n - 1)(q^n - q) \cdots (q^n - q^{k-1})}{(q^k - 1)(q^k - q) \cdots (q^k - q^{k-1})} = \prod_{i=0}^{k-1} \frac{(q^{n-i} - 1)}{(q^{k-i} - 1)}$$

The quantities $\begin{bmatrix} n \\ k \end{bmatrix}$ are called the Gaussian coefficients and satisfy the recursion relations

$$\begin{bmatrix} n \\ k \end{bmatrix} = \begin{bmatrix} n-1 \\ k-1 \end{bmatrix} + q^k \begin{bmatrix} n-1 \\ k \end{bmatrix} \quad \text{and} \quad \begin{bmatrix} n \\ k \end{bmatrix} = \frac{q^n - 1}{q^k - 1} \begin{bmatrix} n-1 \\ k-1 \end{bmatrix}$$

as can be checked by calculation. Notice the similarity of these relations to the binomial coefficient identities

$$\binom{n}{k} = \binom{n-1}{k-1} + \binom{n-1}{k} \quad \text{and} \quad \binom{n}{k} = \frac{n}{k} \binom{n-1}{k-1}$$

Indeed, they are identical if the limit as $q \to 1$ is considered.

As a final counting problem, we derive an expression for the number of l-dimensional subspaces of $V_n(q)$ containing a given k-dimensional subspace, for $n > l > k$. The number of ways of choosing $l - k$ additional independent vectors with which to extend the basis of the given $V_n^k(q)$ is simply

$$(q^n - q^k)(q^n - q^{k+1}) \cdots (q^n - q^{l-1})$$

These $l - k$ additional vectors generate a $V_n^{l-k}(q)$ containing the subspace in

$$(q^{l-k} - 1)(q^{l-k} - q) \cdots (q^{l-k} - q^{l-k-1})q^{k(l-k)}$$

ways and hence the number of l-dimensional subspaces containing a given k-dimensional subspace is

$$\frac{(q^n - q^k)(q^n - q^{k+1}) \cdots (q^n - q^{l-1})}{(q^{l-k} - 1)(q^{l-k} - q) \cdots (q^{l-k} - q^{l-k-1})q^{k(l-k)}}$$

However, this quantity is equal to $\begin{bmatrix} n-k \\ l-k \end{bmatrix}$ since any l-dimensional subspace, say V_1, containing a given k-dimensional subspace V_2 is, by an extension of bases argument, the direct sum of V_2 and another subspace V_3, i.e., $V_1 = V_2 \oplus V_3$, where dim $V_3 = l - k$. The problem is then to find the number of distinct subspaces of dimension $l - k$ in a subspace of dimension $n - k$, i.e., $\begin{bmatrix} n-k \\ l-k \end{bmatrix}$.

Let A be an $n \times n$ nonsingular matrix over $GF(q)$ and let x, y, α be n-tuples over $GF(q)$. It is easily seen that the set of all transformations of the form

$$y = Ax + \alpha$$

which are called affine transformations, forms a group under composition. We shall call it the general linear nonhomogeneous group and denote it by $GLN(n, q)$. The number of nonsingular $n \times n$ matrices over $GF(q)$ is the number of ways that a basis of $V_n(q)$ can be taken to another basis. This is simply the number of bases of $V_n(q)$, which is

$$(q^n - 1)(q^n - q) \cdots (q^n - q^{n-1}) = q^{n(n-1)/2} \prod_{i=1}^{n} (q^i - 1)$$

The number of choices for α is q^n and so

$$|GLN(n, q)| = q^{n + [n(n-1)/2]} \prod_{i=1}^{n} (q^i - 1)$$

The set of all $n \times n$ nonsingular matrices forms a group, the general linear group, denoted by $GL(n, q)$. Its order is clearly

$$|GL(n, q)| = q^{n(n-1)/2} \prod_{i=1}^{n} (q^i - 1)$$

1.8 Linear Transformations of Vector Spaces over Finite Fields

The set of elements of $GL(n, q)$ with determinant unity forms a subgroup of $GL(n, q)$ called the special linear or unimodular group. It will be denoted by $SL(n, q)$ and it can be shown that it is generated by elements of the form

$$i \cdots \begin{bmatrix} 1 & & & \overset{j}{\vdots} & \\ & 1 & & \vdots & \\ & & 1 & \vdots & \\ \cdots & \cdots & \cdots & \lambda & \cdots \\ & & 0 & \vdots & 1 \end{bmatrix}$$

obtained from the $n \times n$ identity matrix by adding a $\lambda \in GF(q)$ in the (i, j) position. In $GL(n, q)$ the number of elements of determinant unity is the same as the number of elements with determinant $\alpha \in GF(q)$, $\alpha \neq 0$. It follows that

$$|SL(n, q)| = \frac{1}{q-1} |GL(n, q)|$$

The center of $GL(n, q)$, $Z(GL(n, q))$, is the set of matrices that commute with all other matrices of $GL(n, q)$. It can be shown that

$$Z(GL(n, q)) = \{\lambda I \mid \lambda \in GF^*(q)\}$$

where I is the $n \times n$ identity matrix. The factor group $GL(n, q)/Z(GL(n, q))$ is called the projective general linear group and is denoted by $PGL(n, q)$. It follows that

$$|PGL(n, q)| = \frac{1}{q-1} |GL(n, q)|$$

The particular case $PGL(2, q)$ is often called the linear fractional group of q letters, while some authors use this term to denote $PGL(n, q)$. We shall consider $PGL(2, q)$ later.

The center of $SL(n, q)$ is the set of matrices

$$Z(SL(n, q)) = \{\alpha I \mid \alpha \in GF^*(q), \ \alpha^n = 1\}$$

If $n \mid (q - 1)$, then we know that there are precisely n solutions to the equation $\alpha^n = 1$ in $GF(q)$. Also, an element $\alpha \in GF(q)$ satisfies this if and only if $\alpha^d = 1$, where $d = (n, q - 1)$. This follows, for suppose that $d = an + b(q - 1)$; then if $\alpha^n = 1$,

$$\alpha^d = \alpha^{an + b(q-1)} = (\alpha^n)^a (\alpha^{q-1})^b = 1$$

Conversely, if $\alpha^d = 1$, then $d|n$ and $\alpha^n = 1$ trivially. The factor group $SL(n, q)/Z(SL(n, q))$ is called the projective special linear group $PSL(n, q)$ and

$$|PSL(n, q)| = \frac{|SL(n, q)|}{d}, \qquad d = (n, q - 1)$$

Many of the above-mentioned groups are of importance for their group-theoretic structure. We single out two types of groups for further study.

By a permutation group of order m and degree k is meant a set of permutations of k letters A that forms a group under composition. The group is said to be t-transitive if for every two ordered t-tuples of distinct letters, say $(a_1, a_2, \ldots, a_t)$ and $(b_1, b_2, \ldots, b_t)$, where $a_i, b_i \in A$, there exists an element σ of the group such that $\sigma(a_i) = b_i$, $i = 1, \ldots, t$.

Consider the special case of $GLN(n, q)$ obtained by setting $n = 1$, i.e., the set of mappings

$$y = \alpha x + \beta$$

where $\alpha, \beta \in GF(q)$ and $\alpha \neq 0$. The order of the group $GLN(1, q)$ is $q(q - 1)$. If for the set of letters A we use the elements of $GF(q)$, we see that the effect of such a mapping is to permute the letters of A. For if $y = \alpha \eta + \beta = \alpha \gamma + \beta$, then $\eta = \gamma$. Furthermore, this group is 2-transitive, or doubly transitive, on the letters of A. Suppose (α_1, α_2) and (β_1, β_2) are any 2-sets; then the equations

$$\beta_1 = \alpha \alpha_1 + \beta \quad \text{and} \quad \beta_2 = \alpha \alpha_2 + \beta$$

can be solved uniquely for α, β to give

$$\alpha = \frac{\beta_2 - \beta_2}{\alpha_2 - \alpha_1}, \qquad \beta = \frac{\alpha_1 \beta_2 - \beta_1 \alpha_2}{\alpha_1 - \alpha_2}$$

We conclude that $GLN(1, q)$ can be represented as a doubly transitive group of order $q(q - 1)$ and degree q. This group is often called the affine group.

Consider now the group of transformations of the form

$$y = \frac{\alpha_1 x + \beta_1}{\alpha_2 x + \beta_2}, \qquad \alpha_1 \beta_2 - \beta_1 \alpha_2 \neq 0$$

We call this the linear fractional group with one variable and it has a natural association with $PGL(2, q)$, which we do not pursue. The order of the group is $q(q^2 - 1)$ and we wish to show that it can be represented as a triply transitive permutation group on $q + 1$ letters. To the symbols of $GF(q)$ we adjoin the symbol ∞ to represent elements of the form $\beta/0$, $\beta \in GF(q)$, $\beta \neq 0$. That transformations of the above form permute the elements of $GF(q) \cup \{\infty\}$ is easily checked. The group is at least doubly transitive on $GF(q)$ since it contains the previous group as a subgroup. Since the group contains the element that maps

0 to ∞ the group is at least 1-transitive on $GF(q) \cup \{\infty\}$. To show that it is 3-transitive on this set requres solving a set of equations for $\alpha_1, \beta_1, \alpha_2, \beta_2 \in GF(q)$ which takes the ordered triple (η_1, η_2, η_3) to $(\gamma_1, \gamma_2, \gamma_3)$, where η_i, $\gamma_i \in GF(q) \cup \{\infty\}$, i.e., solving the equations

$$\gamma_1 = \frac{\alpha_1 \eta_1 + \beta_1}{\alpha_2 \eta_1 + \beta_2}, \qquad \gamma_2 = \frac{\alpha_1 \eta_2 + \beta_1}{\alpha_2 \eta_2 + \beta_2}, \qquad \gamma_3 = \frac{\alpha_1 \eta_3 + \beta_1}{\alpha_2 \eta_3 + \beta_2}$$

That a solution exists follows from the fact that $\alpha_1 \beta_2 - \alpha_2 \beta_1 \neq 0$, the η_i are distinct, the γ_i are distinct, and that we have three equations in four unknowns.

There are many other problems of considerable interest on matrices over finite fields. Rather than extend the treatment here, we shall deal with those problems we require as we meet them.

1.9 Code Invariance under Permutation Groups

The relevance of the problem of finding as large a permutation group as possible on the coordinate positions of the code to the weight enumeration problem has already been indicated. Many of the results in this area tend to be quite specialized and tedious to prove. Instances of this have been observed in previous sections. We shall therefore confine our interest to a very elegant result of Kasami *et al.* (1968c).

It is clear that every cyclic code is invariant under the cyclic group of permutations of appropriate degree. Suppose $c(x)$ is a codeword polynomial of a cyclic (n, k) code over $GF(q)$. Then $c(x^q) = c(x)^q \pmod{x^n - 1}$ and hence $c(x^q) \pmod{x^n - 1}$ is also a codeword. It follows that the code is invariant under the permutation group on n letters generated by the permutation

$$i \longrightarrow qi \bmod n$$

Also, if a linear code is invariant under some permutation group, then its dual code is also. The following theorem is both a simple and powerful result on this problem. If $\mathscr{C}$ is a code of length $q^m - 1$ over $GF(q)$ with generator polynomial $g(x)$, then we denote the extended code obtained by prefixing a digit to each word that is minus the sum of all the digits in the codeword by $\mathscr{C}_e$. Notice that if the unit element is a root of $g(x)$, then every codeword in the cyclic code is such that its digits sum to zero. Thus in this case the first position in each codeword of $\mathscr{C}_e$ is a zero. We exclude this case from consideration.

Assume that $\text{char}(GF(q)) = p$ and $q = p^l$ and suppose that

$$i = \sum_{t=0}^{ml-1} \delta_t p^t, \qquad 0 \leqslant \delta_t \leqslant p - 1, \quad \forall t$$

Then denote by $J(i)$ the set of integers with the representation

$$j = \sum_{t=0}^{ml-1} \sigma_t p^t, \quad 0 \leq \sigma_t \leq \delta_t, \quad \forall t$$

Theorem 9.1 (*Kasami et al.* 1968c) The extended code $\mathscr{C}_e$ of length q^m over $GF(q)$ of a cyclic code $\mathscr{C}$ with generator polynomial $g(x)$, $g(1) \neq 0$, is invariant under the affine group of permutations if and only if for every α^i that is a root of $g(x)$ then for every $j \in J(i)$, $j \neq 0$, α^j is a root of $g(x)$, where α is a primitive root of $GF(q^m)$.

Proof Consider a codeword $c(x) \in \mathscr{C}_e$ of weight ω and let the coordinate positions of its nonzero components be $x_1, \ldots, x_\omega$ and the values of these nonzero components be $y_1, \ldots, y_\omega$. Then since $c(x) \in \mathscr{C}_e$ we must have

$$\delta_0 = \sum_{k=1}^{\omega} y_k = 0, \qquad S_i = \sum_{k=1}^{\omega} y_k x_k^i = 0$$

for each i for which α^i is a root of $g(x)$.

Define the affine transformation π_{ab} of $GF(q^m)$ by

$$\pi_{ab}: \beta \longrightarrow a\beta + b, \quad a \neq 0, \quad a, b \in GF(q^m)$$

and denote by $c'(x)$ the result of the operation on the coordinate positions of $c(x)$ by π_{ab}. If $c'(x)$ is to be in $\mathscr{C}_e$, then defining

$$S_i' = \sum_{k=1}^{\omega} y_k (ax_k + b)^i$$

we must have $S_0' = S_i' = 0$ for each i for which α^i is a zero of $g(x)$. By a theorem of Lucas on the binomial coefficients (see Appendix B)

$$\binom{i}{j} = \prod_{t=0}^{ml-1} \binom{\delta_t}{\sigma_t} \mod p$$

where, as before, δ_t and σ_t are coefficients in the radix p expansions of i and j, respectively. This product is nonzero if and only if each term is nonzero, or, equivalently, if and only if $j \in J(i)$.

Returning to the equation of S_i', we see that

$$S_i' = \sum_{k=1}^{\omega} \sum_{j=0}^{i} y_k \binom{i}{j} a^j b^{i-j} x_k^j$$

$$= \sum_{k=1}^{\omega} \sum_{j \in J(i)} y_k \binom{i}{j} a^j b^{i-j} x_k^j$$

$$= \sum_{j \in J(i)} \binom{i}{j} a^j b^{i-j} S_j$$

Suppose now that we choose $a = 1$ and consider

$$S_i' = \sum_{j \in J(i)} \binom{i}{j} b^{i-j} S_j$$

as a polynomial in b. If the code $\mathscr{C}_e$ is to be invariant under the doubly transitive affine group, then we must have $S_i' = 0$. Since, by definition of $J(i)$, $\binom{i}{j} \neq 0$, this implies that

$$S_j = 0, \quad \forall j \in J(i)$$

and hence that if α^i is a root of $g(x)$ and $\mathscr{C}_e$ is invariant under the doubly transitive affine group, then α^j is also a root of $g(x)$ for each $j \in J(i)$. Conversely, if, whenever α^i is a root of $g(x)$ implies that α^j is also a root for any $j \in J(i)$, then $S_j = 0 \;\forall j \in J(i)$ and it follows that $S_i' = 0$ for every (a, b), implying that $\mathscr{C}_e$ is invariant under the permutation group, which completes the theorem. $\square$

Implicit in the proof of this theorem is the fact that any code of length q^m that is invariant under the doubly transitive permutation group is actually an extended cyclic code, i.e., the code obtained by deleting the first coordinate position is cyclic. An inspection of the conditions on the roots used in defining the cyclic primitive BCH codes over $GF(q)$ reveals that the extended version of this code is invariant under the doubly transitive affine group.

Some other results of a general nature on this problem were obtained by Delsarte et al. (1970) and Delsarte (1970a, b).

In an interesting and significant paper Delsarte (1970a) discusses the invariance problem to some depth and defines classes of codes using these concepts. We prove one of his results here. Let η be a primitive bth root of unity in $GF(q^r)$, where $b \,|\, (q^r - 1)$. Let $x \in V_m(q^r)$ and denote the set of vectors

$$\{x, \eta x, \eta^2 x, \ldots, \eta^{b-1} x\}$$

by (x). Clearly this is an equivalence relation that divides the nonzero elements of $V_m(q^r)$ into $[(q^{rm} - 1)/b] = n$ classes, which are denoted by V_b. The general linear homogeneous group $GL(m, q^r)$ is the set of $m \times m$ nonsingular matrices over $GF(q^r)$ that acts as a permutation group of degree $q^{rm} - 1$ on the nonzero elements of $V_m(q^r)$. It fixes the all-zeros vector. However, it also acts as a permutation group of degree n on the classes of V_b and with this interpretation we denote the group $G_b(m, q^r)$.

Theorem 9.2 Let $\mathscr{C}$ be a linear code of length n over $GF(q)$. If $\mathscr{C}$ is invariant under $G_b(m, q^r)$, then it is equivalent to a cyclic code.

Proof Let σ be a primitive element of $GF(q^{rm})$ and $\boldsymbol{\alpha} = \{\alpha_1, \alpha_2, \ldots, \alpha_m\}$ a basis of $GF(q^{rm})$ over $GF(q^r)$. Since $\sigma\boldsymbol{\alpha} = \{\sigma\alpha_1, \sigma\alpha_2, \ldots, \sigma\alpha_m\}$ is also a basis there must exist a matrix, say M, such that its transpose M^T transforms one basis to the other

$$M^T \alpha = \sigma \alpha$$

where α is considered as a column vector. If ε is a vector such that $(\alpha, \varepsilon) = 1$, then it follows that

$$\sigma^i = \alpha^T M^i \varepsilon, \qquad i = 0, 1, \ldots, q^{rm} - 2$$

which implies that $M^i \varepsilon$, $0 \leq i \leq q^{rm} - 2$, runs through all the elements of $V_m(q^r)$. Now σ^n is a primitive bth root of unity in $GF(q^r)$ and thus $M^n = \sigma^n I = \eta I$. Thus the vectors $M^i \varepsilon$, $0 \leq i \leq n-1$, belong to different classes in V_b. If we relabel the n coordinate positions with these vectors, then since $M \in G_b(m, q^r)$, the new code will be cyclic and equivalent to the original code. □

We consider, without proof, a related result of Delsarte (1970a). Let $GLN(m, q^r)$ be the general linear nonhomogeneous group whose elements are transformations on $V_m(q^r)$ of the form

$$V_m(q^r) \longrightarrow V_m(q^r)$$
$$x \longmapsto Ax + b$$

where A is a nonsingular matrix. This group acts as a permutation group of degree q^{rm} on $V_m(q^r)$. $G_1(m, q^r)$ is the subgroup of $G(m, q^r)$ that fixes the all-zero vector of $V_m(q^r)$. Delsarte (1970a, Theorem 4) shows that if a nontrivial linear code of length q^{rm} over $GF(q)$ is invariant under $GLN(m, q^r)$, then it is equivalent to an extended cyclic code. Using a polynomial approach to codes, he is able to characterize rather completely the codes of appropriate length which are invariant under $G_b(m, q^r)$ and $G(m, q^r)$.

1.10 The Polynomial Approach to Coding

In this section we consider an alternative approach to coding, due to Mattson and Solomon (1961). This approach, introduced first for the single-variable case and then for the multivariable case, will yield the important class of generalized Reed–Muller (GRM) codes and the more general class of polynomial codes. While these are interesting in their own right, they will also lead to the finite geometry codes to be discussed in the next chapter.

Let $\mathscr{C}$ be a cyclic (n, k) code over $GF(q)$ generated by the polynomial $g(x)$ which has the roots $\{\beta^i, i \in k\}$, where β is a primitive nth root of unity and k is a set of q chains mod n. We assume $(n, q) = 1$ unless stated otherwise. The code $\mathscr{C}$ can be described by the set of codeword polynomials

$$\mathscr{C} = \left\{ f(x) \in GF(q)[x]/(x^n - 1) \,\Big|\, g(x) | f(x) \right\}$$

1.10 The Polynomial Approach to Coding

or equivalently,

$$\mathscr{C} = \left\{ f(x) \in GF(q)[x]/(x^n - 1) \,\middle|\, f(\beta^i) = 0, \quad i \in k \right\}$$

Let $c(x) = \sum_i c_i x^i \in \mathscr{C}$, where as usual we identify a codeword and the polynomial. To each such codeword we associate the polynomial

$$F_c(x) = \frac{1}{n} \sum_{j=1}^{n} f_j x^{n-j}$$

where

$$f_j = c(\beta^j) = \sum_{i=0}^{n-1} c_i (\beta^j)^i, \qquad j = 1, \ldots, n$$

By a simple calculation we observe that

$$F_c(\beta^l) = \frac{1}{n} \sum_{j=1}^{n} f_j (\beta^l)^{n-j} = \frac{1}{n} \sum_{j=1}^{n} \left[\sum_{i=0}^{n-1} c_i (\beta^j)^i \right] \beta^{l(n-j)}$$

$$= \frac{1}{n} \sum_{i=0}^{n-1} c_i \left(\sum_{j=1}^{n} \beta^{j(i-l)} \right) = c_l$$

since the sum of all nth roots of unity is zero, for any n, and if $i = l$, then the term in the last set of parentheses is n. Thus, we could characterize the code $\mathscr{C}$ as

$$\mathscr{C} = \{(F_c(1), F_c(\beta), F_c(\beta^2), \ldots, F_c(\beta^{n-1})), \quad c(x) \in \mathscr{C}\}$$

which is not a significant improvement over our original characterization.

To improve upon this characterization, consider first some properties of the polynomials $F_c(x)$, the Mattson–Solomon polynomials. If the set k contains the integers $1, 2, \ldots, d-1$, then

$$c(\beta^i) = 0, \qquad i = 1, 2, \ldots, d-1$$

which implies that the coefficients $f_i = 0$, $i = 1, 2, \ldots, d-1$. Since these are the coefficients of the terms $x^{n-1}, x^{n-2}, \ldots, x^{n-d+1}$ in $F_c(x)$, we conclude that $\deg F_c \leq n - d$ for any $c(x) \in \mathscr{C}$. Now the weight of a codeword $c(x)$ is simply n minus the number of nth roots of unity that are roots of F_c. Since a polynomial of degree $n - d$ cannot have more than $n - d$ such roots, we conclude the weight of any codeword polynomial is at least $n - (n - d) = d$. This, of course, is just the BCH bound on the code distance.

The situation can be viewed in a slightly different manner. We view the set of polynomials in this paragraph as elements of $GF(q)[x]/(x^n - 1)$. As before, we have

$$\mathscr{C} = \{c(x) \,|\, c(\beta^i) = 0, \quad i \in k\}$$

or, equivalently,

$$\mathscr{C} = \{(F(1), F(\beta), \ldots, F(\beta^{n-1})) | F(x) = \sum f_i x^{n-i} \text{ and } f_j = 0, \ j \in k\}$$
$$= \{(F(1), F(\beta), \ldots, F(\beta^{n-1})) | F(x) = \sum_{i_j \in \bar{k}} f_{i_j} x^{n-i_j}\}$$

where $\bar{k}$ is the complement of k in $\{1, 2, \ldots, n\}$. Now one basis of $GF(q)[x]/(x^n - 1)$ is $(x^{n-1}, x^{n-2}, \ldots, x, 1)$ and with respect to this basis the polynomial $F(x)$ can be expressed as $(f_1, \ldots, f_n)$ where $f_j = 0$ if $j \in k$. Rather than this basis, choose the polynomials

$$G_i(x) = \prod_{\substack{j=1 \\ j \neq i}}^{n} \frac{x - \beta^j}{\beta^i - \beta^j}, \qquad i = 1, \ldots, n$$

Clearly, we have $G_i(\beta^j) = \delta_{ij}$ and these polynomials form a basis of $GF(q)[x]/(x^n - 1)$. It is easily verified that

$$F(x) = \sum_{i=0}^{n-1} f_i x^{n-i} = \sum_{i=1}^{n} F(\beta^i) G_i(x)$$

since $F(x)$ is a polynomial of degree n or less. Thus we can characterize the code $\mathscr{C}$ as the set of polynomials

$$\{F(x) = \sum f_i x^{n-i}, \ f_j = 0, \ j \in k\}$$

expressed with respect to the basis $G_i(x)$, $i = 1, \ldots, n$. Although we will make no direct use of this fact, it is interesting to keep in mind.

The idea of associating a polynomial with each codeword in an (n, k) linear code, which when evaluated on the nth roots of unity yields the codeword coordinates, can be extended to the multivariate case. For the remainder of this section we will be concerned with the relationship between these two approaches. The generalized Reed–Muller (GRM) codes (Kasami *et al.* 1968a) are a particularly interesting class of codes in this respect and we will investigate them quite extensively. The polynomial codes also introduced by Kasami *et al.* (1968b) are also defined by a multivariable approach. We give some of their basic properties later in this section but our real interest in them will be in the next chapter where we will show that certain duals of polynomial codes are finite geometry codes.

Denote by $\bar{X}$ the set of variables $X_1, X_2, \ldots, X_m$ and by $P(\bar{X})$ a polynomial in these variables with coefficients from $GF(q)$. The degree of a monomial

$$X_1^{i_1} X_2^{i_2} \cdots X_m^{i_m}$$

is defined as $\sum_{j=1}^{m} i_j$ and the degree of a linear combination over $GF(q)$ of such monomials is the degree of the monomial of largest degree. Since we are interested in the case where X_i assumes values in $GF(q)$, all exponents of X_i

1.10 The Polynomial Approach to Coding

are taken mod $(q-1)$, i.e., $X_i^q = X_i$. We say such a polynomial is in reduced form and hence assume this to be the case unless stated otherwise.

If a polynomial assumes a value of zero for every $\bar{\alpha} = (\alpha_1, \ldots, \alpha_m) \in V_m(q)$, i.e., $X_i = \alpha_i \in GF(q)$, then it is identically zero. A simple proof of this by induction on m is easily constructed.

Recalling that

$$\prod_{\alpha \in GF(q)} (X - \alpha) = X^q - X$$

we see that

$$\prod_{\substack{\alpha \in GF(q) \\ \alpha \neq \omega}} (X - \alpha) = (X - \omega)^{q-1} - 1$$

By setting X equal to ω in this expression, it follows that the product of all nonzero elements of a finite field is equal to -1. This is an extension of Wilson's theorem, which states that $(p-1)! \equiv -1 \bmod p$. We now define the indicator function $F_{\bar{\alpha}}(\bar{X})$ by

$$F_{\bar{\alpha}}(\bar{X}) = \prod_{i=1}^{m} [1 - (X_i - \alpha_i)^{q-1}]$$

so that $F_{\bar{\alpha}}(\bar{X}) = 0$ if $\bar{X} \neq \bar{\alpha}$ and 1 if $\bar{X} = \bar{\alpha}$. Clearly, for a polynomial $P(\bar{X})$ we have

$$P(\bar{X}) = \sum_{\bar{\alpha} \in V_m(q)} P(\bar{\alpha}) F_{\bar{\alpha}}(\bar{X})$$

since X_i is a q-ary variable and P is assumed in reduced form. If we denote by $P(m, q)$ the set of all (reduced form) polynomials over $GF(q)$, then it is clear that $P(m, q)$ is a vector space of dimension q^m over $GF(q)$. An obvious basis is given by the set of monomials

$$X_1^{i_1} X_2^{i_2} \cdots X_m^{i_m}, \quad 0 \leq i_k \leq q - 1, \quad k = 1, \ldots, m$$

Denote by $P_v(m, q)$ the subspace of $P(m, q)$ generated by the monomials of degree v or less.

Following Delsarte *et al.* (1970), as we will for much of the work on GRM codes, we prove the following two lemmas.

Lemma 10.1 If $\deg P(\bar{X}) < m(q - 1)$, then

$$\sum_{\bar{\alpha} \in V_m(q)} P(\bar{\alpha}) = 0$$

Proof We have seen that

$$P(\bar{X}) = \sum_{\bar{\alpha} \in V_m(q)} P(\bar{\alpha}) F_{\bar{\alpha}}(\bar{X})$$

Since the coefficient of the monomial of degree $m(q-1)$ in the expansion

$$F_{\bar{\alpha}}(\overline{X}) = \prod_{i=1}^{m} [1 - (X_i - \alpha_i)^{q-1}] = \prod_{i=1}^{m} \left[1 - \sum_{j=0}^{q-1} X_i{}^j (-\alpha_i)^{q-1-j} \binom{q-1}{j}\right]$$

is $(-1)^m$, and since the coefficient of this monomial in $P(\overline{X})$ is zero by assumption, we conclude that

$$\sum_{\bar{\alpha} \in V_m(q)} P(\bar{\alpha}) = 0$$

Alternatively, we could have shown that since

$$\prod_{\alpha \in GF(q)} (X - \alpha) = X^q - X$$

then, by examining the coefficient of X^{q-1} we have that

$$\sum_{\alpha \in GF(q)} \alpha = 0$$

From this it follows that

$$\sum_{\bar{\alpha} \in V_m(q)} \alpha_1^{i_1} \alpha_2^{i_2} \cdots \alpha_m^{i_m} = 0, \qquad \sum_{j=1}^{m} i_j < m(q-1)$$

and finally that

$$\sum_{\bar{\alpha} \in V_m(q)} P(\bar{\alpha}) = 0 \qquad \deg P < m(q-1) \qquad \square$$

The proof of the following lemma is, in a sense, crucial to the understanding of much of the remainder of this section. It will eventually enable us to relate the important notion of the q weight of an integer to the zeros of a cyclic code. Recall that by the q weight of an integer h we will mean the quantity $\omega_q(h)$, where

$$h = \sum_{i=0}^{\infty} h_i q^i \quad \text{and} \quad \omega_q(h) = \sum_{i=0}^{\infty} h_i$$

Lemma 10.2 If $\omega_q(h) \leq \mu$ and $P(\overline{X}) \in P_\nu(m, q)$, $\mu + \nu < m(q-1)$, then

$$\sum_{\bar{\alpha} \in V_m(q)} (\bar{\alpha}, \bar{\beta})^h P(\bar{\alpha}) = 0 \quad \text{in} \quad GF(q^r)$$

where $(\cdot, \cdot)$ indicates the usual inner product and $\bar{\beta}$ is some fixed element of $V_m(q^r)$.

Proof

$$\sum_{\bar{\alpha} \in V_m(q)} (\bar{\alpha}, \bar{\beta})^h P(\bar{\alpha}) = \sum_{\bar{\alpha} \in V_m(q)} \left(\sum \alpha_i \beta_i\right)^{\sum_k h_k q^k} P(\bar{\alpha})$$

$$= \sum_{\bar{\alpha} \in V_m(q)} \prod_k \left(\sum_i \alpha_i \beta_i^{q^k}\right)^{h_k} P(\bar{\alpha})$$

1.10 The Polynomial Approach to Coding

In the inner summation, raised to the power h_k for fixed k, each term is of the form $C(\bar{\beta})\alpha_1^{i_1}\alpha_2^{i_2}\cdots\alpha_m^{i_m}$, $\sum_j i_j = h_k$. Each term in the product of the sum of such terms is again a term of the form $C'(\bar{\beta})\alpha_1^{j_1}\alpha_2^{j_2}\cdots\alpha_m^{j_m}$, where $\sum_l j_l \leq \sum_i h_i = \omega_q(h)$. The summation is then of the form

$$\sum_{\bar{\alpha}\in V_m(q)} [\sum C'(\bar{\beta})\alpha_1^{j_1}\alpha_2^{j_2}\cdots\alpha_m^{j_m}]P(\bar{\alpha})$$

$$= \sum C'(\bar{\beta})\left[\sum_{\bar{\alpha}\in V_m(q)} \alpha_1^{j_1}\alpha_2^{j_2}\cdots\alpha_m^{j_m}P(\bar{\alpha})\right]$$

where the nonindexed outer summation is over the terms obtained in the inner product. Since $\alpha_1^{j_1}\alpha_2^{j_2}\cdots\alpha_m^{j_m}P(\bar{\alpha})$ is a polynomial in $\bar{\alpha}$ of degree at most $\mu + \nu < m(q-1)$, the summation over $\bar{\alpha}$ is, by the previous lemma, zero. □

We now give the first of three definitions of GRM codes.

Definition 1 The νth-order GRM code, denoted by $C_\nu(m, q)$, is the set of vectors of length q^m over $GF(q)$

$$C_\nu(m, q) = \{(P(\bar{0}), P(\bar{\alpha}_1), \ldots, P(\bar{\alpha}_{q^m-1})),\quad P(\bar{X}) \in P_\nu(m, q)\}$$

where $\bar{0}, \bar{\alpha}_1, \ldots, \bar{\alpha}_{q^m-1}$ is an arbitrary ordering of the elements of $V_m(q)$.

As in the single-variable case, if we identify the polynomial

$$P(\bar{X}) = \sum_{(i_1\cdots i_m)} C_{i_1 i_2 \cdots i_m} X_1^{i_1} X_2^{i_2} \cdots X_m^{i_m}$$

with the q^m-tuple over $GF(q)$ with the coefficients $C_{i_1 i_2 \cdots i_m}$ in some ordering in the coordinate vectors (i.e., w.r.t. the basis of monomials), then the code $C_\nu(m, q)$ is simply the image of $P_\nu(m, q)$ with respect to the basis $F_{\bar{\alpha}}(\bar{X})$, i.e.,

$$P(\bar{X}) = \sum_{\bar{\alpha}\in V_m(q)} P(\bar{\alpha})F_{\bar{\alpha}}(\bar{X})$$

and with respect to this new basis the corresponding coordinate vector contains the elements $P(\bar{\alpha})$, $\bar{\alpha} \in V_m(q)$, again in some ordering.

This code will be shown later to be equivalent to an extension of a cyclic code. Clearly the dimension of $C_\nu(m, q)$ over $GF(q)$ is the same as the dimension of $P_\nu(m, q)$ over $GF(q)$, as a subspace of $P(m, q)$. To determine this dimension, choose the set of monomials

$$\left\{X_1^{i_1}X_2^{i_2}\cdots X_m^{i_m},\quad \sum_{k=1}^m i_k \leq \nu\right\}$$

as a basis of $P_\nu(m, q)$. The number of polynomials in such a basis is just the number of ways we can place ν or fewer objects in m cells where no cell is to contain more than $q - 1$ objects. The number of ways of placing t objects in m cells, no cell to contain more than $q - 1$ objects, is (Riordan, 1958)

$$N(t, m, q) = \sum_{k=0}^{m} (-1)^k \binom{m}{k} \binom{t - kq + m - 1}{t - kq}$$

Thus the dimension of the vth-order GRM code $C_v(m, q)$ is

$$\sum_{t=0}^{v} N(t, m, q) = \sum_{t=0}^{v} \sum_{k=0}^{m} (-1)^k \binom{m}{k} \binom{t - kq + m - 1}{t - kq}$$

To find the dual code of $C_v(m, q)$, we let $\mu = m(q - 1) - v - 1$. The product of a polynomial $P_1(\overline{X}) \in P_v(m, q)$ and $P_2(\overline{X}) \in P_\mu(m, q)$ is of degree less than $m(q - 1)$. Thus, by the first lemma in this section,

$$\sum_{\bar{\alpha} \in V_m(q)} P_1(\bar{\alpha}) P_2(\bar{\alpha}) = 0$$

which implies that the corresponding codewords are orthogonal. Thus if $\bar{x} \in C_v(m, q)$ and $\bar{y} \in C_\mu(m, q)$, $(\bar{x}, \bar{y}) = 0$.

Theorem 10.1 $C_\mu(m, q)$ is the dual code of $C_v(m, q)$.

Proof From the above comments we need only verify that the dimensions of the two codes add to q^m. Let r be the number of monomials of degree less than or equal to v. By replacing the exponent i of each variable by $(q - 1) - i$, for each monomial of degree $\leq v$ we obtain a monomial of degree $\geq \mu + 1$. Thus the number of monomials of degree $\geq \mu + 1$ is again r. The number of monomials of degree $\leq \mu$ is thus $q^m - r$. Thus the dimensions of $C_\mu(m, q)$ and $C_v(m, q)$ add to q^m. □

For some fixed ordering of the elements of $V_m(q)$ we defined

$$C_v(m, q) = \{(P(\bar{0}), P(\bar{\alpha}_1), \ldots, P(\bar{\alpha}_{q^m - 1})), \quad P(\bar{x}) \in P_v(m, q)\}$$

We identify the ith coordinate position of the codeword with $\bar{\alpha}_i$. We prove the following:

Theorem 10.2 The action of $GLN(m, q)$ on the coordinate positions of $C_v(m, q)$ leaves the code invariant.

Proof Consider the permutation which takes $\bar{\alpha}_i$ to $\bar{\alpha}_i'$, where

$$\bar{\alpha}_i' = \bar{\alpha}_i A + \bar{\beta}, \quad \bar{\alpha}_i, \bar{\beta} \in V_m(q)$$

We have to show that the permuted codeword in which $P(\bar{\alpha}_i)$ appears in coordinate position α_i', or equivalently, $P((\bar{\alpha}_i' - \bar{\beta}) A^{-1})$ appears in position

1.10 The Polynomial Approach to Coding

$\bar{\alpha}_i'$, is also a codeword. Consider the polynomial $P'(\bar{x}) = P((\bar{x} - \bar{\beta})A^{-1})$ which is an element of $P_v(m, q)$. The corresponding codeword is

$$(P'(\bar{0}), P'(\bar{\alpha}_1), \ldots, P'(\bar{\alpha}_{q^m-1}))$$
$$= (P(-\bar{\beta}A^{-1}), P((\bar{\alpha}_1' - \bar{\beta})A^{-1}), \ldots, P((\bar{\alpha}_{q^m-1}' - \bar{\beta})A^{-1}))$$

which is thus also a codeword, i.e., $P'(\bar{\alpha}_i') = P(\bar{\alpha}_i)$, as required. □

Since

$$\sum_{\bar{\alpha} \in V_m(q)} P(\bar{\alpha}) = 0, \qquad \deg P < m(q-1)$$

we may view

$$P(\bar{0}) = - \sum_{\substack{\bar{\alpha} \in V_m(q) \\ \bar{\alpha} \neq \bar{0}}} P(\bar{\alpha})$$

as an overall parity check on the code. Also, if $A \in GL(m, q)$, then A acting on the coordinate positions fixes the first position. Now choose an element M of $GL(m, q)$ that is of order $q^m - 1$. This is always possible since, for example, the companion matrix of the minimal polynomial of a primitive element of $GF(q^m)$ over $GF(q)$ is such a matrix. If $\bar{\gamma} \in V_m(q)$ is a fixed nonzero element, then the set $\{\bar{\gamma}M^i, 0 \leq i \leq q^m - 2\}$ exhausts the nonzero elements of $V_m(q)$. It is clear then that the shortened $C_v(m, q)$ code

$$\{(P(\bar{\gamma}), P(\bar{\gamma}M), P(\bar{\gamma}M^2), \ldots, P(\bar{\gamma}M^{q^m-2})), \quad P(\bar{x}) \in P_v(m, q)\}$$

is a cyclic code. We refer to this code as the cyclic GRM code and denote it by $HC_v(m, q)$, following Delsarte *et al.* (1970).

Theorem 10.3 *The code $HC_v(m, q)$ of length $q^m - 1$ is invariant under the action of $GL(m, q)$ on its coordinate positions.*

In order to describe $HC_v(m, q)$ as a cyclic code, it is sufficient to determine the roots of its generator polynomial. As before, let α be a primitive element of $GF(q^m)$, $m(x)$ its minimal polynomial over $GF(q)$, and M its companion matrix. Let $\bar{e} = (1, 0, 0, \ldots, 0) \in V_m(q)$ and define $\bar{\alpha} = (1, \alpha, \alpha^2, \ldots, \alpha^{m-1})$, where it is recognized that this set of elements forms a basis of $GF(q^m)$ over $GF(q)$. Clearly $(\bar{e}M^i, \bar{\alpha}) = \alpha^i$, $i = 0, 1, \ldots, m-1$, and from this it is readily established that the mapping

$$V_m(q) \longrightarrow GF(q^m)$$
$$\bar{e}M^i \longmapsto (\bar{e}M^i, \bar{\alpha})$$

is a vector space [over $GF(q)$] isomorphism and $(\bar{e}M^i, \bar{\alpha}) = \alpha^i$, $i = 0, 1, \ldots, q^m - 2$, e.g.,

$$(\bar{e}M^m, \bar{\alpha}) = (\bar{e}M^{m-1}, \bar{\alpha}M^T) = (\bar{e}M^{m-1}, \alpha\bar{\alpha}) = \alpha \cdot \alpha^{m-1} = \alpha^m$$

The mapping

$$\mathcal{N}: GF(q^m) \longrightarrow \langle M \rangle$$
$$\alpha \longmapsto M$$

is a field isomorphism, where $\langle M \rangle$ is the multiplicative subgroup of $GL(m, q)$ with the zero matrix added and where addition and multiplication are as in a matrix ring.

Now let

$$\bar{P} = (P(\bar{e}), P(\bar{e}M), \ldots, P(\bar{e}M^{q^m-2})), \quad P(\bar{X}) \in P_\nu(m, q)$$

be a codeword of $HC_\nu(m, q)$ and define the corresponding codeword polynomial by

$$P(z) = \sum_{i=0}^{q^m-2} P(\bar{e}M^i) z^i$$

Then α^j is a root of the generator polynomial of $HC_\nu(m, q)$ iff $P(\alpha^j) = 0$ for all $P(\bar{x}) \in P_\nu(m, q)$, i.e.,

$$P(\alpha^j) = \sum_{i=0}^{q^m-2} P(\bar{e}M^i)(\alpha^j)^i$$
$$= \sum_{i=0}^{q^m-2} P(\bar{e}M^i)(\bar{e}M^i, \bar{\alpha})^j$$
$$= \sum_{\substack{\bar{\beta} \in V_m(q) \\ \bar{\beta} \neq \bar{0}}} P(\bar{\beta})(\bar{\beta}, \bar{\alpha})^j \quad (10.1)$$

and, from a previous lemma, this last quantity is zero if $\omega_q(j) \leq \mu = m(q-1) - \nu - 1$. We have proved:

Theorem 10.4 The element α^j is a zero of the generator polynomial of $HC_\nu(m, q)$ iff $0 < \omega_q(j) \leq m(q-1) - \nu - 1$.

The "only if" part of this theorem results from considering the code dimension.

Corollary The element α^j is a zero of the generator polynomial of the dual code of $HC_\nu(m, q)$ iff $0 \leq \omega_q(j) \leq m(q-1) - \mu - 1$.

Notice in the theorem that $\omega_q(j) > 0$. This follows since the summation in (10.1) is over $\bar{\beta} \in V_m(q)$, $\bar{\beta} \neq \bar{0}$, and a previous lemma stated that

$$\sum_{\bar{\beta} \in V_m(q)} P(\bar{\beta}) = 0$$

Since, in general, $P(\bar{0}) \neq 0$, we require the condition $\omega_q(j) > 0$. The corollary is easily derived from the characterization of the dual of the code $C_\nu(m, q)$.

1.10 The Polynomial Approach to Coding

If i is an integer such that $0 < \omega_q(i) \leq m(q-1) - v - 1$, then every integer $j \in J(i)$ (See Section 1.9) also has a q weight less than $m(q-1) - v - 1$ and from Theorem 9.1 we have:

Theorem 10.5 The code $C_v(m, q)$ is invariant under the doubly transitive affine group of permutations.

From Theorem 10.4 we have our second definition of GRM codes:

Definition 2 The cyclic code $HC_v(m, q)$ has α^j as a zero iff $0 < \omega_q(j) \leq \mu = m(q-1) - v - 1$. The code $C_v(m, q)$ is the code $HC_v(m, q)$ extended.

For our third definition we return to the original approach of Kasami et al. (1968a, b). This approach is a more natural generalization of the binary Reed–Muller codes than the previous work but we will only outline it here. Again let α be a primitive element of $GF(q^m)$ and

$$\alpha^j = \sum_{i=0}^{m-1} \alpha_{ij}\alpha^i, \quad 0 \leq j \leq q^m - 2, \quad a_{ij} \in GF(q)$$

Define the matrix G as

$$G = \begin{bmatrix} 1 & 1 & 1 & \cdots & 1 \\ a_{00} & a_{01} & a_{02} & \cdots & a_{0,n-1} \\ a_{10} & a_{11} & a_{12} & \cdots & a_{1,n-1} \\ \vdots & \vdots & \vdots & & \vdots \\ a_{m-1,0} & a_{m-1,1} & a_{m-1,2} & \cdots & a_{m-1,n-1} \end{bmatrix}, \quad n = q^m - 1$$

Label the rows successively as $v_I, v_0, v_1, \ldots, v_{m-1}$. As with the binary Reed–Muller codes, define a componentwise multiplication on $V_n(q)$. Define the matrix G_v to be the matrix G with all additional rows of the form

$$v_0^{i_0} v_1^{i_1} \cdots v_{m-1}^{i_{m-1}}, \quad \sum_{j=0}^{m-1} i_j \leq v$$

added.

Definition 3 The rows of the matrix G_v generate the cyclic code $HC_v(m, q)$.

The equivalence between Definitions 2 and 3 is established in Theorem 1 (Kasami et al., 1968a) and we will not demonstrate it here. With minor modifications this is the same as the multivariable polynomial approach.

Theorem 10.6 The code $HC_v(m, q)$ is a subcode of the BCH code with design distance $(R+1)q^Q - 1$, where $\mu + 1 = Q(q-1) + R$, $0 \leq R < q - 1$.

Proof Recalling that α^j is a zero of $HC_v(m, q)$ iff $0 < \omega_q(j) \leqslant m(q-1) - v - 1 = \mu$, we let h be the smallest integer such that $\omega_q(h) = \mu + 1$. Then we can write

$$h = Rq^Q + \sum_{i=0}^{Q-1} (q-1)q^i = (R+1)q^Q - 1$$

From the construction of h, every integer j, $0 \leqslant j < h$, is such that $\omega_q(j) \leqslant \mu$. Thus the elements $\alpha^1, \alpha^2, \ldots, \alpha^{(R+1)q^Q - 2}$ are all zeros of the code and $HC_v(m, q)$ is a subcode of the BCH code of design distance

$$d = (R+1)q^Q - 1. \quad \square$$

Actually, $HC_v(m, q)$ has exactly this minimum distance, as is shown (Kasami *et al.*, 1968a) by constructing a vector of minimum weight. Notice that for $m = 1$ the code $HC_v(m, q)$ is just the Reed–Solomon code of length $q - 1$ and distance $d = v + 1$.

To see the relationship between the single-variable and multivariable approaches, suppose that $L = \{\alpha^{-j}, j \in k\}$ are the zeros of a cyclic code $\mathscr{C}$. Then an equivalent characterization of $\mathscr{C}$ is

$$\mathscr{C} = \left\{ (F(1), F(\beta), \ldots, F(\beta^{n-1})) \,\Big|\, F(x) = \sum_{i=0}^{n-1} f_i x^i, \; f_i = 0 \; \text{if} \; \alpha^{-i} \in L \right\}$$

(Note: It is convenient in this instance to write $F_e(x)$ as $\sum_{i=0}^{n-1} f_i x^i$ rather than $\sum_{i=1}^{n} f_i x^{n-i}$ as before—hence we write the code zeros as α^{-i}.) We need to generalize the situation slightly. Let $F[z]$ be the set of polynomials

$$F[z] = \left\{ F(z) \in GF(q^m)[z]/(z^{q^m-1} - 1) \,\Big|\, F(\alpha^i) \in GF(q), \; 0 \leqslant i \leqslant q^m - 2 \right\}$$

where α is a primitive element of $GF(q^m)$. Actually, $F[z] \cong GF(q)[z]/(z^{q^m-1} - 1)$. Define the subspace of $F[z]$, $F_v[z]$, to be the set

$$F_v[z] = \left\{ F(z) \in F[z] \,\Big|\, F(z) = \sum_{i=0}^{q^m-2} f_i z^i, \; f_i = 0 \; \text{if} \; \omega_q(i) > v \right\}$$

For the code $HC_v(m, q)$ we had the theorem saying that α^i is a code zero iff $\omega_q(i) \leqslant m(q-1) - v - 1$. Equivalently, since $\omega_q(-i) = m(q-1) - \omega_q(i)$, we can say that α^{-i} is a zero of $HC_v(m, q)$ iff $\omega_q(i) \geqslant v + 1$. It follows then that the single-variable Mattson–Solomon characterization of $HC_v(m, q)$ would be

$$HC_v(m, q) = \{(F(1), F(\alpha), F(\alpha^2), \ldots, F(\alpha^{q^m-2})) \,|\, F(z) \in F_v[z]\}$$

The precise relationship between this single-variable approach and the multi-variable approach is explored in detail by Delsarte *et al.* (1970). We briefly

1.10 The Polynomial Approach to Coding

indicate the relationship here. Clearly the sets of polynomials $P_v(m, q)$ and $F_v[z]$ must somehow be related.

Choose the elements $\lambda_1, \lambda_2, \ldots, \lambda_m \in GF(q^m)$ as a dual basis to $1, \alpha, \alpha^2, \ldots, \alpha^{m-1}$, with α a primitive element of $GF(q^m)$, i.e.,

$$T(\lambda_i \alpha^j) = \delta_{ij}$$

where $T(x) = \sum_{i=0}^{m-1} x^{q^i}$ is the trace function of $GF(q^m)$ over $GF(q)$. It is then established that the mapping

$$\eta: P(m, q) \longrightarrow F[z]$$
$$P(\bar{x}) \longmapsto F(z) = P(T(\lambda_1 z), T(\lambda_2 z), \ldots, T(\lambda_m z))$$

is onto and that

$$F(\alpha^i) = P(\bar{\alpha}_i)$$

where $\bar{\alpha}_i = \bar{e}M^i$, using the previous notation. The key property of the mapping is that if $P(\bar{x}) \in P_v(m, q)$ and

$$F(z) = P(T(\lambda_1 z), T(\lambda_2 z), \ldots, T(\lambda_m z)) = \sum_{i=0}^{q-2} f_i z^i$$

then $f_i = 0$ if $\omega_q(i) > v$. This establishes the connection between the two polynomial characterizations of $HC_v(m, q)$

$$HC_v(m, q) = \{(F(1), F(\alpha), \ldots, F(\alpha^{q^m-2})) \mid F(z) \in F_v[z]\}$$
$$= \{(P(\bar{\gamma}), P(\bar{\gamma}M), \ldots, P(\bar{\gamma}M^{q^m-2})) \mid P(\bar{x}) \in P_v(m, q)\}$$

Consider now the nonprimitive GRM codes, i.e., those whose length is not of the form $q^m - 1$ for some integer m. The construction of these codes is much like that of the nonprimitive BCH codes, although slightly more complicated. We begin by considering the generator matrix of the primitive vth-order GRM code over $GF(q)$ of length $q^m - 1$ and recall that if α is a primitive root of $GF(q^m)$, then α^h is a root of the generator $g_d(x)$ of the dual of the vth-order GRM code iff $\omega_q(h) \leq v$. Thus all code vectors in the dual of the vth-order GRM code are in the null space over $GF(q)$ of the matrix

$$G_v = \begin{bmatrix} 1 & 1 & 1 & \cdots & 1 \\ 1 & \alpha^{h_1} & \alpha^{2h_1} & \cdots & \alpha^{(q^m-2)h_1} \\ 1 & \alpha^{h_2} & \alpha^{2h_2} & \cdots & \alpha^{(q^m-2)h_2} \\ \vdots & \vdots & \vdots & & \vdots \\ 1 & \alpha^{h_i} & \alpha^{2h_i} & \cdots & \alpha^{(q^m-2)h_i} \end{bmatrix}$$

and hence we may take this as a representation of the generator matrix of the vth-order GRM code, where $\{h = 0, h_1, h_2, \ldots, h_i\}$ represent all integers less than $q^m - 1$ whose weight is v or less. If we delete the first row of G_v, then the result will be the parity check matrix of the $[m(q-1)-v-1]$th-order GRM code, as discussed previously.

Now let β be a primitive nth root of unity of $GF(q^m)$, where $b = (q^m - 1)/n$, and consider those rows of G_v for which $b|h_j$ and denote, for these rows $t_j = h_j/b$. Notice that

$$(\alpha^{h_j})^{nl} = (\alpha^{bn})^{t_j l} = (\alpha^{q^m-1})^{t_j l} = 1, \qquad l = 1, \ldots, e-1$$

and hence each of the rows being considered consists of e replications of the first n bits. If there are $n - k$ rows such that $b|h_j$ then define the parity check matrix H to be the $(n-k) \times n$ matrix consisting of the first n bit positions of these $n - k$ rows. Clearly $n - k$ is the number of integers less than $q^m - 1$ that are divisible by b and whose weight is v or less. We can express the matrix H as

$$H = \begin{bmatrix} 1 & \beta^{t_1} & \beta^{2t_1} & \cdots & \beta^{(n-1)t_1} \\ 1 & \beta^{t_2} & \beta^{2t_2} & \cdots & \beta^{(n-1)t_2} \\ \vdots & \vdots & \vdots & & \vdots \\ 1 & \beta^{t_{n-k}} & \beta^{2t_{n-k}} & \cdots & \beta^{(n-1)t_{n-k}} \end{bmatrix}$$

and we define the vth-order nonprimitive GRM code as the null space of this matrix. In other words, the dual of the $((q^m - 1)/b, k)$ cyclic code whose generator polynomial contains α^h as a root iff $b|h$ and $\omega_q(h) \leq v$ will be called a vth-order nonprimitive GRM code.

When b is of the form $b = q^s - 1$ for some positive integer s, then the vth-order GRM code is closely related to the projective geometry codes which will be discussed in the next chapter.

The primitive GRM codes are related to the Euclidean geometry codes, also considered in the next chapter.

We now discuss a rather remarkable class of codes, polynomial codes, which were discovered by Kasami *et. al.* (1968b). Many of the previous classes of codes occur as a subclass of polynomial codes. Historically, they appear as a natural culmination of the work of the GRM codes and the finite geometry codes. While the basic work on finite geometry codes preceded that of polynomial codes, it is convenient to discuss the geometry codes as a subclass of polynomial codes. We shall examine both the Euclidean and projective geometry codes in some detail in the next chapter.

We begin with some preliminary terminology needed to define polynomial codes. Let m and s be two positive integers and α a primitive element of $GF(q^{ms})$. Choosing $1, \alpha, \alpha^2, \ldots, \alpha^{m-1}$ as a basis for $GF(q^{ms})$ over $GF(q^s)$, to each power of α we associate the m-tuple over $GF(q^s)$ by

$$\alpha^j = \sum_{i=1}^m a_{ij} \alpha^{i-1}, \qquad 0 \leq j \leq q^{ms} - 2, \quad a_{ij} \in GF(q^s)$$

1.10 The Polynomial Approach to Coding

and shall designate such an m-tuple as the coordinate vector of α^j over $GF(q^s)$. Let the positive integer b be a divisor of $q^s - 1$ and define

$$z = \frac{q^s - 1}{b}, \qquad n = \frac{q^{ms} - 1}{b}$$

where n will be the code length. Let $X_1, X_2, \ldots, X_m$ be m variables over $GF(q^s)$ and define $\bar{X}$ as $(X_1, X_2, \ldots, X_m)$. Let $Q_m(\mu, b)$ be the set of all polynomials in the variables $X_1, \ldots, X_m$ of the form

$$F(\bar{X}) = \sum_{i, v_i} c_{v_1 v_2 \ldots v_m} X_1^{v_1} X_2^{v_2} \cdots X_m^{v_m}$$

with the properties that:

(i) The coefficients $c_{v_1 v_2 \ldots v_m} \in GF(q^s)$.
(ii) $0 \leq v_i \leq q^s - 1$, $1 \leq i \leq m$.
(iii) $\sum_{i=1}^m v_i = jb$ with $0 \leq j \leq \mu$.
(iv) $f(a_{1l}, a_{2l}, \ldots, a_{ml}) \in GF(q)$, $0 \leq l < n$, where $(a_{1l}, a_{2l}, \ldots, a_{ml})$ is the coordinate vector of α_l.

Now for each such polynomial $f(\bar{X})$ in $Q_m(\mu, b)$ we define an associated n-tuple over $GF(q)$

$$v(f) = (v_0, v_1, \ldots, v_{n-1})$$

whose components are given by

$$v_j = f(a_{1j}, a_{2j}, \ldots, a_{mj}) \in GF(q), \qquad 0 \leq j \leq n - 1$$

Definition An (n, m, s, μ, q) polynomial code over $GF(q)$ of length n is defined as a set of vectors

$$\{v(f) \mid f(\bar{X}) \in Q_m(\mu, b)\}$$

It is clear that the code is linear since the sum of two polynomials in $Q_m(\mu, b)$ is also in $Q_m(\mu, b)$. The following theorem, however, is surprising.

Theorem 10.7 (Kasami et al. 1968b) An (n, m, s, μ, q) polynomial code over $GF(q)$ is cyclic and α^h is a root of its generator polynomial if and only if $b \mid h$ and

$$\min_{0 \leq l < s} \omega_{q^s}(hq^l) = jb$$

with $0 < j < mz - \mu$.

For $s = 1$ this condition is similar to that specifying the roots of GRM codes. Also, conditions specifying roots of the generator polynomial of the cyclic Euclidean and projective geometry codes, which historically appeared before the above theorem, turn out to be disguised versions of this theorem, as we will see in the next chapter. We shall not prove this important theorem, since the notation required is formidable. We refer the reader to the original paper (Kasami *et al.* 1968b, Theorem 6, p. 809). Notice that if α^h is to be a root of the generator polynomial $g(x)$, then, since the code is cyclic and of length n, the order of α^h must divide n. Since the nth roots of unity are $1, \alpha^b, \alpha^{2b}, \ldots, \alpha^{(n-1)b}$, then h is a multiple of b. If h is such that α^h is a root of $g(x)$ then it necessarily follows from the condition in Theorem 10.7, that α^{hq} is also a root and we conclude that the codimension of the code is the number of integers $h, 0 < h \leqslant q^{ms} - 2$, such that $b | h$ and

$$\min_{0 \leqslant l < s} \omega_{q^s}(hq^l) = jb, \qquad 0 < j < mz - \mu$$

Theorem 10.8 The dual code of an (n, m, s, μ, q) polynomial code has α^h as a root of its generator polynomial $g_d(x)$ iff $b | h$ and

$$\max_{0 \leqslant l < s} \omega_{q^s}(hq^l) = jb, \qquad 0 \leqslant j \leqslant \mu$$

Proof The proof is actually an immediate consequence of the previous theorem and the arguments are similar to those used for the GRM codes. However, we shall elaborate a little further. If $g(x)g^*(x) = x^n - 1$, where $g(x)$ is the generator polynomial of the (n, m, s, μ, q) polynomial code of dimension k, say, then $g_d(x) = x^k g^*(1/x)$. From Theorem 10.7, α^h is a root of $g(x)$ iff

$$\min_{0 \leqslant l < s} \omega_{q^s}(hq^l) = jb, \qquad 0 < j < mz - \mu$$

If α^r is an nth root of unity, then $b | r$, and if $b | r$, then $b | \omega_{q^s}(r)$ since, if

$$r = \sum_{i=0}^{m-1} \delta_i q^{is} = \sum_{i=0}^{m-1} \delta_i + \sum_{i=0}^{m-1} \delta_i(q^{is} - 1)$$

and, since $b | (q^{is} - 1)$, this implies $b | \sum_{i=0}^{m-1} \delta_i = \omega_{q^s}(r)$. From the previous theorem we conclude that α^r is a root of $g^*(x)$ iff

$$\min_{0 \leqslant l < s} \omega_{q^s}(rq^l) = jb, \qquad mz - \mu \leqslant j \leqslant mz$$

and in this case α^{-r} will be a root of $g_d(x)$. Letting $r' = -r \equiv q^{ms} - 1 - r$, we have that

$$\omega_{q^s}(r'q^l) = \omega_{q^s}((q^{ms} - 1 - r)q^l) = m(q^s - 1) - \omega_{q^s}(rq^l)$$

and hence α^r is a root of $g_d(x)$ iff

$$\max_{0 \leqslant l < s} \omega_{q^s}(r'q^l) = m(q^s - 1) - jb, \qquad mz - \mu \leqslant j \leqslant mz$$
$$= (mz - j)b$$
$$= j'b, \qquad 0 \leqslant j' \leqslant \mu$$

as required. □

1.10 The Polynomial Approach to Coding

A BCH type of bound on the distance of an (n, m, s, μ, q) polynomial code is readily established by the following reasoning. Let h_0 be the smallest positive integer that is divisible by b such that

$$\min_{0 \leq l < s} \omega_{q^s}(h_0 q^l) = (mz - \mu)b$$

Since the smallest integer with q^s weight $(mz - \mu)b$ is

$$h_0' = (q^s - 1) + (q^s - 1)q^s + \cdots + (q^s - 1)q^{(Q-1)s} + Rq^{Qs}$$

we have that $h_0 \geq h_0'$, where Q and R are the quotient and remainder obtained by dividing $(mz - \mu)b$ by $q^s - 1$ or

$$(mz - \mu)b = Q(q^s - 1) + R, \qquad 0 \leq R < q^s - 1$$

Now consider any positive integer $h < h_0'$ that is divisible by b. Clearly, the q^s weight of any such integer is less than $(mz - \mu)b$ and hence

$$\min_{0 \leq l < s} \omega_{q^s}(h q^l) = jb, \qquad 0 < j < mz - \mu$$

and thus, for any such integer h, α^h is a root of the generator polynomial. This implies that the elements

$$\alpha^b, \alpha^{2b}, \ldots, \alpha^{h_0' - b}$$

are zeros of the generator polynomial.

Since $\beta = \alpha^b$ is a primitive nth root of unity, we have that

$$\beta, \beta^2, \ldots, \beta^{(h_0' - b)/b}$$

are roots of $g(x)$ and hence the minimum distance of the code is at least

$$\frac{h_0'}{b} = \frac{(q^s - 1) + (q^s - 1)q^s + \cdots + (q^s - 1)q^{(Q-1)s} + Rq^{Qs}}{b}$$

$$= \frac{q^{Qs} - 1 + Rq^{Qs}}{b} = \frac{(R + 1)q^{Qs} - 1}{b}$$

Theorem 10.9 An (n, m, s, μ, q) polynomial code has minimum distance at least

$$\frac{(R + 1)q^{Qs} - 1}{b}$$

where Q and R are the quotient and remainder obtained by dividing $(mz - \mu)b$ by $q^s - 1$.

In certain instances the lower bound on the minimum distance given in the previous theorem can be shown to be exact. In particular, if either (i) $R = 0$, or (ii) $s = 1$, or (iii) there exists a BCH code with design distance R/b and of length $(q^s - 1)/b$ whose minimum distance is exactly R/b, then the bound

$$d_{\min} \geq \frac{(R+1)q^{Qs} - 1}{b}$$

is exact. It may also be that the polynomial code is a subcode of the BCH code with this design distance and thus in these instances the design distance of the BCH code is exact.

The relationship between BCH and polynomial codes is further examined by Chen and Lin (1969), who also show that any primitive polynomial code (i.e., $b = 1$) is a subcode of the m-fold direct product of an extended primitive BCH code with itself.

To investigate subclasses of polynomial codes, notice that $b \mid \omega_q^s(h)$ iff $b \mid h$. This follows from the fact that if

$$h = \sum_{i=1}^{m} \delta_i q^{(i-1)s}$$

then

$$h - \omega_{q^s}(h) = \sum_{i=1}^{m} \delta_i q^{(i-1)s} - \sum_{i=1}^{m} \delta_i = \sum_{i=2}^{m} \delta_i [q^{(i-1)s} - 1]$$

and b divides the right-hand side of this equation. It follows that $b \mid [h - \omega_{q^s}(h)]$ and hence if it divides either h or $\omega_{q^s}(h)$, it must also divide the other. Now consider the case when $m = 1$ and $\mu n = -d$. The condition that α^h be a zero of the code then reduces to

$$\min_{0 \leq l < s} \omega_{q^s}(hq^l) = jb, \qquad 0 < j < d$$

If we set $\beta = \alpha^b$, then, since $\omega_{q^s}(b) = b$ and $b \mid \omega_{q^s}(bq^l)$, we have that

$$\min_{0 \leq l < s} \omega_{q^s}(bq^l) = b$$

and α^b is a zero of the code. Similarly $\beta^2, \beta^3, \ldots, \beta^{d-1}$ are zeros of the code of length $n = (q^s - 1)/b$ over $GF(q)$ and β is a primitive nth root of unity. Thus the code is a BCH code with design distance d. If, in addition to the foregoing conditions, $s = 1$, we obtain a Reed–Solomon code of length $(q-1)/b$ over $GF(q)$.

If we set $s = 1$, $b = 1$, then α^h is a zero of the code iff

$$\omega_q(h) = j, \qquad 0 < j < m(q-1) - \mu$$

The code is of length $q^m - 1$ over $GF(q)$ and these conditions describe the GRM code $HC_\mu(m, q)$.

The problem of determining the number of information symbols of polynomial codes has been considered by Chen and Lin (1969), who obtain exact expressions for certain subclasses. Lin (1972b) obtains a combinatorial expression for this quantity.

The GRM codes were the immediate predecessors of the polynomial codes and the two classes are, of course, closely related. To define this relationship, we consider the idea of a subfield subcode. Let $\mathscr{C}(q^s)$ be a cyclic code over $GF(q^s)$ with generator polynomial $g(x)$ and let $\mathscr{C}(q)$ be the set of codewords in $\mathscr{C}(q^s)$ with coordinates from $GF(q)$. Since $\mathscr{C}(q)$ is cyclic, denote its generator polynomial by $g_s(x)$. Suppose that α is a root of $g_s(x)$, so that α^{q^i}, $i = 1, 2, \ldots$, are also roots of $g(x)$. Suppose that α^{q^l} is also a root of $g(x)$ for some l. Since $g(x)|g_s(x)$, α^{q^l} is also a root of $g_s(x)$, as are $(\alpha^{q^l})^{q^j}$. In particular, $(\alpha^{q^l})^{q^{s-l}} = \alpha$ is a root of $g_s(x)$. Conversely, suppose α is a root of $g_s(x)$. If α^{q^i} is not a root of $g(x)$ for any i, then we can factor $g_s(x) = g_{1s}(x)g_{2s}(x)$, where $g_{1s}(x)$ is the minimum polynomial of α over $GF(q)$. Clearly $g_{2s}(x) \in GF(q)[x]$ and $g(x)|g_{2s}(x)$, implying that $g_s(x)$ is not the generator polynomial of $\mathscr{C}(q)$, contrary to assumption. Thus α^{q^i} must be a root of $g(x)$ for some i. Thus α is a root of $g_s(x)$ iff α^{q^i} is a root of $g(x)$ for some i.

This fact makes clear the relationship between GRM and polynomial codes. Let α be a primitive root of $GF(q^{ms})$. Then α^h is a root of the μth-order GRM code of length $(q^{ms} - 1)/b$ over $GF(q^s)$ iff $b|\omega_{q^s}(h)$ and

$$0 < \omega_{q^s}(h) < m(q^s - 1) - \mu b$$

for some m, μ, and b. On the other hand, from Theorem 10.7, $\alpha^{h'}$ is the root of an (n, m, s, μ, q) polynomial code over $GF(q)$ iff $b|h'$, and

$$\min_{0 \leqslant l < s} \omega_{q^s}(h'q^l) = jb, \qquad 0 < j < \frac{m(q^s - 1) - \mu}{b}$$

Note that if $b|(q^s - 1)$, then $b|h'$ iff $b|\omega_{q^s}(h')$. Thus, if $\alpha^{h'}$ is a root of the polynomial code, then for some l, $\alpha^{h'q^l}$ will be a root of the GRM code over $GF(q^s)$ and conversely. Thus the generator of the polynomial code, an element of $GF(q)[x]$, divides the generator of the GRM code, an element of $GF(q^s)[x]$, and the polynomial code is a subfield subcode of the GRM code.

1.11 Bounds on Code Dictionaries

Bounds that have been mentioned or used in this chapter, or that will be used in succeeding chapters, are proven here. The section is then by no means a complete discussion of the results and techniques of bounding. To begin on an optimistic note, we first prove the Gilbert (1952) lower bound on linear codes, which assures the existence of interesting codes. It was discovered independently by Varshamov (1957) and is usually referred to as the Varshamov–Gilbert bound.

In order to demonstrate the existence of a linear (n, k) code with distance d over $GF(q)$, it is only necessary to show the existence of an $(n - k) \times n$ matrix H such that no set of $d - 1$ columns is linearly independent. In finding such a matrix, we can choose the first column as any of the $q^{n-k} - 1$ nonzero $(n - k)$-tuples over $GF(q)$. The second column can be chosen as any nonzero $(n - k)$-tuple over $GF(q)$ which is not a scalar multiple of the first column. In general, suppose $n - 1$ columns have been chosen so that any $d - 1$ of them are linearly independent. There are

$$\sum_{i=0}^{d-2} \binom{n-1}{i}(q-1)^i$$

vectors generated by nonzero linear combinations of $d - 2$ or fewer of the chosen $n - 1$ columns. At worst, these will be distinct, implying that if

$$q^{n-k} > \sum_{i=0}^{d-2} \binom{n-1}{i}(q-1)^i$$

then it will be possible to choose an nth column that is independent of any $d - 2$ of the first $n - 1$ columns. We have shown:

Theorem 11.1 It is possible to construct an (n, k) linear code over $GF(q)$ with minimum distance d if

$$q^{n-k} > \sum_{i=0}^{d-2} \binom{n-1}{i}(q-1)^i \tag{11.1}$$

The bound in the following theorem, called the Plotkin bound, will be of interest in the next chapter, where classes of codes that meet the bound with equality are constructed using balanced incomplete block designs.

Theorem 11.2 If a block code $\mathscr{C}$ of length n, size N, and minimum distance d exists, then

$$d \leq \frac{nN(q-1)}{(N-1)q} \tag{11.2}$$

Proof Form the $N \times n$ matrix D whose rows are the codewords and consider the sum

$$S = \sum_{(u,v) \in \mathscr{C}} d(u, v)$$

1.11 Bounds on Code Dictionaries

Since, if $u \neq v$, we have $d(u, v) \geq d$, we can lower bound S by $S \geq N(N - 1)d$. To obtain an upper bound on S, we consider the first column of D. Label the elements of the alphabet by the integers $0, 1, \ldots q - 1$ and let t_i be the number of times i appears in the first column. For a fixed $u, v \in \mathscr{C}$, if their first coordinates are the same, they contribute nothing to S, while if they are different, they contribute one. If a given word u has first coordinate i, then we have $\sum_{j \neq i} t_j = N - t_i$ since $\sum_{i=0}^{q-1} t_i = N$. Since there are t_i such words, they contribute $t_i(N - t_i)$ to S. Finally, we have

$$\sum_{i=0}^{q-1} t_i(N - t_i) = R \tag{11.3}$$

is the contribution of the first coordinate position to S. An elementary induction argument yields that the expression in Equation (11.3) is maximized by choosing $t_i = N/q$. Since t_i is an integer, we conclude that

$$R = \sum_{i=0}^{q-1} t_i(N - t_i) = N^2 - \sum_{i=0}^{q-1} t_i^2 \leq N^2 - q\left(\frac{N}{q}\right)^2 = N^2 \frac{q-1}{q}$$

Since the same applies for any column, we have

$$N(N-1)d \leq S \leq nN^2 \frac{q-1}{q}$$

which implies that

$$d \leq \frac{nN(q-1)}{(N-1)q} \tag{11.4}$$

and the bound is satisfied iff each element appears N/q times in each column of D, which requires that $q | N$. $\square$

Let $A(n, d)$ be the maximum size of a binary code of length n and minimum distance d. Hamming (1950) showed that for a binary alphabet

$$A(n, 1) = 2^n, \quad A(n, 2) = 2^{n-1}, \quad A(n + 1, 2k) = A(n, 2k - 1)$$

as well as finding the Hamming sphere packing bound for odd distance codes

$$A(n, 2k - 1) \leq \frac{2^n}{\sum_{i=0}^{k-1} \binom{n}{i}}$$

Although Hamming was concerned with linear dictionaries, the results are still valid. The fact that $A(n + 1, 2k) = A(n, 2k - 1)$ is easily seen as follows. Suppose we have an $A(n, 2k - 1)$ code. Adding a parity check position increases both the length and distance by one, giving that $A(n + 1, 2k) \geq A(n, 2k - 1)$. Conversely, suppose that we are given an $A(n + 1, 2k)$ code. If we delete the first coordinate position, we obtain a code of length n and distance at least $2k - 1$, giving $A(n, 2k - 1) \geqslant A(n + 1, 2k)$. Thus we have $A(n + 1, 2k) = A(n, 2k - 1)$. From the Plotkin bound of Eq. (11.4) we have that for $q = 2$

$$2d(N - 1) \leqslant nN \quad \text{or} \quad (2d - n)N \leqslant 2d$$

Thus, if $2d > n$, we conclude that

$$A(n, d) \leqslant 2d/(2d - n)$$

Applying this formula to the various parameters yields:

(i) $A(n, n) = 2$.
(ii) $A(4m - 1, 2m) \leqslant 4m$.
(iii) $A(4m - 2, 2m) \leqslant 2m$.

Lemma $A(n, d) \leqslant 2A(n - 1, d)$.

Proof Let $\mathscr{C}$ be a binary code with $A(n, d)$ words. Suppose, without loss of generality, that at least half the codewords begin with zero. If, from this set of codewords, we delete the first coordinate position, we obtain a code of length $n - 1$, distance at least d, with at least $A(n, d)/2$ words, i.e., $A(n - 1, d) \geqslant A(n, d)/2$. □

Corollary Since $A(4m - 1, 2m) \leqslant 4m$, we have that $A(4m, 2m) \leqslant 8m$. If $A(4m, 2m) = 8m$, then $A(4m - 1, 2m) = 4m$ and $A(4m - 2, 2m) = 2m$.

Plotkin (1960) showed that if $4m - 1$ is a prime, then a code with $8m$ words can be constructed, showing that $A(4m, 2m) = 8m$, in this case. We will discuss this situation further in the next chapter in relating codes that achieve this bound to Hadamard matrices.

Johnson (1962) provides an interesting extension of the Hamming sphere packing bound. Again we are interested in bounding $A(n, d)$ for binary codes. We introduce the function $R(n, d, e)$ to denote the maximum number of binary n-tuples of weight exactly d such that any two of them are distance at least d apart, where $d = 2e + 1$. Without loss of generality we assume that the zero n-tuple is in the code. Let $S_i(x)$ be the sphere of radius i about x. The spheres of radius e about each codeword of our code do not intersect and this argument yields the Hamming bound. To refine this bound, we consider the points in spheres of radius $e + 1$ around codepoints.

There are $\binom{n}{e+1}$ points in $V_n(2)$ of weight $e + 1$, and the maximum number of nearest neighbors of the origin in a code of distance $d = 2e + 1$ is $R(n, d, e)$. Any codeword x of weight d has $\binom{d}{e}$ points of $V_n(2)$ in $S_e(x)$ of weight $e + 1$.

1.11 Bounds on Code Dictionaries

Thus $\binom{n}{e+1} - \binom{d}{e}R(n, d, e)$ points of $e + 1$ are a distance at least $e + 1$ from any codeword. However, each such point can be a distance $e + 1$ from no more than $\lfloor n/(e + 1) \rfloor$ codewords and these codewords would have to be of weight $2(e + 1)$. We obtain our bound by arguing as follows. The spheres of radius e about codewords are nonintersecting. A point of $V_n(2)$ that is a distance $e + 1$ from some codeword could be a distance $e + 1$ from at most $\lfloor n/(e + 1) \rfloor$ codewords. Thus the number of points of $V_n(2)$ that are at a distance $e + 1$ from some codeword is upper-bounded by the quantity

$$\frac{A(n, d)\binom{n}{e+1} - \binom{d}{e}R(n, d, e)}{\lfloor n/(e + 1) \rfloor}$$

where we divide by $\lfloor n/(e + 1) \rfloor$ to ensure that each such point is counted only once. We have shown:

Theorem 11.3

$$A(n, d)\left\{\sum_{i=0}^{e}\binom{n}{i} + \frac{\binom{n}{e+1} - \binom{d}{e}R(n, d, e)}{\lfloor n/(e + 1) \rfloor}\right\} \leq 2^n \quad (11.5)$$

It follows directly from this that the number of minimum weight vectors in a perfect binary code must be $\binom{n}{e+1}/\binom{d}{e}$. This is also demonstrated in Chapter 3, where the relationship between t designs and codes is considered. Codes that meet the bound in Theorem 11.3 will be constructed in Chapter 3.

The quantity $R(n, d, e)$ is crucial to the bound (11.5) and the following theorem gives two interesting upper bounds to it.

Theorem 11.4

(i) $R(n, d, e) \leq \left\lfloor \frac{n}{d}\left\lfloor \frac{n-1}{d-1}\cdots \left\lfloor \frac{n-e}{d-e}\right\rfloor\cdots\right\rfloor\right\rfloor$

(ii) If $d^2 > ne$, then $R(n, d, e) \leq \left\lfloor \frac{n(d-e)}{d^2 - ne}\right\rfloor$

Proof (i) Consider a matrix with $R(n, d, e)$ rows and n columns where the rows are of weight d and are a distance at least d apart. The maximum number of ones in any column is $R(n - 1, d - 1, e - 1)$ since if we consider those rows of the matrix with ones in, say, the first column, then these rows with this column deleted have length $n - 1$, weight $d - 1$, and distance at least d or, equivalently, any two rows have an inner product of at most $e - 1$. The maximum number of ones in the original matrix is $n \cdot R(n - 1, d - 1,$

$e-1$) by counting the maximum number of ones in each column. On the other hand, each row is of weight d and we conclude that

$$dR(n, d, e) \leqslant nR(n-1, d-1, e-1)$$

or

$$R(n, d, e) \leqslant \left\lfloor \frac{n}{d} R(n-1, d-1, e-1) \right\rfloor$$

since $R(n, d, e)$ is an integer. Repeated application of this yields part (i).

(ii) The calculation for this part is almost identical to that for the Plotkin bound. Let λ_{ij} be the inner product of the ith and jth rows of the $R = R(n, d, e) \times n$ matrix described in part (i). Clearly the quantity

$$S = \sum_{\substack{i,j=1 \\ i \neq j}}^{R} \lambda_{ij}$$

may be upper-bounded by $R(R-1)e$ since the inner product of any two distinct rows is at most e. Doing the same calculation on a column basis and letting the ith column have $k_i \leqslant R(n-1, d-1, e-1)$ ones in it, we have

$$S = \sum_{i=1}^{n} k_i(k_i - 1)$$

Since $Rd = \sum_{i=1}^{n} k_i$, then

$$S = \sum_{i=1}^{n} k_i^2 - Rd$$

and, as in the Plotkin bound, the first term is minimized when $k_i = Rd/n$. Comparing the two quantities yields

$$R(R-1)e \geqslant \frac{R^2 d^2}{n} - Rd$$

or

$$R \leqslant \left\lfloor \frac{n(d-e)}{d^2 - ne} \right\rfloor$$

where the integral value signs arise since R is an integer. □

It has been observed that for a linear (n, k) code over $GF(q)$ of distance d it is true that

$$d \leqslant n - k + 1$$

We now prove this bound for nonlinear codes. Let $\mathscr{C}$ be a block code of length n, size N, and distance d. Arranging the codewords in a matrix, observe that in the first column at least one of the alphabet symbols appears at least $[N/q]$ times. If $\mathscr{C}'$ is such a set of $[N/q]$ words with the first digit deleted, then $\mathscr{C}'$ is code of block length $n - 1$, size at least $[N/q]$, and distance at least d. Repeating the argument t times would yield a code of block length $n - t$ with size

$$[\cdots[[N/q]/q]\cdots] \geqslant [N/q^t]$$

and distance d, providing $[N/q^t] \geqslant q$, or equivalently, $t \leqslant \lceil \log_q N \rceil - 1$. Since $d \leqslant n - t$, we conclude that

$$d \leqslant n - \lceil \log_q N \rceil + 1$$

which is the required bound.

1.12 Comments

The aim of the chapter was to provide a reasonably complete account of the theory of finite fields and of polynomials and vector spaces over finite fields, although in some respects the treatment was necessarily shallow. The background material assumed of the reader can be found in any good introductory book on algebra. Particularly good books are those of Artin (1959), Herstein (1964), and Kaplansky (1969b). Several books contain accounts of finite field theory from different points of view. The books on coding theory by Peterson (1961) and Berlekamp (1968) contain chapters devoted to finite fields and polynomials. The classic reference is perhaps the book by Dickson (1958), which is entirely devoted to finite fields and groups of linear transformations defined over them. The books by Albert (1956) and Carmichael (1956) also contain excellent sections on the theory. Van der Waerden (1953) gives a nice account of symmetric functions, among other things.

The initial part of Section 1.4 concerned with the more geometric aspects of vector spaces over finite fields was influenced by the excellent monograph of Kaplansky (1969a). The paper by Conway (1968a) was particularly helpful in the discussion of dual bases of vector spaces as well as for its material on computation over a finite field. Other information on this problem is contained in the paper by Alanen and Knuth (1964). Gaussian coefficients are investigated by Goldman and Rota (1969). Discussions of linear groups can be found in many places, but we followed mainly Artin (1957) and Carmichael (1956).

The sources of the coding material in this chapter are quoted in the text. We mention only the paper of Delsarte *et al.* (1970) for their polynomial approach to coding and to GRM codes, which was followed in Section 1.10.

Exercises

1 Let R be a commutative ring with identity. Show that $R[x]$ is a principal ideal domain iff R is a field.

2 Following Theorem 1.1 it was stated that the splitting field of any polynomial $f(x) \in K[x]$, $\deg f = n$, is at most degree $n!$ over K. Demonstrate that this upper bound can be achieved by showing that the splitting field of $x^3 - 2$ over the rational numbers $\mathbb{Q}$ is of degree six over $\mathbb{Q}$.

3 Show that if the field K has characteristic p not equal to zero, then if $f(x) \in K[x]$ is such that $f'(x) = 0$, then $f(x) = h(x^p)$ for some $h(x) \in K[x]$.

4 Prove that the distinct isomorphisms of the field K_1 onto the field K_2 are linearly independent.

5 (Albert, 1956, p. 133) Let $f(x)$ be an irreducible polynomial of degree m over $GF(q)$ and of exponent $(q^m - 1)/d$. Let t be a prime divisor of e and $t \nmid d$. Then $f(x^t)$ is irreducible over $GF(q)$ and has exponent et.

6 (Dickson, 1958, p. 34) Let $f(x)$ be an irreducible polynomial of degree m over $GF(q)$, $q = p^n$. Show that $f(x^p - x)$ is an irreducible polynomial over $GF(q)$ of degree mp if the trace of α in $GF(q)$ over $GF(p)$ is nonzero, where α is the coefficient of x^{m-1} in $f(x)$.

7 (Dickson, 1958, p. 32) Show that an irreducible polynomial of degree m over $GF(q)$, $q = p^d$, is also irreducible over $GF(q^n)$ if $(n, m) = 1$. Further, show that an irreducible polynomial of degree l over $GF(q)$ decomposes into k irreducible factors of degree l/k over $GF(q^s)$, $k = (l, s)$.

8 (Dickson, 1958, p. 42) Show that $x^p - x - \alpha$ is a primitive irreducible polynomial over $GF(p)$ iff (i) α is a primitive root of $GF(p)$ and (ii) a root of the equation $y^p \equiv y + 1 \pmod{p}$ has order $(p^p - 1)/(p - 1)$.

9 (Albert, 1956, p. 132) Let $f(x)$ be an irreducible polynomial of degree n over $GF(q)$. Let T be the automorphism $x \to x^p$ of $GF(q)$, i.e., $T \in G(q/p)$. Define the polynomial $g(y)$, where $f(T)y = yg(y)$. Then show that $g(y)$, which has degree $q^n - 1$, is irreducible over $GF(q)$ iff $f(x)$ is primitive.

10 (Berlekamp, 1968, p. 243) To find the solutions of a quadratic equation over a finite field, we first note that the equation $x^2 + ax + b$, $a, b \in GF(2^m)$, has a solution over $GF(2^m)$ iff $y^2 + y + \alpha$, $\alpha = a^{-2}b$, has a solution. Show (as in Problem 8) that this equation has a solution iff $\text{tr}(\alpha) = 0$. Let β be a root of an irreducible polynomial of degree m over $GF(2)$ and let β^k be such that

$\operatorname{tr} \beta^k = 1$. Then it is always possible to determine elements y_i, $i = 0, 1, \ldots, m - 1$, such that

$$y_i^2 + y_i = \begin{cases} \beta^i & \text{if } \operatorname{tr} \beta^i = 0 \\ \beta^i + \beta^k & \text{if } \operatorname{tr} \beta^i = 1 \end{cases}$$

If $\alpha = \sum_{i=0}^{m-1} a_i \beta^i$, $a_i \in GF(2)$, then show that the two solutions of the quadratic equation $y^2 + y + \alpha$ are given by $\sum_{i=0}^{m-1} a_i y_i$ and $1 + \sum_{i=0}^{m-1} a_i y_i$.

11 Let V_1 and V_2 be subspaces of $V_n(q)$. Show that $\dim(V_1 \cap V_2) + \dim(V_1 + V_2) = \dim V_1 + \dim V_2$.

12 (Kaplansky, 1969b, p. 47) Show that in a finite field any element can be written as a sum of two squares.

13 Let $f(x) = \sum_{i=0}^{n} f_i x^i$ be an irreducible polynomial over $GF(2)$ of exponent e and let $f^{\alpha}(x) = \sum_{i=0}^{n} f_i x^{2^i - 1}$. Show that all irreducible factors of $f^{\alpha}(x)$ are of exponent e. Show also that $f(x)$ is primitive iff $f^{\alpha}(x)$ is irreducible.

14 (Trinomials)   Let $T_{n,k}(x) = x^n + x^k + 1$, $0 < k < n$.

(i) (Kaplansky, 1969b) For $n \geq 3$ show that $T_{2^n, 1}(x)$ is reducible over $GF(2)$. Show also that the degree of every irreducible factor divides $2n$ but not n.

(ii) (Mills and Zierler, 1969) Show that the degree of every irreducible factor of $T_{2^n+1, 2^{n-1}-1}(x)$ divides either $2(n-1)$ or $3(n-1)$ but not $n-1$.

(iii) (Zierler and Brillhart, 1968) If $n \equiv 1$ or 2 and $k \equiv 2$ or $1 \pmod 3$, then $T_{n,k}(x)$ is divisible by $x^2 + x + 1$ and conversely.

15 (Swan, 1962) Let $f(x)$ be a monic polynomial over $GF(q)$, where q is the power of an odd prime. The discriminant of $f(x)$ is defined to be $D(f) = \delta(f)^2$, where

$$\delta(f) = \prod_{i < j} (\alpha_i - \alpha_j)$$

where $\alpha_1, \ldots, \alpha_n$ are the roots of $f(x)$, including repeated roots in some extension field of $GF(q)$. If $f(x)$ has no repeated roots and has r irreducible factors over $GF(q)$, then show that $r \equiv n \bmod 2$ iff $D(f)$ is a square in $GF(q)$.

16 (Ireland and Rosen, 1972) If $q \equiv 1 \bmod n$, show that the equation $x^n = \alpha \neq 0$, $\alpha \in GF(q)$, has either no solutions or n solutions in $GF(q)$. Show that it has n solutions in $GF(q^n)$.

17 (Ireland and Rosen, 1972) If $(q, n) \equiv 1$, show that the smallest extension field of $GF(q)$ in which $x^n - 1$ splits is $GF(q^a)$, where a is the smallest integer such that $q^a \equiv 1 \bmod n$.

18 Let $\mathscr{C}_1$ be an (n_1, k_1) code with generator matrix G_1 over $GF(q)$ and $\mathscr{C}_2$ an (n_2, k_2) code with generator matrix G_2 over $GF(q)$. Let $\mathscr{C}$ be the code with generator matrix $G_1 \otimes G_2$ (Kronecker product). Show that $\mathscr{C}$ is an $(n_1 n_2, k_1 k_2)$ code with distance $d_1 d_2$.

19 Let α be a root of the irreducible polynomial $x^5 + x^2 + 1$ over $GF(2)$. Find the generator polynomial of the BCH code of length 31 and design distance five.

20 (Relationship between Maximum Length and Hamming Codes) Let A be a $q^k \times n$ matrix over $GF(q)$ whose rows are the codewords of an (n, k) code over $GF(q)$. Show that each (nonzero) column of A contains each field element exactly q^{k-1} times. Let G be a generator matrix of dimension $k \times (q^k - 1)$ whose columns consist of all nonzero k-tuples over $GF(q)$. Show that in the corresponding code all codewords have weight $(q - 1)q^{k-1}$. If G' is the generator matrix whose columns contain one representative from each of the $(q^k - 1)/(q - 1)$ classes, each class containing all nonzero scalar multiples of a given nonzero k-tuple, then all codewords have weight q^{k-1}.

21 In the Mattson–Solomon polynomial description of a code we associated a polynomial $F_{\mathbf{c}}(x)$ with each codeword $\mathbf{c}$ such that $F_{\mathbf{c}}(\beta^i) = c_i$. Show that, in general, for a polynomial $f(x) = \sum f_i x_i \in GF(q^m)[x]$ that if β is a primitive nth root of unity and $(n, q) = 1$, then

$$F_{\mathbf{c}}(\beta^i) \in GF(q) \quad \text{iff} \quad f_{q^i} = (f_i)^q \quad (q^i \text{ taken mod } n)$$

22 (Delsarte, 1973b) The generating function of Krawtchouk polynomials is given by

$$(z - y)^i (z + \lambda y)^{n-i} = \sum_{k=0}^{n} P_k(i) y^k z^{n-k}$$

and the Krawtchouk polynomial of degree k is

$$P_k(x) = \sum_{j=0}^{k} (-1)^j \lambda^{k-j} \binom{x}{j} \binom{n-x}{k-j}$$

where $\binom{x}{j} = x(x - 1) \cdots (x - j + 1)/j!$. Show that these polynomials satisfy the relationships

(i) $\binom{n}{i} P_s(i) = \binom{n}{s} P_i(s)$, with i, s positive integers.

(ii) $\sum_{i=0}^{n} v_i P_r(i) P_s(i) = q^n v_r \delta_{rs}$, where $v_i = \binom{n}{i} \lambda^i$ and $\lambda = q - 1$.

To an $(n + 1)$-tuple $A = (A_0, A_1, \ldots, A_n)$ associate the bivariate homogeneous polynomial

$$A(y, z) = \sum_{i=0}^{n} A_i y^i z^{n-i}$$

Exercises 93

The Krawtchouk or K-transform of this $(n + 1)$-tuple is given by

$$A'(y, z) = A(z - y, z + \lambda y) = \sum_{i=0}^{n} A_i' y^i z^{n-i}$$

If the $(n + 1)$-tuple A is the weight distribution for a code and $B = (B_0, B_1, \ldots, B_n)$ the weight distribution of its dual, then show that $A_i' = q^k B_i$. If A is an arbitrary $(n + 1)$-tuple, A' its K-transform, $d(A)$ the smallest i, $1 \leqslant i \leqslant n$, such that $A_i \neq 0$, and $s(A)$ the number of nonzero components in A, then show that

$$s(A') \geqslant [d(A) - 1]/2$$

23 (Van Lint, 1971) Let β be a primitive nth root of unity in $GF(q)$, where $q = p^k$, p a prime, and k is the multiplicative order of p mod n. Show that

$$\mathscr{C} = \{(\text{tr}(\xi), \text{tr}(\xi\beta), \ldots, \text{tr}(\xi\beta^{n-1})) | \xi \in GF(q)\}$$

is a minimal ideal in $GF(q)[x]/(x^n - 1)$ of dimension k.

24 (Mattson and Solomon, 1961) Let $f(x) = \sum_{i=0}^{k} b_i x^{k-i}$, $b_0 = 1$, be a polynomial over $GF(2)$ such that $f(x) | (x^n + 1)$. Define the set

$$\mathscr{C} = \{(a_0, a_1, \ldots, a_{n-1}) \Big| \sum_{j=0}^{k} a_{i+k-j} b_j = 0; \quad i = 0, 1, \ldots, n - k + 1\}$$

Show that $\mathscr{C}$ is a linear cyclic (n, k) code over $GF(q)$ with generator polynomial $g(x) = (x^n + 1)/f(x)$. [In this case the codeword $(a_0, \ldots, a_{n-1})$ corresponds to the polynomial $\sum_{i=0}^{n-1} a_i x^{n-1-i}$.]

25 Determine the conditions under which a binary cyclic (n, k) code is left invariant under complementation.

26 Let $\mathscr{C}$ be a cyclic binary $(127, 112)$ code. Show that every codeword has even weight.

27 How many distinct binary cyclic codes of length 255 are there? What is the minimum number of zeros necessary to specify a $(255, 239)$ code? How many such codes are there?

28 Let $\mathscr{C}$ be a code of block length n which is invariant under a transitive group of permutations. If A_i is the number of codewords of weight i, show that $n | iA_i$.

29 Let $g(x) \in GF(2)[x]$ be self-reciprocal, i.e., if $\deg g = k$, then $g^*(x) = x^k g(1/x)$ and $g(x) = g^*(x)$. Show that $g(x)$ has at least five consecutive roots.

30 (Kasami *et al.*, 1968c) If a code of length q^m is invariant under the doubly transitive affine group of permutations, then show that the code obtained by

deleting the first (coordinate position zero) digit is cyclic. Show that the extended primitive BCH and GRM codes are invariant under the doubly transitive affine group of permutations.

31 (Kasami et al., 1968c, Corollary 4) Let $\mathscr{C}$ be a cyclic code of length $q^m - 1$ whose extension is invariant under the doubly transitive affine group of permutations, and that has minimum distance less than or equal to $q^s - 1$. Then show that its dual is a subcode of a primitive BCH code with minimum distance greater than or equal to $q^{m-s} + 1$.

32 (Sloane and Whitehead, 1970) Let $X, Y \in V_n(2)$ and define addition by the equation

$$X \oplus' Y = (X + Y, Y)$$

where the operation on the right is one of concatenation. Show that if $\mathscr{C}_1$ is an (n, M_1, d_1) code and $\mathscr{C}_2$ is an $(n, M_2, [\frac{1}{2}(d_1 + 1)])$, then

$$\mathscr{C}_1 \oplus \mathscr{C}_2 = \{X \oplus' Y \mid X \in \mathscr{C}_1, Y \in \mathscr{C}_2\}$$

is an $(2n, M_1 M_2, d_1)$ code.

33 (Griesmer, 1960) Let $\mathscr{C}$ be a linear (n, k) code of distance d over $GF(q)$. Derive a linear code of length $n - d$, dimension $k - 1$, and distance $[d/q]$.

2 Combinatorial Constructions and Coding

2.1 Introduction

Not surprisingly, certain combinatorial structures have played a significant role in coding theory. In this chapter we present a reasonably self-contained account of these structures, their interrelationships, and their relationships to codes. It is interesting to note the part that finite fields play here. There are many deep and intriguing questions concerning some of these configurations that have not yet been answered, mainly to do with existence and enumeration. We avoid these interesting problems here and instead present the basic configurations along with their elementary properties and one or two methods for constructing them.

2.2 Finite Geometries: Their Collineation Groups and Codes

The study of geometries is the study of a set of axioms concerning abstract quantities that we call points, lines, and flats. The axioms are usually framed to satisfy some geometric notions and there is a considerable interplay between the algebraic and geometric properties of such systems. In this section we confine ourselves to the definition of finite projective and Euclidean geometries and an examination of their elementary properties. For the material on projective geometries we will follow quite closely the first few sections of the paper by Veblen and Bussey (1906).

Definition A finite projective geometry consists of a finite set of elements called points and a family of subsets called lines, which satisfy the following axioms:

(i) The set contains a finite number (>2) of points. Each line contains at least three points.

(ii) If A and B are distinct points, there is one and only one line that contains A and B.

(iii) If A, B, and C are noncollinear points and if a line L contains a point D of the line AB and a point E of the line BC but does not contain A, B, or C, then the line L contains a point F of the line CA.

By a plane we mean a collection of points in the projective geometry that are collinear with a point A and any point on the line BC, where A, B, and C are noncollinear points. We define a k space of the geometry inductively by saying that a point is a 0 space and that if the points $A_1, A_2, \ldots, A_{k+1}$ are not all in the same $k-1$ space, then the set of points collinear with A_{k+1} and points in $\langle A_1, \ldots, A_k \rangle$ forms a k space denoted by $\langle A_1, \ldots, A_{k+1} \rangle$. With these axioms it is then possible to prove that in a k space an l space and an m space have at least an r space in common if $l + m - k = r$. To ensure the existence of dimensionality of the k space we add the two axioms to the foregoing definition:

(iv) If l is a positive integer less than k, then not all of the points considered are in the same l space.

(v) If (iv) is satisfied, then there exists in the set of points considered no $k+1$ space.

Finally, we mention that any proposition that we can prove about points and hyperplanes using these five axioms is also true if the words point and hyperplane are interchanged. This is a consequence of the principle of duality, which follows from these axioms. From duality we conclude that the number of points on any line in a projective plane is a constant that equals the number of lines intersecting in a given point. If $n + 1$ is the number of points on a line in a projective plane, i.e., a 2-space, then from the definition of a plane there exists a point A not on a given line L such that the set of points on the set of lines through A and each point of L accounts for all the points of the plane. It follows that there are $n^2 + n + 1$ points in such a finite projective plane and we call n the order of the plane. In general, a projective geometry that is a k space contains $n^k + n^{k-1} + \cdots + n + 1$ points, where $n + 1$ is the number of points on any line.

2.2 Finite Geometries: Their Collineation Groups and Codes

Example One of the simplest projective geometries is the Fano geometry, which is a projective plane of order two. For this geometry we have the helpful diagram shown in Fig. 2. The points of the geometry are A, B, C, D, E, F, and G and the lines are the sets

(A, B, C), (C, D, E), (A, F, E), (B, G, E)
(C, G, F), (A, G, D), (B, F, D)

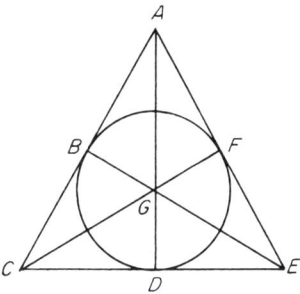

Fig. 2

and the plane, as stated, is of order two. Recall from the axioms that every line must intersect every other line and hence the notion of parallelism does not exist for such geometries.

Fortunately, there exists a construction of projective geometries of any dimension using the elements of a finite field $GF(q)$. Consider the vector space of dimension $n + 1$ over $GF(q)$, $V_{n+1}(q)$, and denote its points by the $(n + 1)$-tuples $(\alpha_1, \alpha_2, \ldots, \alpha_{n+1})$, $\alpha_i \in GF(q)$. For the points of the projective geometry, we take a nonzero point in $V_{n+1}(q)$ and identify all nonzero scalar multiples of it with a single point in the projective geometry. This construction gives

$$\frac{q^{n+1} - 1}{q - 1} = q^n + q^{n-1} + \cdots + q + 1$$

points. For the line containing the two distinct points $P_1 = (\alpha_1, \alpha_2, \ldots, \alpha_{n+1})$ and $P_2 = (\beta_1, \beta_2, \ldots, \beta_{n+1})$ we take the set of points

$$\eta P_1 + \gamma P_2 = (\eta\alpha_1 + \gamma\beta_1, \eta\alpha_2 + \gamma\beta_2, \ldots, \eta\alpha_{n+1} + \gamma\beta_{n+1})$$

where η and γ are not both equal to zero. There are $q^2 - 1$ possible choices for the pair (η, γ), but since we identify scalar multiples, there are $(q^2 - 1)/(q - 1) = q + 1$ points on a line and hence each point has $q + 1$ lines intersecting at it. We leave as an exercise the verification that the set of points, lines, and flats, defined inductively, does indeed give a projective geometry. We denote the geometry constructed in this manner by $PG(n, q)$.

Example If in the preceding example of the Fano geometry we coordinatize the points by assigning a triple over $GF(2)$ to each point in the following manner:

$$A = (0, 0, 1), \quad B = (0, 1, 0), \quad C = (0, 1, 1), \quad D = (1, 0, 1)$$
$$E = (1, 1, 0), \quad F = (1, 1, 1), \quad G = (1, 0, 0)$$

then we can identify the Fano geometry with $PG(2, 2)$.

The interesting property of the above construction technique is that, up to isomorphism (i.e., a permutation of points and lines), all finite projective geometries of dimension three or greater can be obtained in this manner. We sketch the proof of this statement as given by Veblen and Bussey (1906).

When the number of points in the projective geometry is finite and it is of dimension three or more, then the following statement is true:

Let A, B, and C be three collinear points and A', B', and C' be three other collinear points not on the same line. Then if the pairs of lines AB' and $A'B$, BC' and $B'C$, CA' and $C'A$ intersect, the three points of intersection are collinear.

The situation is illustrated in Fig. 3. Such a configuration is often referred to as a Pappus configuration, and if the statement holds for all allowable points in a geometry, we say the geometry has the Pappus property.

We first sketch the proof that all finite projective geometries of dimension greater than two have the Pappus property. From the first four axioms on the projective geometry it is possible to show the truth of Desargues' theorem when the dimension is greater than two and the number of points is finite, i.e., if two triangles A, B, C and A', B', C' are in the same plane and if the lines

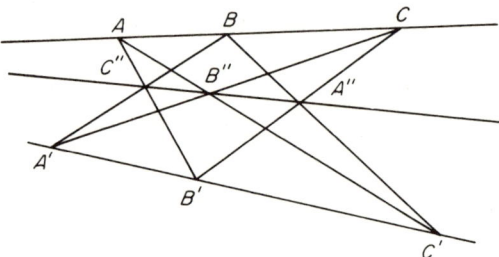

FIG. 3

AA', BB', CC' are concurrent, then the lines AB and $A'B'$, BC and $B'C'$, CA and $C'A'$ intersect in points that are collinear. This statement is illustrated in Fig. 4. Extending the lines AA', BB' and CC', we see that they meet in a point O and the statement is often called the Desargues theorem on perspective triangles. As stated, all finite projective geometries of dimension greater than

2.2 Finite Geometries: Their Collineation Groups and Codes

two have this property and are called Desarguesian. There exist non-Desarguesian planes. However, if the theorem of Desargues is valid in a finite projective plane, then we may identify it as a subgeometry of $PG(n, q)$ for some q, and it follows that the plane is a $PG(2, q)$. An important theorem of finite geometry states that the points in any finite geometry in which the theorem of

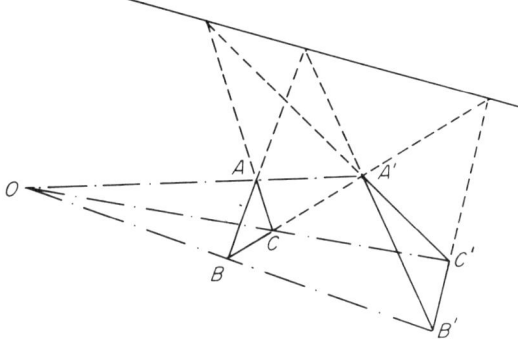

Fig. 4

Desargues is valid can be coordinatized by an $(n + 1)$-tuple over a finite division ring D (which is thus a finite field), where all scalar multiples of a point are identified and lines are defined as previously. Thus any finite projective geometry in which the theorem of Desargues holds is isomorphic, as a geometry, to a $PG(n, q)$ for some n and q. Finally, if the theorem of Pappus is valid in a finite projective geometry, then so is the theorem of Desargues and hence, again, the geometry is $PG(n, q)$ for some n and q.

As stated, in the case of finite projective planes the situation is not quite so simple and consequently this is the case where most of the current interest in finite geometries lies. Indeed a major unsolved problem is the enumeration of all such planes. The order of all known non-Desarguesian planes, however, is the power of a prime. It is known that no projective plane of order six exists. The next lowest order for which the question arises is ten and the answer for this order is as yet unknown. However, a significant result of this problem is the famous Bruck–Ryser theorem, which states that if n is a positive integer, $n \equiv 1$ or $2 \pmod 4$, and p is a prime, $p \equiv 3 \pmod 4$ such that p divides the square free part of n, then there cannot exist a finite projective plane of order n. The theorem tells us nothing about $n = 10$, but excludes, for instance, $n = 14$.

It has become conventional to call an m space in $PG(n, q)$, $m < n$, an m flat, presumably to clearly distinguish the projective geometry spaces from the subspaces of the underlying vector space. It should also be noted that, because of the properties of the underlying vector space, any m flat in $PG(n, q)$ is a $PG(m, q)$.

For future reference we determine some useful information on m flats in $PG(n, q)$. The number of such flats is the number of ways of choosing $m + 1$ independent points in $PG(n, q)$ divided by the number of ways of choosing $m + 1$ independent points in $PG(m, q)$. The number of bases of an m flat is

$$(1 + q + q^2 + \cdots + q^m)(q + \cdots + q^m) \cdots (q^{m-1} + q^m)q^m$$

where the number of ways of choosing the first point is $(1 + q + q^2 + \cdots + q^m)$, the number of ways of choosing the second point $(q + q^2 + \cdots + q^m)$, etc. By similar reasoning the number of ways of choosing $m + 1$ independent points in $PG(n, q)$ is

$$(1 + q + \cdots + q^n)(q + \cdots + q^n) \cdots (q^m + \cdots + q^n)$$

and the number of distinct $PG(m, q)$ in $PG(n, q)$ is

$$\frac{(1 + q + \cdots + q^n)(q + \cdots + q^n) \cdots (q^m + \cdots + q^n)}{(1 + q + \cdots + q^m)(q + \cdots + q^m) \cdots (q^{m-1} + q^m)q^m} = \prod_{t=0}^{m} \frac{q^{n+1-t} - 1}{q^{m+1-t} - 1} \quad (2.1)$$

We shall also require the number of $PG(m, q)$ containing a given $PG(l, q)$ in $PG(n, q)$ where $l < m < n$. The number of ways of adding an independent point to $PG(l, q)$ to give a $PG(l + 1, q)$ is $(q^{l+1} + \cdots + q^n)$. We can add $m - l$ independent points in

$$(q^{l+1} + \cdots + q^n)(q^{l+2} + \cdots + q^n) \cdots (q^m + \cdots + q^n)$$

ways. For any given $PG(m, q)$ the number of ways of choosing the extra $m - l$ independent points to add to the given $PG(l, q)$ is

$$(q^{l+1} + \cdots + q^m)(q^{l+2} + \cdots + q^m) \cdots (q^{m-1} + q^m)q^m$$

and the number of $PG(m, q)$ containing a given $PG(l, q)$ is

$$\frac{(q^{l+1} + \cdots + q^n)(q^{l+2} + \cdots + q^n) \cdots (q^m + \cdots + q^n)}{(q^{l+1} + \cdots + q^m)(q^{l+2} + \cdots + q^m) \cdots (q^{m-1} + q^m)q^m}$$

If $(\alpha_1, \alpha_2, \ldots, \alpha_{n+1})$ represents a point in $PG(n, q)$, then the nonzero solutions to the equation

$$\sum_{i=1}^{n+1} \beta_i \alpha_i = 0$$

form an $n - 1$ flat. Similarly, l independent equations of this form define an $n - l$ flat, where by independence we mean the l points are independent in the underlying vector space.

2.2 Finite Geometries: Their Collineation Groups and Codes

The elements of $GF(q^{n+1})$ can be used to represent the points of $PG(n, q)$ in the following manner. Let ξ be a primitive element of $GF(q^{n+1})$ with minimal polynomial over $GF(q)$

$$m_\xi(x) = \sum_{i=0}^{n+1} m_i x^i, \quad m_i \in GF(q), \quad m_{n+1} = 1$$

Every nonzero element of $GF(q^{n+1})$ can be written uniquely as a power of ξ, and using the minimum polynomial, we can identify uniquely every such power with an $(n + 1)$-tuple over $GF(q)$. Note that $\gamma = \xi^{q-1}$ is a primitive vth root of unity, where $v = (q^{n+1} - 1)/(q - 1)$ and $\beta = \xi^v$ is a primitive element in $GF(q)$. Thus, in $PG(n, q)$ two points ξ^i and ξ^j are identified iff $i \equiv j \mod v$, i.e., iff $\xi^i = \beta^k \xi^j = \xi^{kv+j}$. Thus the first v powers of ξ can be taken as the points in $PG(n, q)$. To determine which of these points are in an m flat of $PG(n, q)$, $m < n$, let $\xi^{s_1}, \xi^{s_2}, \ldots, \xi^{s_{m+1}}$ be a set of $m + 1$ independent points in $PG(n, q)$. Then an m flat is defined as the set of points

$$\alpha_i = \sum_{j=1}^{m+1} \varepsilon_{ij} \xi^{s_j} \tag{2.2}$$

where the ε_{ij} are chosen such that no two vectors $(\varepsilon_{i1}, \varepsilon_{i2}, \ldots, \varepsilon_{i(m+1)})$ are linear multiples over $GF(q)$. There are $(q^{m+1} - 1)/(q - 1)$ such points. Now each such α_i can be expressed in the form

$$\alpha_i = \beta^{k_i} \xi^{l_i}, \quad l_i < v = \frac{q^{n+1} - 1}{q - 1} \tag{2.3}$$

and the $(q^{m+1} - 1)/(q - 1)$ points ξ^{l_i} obtained in this maner form an m flat in $PG(n, q)$. That the points so described are distinct follows easily.

An alternative but equivalent method of describing r flats in $PG(n, q)$ is to consider the set of points $\{\sum_{i=0}^{r} \beta_i \alpha_i\}$, where $\{\alpha_i\}$ is a set of $r + 1$ independent points of $GF(q^{n+1})$ over $GF(q)$ and $\beta_i \in GF(q)$, and the β_i are never all identically zero. The r flat contains $(q^{r+1} - 1)/(q - 1)$ points since scalar multiples over $GF(q)$ are identified. There is an obvious one-to-one correspondence between subspaces of dimension $r + 1$ in a vector space of dimension $n + 1$, $V_{n+1}(q)$, and r flats in $PG(n, q)$.

If from a $PG(n, q)$ we delete the points of an $n - 1$ flat, we obtain a structure called a finite Euclidean geometry, which we denote by $EG(n, q)$. That all $EG(n, q)$ have the same structure follows from the fact that any $n - 1$ flat in $PG(n, q)$ is isomorphic to any other $n - 1$ flat. As an example, consider the points of a $PG(n, q)$, which we may divide into two types, those of the form $(1, \alpha_2, \ldots, \alpha_{n+1})$ and those of the form $(0, \alpha_2, \ldots, \alpha_{n+1})$. The points of the form $(0, \alpha_2, \ldots, \alpha_{n+1})$ are an $n - 1$ flat in $PG(n, q)$ and the remaining points form an $EG(n, q)$. We can therefore associate each point in $EG(n, q)$ with an n-tuple $(\alpha_2, \ldots, \alpha_{n+1})$ and there are q^n points in $EG(n, q)$.

We call the $n-1$ flat in $PG(n, q)$ that we delete to form $EG(n, q)$ the flat at infinity. The lines in $EG(n, q)$ are simply those lines in $PG(n, q)$ that are not in the flat at infinity with the points in the flat at infinity removed. The original $PG(n, q)$ is generated by the $n-1$ flat and a point A external to the flat. The lines collinear with A and each point of the $n-1$ flat are the lines of the $EG(n, q)$ when the points of the $n-1$ flat are removed. Similarly, to form an l flat in $EG(n, q)$ consider an l flat in $PG(n, q)$. If it lies entirely in the flat at infinity, ignore it. Otherwise we define an l flat in $EG(n, q)$ as the points of the l flat in $PG(n, q)$ with the points of the flat at infinity deleted. To see that each such l flat has the same number of points, we consider the properties of the underlying vector spaces and denote the deleted $n-1$ flat by V and the l flat not entirely contained in the $n-1$ flat by W. Then $V + W$ is the entire $PG(n, q)$ and

$$\dim(V \cap W) = \dim V + \dim W - \dim(V + W)$$

and so

$$\dim(V \cap W) = n - 1 + l - n = l - 1$$

which implies that the number of points in V in common with W is $(1 + q + \cdots + q^{l-1})$ and hence $W \setminus (V \cap W)$ contains q^l points and is an l flat in $EG(n, q)$.

By a similar type of reasoning we can see that any l flat in $EG(n, q)$ is an $EG(l, q)$. For suppose the l flat in $EG(n, q)$ is obtained from the residue of some $PG(l, q)$ in $PG(n, q)$. Let V be the $n-1$ flat deleted from $PG(n, q)$ to form $EG(n, q)$ and W the $PG(l, q)$. Then again we have

$$\dim(V \cap W) = l - 1$$

and hence $V \cap W$ is an $l-1$ flat in $PG(n, q)$. But $V \cap W$ is also an $l-1$ flat in $W = PG(l, q)$ and hence the l flat in $EG(n, q)$ is an $EG(l, q)$.

Example Consider the previous example of the Fano geometry $PG(2, 2)$ and delete the line (A, B, C) to form $EG(2, 2)$ (Fig. 5). The lines that are left

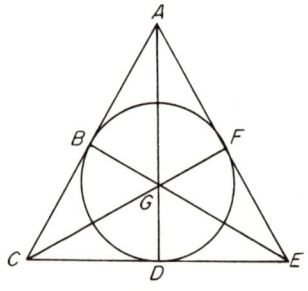

FIG. 5.

each have two points and are

$$(E, F) \quad (D, E) \quad (E, G) \quad (D, F) \quad (D, G) \quad (F, G)$$

In the $EG(2, 2)$ obtained we have the interesting property that it is no longer necessary for lines to intersect, and hence we have the idea of parallelism, which of course was lacking in the projective geometries. The lines of a Euclidean geometry can be divided into equivalence classes according to parallelism, since parallelism is an equivalence relation. For the above example these classes are

$$\{(E, F) \text{ and } (D, G)\}, \quad \{(E, G) \text{ and } (D, F)\}, \quad \{(D, E) \text{ and } (F, G)\}$$

As for projective geometries, we shall have need of certain information on l flats in $EG(n, q)$. To determine the number of l flats in $EG(n, q)$, we recall that every l flat in $EG(n, q)$ is the residue of an l flat in $PG(n, q)$ that is not contained in the $n - 1$ flat at infinity. The number of such flats is

$$\frac{(1 + q + \cdots + q^n) \cdots (q^l + \cdots + q^n)}{(1 + q + \cdots + q^l) \cdots (q^{l-1} + q^l)q^l}$$
$$- \frac{(1 + q + \cdots + q^{n-1}) \cdots (q^l + \cdots + q^{n-1})}{(1 + q + \cdots + q^l) \cdots (q^{l-1} + q^l)q^l}$$

which may be more conveniently written as

$$q^{n-l} \prod_{k=1}^{l} \frac{q^{n+1-k} - 1}{q^{l+1-k} - 1}$$

The number of m flats containing a given l flat in $EG(n, q)$ is just the number of m flats in $PG(n, q)$ containing a given l flat in $PG(n, q)$, which follows since the given l flat in $EG(n, q)$ cannot be in the flat at infinity and hence any m flat containing it cannot be in it either. Thus the number is

$$\frac{(q^{l+1} + \cdots + q^n)(q^{l+2} + \cdots + q^n) \cdots (q^m + \cdots + q^n)}{(q^{l+1} + \cdots + q^m)(q^{l+2} + \cdots + q^m) \cdots (q^{m-1} + q^m)q^m} = \prod_{k=l+1}^{m} \frac{q^{n-k+1} - 1}{q^{m-k+1} - 1}$$

(2.4)

From the previous equation we see that there are

$$q^{n-1} \frac{q^n - 1}{q - 1}$$

lines in $EG(n, q)$ and from the analytic description of the geometry each line contain q points. As seen before, each line of a $PG(n, q)$ is either entirely contained in a given $n - 1$ flat of $PG(n, q)$ or else has precisely one point in the flat.

Much as we did for projective geometries, we can obtain a representation of $EG(n, q)$ in terms of elements of $GF(q^n)$. We have already observed that for $n \geq 3$ the points of $EG(n, q)$ can be taken to be the points of $V_n(q)$. If α is a primitive element of $GF(q^n)$, then each n-tuple over $GF(q)$ can be uniquely identified with a power of α. In this representation a line through the point α^i is the set of all points of the form

$$\alpha^j = \alpha^i + \gamma \alpha^{i_1}, \qquad \gamma \in GF(q)$$

In a similar fashion an m flat through α^i is the set of points

$$\alpha^j = \alpha^i + \gamma_1 \alpha^{i_1} + \gamma_2 \alpha^{i_2} + \cdots + \gamma_m \alpha^{i_m}, \qquad \gamma_i \in GF(q)$$

where the points $\alpha^i, \alpha^{i_1}, \alpha^{i_2}, \ldots, \alpha^{i_m}$ are independent and $i_j \in \{\infty, 0, 1, \ldots, q^n - 2\}$. Similarly a line through the (distinct) points α^i and α^{i_1} is the set of points

$$\{\beta \alpha^i + (1 - \beta)\alpha^{i_1}, \qquad \beta \in GF(q)\}$$

and an m flat through the $m + 1$ points $\alpha^i, \alpha^{i_1}, \ldots, \alpha^{i_m}$ is the set of points

$$\{\beta_0 \alpha^i + \beta_1 \alpha^{i_1} + \cdots + \beta_m \alpha^{i_m}, \qquad \beta_i \in GF(q)\}$$

where $\sum_{i=0}^{m} \beta_i = 1$.

We consider now some groups of transformations that it is possible to define on finite geometries. From Section 1.8 in Chapter 1 the general linear group $GL(n, q)$ (called the general linear homogeneous groups by some authors) is the set of $n \times n$ nonsingular matrices over $GF(q)$ and has order

$$|GL(n, q)| = q^{n(n-1)/2} \prod_{i=1}^{n} (q^i - 1)$$

Now consider the transformation

$$Ay_i = \sum_{j=0}^{n} \alpha_{ij} x_j, \qquad i = 0, 1, \ldots, n$$

defined on $V_{n+1}(q)$, where the transformation is nonsingular and we adopt the notation Ay_i to indicate that we identify transformations that are nonzero scalar multiples of one another. The set of such transformations forms a group, the projective group, which we denote by $P(n, q)$ and it is clear that

$$|P(n, q)| = \frac{|GL(n+1, q)|}{q - 1}$$

The elements of $P(n, q)$ are, of course, intimately connected with the properties of $PG(n, q)$. Indeed, each element of $P(n, q)$ is a one-to-one transformation of $PG(n, q)$ onto itself. Furthermore, from the definition of a line in $PG(n, q)$ and the linearity (of a sort) of the transformation in $P(n, q)$ it follows that

2.2 Finite Geometries: Their Collineation Groups and Codes

each element of $P(n, q)$ takes a line of $PG(n, q)$ into a line. The elements of $P(n, q)$ permute the points of $PG(n, q)$, and hence the group has a natural representation as a permutation group on these points, and the degree of the permutation group is $(1 + q + \cdots + q^n)$.

For $n > 0$, $P(n, q)$ is doubly transitive, for consider the action of a group element on the two $(n + 1)$-tuples $(1, 0, \ldots, 0)$ and $(0, 1, 0, \ldots, 0)$. If the element is (α_{ij}), then these two $(n + 1)$-tuples are taken to $(\alpha_{00}, \alpha_{10}, \ldots, \alpha_{n0})$ and $(\alpha_{01}, \alpha_{11}, \ldots, \alpha_{n1})$, respectively. Since these may be chosen independently, there exists an element of $P(n, q)$ that takes any two points of $PG(n, q)$ to any other two points of $PG(n, q)$, and thus, for $n > 0$, the group is doubly transitive. It can be verified that $P(1, q)$ is triply transitive.

By a collineation in $PG(n, q)$ we mean a point transformation that takes lines into lines. We have observed that elements of $P(n, q)$ are collineations and we ask if there are any others. Consider the transformation

$$\alpha y_i = x_i^p, \quad i = 0, 1, \ldots, n$$

of the point $(x_0, x_1, \ldots, x_n)$ in a $PG(n, q)$, where again we identify scalar multiples and the characteristic of $GF(q)$ is p, i.e., $q = p^k$. If $\mathbf{x}_1 = (\alpha_0, \alpha_1, \ldots, \alpha_n)$ and $\mathbf{x}_2 = (\beta_0, \beta_1, \ldots, \beta_n)$ are points of $PG(n, q)$ then the line through these points is defined by

$$\{\gamma \mathbf{x}_1 + \sigma \mathbf{x}_2, \quad \gamma, \sigma \in GF(q)\}$$

The above transformation, defined on the coordinates of each point, takes a point on this line to the point

$$(\gamma^p \alpha_0^p + \sigma^p \beta_0^p, \gamma^p \alpha_1^p + \sigma^p \beta_1^p, \ldots, \gamma^p \alpha_n^p + \sigma^p \beta_n^p)$$

since $\binom{p}{i} = 0$ in a field of characteristic p if $i \neq 0$ or p. Since the mapping $\gamma \to \gamma^p$ is an automorphism of $GF(q)$, the set of transformed points lies on the line $\alpha' \mathbf{x}_1' + \sigma' \mathbf{x}_2'$, where

$$\mathbf{x}_1' = (\alpha_0^p, \alpha_1^p, \ldots, \alpha_n^p) \quad \text{and} \quad \mathbf{x}_2' = (\beta_0^p, \beta_1^p, \ldots, \beta_n^p)$$

and the transformation in question is a collineation. It follows that a transformation of the form

$$\alpha y_i = \sum_{j=0}^{n} \alpha_{ij} x_j^{p^l}, \quad i = 0, 1, \ldots, n$$

where $l = 0, 1, \ldots, k - 1$ and $|\alpha_{ij}| \neq 0$, is a collineation. Clearly, the set of all collineations is a group. An important theorem states that every collineation of $PG(n, q)$ is of the above form and we denote the group of collineations by $C(n, q)$. The order of $C(n, q)$ is of course k times the order of $P(n, q)$ since the only new factors introduced into the argument are the k possible powers of p in the exponent. Collineation groups and their properties are rather more completely described by Carmichael (1956 Chapter 12), and the reader is referred there for more information.

Example The smallest example of a projective geometry over a non-prime field is $PG(2, 2^2)$, which we discuss here. Denote the elements of $GF(2^2)$ by $\{0, 1, \alpha, \alpha^2\}$, where, of necessity, $\alpha + 1 = \alpha^2$ and α is a primitive element. The geometry contains 21 points (Table V). There are five points on any line and the 21 lines are given by Table VI.

TABLE V

$P_1 = \{1, 0, 1\}$	$P_8 = \{1, 1, 0\}$	$P_{15} = \{1, \alpha^2, \alpha^2\}$
$P_2 = \{1, 0, \alpha\}$	$P_9 = \{1, \alpha, 1\}$	$P_{16} = \{1, \alpha^2\ 0\}$
$P_3 = \{1, 0, \alpha^2\}$	$P_{10} = \{1, \alpha, \alpha\}$	$P_{17} = \{0, 0, 1\}$
$P_4 = \{1, 0, 0\}$	$P_{11} = \{1, \alpha, \alpha^2\}$	$P_{18} = \{0, 1, 1\}$
$P_5 = \{1, 1, 1\}$	$P_{12} = \{1, \alpha, 0\}$	$P_{19} = \{0, 1, \alpha\}$
$P_6 = \{1, 1, \alpha\}$	$P_{13} = \{1, \alpha^2, 1\}$	$P_{20} = \{0, 1, \alpha^2\}$
$P_7 = \{1, 1, \alpha^2\}$	$P_{14} = \{1, \alpha^2, \alpha\}$	$P_{21} = \{0, 1, 0\}$

TABLE VI

$L_1 = \{P_1, P_2, P_{17}, P_4, P_3\}$	$L_8 = \{P_2, P_7, P_{18}, P_{13}, P_{12}\}$	$L_{15} = \{P_4, P_6, P_{19}, P_{13}, P_{11}\}$
$L_2 = \{P_1, P_5, P_{21}, P_9, P_{13}\}$	$L_9 = \{P_2, P_8, P_{19}, P_{15}, P_9\}$	$L_{16} = \{P_4, P_7, P_{20}, P_{14}, P_9\}$
$L_3 = \{P_1, P_6, P_{20}, P_{15}, P_{12}\}$	$L_{10} = \{P_3, P_5, P_{19}, P_{14}, P_{12}\}$	$L_{17} = \{P_4, P_8, P_{21}, P_{16}, P_{12}\}$
$L_4 = \{P_1, P_7, P_{19}, P_{16}, P_{10}\}$	$L_{11} = \{P_3, P_6, P_{18}, P_{16}, P_9\}$	$L_{18} = \{P_5, P_6, P_{17}, P_7, P_8\}$
$L_5 = \{P_1, P_8, P_{18}, P_{14}, P_{11}\}$	$L_{12} = \{P_3, P_7, P_{21}, P_{15}, P_{11}\}$	$L_{19} = \{P_9, P_{10}, P_{17}, P_{11}, P_{12}\}$
$L_6 = \{P_2, P_5, P_{20}, P_{16}, P_{11}\}$	$L_{13} = \{P_3, P_8, P_{20}, P_{13}, P_{10}\}$	$L_{20} = \{P_{13}, P_{14}, P_{17}, P_{16}, P_{15}\}$
$L_7 = \{P_2, P_6, P_{21}, P_{14}, P_{10}\}$	$L_{14} = \{P_4, P_5, P_{18}, P_{15}, P_{10}\}$	$L_{21} = \{P_{18}, P_{19}, P_{17}, P_{20}, P_{21}\}$

Consider the points of the geometry containing only elements of $GF(2)$, i.e., $P_1, P_4, P_5, P_8, P_{17}, P_{18}, P_{21}$. The lines of this subgeometry are "sublines" of the previous geometry, i.e.,

$$L_1' = \{P_1, P_4, P_{17}\}, \quad L_2' = \{P_1, P_5, P_{21}\}, \quad L_3' = \{P_1, P_8, P_{18}\}$$
$$L_4' = \{P_4, P_5, P_{18}\}, \quad L_5' = \{P_4, P_8, P_{21}\}, \quad L_6' = \{P_5, P_8, P_{17}\}$$
$$L_7' = \{P_{17}, P_{18}, P_{21}\}$$

This, of course, is just $PG(2, 2)$, the Fano geometry. In general $PG(m, q)$ is contained in $PG(m, q^t)$ as a subgeometry. The points $P_{17}, P_{18}, P_{19}, P_{20}$, and P_{21} form a hyperplane and subtracting these points leaves the Euclidean geometry $EG(2, 2^2)$. The lines L_i', $i = 1, \ldots, 20$, of the geometry are those of

$PG(2, 2^2)$ with the line L_{21} and its points removed. The parallelism classes of $EG(2, 2^2)$ are

$$\{L_1', L_{18}', L_{19}', L_{20}'\}, \quad \{L_2', L_{12}', L_7', L_{17}'\}$$

$$\{L_3', L_6', L_{13}', L_{16}'\}, \quad \{L_4', L_{10}', L_9', L_{15}'\}, \quad \{L_5', L_8', L_{11}', L_{14}'\}$$

For the remainder of the section we will discuss majority logic decoding and the application of concepts of finite geometry to construct and analyze codes that are majority logic decodable. The forerunners of most of these ideas are the Reed–Muller codes discovered by Muller (1954) and provided with a decoding algorithm by Reed (1954). The work of Rudolph (1967) and Weldon (1969) has prompted the more recent interest in these codes.

To introduce majority logic decoding, we consider the following simple situation. Let $c(x) = \sum_{i=0}^{n-1} c_i x^i$ be a codeword in the (n, k) code $\mathscr{C}$ over $GF(q)$ with dual code $\mathscr{C}^\perp$ and let the error polynomial be $e(x) = \sum_{i=0}^{n-1} e_i x^i$ so that the received word polynomial is

$$r(x) = c(x) + e(x) = \sum r_i x^i = \sum (c_i + e_i) x^i.$$

Decoding the received word is equivalent to determining the error polynomial $e(x)$. The codeword $c(x)$ is orthogonal to every codeword in $\mathscr{C}^\perp$. Let $c'(x) = \sum_{i=0}^{n-1} c_i' x^i \in \mathscr{C}^\perp$; then

$$\langle r(x), c'(x) \rangle \triangleq \sum_{i=0}^{n-1} r_i c_i' = \sum_{i=0}^{n-1} e_i c_i'$$

Suppose that $\mathscr{C}$ has a distance three and that we can find two codewords $c'(x)$ and $c''(x)$ in $\mathscr{C}^\perp$ such that $c_0' = 1$ and $c_0'' = 1$ and if $c_i' \neq 0$, then $c_i'' = 0$ and if $c_j'' \neq 0$, then $c_j' = 0$. This leads to two equations such that e_0 appears in both and if e_i appears in one it cannot appear in the other, $i > 0$. Now suppose only one error occurs in transmission, i.e., the polynomial $e(x)$ has precisely one nonzero coefficient. If this error occurs in the zeroth position, then $e_0 = \alpha \in GF(q)$ and the two equations read

$$\langle r(x), c'(x) \rangle = \alpha = \langle r(x), c''(x) \rangle$$

If the error appears in the jth position, then by the assumptions on $c'(x)$ and $c''(x)$, c_j' and c_j'' cannot both be nonzero. If $c_j' \neq 0$, then the equations read

$$\langle r(x), c'(x) \rangle = \alpha c_j' \neq 0, \quad \langle r(x), c''(x) \rangle = 0$$

If both $c_j' = 0 = c_j''$, then both equations will be equal to zero. We draw the following conclusions if one error or less occurs:

(i) $\langle r(x), c'(x) \rangle = \langle r(x), c''(x) \rangle = \alpha$, then $e_0 = \alpha$.

(ii) $\langle r(x), c'(x) \rangle = \beta$, $\langle r(x), c''(x) \rangle = \gamma$, where one or both of β and γ are zero, then $e_0 = 0$.

Thus, contingent upon finding the polynomials $c'(x)$ and $c''(x)$, we have a criterion for correcting an error occurring in the zeroth position. If we can carry out a procedure for the other error coefficients e_j, $j = 1, \ldots, n - 1$, then we can correct any single error.

We generalize this simple procedure and consider $\mathscr{C}$ as an (n, k) code with distance d over $GF(q)$. Any sum of the form $\langle r(x), c'(x) \rangle$, where $c'(x) \in \mathscr{C}^\perp$, is called a parity check sum.

Definition A set of parity check sums $\langle r(x), c^{(i)}(x) \rangle, i = 1, 2, \ldots, J$, $c^{(i)}(x) \in \mathscr{C}^\perp$, is said to be orthogonal on the jth position (or on e_j) if:

(i) $c_j^{(i)} = 1, i = 1, \ldots, J$.
(ii) $c_k^{(i)} \neq 0$ in one sum, then $c_k^{(l)} = 0, \forall l \neq i$.

If $J = d - 1$ and $(d - 1)/2$ or fewer errors occur, then if $e_j = \alpha \neq 0$ since fewer than $(d - 1)/2$ other errors occur, fewer than $(d - 1)/2$ parity check sums will be different from α, i.e., in this case a majority of the sums will equal α. Similarly, if $e_j = 0$, then a majority (or at least half) of the sums will be zero and hence from a majority count of the values $\langle r(x), c^{(i)}(x) \rangle$ we can determine the value of e_j under the stated assumptions.

Definition If a set of $d - 1$ parity check sums orthogonal on e_i can be found for each $i = 0, 1, \ldots, n - 1$ for an (n, k, d) linear code, then the code is said to be completely or one-step orthogonalizable. If a set of $t - 1$ parity check sums orthogonal on e_i can be found for each $i = 0, 1, \ldots, n - 1$ for an (n, k, d) code, $t < d$, then we say the code is a one-step majority-logic-decodable code capable of correcting $\lfloor (t - 1)/2 \rfloor$ errors.

The term majority-logic-decodable code in general implies that majority logic decoding of the code may not correct all the errors that the code is capable of correcting. Massey (1963) uses the term *threshold decoding* to encompass methods using sets of orthogonal parity checks to achieve decoding.

There are few classes of codes that are completely one-step orthogonalizable. For example, the binary maximum length codes are completely one-step orthogonalizable.

We extend the notion of one-step majority logic decodability by first defining:

Definition A set of parity check sums is orthogonal on a set of positions $A = \{i_1, i_2, \ldots, i_k\}$ if:

(i) For each $i_j \in A$ the corresponding error term e_j appears in each parity check sum, and with the same nonzero coefficient in each sum.

(ii) For each coordinate position $l \notin A$, e_l appears in at most one sum of the set with a nonzero coefficient.

Thus, rather than an estimate of a single error bit, we now obtain a majority vote on a weighted sum of the error positions in A. We now define an L-step majority-logic-decodable code recursively, using Berlekamp's (1968) definition, and restrict our attention to binary codes.

Definition A linear code with distance d is said to be L-step orthogonalizable if and only if the code contains sets of positions $A_1, A_2, \ldots$ such that

(i) For each i the code contains $d - 1$ parity check sums orthogonal on A_i.

(ii) The subcode of the original code that satisfies all these additional parity check sums is $(L - 1)$-step orthogonalizable.

When we talk of a nonbinary code being L-step majority logic decodable, the generalization will be intuitively straightforward. Basically, all coefficients of error terms in a set of parity check sums orthogonal on a set of error positions will be identical for these positions. This generalization of one-step majority logic decodability has led to the discovery of several interesting new classes of codes, including the finite geometry codes to be discussed in this section.

We begin the discussion of finite geometry codes with the projective geometry codes. It is convenient to consider the finite geometry $PG(m - 1, p^s)$ and describe its points as nonzero m-tuples over $GF(p^s)$ with scalar multiples identified. Let $n = (p^{ms} - 1)/(p^s - 1)$. The projective geometry code will be a code of length n, and we identify each coordinate position of an n-tuple with a point in the geometry. By an incidence vector of a t flat of $PG(m - 1, p^s)$ is meant a binary n-tuple with ones in those positions corresponding to points in the t flat and zeros elsewhere.

Definition A projective geometry code of order r and length $n = (p^{ms} - 1)/(p^s - 1)$ over $GF(p)$ is the largest cyclic code whose null space contains all the incidence vectors of all the r flats in $PG(m - 1, p^s)$.

The significance of the definition will become apparent later when majority logic decoding is discussed. At the moment it is important to establish the connection between these codes and the polynomial codes of Chapter 1.

Some authors define the rth-order p-ary projective geometry code to have length $(p^{(m+1)s} - 1)/(p^s - 1)$, containing all the flats of degree r of $PG(m, p^s)$ in its null space. While this relative difference of one in the dimension of the geometry affects the calculations, it makes little difference to the ideas. We choose our definition to preserve a certain symmetry with Euclidean geometry codes, whose definition will follow. With our definition the difference between the dimension of the geometry and the order of the flats contained in its null space will be the same.

That the coordinate positions can be labeled so that the incidence matrix of r flats in $PG(m, q)$ is cyclic can easily be demonstrated from the description of flats given in Equations (2.2) and (2.3). Thus if $\zeta^{s_1}, \zeta^{s_2}, \ldots, \zeta^{s_{m+1}}$ are independent points in $PG(n, q)$, then so are $\zeta\zeta^{s_1}, \zeta\zeta^{s_2}, \ldots, \zeta\zeta^{s_{m+1}}$, and if the points

$$\alpha_i = \sum_{j=1}^{m+1} \varepsilon_{ij} \zeta^{s_j}$$

form an m flat, then the points

$$\zeta\alpha_i = \sum_{j=1}^{m+1} \varepsilon_{ij} \zeta^{s_j+1}$$

form another m flat. If the coordinate positions are labeled with the first v distinct powers of ζ, the cyclic nature of the matrix is demonstrated.

Let L be a t flat in $PG(m-1, p^s)$ generated by the $t+1$ independent points $\{\mathbf{a}_0, \mathbf{a}_1, \ldots, \mathbf{a}_t\}$. Define $L^\perp$ to be the set of points $\mathbf{X}$ such that

$$\mathbf{a}_i \cdot \mathbf{X}^T = 0, \qquad 0 \leqslant i \leqslant t$$

which is, of course, an $m - t - 2$ flat in $PG(m-1, p^s)$. Consider the multivariable polynomial

$$f(\mathbf{X}) = \prod_{i=0}^{t} \{1 - (\mathbf{a}_i \cdot \mathbf{X}^T)^{p^s - 1}\}$$

and observe that

$$f(\mathbf{X}) = \begin{cases} 1, & \mathbf{X} \in L^\perp \\ 0, & \mathbf{X} \notin L^\perp \end{cases}$$

Now consider an (n, m, s, μ, p) polynomial code with $b = p^s - 1$, implying that $n = (p^{ms} - 1)/(p^s - 1)$. Trivially the polynomial $f(\mathbf{X})$ is an element of $Q_m(\mu, p^s - 1)$ for $\mu \geqslant t + 1$ and hence the codeword $v(f)$ corresponding to this polynomial is in the polynomial code. It is clear that this codeword can be interpreted as the incidence vector of the $m - t - 2$ flat $L^\perp$. Thus the incidence vector of every $m - t - 2$ flat of $PG(m-1, p^s)$ is in the (n, m, s, μ, p) polynomial code if $0 \leqslant t < \mu$. Thus the dual of a $((p^{ms} - 1)/(p^s - 1), m, s, \mu, p)$ polynomial code is certainly contained in the projective geometry code of order $m - \mu - 1$.

The BCH bound on the (n, m, s, μ, p) code with $n = (p^{ms} - 1)/(p^s - 1)$ and $b = p^s - 1$ is given by Theorem 10.9 in Chapter 1:

$$d_{\min} \geqslant \frac{(R+1)p^{Qs} - 1}{b}$$

2.2 Finite Geometries: Their Collineation Groups and Codes

where R and Q are the remainder and quotient, respectively, obtained by dividing $m(p^s - 1) - \mu(p^s - 1)$ by $p^s - 1$. Clearly $R = 0$ and $Q = m - \mu$, to yield

$$d_{\min} \geq \frac{p^{(m-\mu)s} - 1}{p^s - 1}$$

Since the $m - \mu - 1$ flats are in the code and have precisely this weight, we conclude that this is the exact minimum distance of the code. Since this polynomial code is a subfield subcode of a GRM code, it follows from Delsarte (1970a, Theorem 12) that the minimum weight codewords generate the code. Thus the polynomial code is the minimal cyclic code containing the required flats, which implies that the dual code is the maximal code with the required flats in its null space, i.e., the projective geometry code. In general, the projective geometry code of order r has a null space generated by the incidence vectors of the r flats and this is the dual of the polynomial code $((p^{ms} - 1)/(p^s - 1), m, s, m - r - 1, p)$.

To see the relevance of this to majority logic decoding consider a projective geometry code of order r. There are

$$\frac{(1 + p^s + p^{2s} + \cdots + p^{(m-1)s})(p^s + \cdots + p^{(m-1)s}) \cdots (p^{rs} + \cdots + p^{(m-1)s})}{(1 + p^s + \cdots + p^{rs})(p^s + \cdots + p^{rs}) \cdots (p^{(r-1)s} + p^{rs})p^{rs}}$$

distinct r flats in $PG(m - 1, p^s)$. Now every $r - 1$ flat of $PG(m - 1, p^s)$ is contained in

$$\frac{p^{sr} + \cdots + p^{s(m-1)}}{p^{sr}} = 1 + \cdots + p^{s(m-r-1)} = \frac{p^{s(m-r)} - 1}{p^s - 1} = J$$

distinct r flats. If we fix an $r - 1$ flat L in $PG(m - 1, p^s)$, then every point of $PG(m - 1, p^s)$ is either in the $r - 1$ flat L or else in precisely one r flat containing L. Thus we use the J r-flats containing L to obtain a set of parity checks which are orthogonal on L. If e_i is the error digit on the ith coordinate position, then if $\lfloor J/2 \rfloor$ or fewer errors occur, the value of the sum

$$s_i = \sum_{j \in L} e_j$$

is given correctly by a majority of the J error sums on the r-flats containing L. By similar reasoning there are precisely J $(r - 1)$-flats containing a given $r - 2$ flat and, again assuming that $\lfloor J/2 \rfloor$ or fewer errors occur, we obtain correct estimates of error sums on the $r - 2$ flats. Clearly, in r steps we obtain correct error estimates, under the same conditions, of the 0 flats, i.e., the error digits themselves. The rth-order projective geometry code is thus r-step orthogonalizable and r-step majority logic decodable with distance at least $J + 1$. Interestingly, it can be shown that this is also the BCH bound on the minimum distance of the rth-order projective geometry code, which can be shown by considering the description of the roots of the associated polynomial code. These codes were originally considered by Rudolph (1964, 1967), who observed that the incidence matrix of r flats in a projective geometry can be made cyclic. Goethals and Delsarte (1968) approached the problem from a polynomial point of view and obtained an interesting characterization of the codeword zeros. Until recently the dimensions of these codes were known in only a few cases. The result of Hamada (1968), however, establishes the dimension for all cases.

The development of Euclidean geometry codes proceeds along lines similar to those of projective geometry codes. This time we label the $n = p^{ms} - 1$ coordinate positions with the nonzero points of the Euclidean geometry $EG(m, p^s)$.

Definition The Euclidean geometry code of order r and length $p^{ms} - 1$ over $GF(p)$ is the largest cyclic code whose null space contains the incidence vectors of all $r + 1$ flats of $EG(m, p^s)$.

Again, we first consider the relationship between these codes and polynomial codes. Let L be a t flat in $EG(m, p^s)$ and $\{\mathbf{a}_1, \mathbf{a}_2, \ldots, \mathbf{a}_t\}$ a basis. The polynomial

$$f(\mathbf{X}) = \prod_{i=1}^{t} \{1 - (\mathbf{a}_i \cdot \mathbf{X}^T)^{p^s - 1}\}$$

is of degree $t(p^s - 1)$. If $L^\perp$ is the null space of L, then $f(\mathbf{X})$ is the indicator polynomial of $L^\perp$, which is an $m - t$ flat. If $t(p^s - 1) \leq \mu$, then $f(\mathbf{X}) \in Q_m(\mu, 1)$ and the corresponding $(p^{ms} - 1)$-tuple is in the polynomial code $((p^{ms} - 1), m, s, \mu, p)$ for $b = 1$ and $\mu = D(p^s - 1)$ for some positive integer D. The flat $L^\perp$ goes through the origin since the origin is a solution to the equations $(\mathbf{a}_i \cdot \mathbf{X}^T) = 0$, $1 \leq i \leq t$. Notice that since coordinate positions are labeled only with the nonzero points of $EG(m, p^s)$, the incidence vector of an $m - t$ flat through the origin is of weight $p^{m-t} - 1$, since the origin is deleted. The weight of an $m - t$ flat not through the origin is p^{m-t}. Similarly, let $L'^\perp$ be the solutions to the set of equations

$$\mathbf{a}_i \cdot (\mathbf{X} - \mathbf{b})^T = 0, \quad 1 \leq i \leq t$$

The solutions form an $m - t$ flat through the point $\mathbf{b}$. The polynomial

$$f'(X) = \prod_{i=1}^{t} \{1 - [\mathbf{a}_i \cdot (\mathbf{X} - \mathbf{b})^T]^{p^s - 1}\}$$

is of degree $t(p^s - 1)$ and is the indicator function of the $m - t$ flat $L'^\perp$. The corresponding codeword $v(f')$ is the incidence vector of this flat.

2.2 Finite Geometries: Their Collineation Groups and Codes

For an (n, m, s, μ, p) polynomial code with $b = 1$ and $n = p^{ms} - 1$ suppose that

$$\mu = D(p^s - 1) + N, \qquad 0 \leq N < p^s - 1$$

From the previous considerations it follows that such a code contains every $m - t$ flat of $EG(m, p^s)$ for $0 \leq t \leq D$, i.e., all flats of order $m - D, m - D + 1, \ldots, m$.

Using precisely the decoding scheme as for projective geometry codes and noting that the number of $m - D$ flats that intersect a given $m - D - 1$ flat in $EG(m, p^s)$ is

$$J = \frac{p^{(D+1)s} - 1}{p^s - 1}$$

we conclude that the dual of the polynomial code is $(m - D)$-step majority logic decodable with minimum distance at least

$$J + 1 = \frac{p^{(D+1)s} - 1}{p^s - 1} + 1$$

Actually, with arguments similar to those used in deriving the BCH bound for an arbitrary polynomial code, Lin (1968, Theorem 4) showed that the dual code of a $(p^{ms} - 1, m, s, \mu, p)$ polynomial code has

$$d_{\min} \geq (\lambda + 1)p^{Ds} + p \cdot p^{(D-1)s}$$

where

$$\mu = D(p^s - 1) + N, \qquad 0 \leq N < p^s - 1$$

and

$$N = \lambda p^{s-1} + \sigma, \qquad 0 \leq \sigma < p^{s-1}$$

Choosing μ to be minimum for a given D, i.e., choosing $N = 0$, yields the bound

$$d_{\min} \geq p^{Ds} + p \cdot p^{(D-1)s}$$

The difference between this bound and the bound given by majority logic decoding is

$$(p^s - 2) + (p^s - 2)p^s + (p^s - 2)p^{2s} + \cdots + (p^s - 2)p^{(D-2)s} + (p - 2)p^{(D-1)s}$$

which indicates that for large s and D, majority logic decoding of the codes is falling far short of using the full error-correcting capabilities of the code.

It has been shown that a polynomial code of length $p^{ms} - 1$, $b = 1$, and $\mu = D(p^s - 1)$ contains all the $m - D$ flats of $EG(m, p^s)$. From Theorem 10.9 of Chapter 1 the BCH bound for such a code is given by

$$d_{\min} \geqslant \frac{(R+1)p^{Qs} - 1}{b}$$

where $b = 1$, and R and Q are the remainder and quotient obtained by dividing $m(p^s - 1) - \mu$ by $p^s - 1$. For our situation $R = 0$ and $Q = m - D$, yielding

$$d_{\min} \geqslant p^{(m-D)s} - 1$$

However, an $m - D$ flat through the origin has weight $p^{(m-D)s} - 1$ and we conclude that this is exactly the minimum weight of the polynomial code. Recalling that a polynomial code is a subfield subcode of a GRM code Delsarte (1970a, Theorem 11) shows that the minimum weight vectors actually generate the code. Thus the polynomial code is the smallest code that contains the required flats, and we conclude that the dual of the polynomial code of length $p^{ms} - 1$, $b = 1$, $\mu = (m - r - 1)(p^s - 1)$ over $GF(p)$ is the rth-order Euclidean geometry code.

Now let α be a primitive root of $GF(q^{ms})$ and let α^h be a zero of the polynomial code of length $q^{ms} - 1$, $b = 1$. Then, from a characterization of the roots it follows that

$$\min_{0 \leqslant l < s} \omega_{q^s}(hq^l) = j, \qquad 0 < j < m(q^s - 1) - \mu$$

Suppose the minimization is achieved with hq^l for some integer l and let

$$h = \sum \alpha_i q^{si} = \sum \beta_i p^i, \qquad 0 \leqslant \alpha_i \leqslant q^s - 1, \quad 0 \leqslant \beta_i \leqslant p - 1$$

Let $h' \in J(h)$, where $J(\cdot)$ is defined in Section 1.9 of Chapter 1. Then

$$h' = \sum \beta_i' p^i = \sum \alpha_i' q^{si}$$

and since $0 \leqslant \beta_i' \leqslant \beta_i$ we have that $0 \leqslant \alpha_i' \leqslant \alpha_i$ and hence that $\omega_{q^s}(h') \leqslant \omega_{q^s}(h)$. From the construction it follows that $\omega_{q^s}(h'q^l) \leqslant \omega_{q^s}(hq^l)$ and hence that $\alpha^{h'}$ is also a zero of the code. From Theorem 9.1 of Chapter 1 it follows that the extended polynomial code with $b = 1$ is invariant under the doubly transitive affine group of permutations.

Many authors refer to what we have defined as an rth-order Euclidean geometry code as a type 0, rth-order Euclidean geometry code. This is to distinguish them from the following:

Definition A type 1 Euclidean geometry code of order r and length $p^{ms} - 1$ over $GF(p)$ is the largest cyclic code whose null space contains the incidence vectors of all the $r + 1$ flats of $EG(m, p^s)$ that do not pass through the origin.

2.2 Finite Geometries: Their Collineation Groups and Codes

We have observed already the problem of flats which do or do not pass through the origin with respect to the fact that coordinate positions are labeled with only the nonzero elements of $EG(m, p^s)$. It is instructive to consider the problem a little further. Number p^{ms} coordinate positions with p^{ms} elements of $EG(m, p^s)$. Let H_1 be the incidence matrix of all the $r + 1$ flats in $EG(m, p^s)$ and H_2 the incidence matrix of all those $r + 1$ flats in $EG(m, p^s)$ that do not pass through the origin. Let $\mathscr{C}_1$ and $\mathscr{C}_2$ be the codes that have H_1 and H_2 as generator matrices, respectively. Let the first coordinate position be labeled with the origin of $EG(m, p^s)$ and denote by H_1', H_2', $\mathscr{C}_1'$, and $\mathscr{C}_2'$ the respective matrices and codes with the first position deleted. From the foregoing, the code $\mathscr{C}_1'$ is the polynomial code of length $p^{ms} - 1$, $\mu = (m - r - 1)(p^s - 1)$, and $b = 1$ over $GF(p)$. The dual of $\mathscr{C}_1'$ is the rth-order Euclidean geometry code if $g(X)$ is the generator polynomial of the dual of $\mathscr{C}_1'$, then α^h is a root iff

$$\max_{0 \leq l < s} \omega_{p^s}(hp^l) \leq (m - r - 1)(p^s - 1)$$

where α is a primitive element of $GF(p^{ms})$. $\mathscr{C}_2$ is obviously a proper subcode of $\mathscr{C}_1$ since it does not contain the incidence vector of any flat through the origin. Actually $\mathscr{C}_2$ has dimension precisely one less than that of $\mathscr{C}_1$. To see this, suppose F_0 is an $r + 1$ flat through the origin. It contains $p^{s(r+1)}$ points and it is possible to find $p^{(m-r-1)s} - 1$ other flats F_i, $1 \leq i \leq p^{(m-r-1)s} - 1$, not through the origin, which are parallel to F_0 so that, as sets,

$$EG(m, p^s) = \bigcup_{i=0}^{p^{(m-r-1)s}} F_i$$

If U is the all-ones vector and U_i the incidence vector of F_i, then

$$U = \sum_{i=0}^{p^{(m-r-1)s}-1} U_i$$

However U, which is a codeword of $\mathscr{C}_1$, cannot be a codeword of $\mathscr{C}_2$ since this would imply

$$U_0 = U - \sum_{i=1}^{p^{(m-r-1)s}} U_i$$

which says a flat through the origin is in $\mathscr{C}_2$. Since any flat through the origin can be obtained in this way, we conclude that the closure of U and $\mathscr{C}_2$ is $\mathscr{C}_1$ and hence the dimensions of $\mathscr{C}_1$ and $\mathscr{C}_2$ differ by exactly one.

Since an affine transformation of $EG(m, q^s)$ takes a t flat to a t flat, then $\mathscr{C}_1$ is invariant under the group of affine transformations. Similarly $\mathscr{C}_2$ is invariant under the subgroup that fixes the origin. This implies that $\mathscr{C}_2'$ is cyclic. Let $g_1(x)$ and $g_2(x)$ be the generator polynomials of $\mathscr{C}_1'$ and $\mathscr{C}_2'$

respectively. The generator polynomial of the dual of $\mathscr{C}_1'$ clearly does not have the unit element as a root since $\mathscr{C}_1'$ contains the all-ones vector. Thus the generator polynomial of $\mathscr{C}_1'$ does not have 1 as a root. On the other hand, every codeword polynomial corresponding to a row of H_2 has weight $p^{s(r+1)}$, which is zero mod p, implying that one is a zero of $g_2(x)$. We conclude that

$$g_2(x) = (x - 1)g_1(x)$$

The dual of $\mathscr{C}_2'$ is a type 1 Euclidean geometry code of order r. From the characterization of the roots of the type 0 code we can conclude that α^h is a root of the generator polynomial of a type 1 Euclidean geometry code iff

$$0 < \max_{0 \leq l < s} \omega_{p^s}(hp^l) \leq (m - r - 1)(p^s - 1)$$

Notice that both the type 0 and type 1 Euclidean geometry codes are r-step orthogonalizable and, using r-step majority logic decoding, are capable of correcting

$$\left\lfloor \frac{p^{s(m-r+1)} - 1}{2(p^s - 1)} \right\rfloor$$

errors.

The original rth-order Reed–Muller codes (Reed, 1954; Muller, 1954) were binary, noncyclic (i.e., extended), type 0 Euclidean geometry codes. The null space of the codes of length 2^m contained every $r + 1$ flat of $EG(m, 2)$. The dimension of the code was known to be

$$\sum_{i=0}^{r} \binom{m}{i}$$

and its distance 2^{m-r}. This approach to Reed–Muller codes is discussed in Exercise 6. The natural generalizations of these codes, the GRM codes, has been discussed in the previous chapter.

Slightly before the development of polynomial and geometry codes, Weldon (1966) considered planar difference set codes. These however, correspond to projective geometry codes with a parity check matrix containing the incidence vectors of lines in a projective plane. These p-ary codes, which have length $n = p^{2s} + p^s + 1$ and dimension (Graham and MacWilliams, 1966)

$$k = \binom{p+1}{2}^s + 1$$

will be considered in a later section. The more general class of difference set codes, whose parity check matrices contain all the incidence vectors of hyperplanes in $PG(m, p^s)$, will also be discussed there. The dimensions of these codes are

$$k = \binom{p+m-1}{p-1}^s + 1$$

where the codes are of length $(p^{ms} - 1)/(p^s - 1)$ (Smith, 1969; Goethals and Delsarte, 1968; MacWilliams and Mann, 1968). This latter reference also shows that the rank over $GF(p)$ of the hyperplanes in $EG(m, p^s)$ is

$$\binom{p+m-1}{p-1}^s - 1$$

A problem that has received attention recently is reducing the number of steps required in majority logic decoding of the geometry codes. Weldon (1968) described a scheme, applicable to RM and Euclidean geometry codes, that provided some improvement. He also demonstrated that nonorthogonal parity check sums could be used in decoding the geometry codes in fewer steps. Perhaps the most impressive results on this problem are those of Chen (1971, 1972), who showed that a type 1, rth-order Euclidean geometry code of length $p^{ms} - 1$ can be majority logic decoded in N steps, where

$$N = \begin{cases} 1, & r = 0 \\ 2, & \tfrac{1}{2}m \geqslant r > 0 \\ i+1 = 1 + \log_2\left\lceil \dfrac{m}{m-r} \right\rceil, & (1-2^{-i})m \geqslant r > (1-2^{-(i-1)})m \end{cases}$$

The result is obtained essentially by a flat counting argument. A similar result also holds for the projective geometry codes. Lin (1972a) was also able to give a shortening algorithm for the geometry codes, which resulted in majority logic decodable codes able to correct the same number of errors as the original code.

Delsarte (1969) generalizes the concept of a Euclidean geometry in an unusual way and obtains majority logic decodable codes. In another paper (Delsarte, 1971a) he defines a class of linear binary codes using the finite inversive planes [e.g., see Dembowski (1968)] and these codes are one-step orthogonalizable. Bose and Burton (1966) use projective geometries to show that the binary codes of maximum length n for a minimum distance $d = 4$ are Hamming codes and are unique.

The projective and Euclidean geometry codes are, of course, closely related and we consider this relationship further. Let α be a primitive element of $GF(p^{ms})$ and let $\beta = \alpha^n$, $n = (p^{ms} - 1)/(p^s - 1)$ be the corresponding primitive element of $GF(p^s)$. Let $\alpha^{s_1}, \ldots, \alpha^{s_{r+1}}$ be $r + 1$ independent points of $GF(p^{ms})$ over $GF(p^s)$. An r flat of $PG(m - 1, p^s)$ is the set of points α^j described by

$$\alpha^j = \sum_{k=1}^{r+1} \beta^{i_k} \alpha^{s_k} \tag{2.5}$$

as β^{i_k}, $k = 1, \ldots, r + 1$, assume all possible values subject to the condition that they not be simultaneously zero. In the projective geometry the set of $p^s - 1$ points $\{\alpha^j, \alpha^{j+n}, \alpha^{j+2n}, \ldots, \alpha^{j+(p^s-2)n}\}$ are identified since they are scalar multiples of one another over $GF(p^s)$. We say the set consists of $p^s - 1$ replications of the point α^j. On the other hand, the set of all points α^j satisfying Equation (2.5) for some set of β^{i_k}, $k = 1, \ldots, r + 1$, including the all-zero combination, forms an $r + 1$ flat through the origin in $EG(m, p^s)$. This flat has $p^{(r+1)s}$ points, while the r flat in $PG(m - 1, p^s)$ has $(p^{(r+1)s} - 1)/(p^s - 1)$. Clearly the $p^s - 1$ replications of points in an r flat in $PG(m - 1, p^s)$ together with the origin form an $r + 1$ flat in $EG(m, p^s)$ which passes through the origin. Since the number of r flats in $PG(m - 1, p^s)$ [by Eq. (2.1)] is

$$\frac{(1 + p^s + \cdots + p^{s(m-1)})(p^s + \cdots + p^{s(m-1)}) \cdots (p^{sr} + \cdots + p^{s(m-1)})}{(1 + p^s + \cdots + p^{sr})(p^s + \cdots + p^{sr}) \cdots (p^{s(r-1)} + p^{sr})p^{sr}}$$

is the same as the number of $r + 1$ flats through the origin in $EG(m, p^s)$ [by Eq. (2.4)] we conclude that the converse is also true, i.e., every $(r + 1)$ flat of $EG(m, p^s)$ that goes through the origin consists of $p^s - 1$ replications of an r flat of $PG(m - 1, p^s)$ plus the origin.

Notice, finally, that all the codes in this section were formed over $GF(p)$. The codes are the null spaces of certain incidence matrices containing only zeros and ones. The rank of this matrix is the same over $GF(p^l)$, l any positive integer, as it is over $GF(p)$, since all calculations are done in the prime subfield. The dimension of the code generated by the matrix, using $GF(p^l)$, is the same [over $GF(p^l)$] as that using $GF(p)$ [over $GF(p)$]. In particular the two codes have the same generator polynomial, which is a polynomial over $GF(p)$. Our main reason for using $GF(p)$ was that in this case it has been established that the respective polynomial codes described in this section are minimal, in the sense that they are the smallest cyclic codes containing the required flats. Their duals are then the geometry codes. If the codes are generated over $GF(p^l)$ rather than $GF(p)$, but using the same geometries, then the resulting code is closely related to the $GF(p)$ code. Specifically, if we view $GF(p^l)$ as a vector space over $GF(p)$, then an arbitrary linear combination of vectors over $GF(p)$ of the $GF(p)$ code yields a vector in the $GF(p^l)$ code, by associating with each of the code vectors a basis element in the vector space of $GF(p^l)$ over $GF(p)$. Alternatively, we could use the subfield subcode concept of the previous chapter to discuss the code over $GF(p)$.

2.3 Balanced Incomplete Block Designs and Codes

The arrangement of the elements of some set into blocks or subsets with certain properties is a problem that attracts much attention, both in mathematics and the applied sciences. Many of the applications lie in the theory of experimental design, but the problems encountered in the study of such systems are of considerable mathematical complexity. In this section we introduce the idea of a balanced incomplete block design (BIBD hereafter) and examine some of its more elementary properties.

A BIBD is a special, but very important, case of the more general incidence system, which may be described as a set of blocks B_i, $i = 1, \ldots, b$, of elements taken from the set $A = \{a_1, a_2, \ldots, a_v\}$ with an incidence relation indicating which elements are in which blocks. An element is, in general, in more than one block. If there are v elements in the set A, it is somewhat customary to refer to them by the integers one through v and we shall do so. The incidence system is a little too general to study and we define the following special case, a BIBD.

Definition A balanced incomplete block design is an incidence system on v elements with b blocks such that (i) each block contains the same number of objects $k < v$, (ii) each element appears in the same number of blocks r, and (iii) every unordered pair of distinct elements appears in precisely λ blocks.

Very often a BIBD is referred to as a (v, b, r, k, λ) configuration. In the following we will often refer to such a configuration simply as a design. The theory of such designs has a very intimate relationship with both number theory and group theory. As mentioned previously, BIBD's arise from problems in the design of experiments. The term balanced refers to the fact that each pair of elements occurs in precisely the same number of blocks, while the term incomplete implies that each block contains fewer than v elements. Before proceeding we give a simple example to verify the existence of such designs.

Example Consider the Fano geometry introduced in the previous section. We reproduce its diagram here with letters replaced by integers (Fig. 6). The lines of the geometry will be taken as the blocks of the design and are

(1, 2, 3), (3, 4, 5), (1, 5, 6), (1, 4, 7) (3, 6, 7), (2, 5, 7), (2, 4, 6)

Each element appears three times and each pair of elements appears in exactly one block. This system is a (7, 7, 3, 3, 1) configuration. The Fano geometry is the projective geometry $PG(2, 2)$, and we constructed the design from the incidence relations between points and lines. Later in the section we shall construct BIBD's from the incidence relations of the points in r flats of any finite geometry.

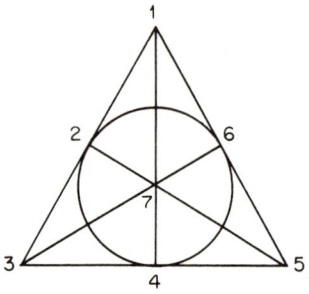

Fig. 6

To further verify the existence of such designs, we note that if one takes all possible combinations of k elements as the blocks, then a BIBD is obtained with parameters

$$b = \frac{v!}{k!(v-k)!}, \qquad r = \frac{(v-1)!}{(k-1)!(v-k)!}, \qquad \lambda = \frac{(v-2)!}{(k-2)!(v-k)!}$$

However, such a design is uninteresting, both mathematically and practically.

It is clear that the parameters of a design must satisfy certain relationships. Each of the b blocks contains k elements and the total number of elements in the array of blocks is bk. Since each element appears r times (the number of replications of the element) in the array and there are v elements, we have

(i) $bk = rv$.

Considering the r blocks containing a given element, we can form $r(k-1)$ pairs containing this element. Since there are $v - 1$ possible sets of unordered pairs of elements containing the given element and each such pair occurs λ times in the array, we have

(ii) $r(k-1) = \lambda(v-1)$.

These are the basic necessary conditions for the existence of (v, b, r, k, λ) configuration. They are not, however, sufficient, as can be shown by example, and the determination of necessary and sufficient conditions for the existence of designs is an unsolved problem. For any given set of parameters of a design

2.3 Balanced Incomplete Block Designs and Codes 121

it must, of course, be true that $k < v$ and $\lambda < r$. In the case when $b = v$, then $k = r$ and we say that the design is symmetric.

The relationships (i) and (ii) imply that the design is specified by the three parameters (v, k, λ) (although any other set of three parameters can also be used to specify the design). It is also possible to show that $b \geq v$, an inequality due to Fisher, which is proven after the following theorem.

We define the incidence matrix $\Gamma = (\gamma_{ij})$ of a (v, b, r, k, λ) configuration as the $v \times b$ matrix of zeros and ones, where

$$\gamma_{ij} = \begin{cases} 1 & \text{if } i \in B_j \\ 0 & \text{otherwise} \end{cases}$$

where, for the ith element, we take the integer i. Some of the basic properties of designs can be derived using incidence matrices. It will also have significance in some problems of coding. We consider some of its properties in the following theorem.

Theorem 3.1 Let Γ be the $v \times b$ incidence matrix of a (v, b, r, k, λ) configuration. Then

(i) $\Gamma\Gamma^T = (r - \lambda)I_v + \lambda J_{vv}$;
(ii) $\det(\Gamma\Gamma^T) = [r + (v - 1)\lambda](r - \lambda)^{v-1}$;
(iii) $\Gamma J_{bb} = rJ_{vb}$;
(iv) $J_{vv}\Gamma = kJ_{vb}$;

where J_{mn} is the $m \times n$ matrix of all ones and I_n is the $n \times n$ identity matrix.

Proof To show (i), we notice that in the ith row of Γ a one appears in the jth position if and only if the element i is in the jth block. Thus, if $\Gamma\Gamma^T = \Sigma = (\sigma_{ij})$, then, since each row of Γ has r ones, we have $\sigma_{ii} = r$ for $i = 1, 2, \ldots, v$. The inner product of the ith row of Γ with the jth row, $i \neq j$, is the number of blocks in which both the elements i and j occur, which by definition is λ, and so $\sigma_{ij} = \lambda$, $i \neq j$. The resulting matrix is then most conveniently described by

$$\Gamma\Gamma^T = \Sigma = (r - \lambda)I_v + \lambda J_{vv}$$

To find the determinant of Σ, which has the form

$$\Sigma = \begin{bmatrix} r & \lambda & \lambda & \cdots & \lambda \\ \lambda & r & \lambda & \cdots & \lambda \\ \lambda & \lambda & r & \cdots & \lambda \\ \vdots & \vdots & \vdots & & \vdots \\ \lambda & \lambda & \lambda & \cdots & r \end{bmatrix}$$

we subtract the first column from each of the other columns and then add to the first row all rows below it, to give the matrix

$$\begin{bmatrix} r+(v-1)\lambda & 0 & 0 & \cdots & 0 \\ \hdashline \lambda & r-\lambda & & & \\ \lambda & & r-\lambda & & 0 \\ \vdots & & & \ddots & \\ \lambda & & 0 & & r-\lambda \end{bmatrix}$$

and the determinant of $\Gamma\Gamma^T$ is $[r+(v-1)\lambda](r-\lambda)^{v-1}$.

The third and fourth relationships in the theorem merely indicate that each row of Γ contains r ones and each column k ones. □

The fact that $r > \lambda$ implies that $\Gamma\Gamma^T$ is of rank v, by (ii). However, the rank of Γ is at most b and since rank $\Gamma \geqslant \mathrm{rank}(\Gamma\Gamma^T) = v$, it follows that $b \geqslant v$.

We should perhaps mention that there are many interesting results on BIBD's which are pertinent to both number theory and matrix theory. For example, it can be shown [e.g., Ryser (1963, p. 111)] that in a symmetric BIBD with parameters $v = b$, $k = r$, and λ, if v is even, then $k - \lambda$ is a square, while if v is odd, then the Diophantine equation

$$x^2 = (k-\lambda)y^2 + (-1)^{(v-1)/2}\lambda z^2$$

has a nontrivial solution in integers for x, y, and z. Such a statement serves as a nonexistence theorem for symmetric BIBD's since for any v, k, and λ the foregoing conditions are certainly necessary for the existence of such a design. It is not known whether they are sufficient conditions.

If we are given a BIBD, there are several procedures for constructing other BIBD's from it and we consider three of them here. Perhaps we should first mention that two BIBD's are said to be isomorphic if one can be obtained from the other by a relabeling of the elements if the order in which the blocks are written down is immaterial.

If Γ is the incidence matrix of the given design, then the complement of Γ, which we denote by $\bar{\Gamma}$, obtained by replacing a zero in Γ by a one and a one by a zero, will be the incidence matrix of a design, which we call the complementary design. To verify that $\bar{\Gamma}$ is the incidence matrix of a design and to find its parameters, we proceed as follows. Each row of $\bar{\Gamma}$ has $b - r$ ones and each column has $v - k$ ones, indicating that for the new design $\bar{r} = b - r$ and $\bar{k} = v - k$. Furthermore, since two distinct rows of Γ have ones in precisely λ places at the same time, then they differ in $2(r - \lambda)$ places and hence any

2.3 Balanced Incomplete Block Designs and Codes

two rows of $\bar{\Gamma}$ have ones in $b - (2r - \lambda)$ places at the same time. Thus $\bar{\Gamma}$ is the incidence matrix of a $(v, b, b - r, v - k, b - 2r + \lambda)$ configuration if Γ is the incidence matrix of a (v, b, r, k, λ) configuration.

The residual design is another configuration that may be obtained from a given design, provided the given design is symmetric, i.e., $b = v$. If Γ is the incidence matrix of such a design, then, it can be shown that [see, for example, Ryser (1963, p. 103)].

$$\Gamma\Gamma^T = \Gamma^T\Gamma = (r - \lambda)I_v + \lambda J_{vv}$$

where Γ is a $v \times v$ matrix. The inner product of any two distinct rows of Γ^T is λ, implying that in a symmetric design any two distinct blocks have precisely λ elements in common. Now, from the given design with parameters (v, b, r, k, λ) ($b = v$ and $k = r$) delete a block and all elements occurring in that block from all other blocks. Thus we have $b - 1$ blocks remaining, and since we have removed precisely λ elements from each block, they contain $k - \lambda$ elements. This system clearly forms a design, called the residual design, and has parameters $(v - k, b - 1, r, k - \lambda, \lambda)$ where, again $b = v$ and $k = r$. It is important to note that the properties of the residual design may depend on which block of the original design was deleted and the deletion of a different block may not lead to an isomorphic design.

Suppose we start again with a symmetric (v, b, r, k, λ) design. To form the derived design, we choose a block and for the blocks of the derived design we take the sets of elements which each of the other blocks have in common with the chosen block. This gives a design with parameters $(k, b - 1, r - 1, \lambda, \lambda - 1)$ and again the properties of the derived design depend on the initial block chosen.

There are a wide variety of schemes available for the construction of BIBD's and the interested reader should consult Hall (1964, 1967a, b). We consider only one more technique since it uses the finite geometries which we have already investigated. Consider the case of a projective geometry $PG(n, q)$ first and for the elements of the design we take the points of the geometry. For the elements of a block we take the points of an m flat, where m is a constant for a given design. From the previous section we have that

$$v = 1 + q + q^2 + \cdots + q^n \quad \text{and} \quad k = 1 + q + q^2 + \cdots + q^m$$

where we are using the m flats in $PG(n, q)$ for the blocks of the design. The number of blocks is the number of distinct m flats in $PG(n, q)$, which we found to be

$$b = \frac{(1 + q + \cdots + q^n)(q + \cdots + q^n) \cdots (q^m + \cdots + q^n)}{(1 + q + \cdots + q^m)(q + \cdots + q^m) \cdots (q^{m-1} + q^m)q^m}$$

In the previous section we found that the number of $PG(m, q)$ in $PG(n, q)$ containing a given $PG(l, q)$ is

$$\frac{(q^{l+1} + \cdots + q^n)(q^{l+2} + \cdots + q^n) \cdots (q^m + \cdots + q^n)}{(q^{l+1} + \cdots + q^m)(q^{l+2} + \cdots + q^m) \cdots (q^{m-1} + q^m)q^m}$$

Thus, the number of m flats that are the blocks of the design containing a given point is, setting $l = 0$ in the above equation,

$$r = \frac{(q + \cdots + q^n)(q^2 + \cdots + q^n) \cdots (q^m + \cdots + q^n)}{(q + \cdots + q^m)(q^2 + \cdots + q^m) \cdots (q^{m-1} + q^m)q^m}$$

which is, of course, the number of replications of each point in the design. The parameter λ for the design is the number of m flats containing a given pair of points. However, any m flat containing the pair of points also contains the line joining the points and hence λ is the number of m flats containing a given line. This quantity is found by setting $l = 1$ in the above equation to give

$$\lambda = \frac{(q^2 + \cdots + q^n)(q^3 + \cdots + q^n) \cdots (q^m + \cdots + q^n)}{(q^2 + \cdots + q^m)(q^3 + \cdots + q^m) \cdots (q^{m-1} + q^m)q^m}$$

and $\lambda = 1$ for $m = 1$, and we have found all the parameters of the design.

In precisely the same manner we can use the m flats of $EG(n, q)$ to give a design with parameters

$$v = q^n, \quad k = q^m, \quad b = q^{n-m} \prod_{j=1}^{m} \frac{(q^{n+1-j} - 1)}{(q^{m+1-j} - 1)}$$

$$r = \frac{(q + \cdots + q^n)(q^2 + \cdots + q^n) \cdots (q^m + \cdots + q^n)}{(q + \cdots + q^m)(q^2 + \cdots + q^m) \cdots (q^{m-1} + q^m)q^m}$$

$$\lambda = \begin{cases} 1 & \text{if } m = 1 \\ \dfrac{(q^2 + \cdots + q^n)(q^3 + \cdots + q^n) \cdots (q^m + \cdots + q^n)}{(q^2 + \cdots + q^m)(q^3 + \cdots + q^m) \cdots (q^{m-1} + q^m)q^m} & \text{otherwise} \end{cases}$$

We have observed that when $b = v$, and hence $k = r$, the design is said to be symmetric and its incidence matrix is square. From the parameters of the designs derived from the projective geometries $PG(n, q)$ it follows that when $m = n - 1$, i.e., when the blocks of the design are determined by points in hyperplanes, then $b = v = 1 + q + q^2 + \cdots + q^n$ and hence these designs are symmetric with $\lambda = (q^{n-1} - 1)/(q - 1)$. In particular, the lines of any projective plane [not just $PG(2, q)$] determine a symmetric BIBD with $\lambda = 1$. The converse of this statement is also true, i.e., if we have a symmetric BIBD with $v = n^2 + n + 1$ and $k = n + 1$ and $\lambda = 1$, then we can form a projective plane of order n by identifying the elements of the designs with points of the

2.3 Balanced Incomplete Block Designs and Codes

geometry and the blocks of the design with the lines of the geometry. For a proof of this see Ryser (1963, p. 104).

In the next two sections of this chapter we shall consider some other combinatorial structures that may also be used to derive some combinatorial designs. However, rather than treat them as special cases of BIBD's, we prefer to present them in their original setting and deduce the associated design from them.

If it is possible to separate the b blocks of a BIBD into r sets of n blocks each such that each variety occurs exactly once in each set, then $b = nr$ and we say the design is resolvable (RBIBD). Such designs were studied by Bose (1942). It can be shown that for such designs

$$b \geqslant v + r - 1 \tag{3.1}$$

and since $r \geqslant 1$, this is a stronger version of Fisher's inequality. For an ordinary BIBD (i.e., not necessarily resolvable), if Fisher's inequality (i.e., $b \geqslant v$) holds with equality, then any two blocks in the design have the same number of elements in common. If Eq. (3.1) holds with equality for an RBIBD, then it can be shown that any two blocks belonging to different sets have exactly the same number of elements in common. A resolvable design with this property is called an affine resolvable BIBD (ARBIBD). The converse is also true, i.e., if the design is affine resolvable then Eq. (3.1) holds with equality. We state this as a theorem [due to Bose (1942)]:

Theorem 3.2 If a balanced incomplete block design D with parameters (v, b, r, k, λ) is resolvable, then $b \geqslant v + r - 1$, and equality holds if and only if D is affine resolvable.

Proof Since D is resolvable, then $v = nk$ and $b = nr$. Let R be a resolution class. Let B be a block of the class, and let $B_1, B_2, \ldots, B_t$, $t = (r - 1)n$, be the blocks of the remaining classes. Let $x_i = |B \cap B_i|$, $i = 1, 2, \ldots, t$. Since each variety of B occurs $r - 1$ more times,

$$\sum_{i=1}^{t} x_i = k(r - 1)$$

Also, since each pair of varieties of B occurs $\lambda - 1$ times elsewhere,

$$\sum_{i=1}^{t} x_i(x_i - 1) = (\lambda - 1)k(k - 1)$$

If $\bar{x}$ denotes the mean of the x_i, then

$$\bar{x} = \frac{k(r-1)}{t} = \frac{k}{n} = \frac{k^2}{v}$$

Now

$$\sum_{i=1}^{t} (x_i - \bar{x})^2 = \sum x_i^2 - t\bar{x}^2$$

Since $v > k$, $b \geq v + r - 1$. If $b = v + r - 1$, each $x_i = k^2/v$, and the design is affine resolvable. Conversely, if the design is affine resolvable, each $x_i = \bar{x}$, and therefore $b = v + r - 1$. □

The following lemma will be used in the next chapter.

Lemma 3.1 Let D be a balanced incomplete block design with parameters (v, b, r, k, λ) which satisfy $b = v + r - 1$. If every pair of blocks intersect in either zero or k^2/v varieties, then D is affine resolvable.

Proof Since $b = v + r - 1$, the basic relations can be used to prove

$$v = \frac{(r-1)k}{r-k}, \qquad b = \frac{r(r-1)}{r-k}, \qquad \lambda = r - k$$

Let B be a block of D. Remove B and all varieties of B from D. The result is a configuration D' with $v' = v - k = k(k-1)/(r-k)$ varieties in which every variety of D' occurs in r blocks and every pair of distinct varieties of D' occurs in λ blocks of D'. The configuration D' has two block sizes, k and $k' = k - k^2/v$. Let x be a variety of D' and let $s(x)$ denote the number of blocks of size k' that contain x. Since every other variety of D' occurs with x exactly λ times, one obtains

$$s(x)(k' - 1) + [r - s(x)](k - 1) = \lambda(v' - 1)$$

$$s(x) = \frac{-\lambda k}{k' - k} = \frac{\lambda v}{k} = r - 1$$

Thus every variety of D' occurs in exactly one block of size k. But these blocks are the blocks of D that do not meet B. Therefore the block B and those that are disjoint from it form a resolution class. But B was arbitrary; hence every block can be assigned to a resolution class. □

Example An example of an ARBIBD with $b = 12$, $v = 9$, $r = 4$, $k = 3$, and $\lambda = 1$ is

$$\begin{aligned}
b_1 &= \{1, 2, 3\} \\
b_2 &= \{4, 5, 6\} \quad \text{set 1} \\
b_3 &= \{7, 8, 9\}
\end{aligned} \qquad \begin{aligned}
b_7 &= \{1, 5, 9\} \\
b_8 &= \{2, 6, 7\} \quad \text{set 3} \\
b_9 &= \{3, 4, 8\}
\end{aligned}$$

$$\begin{aligned}
b_4 &= \{1, 4, 7\} \\
b_5 &= \{2, 5, 8\} \quad \text{set 2} \\
b_6 &= \{3, 6, 9\}
\end{aligned} \qquad \begin{aligned}
b_{10} &= \{1, 6, 8\} \\
b_{11} &= \{2, 4, 9\} \quad \text{set 4} \\
b_{12} &= \{3, 5, 7\}
\end{aligned}$$

2.3 Balanced Incomplete Block Designs and Codes

The number of varieties in common with any two blocks of different sets of an ARBIBD is k^2/v, implying that $v \mid k^2$. For an arbitrary BIBD, if it has the property that any two blocks have the same number of elements in common, then $b = v$ and the design is symmetric. The converse also holds and any two blocks in a symmetric design must have precisely λ elements in common.

While three parameters specify the other two parameters of a BIBD, for an ARBIBD we only require two parameters. If an ARBIBD has parameters (v, b, r, k, λ), then these parameters must be of the form

$$v = n^2(n-1)t + n^2, \quad b = n(n^2t + n + 1), \quad r = n^2t + n + 1$$
$$k = n(n-1)t + n, \quad \lambda = nt + 1$$

A design that is associated with the BIBD's and also with the Latin squares to be considered in the next section is the orthogonal array, which we require later in this section for our discussion of equidistant codes.

Definition Let $\mathbf{A}$ be a $k \times N$ matrix with entries from the set $\{0, 1, \ldots, s-1\}$. We say that $\mathbf{A}$ is an orthogonal array of strength t, size N, with k constraints and s levels if each $t \times N$ submatrix of $\mathbf{A}$ contains all possible $t \times 1$ column vectors with the same frequency λ, where λ is called the index of the array. We denote such an array by $OA(N, k, s, t)$.

This is the definition given by Bose and Bush (1952). Hall (1967a) defines an orthogonal array as the special case of the foregoing definition for $t = 2$ and $\lambda = 1$, $N = n^2$, and $s = n$. Certain orthogonal arrays are closely related to transversal systems.

Definition Let S be a class of m mutually disjoint t-sets w_i, $i = 1, 2, \ldots, m$. A transversal system $\Gamma_0(m, t)$ consists of t^2 sets Y_j, $j = 1, 2, \ldots, t^2$, each containing m elements such that $|w_i \cap Y_j| = 1$, $i = 1, 2, \ldots, m$ and $j = 1, 2, \ldots, t^2$, and if $j \neq k$, then $|Y_j \cap Y_k| \leq 1$. The sets Y_j are called *transversals*.

Lemma 3.2 There exists a transversal system $\Gamma_0(m, t)$ if and only if there exists an orthogonal array $OA(t^2, m, t, 2)$ of index one.

Proof Let us assume that there exists an orthogonal array $OA(t^2, m, t, 2)$ on the set of symbols $1, 2, \ldots, t$. Let sets $w_i = \{a_{ij}, j = 1, 2, \ldots, t\}$ be given. Form an array A of the symbols of $V = \bigcup_{i=0}^{m} w_i$ by replacing the symbol j in the ith row of the $m \times t^2$ orthogonal array by the element a_{ij}. Let Y_k be the set of elements in the kth column of A. Then these sets form a transversal system $\Gamma_0(m, t)$. Indeed, it is clear that $|w_i \cap Y_k| = 1$, and if Y_k and Y_l, $k \neq l$, intersect in two or more elements, say $\{a_{ij}, a_{rs}\} \subseteq Y_k \cap Y_l$, then the pair of symbols (j, s) occurs twice in rows i and r of the array in columns k and l, contradicting the definition of orthogonal array. Conversely, given the transversal system, it is evident that the elements of the sets Y_k can be ordered to form the rows of an orthogonal array. □

Definition A set of t transversals of a transversal system $\Gamma_0(m, t)$ is a parallel class if no two have a common element.

If $\Gamma_0(m, t)$ contains e (or more) parallel sets of transversals, it is denoted by $\Gamma_e(m, t)$.

Lemma 3.3 There is a system $\Gamma_t(m - 1, t)$ if and only if there is a system $\Gamma_0(m, t)$.

Proof Let a transversal system $\Gamma_0(m, t)$ defined on sets $w_i = \{a_{ij}\}$ be given. Let P_j be the class of transversals containing the element a_{mj}, $j = 1, 2, \ldots, t$. The sets of P_j correspond to a parallel class in the transversal system $\Gamma_0(m - 1, t)$ obtained by removing the elements of a_m from $\Gamma_0(m, t)$. Hence this system has t parallel classes and can be denoted by $\Gamma_t(m - 1, t)$. Clearly the construction can be reversed to prove the converse. □

Theorem 3.3 There exists a projective plane or order k if and only if there exists an orthogonal array $OA(k^2, (k + 1), k, 2)$ of index one.

Proof Let us assume that there exists a projective plane of order k. Then there exists an affine plane A of order k. Let $l_1, l_2, \ldots, l_k$ be the lines of a parallel class of A. Then the remaining lines form a transversal system $\Gamma_0(k, k)$. Since these lines can be resolved into k parallel classes, this system is a system $\Gamma_k(k, k)$. Hence there exists a transversal system $\Gamma_0(k + 1, k)$ and therefore an orthogonal array $OA(k^2, (k + 1), k, 2)$. The argument can be reversed to establish the converse. □

Example The matrix

$$\mathbf{A} = \begin{bmatrix} 0 & 1 & 0 & 0 & 0 & 1 & 1 & 1 \\ 0 & 0 & 1 & 0 & 1 & 0 & 1 & 1 \\ 0 & 0 & 0 & 1 & 1 & 1 & 0 & 1 \\ 0 & 1 & 1 & 1 & 0 & 0 & 0 & 1 \end{bmatrix}$$

is an $OA(8, 4, 2, 3)$ of strength three and index one.

We give a construction for such arrays, using the results of Bose and Bush (1952). Let $\mathbf{C}$ be a $k \times r$ matrix over $GF(q)$ with the property that every t rows are linearly independent. Label all the elements of $V_r(q)$, viewed as column vectors, by $\mathbf{X}_1, \mathbf{X}_2, \ldots, \mathbf{X}_{q^r}$. We claim that the $k \times q^r$ matrix $\mathbf{A}$,

2.3 Balanced Incomplete Block Designs and Codes

whose ith row is $\mathbf{CX}_i$, is an $OA(q^r, k, q, t)$ of index q^{r-t}. Let $\mathbf{A}'$ be a $t \times q^r$ submatrix of $\mathbf{A}$ and let $\mathbf{C}'$ be the corresponding submatrix of $\mathbf{C}$ consisting of rows of $\mathbf{C}$ corresponding to those chosen for $\mathbf{A}'$. Since $\mathbf{C}'$ has rank t, the equation $\mathbf{C}'\mathbf{X} = \mathbf{y}$ has q^{r-t} solutions for each $\mathbf{y} \, \varepsilon \, V_t(q)$, implying $\mathbf{A}$ is an $OA(q^r, k, q, t)$ of index q^{r-t}. Since nonzero scalar multiples of a row of $\mathbf{C}$ do not affect the independence of the rows, we can view the problem of constructing $\mathbf{C}$ as choosing k points of $PG(r-1, q)$ so that no t of them lie in a μ flat for $\mu \leqslant t - 2$. Notice the similarity of this argument to that used in proving the Varshamov–Gilbert bound.

It follows immediately from the definition that an $OA(N, k, s, t)$ of index λ has $N = \lambda s^t$. It can be shown (Bose and Bush, 1952) that for $t = 2$ the number of constraints is bounded by

$$k \leqslant \left\lfloor \frac{\lambda s^2 - 1}{s - 1} \right\rfloor$$

while for $t = 3$ it must be true that

$$k \leqslant \left\lfloor \frac{\lambda s^2 - 1}{s - 1} \right\rfloor + 1$$

There are several close connections between codes and BIBD's and in the remainder of this section we discuss two of them. Let C be a binary, linear (n, k) code and suppose it is invariant under a doubly transitive permutation group. Let D_i be the set of vectors of weight i, $|D_i| = N_i$. Let $\mathbf{A}$ be the $N_i \times n$ matrix whose rows are the codewords of D_i. Since a permutation of coordinate positions does not affect the weight of a codeword, the set D_i is also invariant under the permutation group. There exists in the group a permutation which takes column one of $\mathbf{A}$ to column j and this permutation has the same effect as rearranging the rows of $\mathbf{A}$. Thus the number of ones in the first column is the same as the number in the jth column and we conclude that each column has $r = iN_i/n$ ones, since the total number of ones in $\mathbf{A}$ is iN_i. Similarly, let λ be the number of rows in which the first two columns of $\mathbf{A}$ both have ones. There exists a permutation that takes column one to column j and column two to column k. Again, this permutation can be effected by a rearrangement of the rows in which any two columns both have ones. Thus columns j and k both have ones in λ rows. Permute the rows of $\mathbf{A}$ so that the r ones in the first column of $\mathbf{A}$ are in the first r rows. From the preceding every other column of $\mathbf{A}$ must have exactly λ ones in the first r rows. Since each row has i ones, by counting the number of ones two ways, we obtain

$$(n - 1)\lambda + r = ri$$

or

$$\lambda = \frac{i(i - 1)}{n(n - 1)} N_i$$

Clearly, if we treat the column positions of **A** as the varieties, then **A** is the incidence matrix of a BIBD with parameters

$$v = n, \quad b = N_i, \quad k = i, \quad r = \frac{iN_i}{n}, \quad \lambda = \frac{r(i-1)}{n}$$

Thus the codewords of a given weight of any code that is invariant under a doubly transitive group yield a BIBD. We have encountered several classes of codes that are invariant under doubly transitive groups. These include the primitive BCH code (a simple consequence of Theorem 9.1 in Chapter 1), the GRM codes, and the type 0 Euclidean geometry codes. In later sections and the next chapter we will consider the relationship between t designs, which are particular types of BIBD's and codewords of constant weight in a code. Generally speaking, the conditions required to obtain t designs are far more severe than those required to obtain BIBD's.

For the remainder of the section we will consider the work of Semakov and Zinov'ev (1968) on the relationships between equidistant (ED) codes, RBIB and ARBIB designs, and orthogonal arrays of strength two. From Theorem 11.2 of Chapter 1 we have that in any code of length n with N codewords over an alphabet of q symbols and with minimum distance d [an (n, N, q, d) code]

$$d \leqslant nN(q-1)/(N-1)q \tag{3.2}$$

If we form the $N \times n$ matrix **A** whose rows are the codewords, then equality is achieved in (3.2) only if each of the q symbols appears the same number of times in each column, i.e., $N = qt$, where each symbol appears t times in each column. A code that attains equality in the bound of (3.2) is called a maximal ED code and denoted as an ED_m code. In an ED_m code we have $N = qt$ and

$$d = nqt(q-1)/(qt-1)q$$

Since $qt - 1 = (q-1)(t-1) + (q-1) + (t-1)$, we can reduce this by the quantity $(q-1, t-1)$. If we can write

$$n = c(qt-1)/(q-1, t-1)$$

then

$$d = ct(q-1)/(q-1, t-1) \quad c \text{ an integer}, \quad c \geqslant 1$$

We exclude the case where $t = 1$ from consideration since this corresponds to the trivial situation of each codeword containing n repetitions of the same symbol. Notice that when $c = 1$ we must have that

$$(N-1) \geqslant n \geqslant \max\left\{\frac{(N-1)}{(q-1)}, \frac{(N-1)}{(t-1)}\right\}$$

2.3 Balanced Incomplete Block Designs and Codes

We now establish the equivalence between a (v, b, r, k, λ) RBIB, D, and an (n, N, q, d) ED_m code $\mathscr{C}$. Let $\mathbf{A}$ be the $N \times n$ code matrix and let $\mathbf{B}$ be the $v \times b$ incidence matrix of D with r ones in each row and k ones in each column. Suppose we are given the design D and let $b = qr$ and $v = qk$. Denote by $S_1, S_2, \ldots, S_r$ the sets of blocks with the property that each of the v elements appears precisely once in each set. Each set S_i contains q blocks and suppose the first q columns of the incidence matrix $\mathbf{B}$ of the design correspond to S_1. Let $\mathbf{B}'$ be the $v \times q$ submatrix of $\mathbf{B}$ containing its first q columns. Each row of $\mathbf{B}'$ contains one one while each column contains k ones. Label the rows of the $q \times q$ identity matrix by the elements of $X = \{0, 1, \ldots, q-1)\}$ in some arbitrary but fixed manner. Then replace each row of $\mathbf{B}'$ by its corresponding element of X. Doing this for the other sets S_i yields a $v \times r$ matrix $\mathbf{C}$ with elements from X. Since in any design every pair of elements appears in precisely λ blocks, and since these λ blocks must appear in different sets, it follows that any two rows of $\mathbf{C}$ agree in exactly λ places. Viewing the rows of $\mathbf{C}$ as a code over X yields an ED code with

$$N = v = qk, \quad d = r - \lambda, \quad n = r$$

However, for any design

$$\lambda = r(k - 1)/(v - 1)$$

and it follows that

$$d = r - \lambda = r(v - k)/(v - 1) = rk(q - 1)/(qk - 1) = nN(q - 1)/q(N - 1)$$

and the code is maximal.

The converse statement is also true and is shown simply by retracing these arguments, i.e., in the code matrix $\mathbf{A}$ replace each element of X by its associated row of I_q and the resulting matrix is the incidence matrix of an RBIBD. We have shown the following theorem.

Theorem 3.4 An ED_m code $\mathscr{C}$ with parameters $(n, N = qt, q, d)$ is equivalent to an RBIBD with parameters $(v = qk, b = qr, r, k, \lambda)$ and

$$t = k, \quad N = qt = v, \quad n = r, \quad qn = b, \quad d = n - \lambda = r - \lambda$$

Suppose now that we are given an ARBIBD with incidence matrix $\mathbf{B}$ and consider the ith column of the set S_1 and the jth column of the set S_2. The blocks corresponding to these two columns have precisely μ elements in common, implying that when we replace rows of $\mathbf{B}$ by r-tuples of elements of X the same ordered pair of elements in the first and second columns of the code will appear μ times. Since there are q^2 such ordered pairs, we must have that $v = q^2\mu$. Hence in a code corresponding to an ARBIBD in any two columns each ordered pair of elements from X appears μ times. Retracing the argument yields the converse, i.e., given a code with the property that in any two columns of its code matrix every ordered pair of elements appears μ times, then an ARBIBD can be obtained from it.

Let J be the transpose of the matrix over X of an $OA(N, k, S, 2)$ of index λ'. Thus J is an $N \times k$ matrix with the property that every ordered pair of elements of X appears λ' times in every pair of columns. But, using the correspondence between the rows of the identity matrix and elements of X, we see that an ARBIBD with parameters (v, b, r, k, λ) with $b = qr$ and $v = qk$ is equivalent to an $OA(v, r, q, 2)$ of index k^2/v.

Semakov and Zinov'ev (1968) further show that ED_m codes with $n = (N - 1)/(q - 1)$ are equivalent to ARBIBD's and hence to orthogonal arrays of appropriate parameters.

There are many other interesting relationships between balanced codes (all codewords have the same weight) and combinatorial configurations. The important t designs will be considered in the context of coding in the next chapter. We mention one other result on equidistant codes. Deza (1973) showed that a binary equidistant code of length n with m codewords at a mutual distance of $2k$ must have $m \leqslant k^2 + k + 2$ unless the code is trivial (i.e., each column of its code matrix contains m or $m - 1$ equal entries). Van Lint (1973) then showed that for $k > 1$ a code of length n, mutual distance $2k$, and with $m = k^2 + k + 2$ exists for sufficiently large n iff a $PG(2, k)$ exists. These results will be considered in the next chapter.

2.4 Latin Squares and Steiner Triple Systems

We shall refer to a symmetric BIBD with parameters $b = v$, $k = r$ as a (v, k, λ) configuration.

Definition Let x be a set of n elements $\{x_1, x_2, \ldots, x_n\}$. A Latin square of order n is then an $n \times n$ array of elements of x such that each row and each column of the array contains each element of x exactly once.

Example Let $x = \{1, 2, 3, 4\}$; then an example of a Latin square of order four is

$$\begin{array}{cccc} 1 & 3 & 2 & 4 \\ 4 & 2 & 3 & 1 \\ 2 & 4 & 1 & 3 \\ 3 & 1 & 4 & 2 \end{array}$$

2.4 Latin Squares and Steiner Triple Systems

Notice that we can permute rows and columns of the array without destroying the Latin square property. This implies that we can always permute the rows and columns of the array so that the elements in the first row and first column are ordered. Thus the foregoing array can be put into the form

$$\begin{array}{cccc} 1 & 2 & 3 & 4 \\ 2 & 1 & 4 & 3 \\ 3 & 4 & 1 & 2 \\ 4 & 3 & 2 & 1 \end{array}$$

Notice also that the group multiplication table of any group is, by definition, a Latin square.

Definition A pair of Latin squares of order n is said to be orthogonal if, when one square is superimposed on the other so that each cell of the $n \times n$ array contains an ordered pair, each of the n^2 possible ordered pairs occurs exactly once in the array.

Similarly, we say that a set of Latin squares is an orthogonal set if the squares are pairwise orthogonal.

Example The two Latin squares L_1 and L_2 of order four

$$L_1: \begin{array}{cccc} 1 & 2 & 3 & 4 \\ 2 & 1 & 4 & 3 \\ 3 & 4 & 1 & 2 \\ 4 & 3 & 2 & 1 \end{array} \qquad L_2: \begin{array}{cccc} \alpha & \beta & \gamma & \delta \\ \gamma & \delta & \alpha & \beta \\ \delta & \gamma & \beta & \alpha \\ \beta & \alpha & \delta & \gamma \end{array}$$

when superimposed give

$$\begin{array}{cccc} (1,\alpha) & (2,\beta) & (3,\gamma) & (4,\delta) \\ (2,\gamma) & (1,\delta) & (4,\alpha) & (3,\beta) \\ (3,\delta) & (4,\gamma) & (1,\beta) & (2,\alpha) \\ (4,\beta) & (3,\alpha) & (2,\delta) & (1,\gamma) \end{array}$$

and hence L_1 and L_2 are orthogonal.

The orthogonality of two Latin squares is not destroyed by a relabeling of the elements. Thus, if we have a set of r orthogonal Latin squares of order n, we can relabel the elements of each square so that the first row contains in order the elements $1, 2, \ldots, n$ and i appears in the ith column of each square. The set of elements in any given cell not in the first row of each square must be distinct since all identical pairs appear in the first row for any two given squares. Furthermore, the element i cannot appear in the ith column of any square, and we conclude that $r \leq n - 1$ and we can never have more than $n - 1$

pairwise orthogonal Latin squares (pols) of order n. A set of $n-1$ orthogonal Latin squares is said to be complete.

There are many techniques for constructing orthogonal Latin squares, but we limit ourselves to those using finite fields. The first result concerns complete sets of orthogonal squares.

Theorem 4.1 If $n \geq 3$ is a prime power, then there exists a complete set of orthogonal Latin squares of order n.

Proof We prove the theorem by actual construction of the complete set of squares using $GF(p^e)$, where $n = p^e$, p a prime. Let α be a primitive root of $GF(p^e)$ and by convention, let $\alpha^\infty = 0$. Define the $n \times n$ arrays

$$L_k = (l_{ij}^{(k)}), \qquad i, j = 1, 2, \ldots, p^e - 1, \infty, \quad k = 1, 2, \ldots, p^e - 1$$

where the last row and column are for convenience labeled ∞, and $l_{ij}^{(k)}$ is defined by the relation

$$l_{ij}^{(k)} = \alpha^k \cdot \alpha^i + \alpha^j, \qquad i, j = 1, 2, \ldots, p^e - 1, \infty, \quad k = 1, 2, \ldots, p^e - 1$$

We first verify that the L_k, $k = 1, 2, \ldots, p^e - 1$ are Latin squares. If two elements in the same row are identical, then we would have

$$\alpha^k \cdot \alpha^i + \alpha^j = \alpha^k \cdot \alpha^i + \alpha^{j'} \quad \text{or} \quad \alpha^j = \alpha^{j'}$$

implying that $j = j'$. Similarly, if two elements in the same column are identical, then

$$\alpha^k \cdot \alpha^i + \alpha^j = \alpha^k \cdot \alpha^{i'} + \alpha^j$$

implying that $i = i'$. Thus L_k is a Latin square. To show that L_{k_1} and L_{k_2} are orthogonal for any two distinct integers less than $n - 1$, suppose on the contrary that

$$(l_{ij}^{(k_1)}, l_{ij}^{(k_2)}) = (l_{i'j'}^{(k_1)}, l_{i'j'}^{(k_2)})$$

i.e., assume that the same ordered pair appears twice in the superposition of the squares. This equation implies that

$$\alpha^{k_1} \cdot \alpha^i + \alpha^j = \alpha^{k_1} \cdot \alpha^{i'} + \alpha^{j'}$$
$$\alpha^{k_2} \cdot \alpha^i + \alpha^j = \alpha^{k_2} \cdot \alpha^{i'} + \alpha^{j'}$$

which on subtraction implies that

$$(\alpha^{k_1} - \alpha^{k_2})(\alpha^i - \alpha^{i'}) = 0$$

and since k_1 and k_2 were assumed distinct, $i = i'$ and, consequently, $j = j'$. Thus we have a complete set of $n - 1$ orthogonal Latin squares of order n. □

2.4 Latin Squares and Steiner Triple Systems

It is not possible to construct a complete set of orthogonal Latin squares of order n for arbitrary n. However, the following is possible; let the prime factorization of n be

$$n = p_1^{e_1} p_2^{e_2} \cdots p_k^{e_k}$$

where the p_i are distinct primes and the e_i are positive integers. Then if

$$r = \min_i (p^{e_i} - 1), \quad r \geq 2$$

it is possible to construct r pairwise orthogonal Latin squares of order n. We give the construction of these squares given by Hall (1964). Let M be the set of elements of the form $(\alpha_1, \alpha_2, \ldots, \alpha_k)$, $\alpha_i \in GF(p^{e_i})$ and define addition and multiplication of elements of the set componentwise, i.e.,

$$(\gamma_1, \gamma_2, \ldots, \gamma_k) + (\beta_1, \beta_2, \ldots, \beta_k) = (\gamma_1 + \beta_1, \gamma_2 + \beta_2, \ldots, \gamma_k + \beta_k)$$
$$(\gamma_1, \gamma_2, \ldots, \gamma_k)(\beta_1, \beta_2, \ldots, \beta_k) = (\gamma_1 \beta_1, \gamma_2 \beta_2, \ldots, \gamma_k \beta_k)$$

Notice that the set M contains precisely n elements. Now let α_i be a primitive element of $GF(p_i^{e_i})$, $i = 1, \ldots, k$, and let $z = (\alpha_1, \alpha_2, \ldots, \alpha_k)$. From the definition of r we see that the ith components of z^j, $j = 0, 1, \ldots, r-1$, are distinct for $i = 1, \ldots, k$. We construct r arrays L_i, $i = 0, 1, \ldots, r-1$, in the following manner. Designate the n elements of M by $a_0, a_1, a_2, \ldots, a_{n-1}$. The cell of each array will contain an element of M determined in the following manner: In the (i, j) square of the array L_l, $l = 0, 1, \ldots, r-1$, we put the element b of M, where

$$a_i = z^l a_j + b, \quad i, j = 0, 1, \ldots, n-1, \quad l = 0, 1, \ldots, r-1$$

We first check that L_l is a Latin square. If the element b occurs twice in the same row of L_l then

$$a_i = z^l a_j + b = z^l a_{j'} + b$$

which implies $j = j'$. Similarly if b occurs twice in the same column, then

$$a_i = z^l a_j + b, \quad a_{i'} = z^l a_j + b$$

implying that $i = i'$. Thus L_l, $l = 0, 1, \ldots, r-1$, is a Latin square. To show that the squares are orthogonal, consider L_{l_1} and L_{l_2}, l_1 and l_2 distinct, and suppose in their superposition that the ordered pair (b_1, b_2) occurs in cells (i, j) and (i', j'). This implies the equations

$$a_i = z^{l_1} a_j + b_1, \quad a_{i'} = z^{l_1} a_{j'} + b_1$$
$$a_i = z^{l_2} a_j + b_2, \quad a_{i'} = z^{l_2} a_{j'} + b_2$$

Using the first set of equations, we find that

$$(b_1 - b_2) + a_j(z^{l_1} - z^{l_2}) = 0$$

and from the second set

$$(b_1 - b_2) + a_{j'}(z^{l_1} - z^{l_2}) = 0$$

Subtracting these equations gives

$$(a_j - a_{j'})(z^{l_1} - z^{l_2}) = 0$$

and since $l_1 \neq l_2$, $j = j'$ and consequently $i = i'$ and the set is orthogonal. Notice the dependence of the argument on the form of z.

From a complete set of Latin squares of order $n \geq 3$ it is possible to construct a projective plane of order n and, conversely, from a projective plane of order n it is possible to construct a complete set of Latin squares of order n [cf. Ryser, (1963, p. 92)]. However, we have already seen that from a projective plane of order n we can construct an $(n^2 + n + 1, n + 1, 1)$ configuration, and in this manner we establish the connection between symmetric BIBD's and complete sets of orthogonal Latin squares. If we have a set of r orthogonal Latin squares of order n, $r < n$, then construction techniques exist for partially balanced designs, i.e., a design where the frequency of appearance of a given pair varies depending on the pair. The interested reader is referred to the work of Hall (1964). Many other construction techniques for sets of orthogonal Latin squares exist, and again the reader is referred to the work of Hall (1964, 1967a).

For many years there had been a question of the existence of orthogonal Latin squares. Euler in 1782 had conjectured that when n is equal to 2 mod 4 ("unevenly even" numbers) then no pair of orthogonal Latin squares of order n would exist. For $n = 6$ Tarry (1901) verified this by the complete enumeration of all possibilities. The falsity of the conjecture, however, was demonstrated by the result, due to Bose *et al.* (1960), that for n equal to 2 mod 4 and for $n > 6$ there exists a pair of orthogonal Latin squares of order n. The equivalence between complete sets of orthogonal Latin squares and projective planes might indicate that one method of constructing a projective plane of order ten, the lowest-order unknown case, is to try and find a set of nine pairwise-orthogonal Latin squares. This approach has not yet proven fruitful.

We briefly mention here Steiner triple systems, although we will not require them until the next chapter. These triple systems are special cases of t designs where a λ-(t, d, n) t-design D is a collection of d-subsets of a set X, $|X| = n$, such that any t-subset of X is in exactly λ subsets of D. There are some new and interesting relationships between t designs and codewords of certain fixed weights in particular codes which we will consider in a later section and the next chapter.

A Steiner system S of order n is a family of subsets of a set of elements of order n, such that each subset in the family contains k elements and each t-

2.4 Latin Squares and Steiner Triple Systems

element subset is contained in precisely one of the k-element subsets, i.e., it is a λ-(t, k, n) design where $\lambda = 1$. For convenience we designate a Steiner system by $S(t, k, n)$. Of particular interest are the Steiner triple systems for which $k = 3$ and $t = 2$. It follows immediately that a Steiner triple system is a BIBD with $k = 3$ and $\lambda = 1$, $v > 3$, and conversely. From the basic relationships between the parameters of a BIBD we find that

$$b = \tfrac{1}{6}v(v-1), \qquad r = \tfrac{1}{2}(v-1)$$

from which it follows that $v \equiv 1$ or $3 \mod 6$, i.e., v is of the form $6n + 1$ or $6n + 3$ for some positive integer n. Since Steiner triple systems can be constructed for all such values, these conditions are both necessary and sufficient for the existence of such systems.

We give two recursive techniques for constructing Steiner triple systems from given ones. Suppose we are given two Steiner triple systems S_1 of order v_1 defined on the set $\{a_1, a_2, \ldots, a_{v_1}\}$ and S_2 of order v_2 defined on the set $\{b_1, b_2, \ldots, b_{v_2}\}$. To construct a Steiner system S of order $v_1 v_2$ we take as the elements on which S is defined the $v_1 v_2$ ordered 2-tuples (a_i, b_j). A triple of these elements $\{(a_i, b_r), (a_j, b_s), (a_k, b_t)\}$ will be in S if it satisfies one of the following conditions:

(i) If $r = s = t$ and (a_i, a_j, a_k) is in S_1. Thus triples of the form $\{(a_i, b_r), (a_j, b_r), (a_k, b_r)\}$, $r = 1, 2, \ldots, v_2$, are in S if (a_i, a_j, a_k) is in S_1.
(ii) If $i = j = k$ and (b_r, b_s, b_t) is in S_2.
(iii) If (a_i, a_j, a_k) is in S_1 and (b_r, b_s, b_t) is in S_2.

That S is a Steiner triple system of order $v_1 v_2$ follows easily. Notice that isomorphic copies of both S_1 and S_2 are contained in S.

A second powerful construction of Steiner triple systems, given by Hall (1967a, p. 238), shows that given a system of order v_2 containing a subsystem of order v_3, and a system of order v_1, then we can construct a system of order $v = v_3 + v_1(v_2 - v_3)$. The first construction is just a special case of this last one, as is seen by choosing a subdesign, i.e., $v_3 = 0$. Finally, we note that the points on the lines of the Fano geometry, considered in the previous two sections, also form a Steiner triple system, and that any BIBD with $k = 3$ and $\lambda = 1$ forms a Steiner triple system.

Consider an orthogonal array $OA(n^2, k, n, 2)$ of index one and let $\mathbf{A}$ be the $k \times n^2$ array matrix with elements from the set $\{1, 2, \ldots, n\}$. From the ith row of $\mathbf{A}$ we form an $n \times n$ matrix $\mathbf{B}_i$ where the first n entries of the row form the first row of $\mathbf{B}_i$, the second n entries form the second row of $\mathbf{B}_i$, etc. From the definition of the orthogonal array the matrices $\mathbf{B}_i$, $i = 1, \ldots, k$, form a set of k pols. Hence an $OA(n^2, n-1, n, 2)$ of index one is equivalent to a projective plane of order n, $n \geq 3$.

We have already observed the equivalence between a set of $n - 1$ pols of order n and a projective plane of order n. Also, the relationship between coding, block designs, and projective planes has been considered. We consider further the relationship between sets of pols and coding and commence by proving a theorem given by Singleton (1964), attributed to Golomb and Posner.

Theorem 4.2 An $(n, q^2, n - 1)$ code over an alphabet on q symbols is equivalent to a set of $n - 2$ pols of order q.

Proof Suppose we are given a set of $n - 2$ pols of order q. Number the rows and columns in the same fashion with the q alphabet symbols on which the squares are defined. Let $L_1, L_2, \ldots, L_{n-2}$ be the set of pols and L the set of pols superimposed, so that each of the q^2 cells of L contains an ordered $n - 2$-tuple the ith position of which contains the alphabet symbol in the same cell of L_i. Suppose cell (a_i, a_j) of L contains the $(n - 2)$-tuple $(a_{ij}^1, a_{ij}^2, \ldots, a_{ij}^{n-2})$, where a_i, a_j, and a_{ij}^k are elements of the q-ary alphabet. Form the code C with q^2 codewords:

$$C = \{X_{ij} = (a_i, a_j, a_{ij}^1, a_{ij}^2, \ldots, a_{ij}^{n-2}), \quad 1 \le i, j \le q\}$$

Consider the distance between two distinct codewords X_{ij} and X_{rs}. These two codewords can agree in at most one place in the last $n - 2$ places since if they agreed in two places, the corresponding Latin squares when superimposed would contain a repeated ordered 2-tuple, contrary to the assumed orthogonality. However, if X_{ij} and X_{rs} agree in either the first or second position, then they can agree in none of the last $n - 2$ places since if they did, it would imply that a symbol is repeated in either a row or a column of one of the squares, depending on whether the first or second symbols of the two codewords are the same. Thus the resulting code has distance $n - 1$ and is maximum distance separable.

For the converse, suppose we are given a code of block length n with q^2 codewords, distance $n - 1$, over a q-ary alphabet. Reversing the above process, we identify a cell in L, with rows and columns labeled as before, by the first two coordinate positions and place the ordered $(n - 2)$-tuple consisting of the last $n - 2$ positions in that cell. The ith coordinates yield a Latin square L_i, $1 \le i \le n - 2$, and their pairwise orthogonality follows from the distance properties of the code. □

The method of the above theorem can be extended to Latin hypercubes, yielding codes with higher dimension. Golomb and Posner (1964) laid to rest a question of Golay (1958) concerning the existence of a perfect single-error-correcting code of length seven over an alphabet of six symbols containing 6^5 codewords. The sphere-packing condition is, of course, satisfied for these parameters. Since $d = n - k + 1$, the code is maximum distance separable and any five coordinate positions contain all 6^5 possible 5-tuples over the alphabet. Take, for convenience, the first five positions and consider the 36 codewords that begin with a fixed triple. If we delete the (identical) first three positions from each of the 36 codewords, a code of length four and distance three over an alphabet of six symbols results. From the previous theorem this implies the existence of two pols of order six. However, as previously mentioned, Tarry (1901), by exhaustive search, showed that two pols of order six do not exist. Hence no perfect single error-correcting code of length seven over an alphabet of six symbols exists.

2.5 Quadratic Residues and Codes

Let p be an odd prime and consider the integers mod p. We say that a is a quadratic residue of p if $a \not\equiv 0 \bmod p$ and there is a solution to the equation

$$x^2 \equiv a \bmod p$$

If no solution exists, a is called a quadratic nonresidue of p. Consider the $(p - 1)/2$ integers, taken mod p,

$$1^2, 2^2, 3^2, \ldots, [(p-1)/2]^2$$

These must be distinct integers mod p, for if $a^2 = b^2$, mod p, then $a = b$ or $a = p - b$ and since $a, b \leq (p - 1)/2$ by assumption, $a = b$. Since $a^2 = (p - a)^2$ mod p, it follows that there are precisely $(p - 1)/2$ quadratic residues mod p, which are the above set of numbers. Consequently, there must be $(p - 1)/2$ quadratic nonresidues of p.

The Legendre symbol is a useful notation in the investigation of quadratic residues. If a is a quadratic residue of p, $p \nmid a$, then we denote this fact by writing $(a/p) = +1$. If a is a quadratic nonresidue of p, then $(a/p) = -1$. There are many interesting properties that can be proved about this symbol and we state only a few of them. For any odd prime p, it is true that

$$(a/p) = a^{(p-1)/2} \bmod p$$

To see this, we observe that from Fermat's theorem, for any nonzero integer a and prime p such that $p \nmid a$, $a^{p-1} \equiv 1 \bmod p$. It follows that $a^{(p-1)/2} \equiv \pm 1$ mod p. If a is a quadratic residue, then $a \equiv x^2$ for some x and hence $a^{(p-1)/2} \equiv 1 \bmod p$. But the equation $y^{(p-1)/2} \equiv 1$ cannot have more than $(p - 1)/2$ distinct solutions mod p and hence these solutions are precisely the quadratic residues. Since every nonzero element satisfies the equation

$$y^{(p-1)} - 1 = (y^{(p-1)/2} - 1)(y^{(p-1)/2} + 1)$$

it follows that every quadratic nonresidue satisfies $a^{(p-1)/2} \equiv -1 \mod p$. From this relationship it readily follows that

$$(a/p)(b/p) = (ab/p) \quad \text{and} \quad (-1/p) = (-1)^{(p-1)/2}$$

implying that $-1 \equiv (p-1) \pmod{p}$ is a quadratic residue if $p \equiv 1 \mod 4$ and a nonresidue if $p \equiv 3 \mod 4$. Thus if a and b are two quadratic residues or two quadratic nonresidues, then their product will be a quadratic residue. Similarly, the product of a residue and a nonresidue is a nonresidue.

The law of quadratic reciprocity states that if p and q are distinct odd primes, then

$$(p/q)(q/p) = (-1)^{(p-1)(q-1)/4}$$

Since the proof is quite lengthy and can be found in many books on number theory, we omit it.

There is an interesting property of factorials using quadratic residues, which we consider. Let a be a fixed element mod p and suppose it is a quadratic residue and $x_1^2 \equiv a \mod p$. Also, $p - x_1$ is a solution since $(p - x_1)^2 \equiv a \mod p$ and $x_1(p - x_1) \equiv -a \mod p$. The elements x_1 and $p - x_1$ are the only solutions to the congruence $x^2 \equiv a \mod p$. For any other element x' mod p there is precisely one element x'' such that $x'x'' \equiv a \mod p$. Thus the elements $1, 2, \ldots, p - 1$ can be divided into x_1 and $p - x_1$ [for which $x_1(p - x_1) \equiv -a \mod p$] and $(p - 3)/2$ classes each of two elements x' and x'' such that $x'x'' \equiv a \mod p$. Thus if a is a quadratic residue, we conclude that

$$(p-1)! = \Pi x \equiv -a \cdot a^{(p-3)/2} \equiv -a^{(p-1)/2}$$

If a is a quadratic nonresidue, however, we can divide the elements $1, 2, \ldots, p - 1$ into $(p - 1)/2$ classes x' and x'' such that $x'x'' \equiv a \mod p$ for each class, from which it follows that

$$(p-1)! \equiv -(a/p)a^{(p-1)/2} \mod p$$

Since unity is always a quadratic residue, we have

$$(p-1)! \equiv -1 \mod p$$

which is just Wilson's theorem. From these relations it also follows directly that

$$(a/p) \equiv a^{(p-1)/2} \mod p$$

a fact shown previously.

For another interesting interpretation of the Legendre symbol, we say that the (ordinary) residue of an integer k mod p is minimal if it lies between

2.5 Quadratic Residues and Codes

$-p/2$ and $+p/2$. For some fixed integer k, $p \nmid k$, consider the set of minimal residues of the set

$$k, 2 \cdot k, 3 \cdot k, \ldots, [(p-1)/2] \cdot k$$

which we denote by $r_1, r_2, \ldots, r_a, -s_1, -s_2, \ldots, -s_b$, where $0 < r_i$, $s_j < p/2$ and $a + b = (p-1)/2$. Since $p \nmid k$, if $r_i = r_j$, $i \neq j$, then we would have $u \cdot k \equiv v \cdot k \pmod{p}$, which would imply $p | (u-v)k$, which is impossible since $0 < u, v < p/2$. Similarly, no two of the s_i are equal. If $r_i = s_j$, then, for some u, v we have that

$$uk \equiv r_i \bmod p \quad \text{and} \quad vk \equiv -s_j \bmod p$$

or

$$(u + v)k \equiv 0 \bmod p$$

Since $p \nmid k$, this equation implies that

$$u + v \equiv 0 \bmod p$$

which, again, is impossible since $0 < u, v < p/2$. Thus the minimal residues are distinct and the set $\{r_1, r_2, \ldots, r_a, s_1, s_2, \ldots, s_b\}$ accounts for all the integers $\{1, 2, \ldots, (p-1)/2\}$. It follows that

$$k \cdot 2k \cdot 3k \cdots [(p-1)/2]k \equiv (-1)^b \cdot 1 \cdot 2 \cdots [(p-1)/2] \bmod p$$

or equivalently

$$k^{(p-1)/2} \equiv (-1)^b \bmod p$$

However, since

$$(k/p) = k^{(p-1)/2} \bmod p$$

we conclude that

$$(k/p) \equiv (-1)^b \bmod p$$

a result that is referred to as Gauss's lemma. For $k = 2$ we can find $(2/p)$ by considering the minimal residues of the set

$$\{2, 4, 6, \ldots, p-1\}$$

It is easily established that $(2/p) = 1$ if p is a prime of the form $8n \pm 1$ and $(2/p) = -1$ if p is a prime of the form $8n \pm 3$. Since $\frac{1}{8}(p^2 - 1)$ is even if p is of the form $8n \pm 1$ and odd otherwise,

$$(2/p) = (-1)^{(p^2-1)/2}$$

Notice that from the law of reciprocity

$$(p/q)(q/p) = (-1)^{(p-1)(q-1)/4}$$

and thus if either $(p-1)/2$ or $(q-1)/2$ is an even integer, then $(p/q) = (q/p)$. If they are both odd, then $(p/q) = -(q/p)$ and this occurs only when the odd primes p and q are of the form $4n + 3$.

The theory of quadratic residues has been put to some interesting uses in the solution of certain congruences. Berlekamp (1968) uses the law of reciprocity in factoring the polynomial $x^n - 1$ over $GF(p)$, where p and n are distinct odd primes (see Exercise 16).

Recall that there are $(p - 1)/2$ quadratic residues of the odd prime p, which are $1^2, 2^2, \ldots, [(p - 1)/2]^2$ and which we denote by R_0. We now use these to construct some $(p, (p - 1)/2)$ codes over $GF(q)$ that have good distance properties.

Let η be a primitive pth root of unity in some extension field of $GF(q)$, $(q, p) = 1$, and denote the set of quadratic nonresidues by R_1. Assume that the order of q mod p divides $(p - 1)/2$, i.e., $q \in R_0$, and notice that char$(GF(q))$ is not related to p except that it is relatively prime to p. Define the two polynomials

$$f_1(x) = \prod_{i \in R_0} (x - \eta^i), \qquad f_2(x) = \prod_{i \in R_1} (x - \eta^i)$$

and observe that these polynomials will have coefficients in $GF(q)$ and that

$$x^p - 1 = (x - 1)f_1(x)f_2(x)$$

The polynomials $f_i(x)$ will be irreducible over $GF(q)$ iff the multiplicative order of q mod p is $(p - 1)/2$. With these polynomials we define the following codes.

(i) $\mathscr{C}_1$ is the quadratic residue code with parameters $(p, (p + 1)/2)$ generated by $f_1(x)$.

(ii) $\mathscr{C}_2$ is the expurgated quadratic residue code with parameters $(p, (p - 1)/2)$ generated by $(x - 1)f_1(x)$.

(iii) $\mathscr{C}_3$ is the extended quadratic residue code with parameters $(p + 1, (p + 1)/2)$ obtained by annexing an overall parity check to $\mathscr{C}_1$.

The code $\mathscr{C}_2$ is, of course, a subcode of $\mathscr{C}_1$ consisting of all those codewords $c(x) = \sum_{i=0}^{p-1} c_i x^i$ such that $\sum_{i=0}^{p-1} c_i = 0$, whence the name expurgated. The original investigation of Mattson and Solomon (1961) was restricted to the binary case and $f_i(x)$ irreducible. In this case if the roots of $f_i(x)$ expressed as powers of a primitive pth root of unity, then these powers are either all quadratic residues or all quadratic nonresidues. The BCH bound on the minimum distance of these codes is, generally speaking, not very good. We proceed to obtain a better bound. We do not restrict the discussion to $f_i(x)$ irreducible.

2.5 Quadratic Residues and Codes

Lemma 5.1 Let $c(x) \in \mathscr{C}_1 \backslash \mathscr{C}_2$ be a codeword of weight d; then $d^2 \geqslant p$ and if -1 is a quadratic nonresidue mod p, i.e., $p \equiv -1 \mod 4$, then this bound can be improved to $d^2 - d + 1 \geqslant p$.

Proof Since multiplication of a quadratic residue by a quadratic nonresidue is a quadratic nonresidue, the codes generated by $f_1(x)$ and $f_2(x)$ are equivalent, as can be seen by applying Theorem 7.5 of Chapter 1. Let $c(x)$ by a codeword of weight d in $\mathscr{C}_1 \backslash \mathscr{C}_2$ and let $c'(x)$ be a codeword of weight d in the code $\mathscr{C}_1'$ generated by $f_2(x)$ but not in the expurgated code generated by $(x-1)f_2(x)$. Then $f_1(x)|c(x)$, $(x-1) \nmid c(x)$, $f_2(x)|c'(x)$, and $(x-1) \nmid c'(x)$ and we consider the product $c(x)c'(x)$. We write

$$c(x)c'(x) = q(x)(x^p - 1) + r(x), \qquad \deg r < p$$

Since $(x-1) \nmid c(x)c'(x)$ and $f_1(x)f_2(x)|c(x)c'(x)$ it follows that $f_1(x)f_2(x)|r(x)$ and hence, since $\deg(f_1 f_2) = p - 1$,

$$\alpha f_1(x)f_2(x) = r(x) = \alpha(1 + x + \cdots + x^{p-1}), \qquad \alpha \in GF(q), \quad \alpha \neq 0$$

However, the Hamming weight of the product of these two polynomials $\omega_H(c(x)'c(x))$ cannot be greater than $\omega_H(c(x))\omega_H(c'(x))$ and we conclude that

$$p \leqslant d^2$$

If $p \equiv 3 \mod 4$, then we have seen that -1 is a quadratic nonresidue, in which case the above bound can be sharpened as follows. For $c'(x)$ we take the codeword $c(x^{-1})$, which is in the desired code and of weight d. In the product $c(x)c(x^{-1})$, d of the terms collapse into unity, of which $d-1$ were not taken into account by the above argument. Hence, the weight of $c(x)c(x^{-1})$ is at most $d^2 - (d-1)$ and we conclude that

$$p \leqslant d^2 - d + 1 \qquad \square$$

Berlekamp (1968) shows that every extended binary QR code is invariant under the doubly transitive projective unimodular group and uses this fact to show that the minimum weight of an augmented binary QR code of length n is an odd number d bounded by

$$d^2 > n \qquad \text{if} \quad n \equiv +1 \mod 8$$
$$d(d-1) \geqslant n - 1 \qquad \text{if} \quad n \equiv -1 \mod 8$$

Two particularly interesting examples of QR codes are the so-called Golay codes. One is a binary (23,12) code of weight seven and the other is an (11, 6) code over $GF(3)$ of weight five. They are both perfect codes and will be considered further in Section 2.8.

There is a close connection between quadratic residue codes and the quasi-cyclic codes, introduced in Section 2.7. Also, certain extended quadratic residue codes are self-dual, a concept also introduced in Section 2.7. The relationships between quadratic residue codes, quasicyclic codes, and self-dual codes are interesting and not yet fully investigated. Assmus and Mattson (1972a, b) investigate some of these relationships in determining minimum weights of quadratic residue codes. Automorphism groups of quadratic residue codes are studied extensively by Assmus and Mattson (1969). In this regard notice that the permutation

$$\eta: \quad X \to X^r \quad r \text{ a quadratic residue}$$

certainly preserves the code C_1. In fact, the extended quadratic residue codes are invariant under certain projective special linear groups and this can be used to give information on the minimum weight of the code [see Assmus and Mattson (1969)].

2.6 Hadamard Matrices, Difference Sets, and Their Codes

Let H be an $m \times m$ matrix with elements of plus one and minus one such that

$$HH^T = mI$$

where I is the $m \times m$ identity matrix. Equivalently, H is a matrix of plus ones and minus ones whose rows are orthogonal. It follows directly from the definition that the determinant $|H|$ of such a matrix is

$$|H| = \pm m^{m/2}$$

For any real, square, $n \times n$ nonsingular matrix $A = (a_{ij})$ Hadamard's inequality states that

$$\det A \leq \left[\prod_{i=1}^{n} \left(\sum_{j=1}^{n} a_{ij}^2\right)\right]^{1/2}$$

Since a matrix H of the form described satisfies the bound with equality, we refer to it as a Hadamard matrix. Complex Hadamard matrices and Hadamard matrices over the set of pth roots of unity have also been considered in the literature, but they will not be considered here. Multiplying a row or a column by minus one does not destroy the Hadamard property, and, similarly, permuting rows and columns does not destroy the property. Multiplying the appropriate rows and columns by minus one, we can always obtain a

2.6 Hadamard Matrices, Difference Sets, and Their Codes

matrix H with the first row and first column all plus ones, and we call this a normalized Hadamard matrix. Except for the trivial Hadamard matrix

$$H_1 = [1]$$

this implies immediately that the order of a Hadamard matrix must be even, since for orthogonality, the second row must contain an even number of plus and minus ones. The normalized Hadamard matrix of order two is

$$H_2 = \begin{bmatrix} 1 & 1 \\ 1 & -1 \end{bmatrix}$$

Now suppose H_m is a normalized Hadamard matrix of order m, $m \geq 3$, and consider the first three rows of this matrix. Rows two through m must have an equal number of plus and minus ones and permute the columns of H_m so that the first $m/2$ elements of the second row are plus one and the remaining $m/2$ elements are minus one. Suppose there are x elements of $+1$ in the first $m/2$ elements of the third row and permute the columns so that the first x elements of the third row are plus one and the elements in the third row in columns $\frac{1}{2}m + 1$ to $\frac{1}{2}m + \frac{1}{2}(m - 2x)$ are plus ones. Now, for the second and third row to be orthogonal, we must have

$$2[x - (\tfrac{1}{2}m - x)] = 0$$

which implies that $m = 4x$. We conclude that the order of any Hadamard matrix of order greater than two is divisible by four. It remains an open question as to whether a Hadamard matrix of order $4t$ exists for all positive integers t, despite the many construction techniques known. We mention that if H_{m_1} and H_{m_2} are Hadamard matrices of orders m_1 and m_2, respectively, then the Kronecker product matrix $H_{m_1} \otimes H_{m_2}$ is easily shown to be a Hadamard matrix of order $m_1 m_2$.

We now consider the relationship between Hadamard matrices and designs. Suppose H is a normalized Hadamard matrix of order $4t$, $t \geq 2$. We form an incidence matrix Γ by replacing the minus ones by zeros and delete the first row and column. As we have seen, in a normalized Hadamard matrix H each row and each column contains the same number of plus and minus ones. This implies that the $(4t - 1) \times (4t - 1)$ matrix Γ is such that each row and each column contains $2t$ zeros and $2t - 1$ ones. It readily follows that

$$\Gamma\Gamma^T = tI_{4t-1} + (t - 1)J_{(4t-1)(4t-1)}$$

since in the normalized matrix H, plus ones in any two distinct rows match up in precisely t places and hence the inner product of any two distinct rows (or columns) of Γ is $t - 1$. Thus Γ is the incidence matrix of a $(4t - 1, 4t - 1, 2t - 1, 2t - 1, t - 1)$ symmetric BIBD. Conversely, a Hadamard matrix of order $4t$ can be obtained from a symmetric design with the above parameters by replacing the zeros of its incidence matrix by minus ones and adding a row and column of all ones. There are other methods of obtaining BIBD's from Hadamard matrices. For example, the complement of the above design is also a symmetric BIBD.

Example Consider again the BIBD formed from the Fano geometry as given in the previous section. The blocks are

$$B_1 = (1, 2, 3), \quad B_2 = (3, 4, 5), \quad B_3 = (1, 5, 6), \quad B_4 = (1, 4, 7)$$
$$B_5 = (3, 6, 7), \quad B_6 = (2, 5, 7), \quad B_7 = (2, 4, 6)$$

and using the integers to label the columns and rows, this design has the incidence matrix

$$\Gamma = \begin{bmatrix} 1 & 1 & 1 & 0 & 0 & 0 & 0 \\ 0 & 0 & 1 & 1 & 1 & 0 & 0 \\ 1 & 0 & 0 & 0 & 1 & 1 & 0 \\ 1 & 0 & 0 & 1 & 0 & 0 & 1 \\ 0 & 0 & 1 & 0 & 0 & 1 & 1 \\ 0 & 1 & 0 & 0 & 1 & 0 & 1 \\ 0 & 1 & 0 & 1 & 0 & 1 & 0 \end{bmatrix}$$

Changing the zeros to minus ones and adding a column and a row of all ones gives the normalized Hadamard matrix of order eight

$$H_8 = \begin{bmatrix} 1 & 1 & 1 & 1 & 1 & 1 & 1 & 1 \\ 1 & 1 & 1 & 1 & -1 & -1 & -1 & -1 \\ 1 & -1 & -1 & 1 & 1 & 1 & -1 & -1 \\ 1 & 1 & -1 & -1 & -1 & 1 & 1 & -1 \\ 1 & 1 & -1 & -1 & 1 & -1 & -1 & 1 \\ 1 & -1 & -1 & 1 & -1 & -1 & 1 & 1 \\ 1 & -1 & 1 & -1 & -1 & 1 & -1 & 1 \\ 1 & -1 & 1 & -1 & 1 & -1 & 1 & -1 \end{bmatrix}$$

Thus the Fano geometry is a projective plane, a Steiner triple system, a BIBD, and also yields an Hadamard matrix.

If one Hadamard matrix can be obtained from another by multiplying a row or a column by minus one or by permuting any set of the rows or the columns, we call them equivalent. It is not true that any two Hadamard matrices of the same order are equivalent.

The matrix

$$H = \begin{bmatrix} -1 & 1 & 1 & 1 \\ 1 & -1 & 1 & 1 \\ 1 & 1 & -1 & 1 \\ 1 & 1 & 1 & -1 \end{bmatrix}$$

2.6 Hadamard Matrices, Difference Sets, and Their Codes

is both Hadamard and a circulant. It is conjectured that a Hadamard matrix of order $n > 4$ cannot be circulant, although it is possible that a normalized Hadamard matrix with its first row and column removed is circulant. A Hadamard matrix is said to be regular if the sum of all the elements in each row or column is constant. It is possible to show that a regular, symmetric Hadamard matrix of order $4s$ exists only if s is an integer square. The existence of a regular Hadamard matrix H, of order $4k'^2$, where $HJ = \pm 2k'J$, is equivalent to the existence of an SBIBD with parameters $v = 4k^2$, $k = 2k'^2 \pm k'$, $\lambda = k^2 + k$ (Wallis et al., 1972; Hall, 1967a).

Since we have observed that the existence of a Hadamard matrix of order $4t$ is equivalent to the existence of a symmetric, balanced, incomplete block design with parameters $v = b = 4t - 1$, $r = k = 2t - 1$, $\lambda = t - 1$, all statements referring to codes and Hadamard matrices refer equally well to codes and SBIBD's with the appropriate parameters. In Section 1.11 we proved the bounds, due to Plotkin (1960),

(i) $A(4t - 2, 2t) \leqslant 2t$
(ii) $A(4t - 1, 2t) \leqslant 4t$ (6.1)
(iii) $A(4t, 2t) \leqslant 8t$

where $A(n, d)$ is the maximum number of binary codewords of length n and minimum distance d, and t is some positive integer. If equality in (iii) holds, then it must also hold in (i) and (ii) and equality will hold in (iii) when $4t - 1$ is a prime.

Suppose we are given a Hadamard matrix H of order $4t$. Assume it to be in normalized form so that its first row and column are plus ones. Each row has $2t$ plus ones and $2t$ minus ones. Form the matrix H' by replacing the minus ones with zeros. Form the $8t \times 4t$ matrix

$$H_1 = \left[\frac{H'}{H_c'} \right]$$

where H_c' is the complement of H' obtained by interchanging zeros and ones. Any two rows of H' are a distance $2t$ apart, as are any two rows of H_c'. A row of H' is also a distance $2t$ from a row of H_c' unless the two are complements, in which case the two are a distance $4t$ apart. In this manner the existence of a Hadamard matrix of order $4t$ implies the existence of a $(4t, 8t, 2t)$ code, i.e., a code of length $4t$, distance $2t$, and with $8t$ codewords. The rows of H' with the first column removed form a $(4t - 1, 4t, 2t)$ code. In this code half the words begin with a one and half with a zero, since in H' each column except the first has $2t$ zeros and $2t$ ones. Choosing the $2t$ words that begin with a one and deleting these ones yields a $(4t - 2, 2t, 2t)$ code. Thus the existence of a Hadamard matrix of order $4t$ implies the existence of codes that satisfy the bounds of (6.1) with equality.

Conversely, suppose $\mathscr{C}$ is a binary $(4t, 8t, 2t)$ code and let M be the $8t \times 4t$ matrix which has the codewords as rows. Again half of the rows have a first coordinate of zero and half have one. Permute the rows until the first $4t$ rows begin with a one. If in the first row a column has a zero, interchange zeros and ones in that column, so that the first row will be all ones. Let H be the $4t \times 4t$ matrix obtained from the first $4t$ rows of the modified matrix M by replacing zeros by minus ones. From the properties of the code it follows immediately that H is a Hadamard matrix. Using similar reasoning, we can conclude that the existence of either a $(4t, 8t, 2t)$ code or a $(4t - 1, 4t, 2t)$ code is entirely equivalent to a Hadamard matrix of order $4t$ and hence to a certain SBIBD.

The role of Hadamard matrices in coding is far deeper then these elementary results would indicate [see, for example, the work of Semakov and Zinov'ev (1969a, b)]. Since, at the moment, many of the applications of Hadamard matrices involve particular rather than general constructions, we will not report on other work here.

As mentioned previously, a Steiner system is a λ-(t, d, n) design with $\lambda = 1$. Many of the interesting connections between codes and t designs will be discussed in the next chapter, where Steiner systems will arise as particular cases. However, there is one interesting observation to be made with regard to Steiner systems.

Definition An (n, w, λ) binary balanced code is a set of binary n-tuples, each of weight w, such that any two words agree in at most λ positions.

Let the maximum number of words in a balanced code be N. It follows directly from the bound on the quantity $R(n, d, e)$ given in Theorem 11.4 of Chapter 1 that

$$N \leqslant \left\lfloor \frac{n}{w} \left\lfloor \frac{n-1}{w-1} \left\lfloor \cdots \left\lfloor \frac{n-\lambda}{w-\lambda} \right\rfloor \cdots \right\rfloor \right\rfloor \right\rfloor \leqslant \binom{n}{\lambda+1} \bigg/ \binom{w}{\lambda+1}$$

where the right-hand bound follows trivially from the left-hand bound.

A balanced (n, w, λ) code with $\binom{n}{\lambda+1}/\binom{w}{\lambda+1}$ codewords is called a complete balanced code. There are $\binom{n}{\lambda+1}$ binary n-tuples of weight $\lambda + 1$ possible. An n-tuple of weight w "contains" $\binom{w}{\lambda+1}$ such n-tuples. Since in a balanced (n, w, λ) code no two words can agree in more than λ positions, the equivalence between an (n, w, λ) complete balanced code and a 1-$((\lambda + 1), w, n))$ Steiner system is established, since such a Steiner system also contains the requisite number of $\binom{n}{\lambda+1}/\binom{w}{\lambda+1}$ blocks.

We consider now another interesting combinatorial structure, the difference set, which will also have significant applications in coding.

2.6 Hadamard Matrices, Difference Sets, and Their Codes

Definition If the set of k integers mod v, $D = \{a_1, a_2, \ldots, a_k\}$, is such that for any nonzero integer a mod v there exist precisely λ pairs (a_i, a_j) where

$$a_i - a_j = a \text{ mod } v$$

then we call D a (v, k, λ) or perfect difference set. If $\lambda = 1$, D is called a planar difference set. In such a difference set $\lambda = k(k-1)/(v-1)$.

Once again, an important problem is the enumeration of all difference sets and this problem is unsolved, although several plausible conjectures exist. As with other structures, we consider the connection between difference sets and configurations and give two important methods for constructing difference sets.

A circulant matrix is an $n \times n$ matrix whose $(i + 1)$th row is a cyclic shift of the ith row, i.e., one of the form

$$\begin{bmatrix} \alpha_1 & \alpha_2 & \alpha_3 & \cdots & \alpha_n \\ \alpha_n & \alpha_1 & \alpha_2 & \cdots & \alpha_{n-1} \\ \vdots & \vdots & \vdots & & \vdots \\ \alpha_2 & \alpha_3 & \alpha_4 & \cdots & \alpha_1 \end{bmatrix}$$

We now show that there is a one-to-one correspondence between the difference sets defined above and those (v, k, λ) configurations whose incidence matrices are circulants.

Let D be a (v, k, λ) configuration defined on the integers mod v. Clearly, adding any integer mod v to each element of D also yields a (v, k, λ) difference set and hence from D we can form $v - 1$ other difference sets

$$D_i = \{a_1 + i, a_2 + i, \ldots, a_k + i\}, \quad i = 1, \ldots, v - 1$$

Each integer mod v appears in precisely k of the sets $D, D_1, \ldots, D_{v-1}$. To show that every pair of integers (a, b) mod v appears in λ of these sets, let $a - b \equiv c$ mod v, where $c \not\equiv 0$ mod v. Then for precisely λ pairs (a_i, a_j), $a_i, a_j \in D$, we have

$$a - b \equiv a_i - a_j \text{ mod } v$$

Thus, if we let $d \equiv a - a_i \equiv b - a_j$ mod v, then $a \equiv a_i + d$ and $b = a_j + d$ and hence both a and b belong to D_d. Since we can do this for each pair (a_i, a_j), the pair (a, b) belong to λ of the sets $D, D_1, D_2, \ldots, D_{v-1}$. Consequently these sets form a (v, k, λ) configuration, and its incidence matrix is a circulant.

Conversely, suppose we are given a (v, k, λ) configuration whose incidence matrix is a circulant. Suppose the elements are the integers $0, 1, \ldots, v - 1$ and denote the blocks by $B_0, B_1, B_2, \ldots, B_{v-1}$. If block B_0 contains the elements $\{a_1, a_2, \ldots, a_k\}$ then, from the circulant property of the incidence matrix, block B_i contains the elements $a_1 + i, a_2 + i, \ldots, a_k + i$, mod v. There are λ blocks that contain the pair of elements $(0, d)$ $d \not\equiv 0$ mod v, which means there are precisely λ triples (j, a_k, a_l) such that $a_k + j \equiv d$ mod v and $a_l + j \equiv 0$ mod v, i.e., there are λ pairs (a_k, a_l) such that

$$a_k - a_l \equiv d \bmod v$$

which, of course, implies that B_0 is a (v, k, λ) difference set. We have shown that a (v, k, λ) difference set is equivalent to a (v, k, λ) configuration that has a circulant incidence matrix.

There is also an interesting relationship between quadratic residues and difference sets, and hence between quadratic residues and (v, k, λ) configurations with circulant incidence matrices. Recall that in the discussion of quadratic residues we showed that $(a/p) = a^{(p-1)/2}$ and hence if p is an odd prime of the form $p = 4n + 3$, then $-1 \equiv p - 1$ is a quadratic nonresidue of p. Also, if r is a quadratic residue of p, p of the form $4n + 3$, then $-r \equiv p - r$ is a quadratic nonresidue and if r runs through the quadratic residues of p, then $-r$ runs through the quadratic nonresidues. We wish to show that when p is a prime of this form then its quadratic residues $R = \{r_1, r_2, \ldots, r_{(p-1)/2}\}$ form a difference set with parameters $v = p = 4n + 3$, $k = 2n + 1$, and $\lambda = n$. This is often called a Hadamard difference set, or equivalently, a Hadamard design, since it is an SBIBD with the right parameters that yields a $4(n + 1) \times 4(n + 1)$ Hadamard matrix.

Let r_i and r_j be two distinct quadratic residues of p, and suppose $r_i - r_j \equiv r$ mod p, where r is a quadratic residue. Then $r^{-1}r_i - r^{-1}r_j = r_i' - r_j' \equiv 1$ mod p, where $r_i' = r^{-1}r_i$ and $r_j' = r^{-1}r_j$, and r_i' and r_j' are also quadratic residues, i.e., elements of R. Also, if r_i and r_j are two elements of R such that $r_i - r_j \equiv 1$ mod p, then $rr_i - rr_j = r$ mod p for any quadratic residue of p and both rr_i and rr_j are in R. Thus the number of ordered pairs of elements of R, (r_i, r_j), whose difference equals a given quadratic residue is the same as for any other quadratic residue. If $r_i - r_j \equiv r$ mod p, r a quadratic residue, then $r_j - r_i \equiv -r$ mod p, where $-r$ is a quadratic nonresidue, and precisely the same argument holds. Thus, for any integer m mod p, the number of pairs of R whose difference equals m is the same for any m, and this, of course, is the definition of a difference set. To determine the parameters of the set, v is clearly equal to p and k to $(p - 1)/2$. Since there are $\frac{1}{2}(p - 1)\frac{1}{2}(p - 3)$ pairs of elements from R, we must have

$$\lambda = \frac{\frac{1}{2}(p-1)\frac{1}{2}(p-3)}{p-1} = \frac{p-3}{4} = n$$

It was shown that the incidence matrix of the Hadamard design associated with this difference set can be made circulant. Adding the row and column of ones to form the Hadamard matrix, however, destroys the circulant property.

2.6 Hadamard Matrices, Difference Sets, and Their Codes

Example The quadratic residues mod 19 are

$$\{1, 4, 5, 6, 7, 9, 11, 16, 17\}$$

and it is readily verified that these form a (v, k, λ) difference set with $v = 19$, $k = 9$, and $\lambda = 4$.

It was seen in an earlier section that the hyperplanes in $PG(n, q)$ can be used to form a symmetric block design. We show now that this design has an incidence matrix that is a circulant and hence the design determines a (v, k, λ) difference set, where

$$v = \frac{q^{n+1} - 1}{q - 1}, \qquad k = \frac{q^n - 1}{q - 1}, \qquad \lambda = \frac{q^{n-1} - 1}{q - 1}$$

if the hyperplanes in $PG(n, q)$ are used. Recall the representation of $PG(n, q)$ given earlier, where, if ξ is a primitive root of $GF(q^{n+1})$, then the first $v = (q^{n+1} - 1)/(q - 1)$ powers of ξ can be taken as the points of $PG(n, q)$. The elements ξ^i and ξ^j represent the same point iff $i \equiv j$ mod v and the elements of the form ξ^{iv}, $i = 1, \ldots, q - 1$, with the zero element, form $GF(q)$. Consider the mapping on $GF(q^{n+1})$ defined by

$$\tau: \quad 0 \longmapsto 0$$
$$\xi^i \longmapsto \xi^{i+1}$$

This is a pointwise map of $GF(q^{n+1})$ which takes m flats into m flats since it preserves the independence of points. Now suppose τ^j maps a hyperplane onto itself. Then it must permute the points of a hyperplane in cycles of length, say, t, where $t|k$, k the number of points in a hyperplane. Since $\tau^v = 1$, the identity map, $t|v$ and since v and k are relatively prime, $t = 1$. Thus the map τ maps the hyperplanes in a chain of length v, i.e., if $V = PG(n-1, q)$ is a particular hyperplane, then the other hyperplanes are $\tau(V)$, $\tau^2(V), \ldots, \tau^{v-1}(V)$. This, of course, is precisely the condition needed to verify that the incidence matrix of the design is a circulant. There are many other constructions known for difference sets. Since they tend to use concepts that are not important for our purpose, we will not discuss them here.

Example Consider the Fano geometry (Fig. 7). The lines of the geometry are

$$\{0, 1, 3\}, \quad \{1, 2, 4\}, \quad \{2, 3, 5\}, \quad \{3, 4, 6\}, \quad \{4, 5, 0\}, \quad \{6, 5, 1\}, \quad \{6, 0, 2\}$$

and in this representation the associated design is cyclic. The set or line $\{0, 1, 3\}$ is a planar difference set.

An important and useful notion in the investigation of a difference set is that of a multiplier. If $D = \{d_1, d_2, \ldots, d_k\}$ is a difference set, then every translation, mod v, is also a difference set, where the translation is $D' = \{d_1 + r, d_2 + r, \ldots, d_k + r\}$ for some integer r. If there exists an integer S with $(S, v) = 1$ such that the sets of elements, mod v, $D' = \{d_1 + r, d_2 + r, \ldots, d_k + r\}$ and $D'' = \{d_1 S, d_2 S, \ldots, d_s S\}$ are identical, then we call S a multiplier of the difference set D. It can be shown that if D is a (v, k, λ) difference set and p a prime such that $p | (k - \lambda)$, $p \nmid v$, and $p > \lambda$, then p is a multiplier of D.

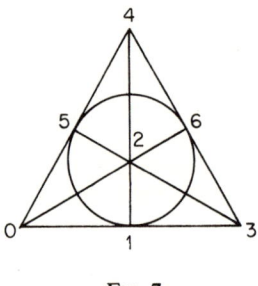

Fig. 7

A planar difference $(v, k, \lambda = 1)$ set can be shown to be equivalent to a projective plane of order $n = k - 1$. Singer (1938) constructed such difference sets using projective planes of order $n = p^s$, p a prime and s a positive integer. These sets are cyclic in the sense discussed previously and it is conjectured that every finite cyclic projective plane is Desarguesian and hence must have order $n = p^s$ for some prime p and integer s.

Weldon (1966) defined a difference-set cyclic code to be the null space of the incidence matrix of the associated design. However, the only cyclic difference sets used are those generated from the hyperplanes of a projective geometry, hence the only difference-set codes that have been considered are the projective geometry codes of the appropriate order. The dimensions of these codes were given by Graham and MacWilliams (1966), Smith (1969), and MacWilliams and Mann (1968). Since these codes are subsumed by the projective geometry codes, we consider them no further.

2.7 Self-Dual and Quasicyclic Codes

Let $\mathscr{C}$ be a linear code with block length n over $GF(q)$. As defined previously, the dual of $\mathscr{C}$ is

$$\mathscr{C}^\perp = \{u \in V_n(q); \ (u, v) = 0, \ \forall v \in \mathscr{C}\}$$

2.7 Self-Dual and Quasicyclic Codes

We say that $\mathscr{C}$ is self-dual if $\mathscr{C} = \mathscr{C}^\perp$. Notice that $\mathscr{C}^\perp$ is a subspace even if $\mathscr{C}$ is not a linear code; thus a self-dual code is automatically linear. If $\mathscr{C}$ is self-dual, then its block length n must be even since its dimension is $n/2$. Furthermore, the weight of each codeword is even if $q = 2$ since an odd-weight codeword cannot be orthogonal to itself. Thus over $GF(2)$ the all-ones vector is always in a self-dual code.

MacWilliams *et al.* (1972b) define $\mathscr{C}$ to be a weakly self-dual code over $GF(2)$ if it is linear, $\mathscr{C} \subset \mathscr{C}^\perp$, and the all-one vector is in $\mathscr{C}$. Clearly every self-dual code is weakly self-dual.

There are many known self-dual codes. For example, the extended binary (24, 12) Golay code is self-dual, as is the extended (12, 6) ternary Golay code. Both these codes are related to quadratic residue codes and the latter code is a symmetry code. In this section we consider classes of codes that are self-dual. We begin with the symmetry codes of Pless (1969, 1970, 1972a).

The symmetry codes will be a class of self-dual codes over $GF(3)$ with parameters $(2q + 2, q + 1)$ where $q \equiv -1 \mod 3$ and q is the power of an odd prime. We first construct a $(q + 1) \times (q + 1)$ matrix S_q over $GF(3)$ and will write its entries as either 0 or ± 1. Let a be an arbitrary (but fixed) mapping of the integers $0, 1, 2, \ldots, q - 1$ onto $GF(q)$ with the condition that $a(0) = 0$ and $a(1) = 1$. Let a^{-1} be the inverse mapping. To $GF(q)$ we adjoin an exceptional element ∞ and let $a(\infty) = \infty$. Label the rows and columns of $S_q = (s_{ij})$ with the elements $\infty, 0, 1, 2, \ldots, q - 1$ consecutively.

Define the function χ on $GF(q)$ such that $\chi(\eta) = 1$ if η is a square, -1 if η is a nonsquare, and 0 if $\eta = 0$. The matrix entries are then defined by

$$s_{\infty, \infty} = 0, \qquad s_{i, \infty} = \chi(-1), \qquad s_{\infty, i} = 1$$
$$s_{i, j} = \chi(a(j) - a(i)), \qquad i, j = 0, 1, \ldots, q - 1$$

Definition The code with generator matrix $[I, S_q]$, I the identity matrix of order $q + 1$, is a symmetry code which we denote by $C(q)$.

Notice that if q is a prime, then we can take the map a to be the identity map. For example, if $q = 5$, then the matrix S_q is, with a the identity map,

	∞	0	1	2	3	4
∞	0	1	1	1	1	1
0	1	0	1	−1	−1	1
1	1	1	0	1	−1	−1
2	1	−1	1	0	1	−1
3	1	−1	−1	1	0	1
4	1	1	−1	−1	1	0

The following theorem gives the basic properties of the matrix S_q.

Theorem 7.1 If q is an odd power of a prime and S_q is as described above, then

(a) $S_q S_q^T = qI_{q+1}$ over $\mathbb{R}$ and hence $S_q S_q^T = -I_{q+1}$ over $GF(3)$. It follows that S_q is nonsingular and $S_q^{-1} = -S_q^T$ over $GF(3)$.
(b) If $q \equiv 1 \mod 4$, then $S_q = S_q^T$.
(c) If $q \equiv 3 \mod 4$, then $S_q = -S_q^T$.

Proof Notice that -1 is a square if $q \equiv 1 \mod 4$ and is a nonsquare if $q \equiv 3 \mod 4$. Also, if α and β are any two field elements, then $\chi(\alpha\beta) = \chi(\alpha)\chi(\beta)$. For q the power of an odd prime, there are precisely $(q-1)/2$ squares and nonsquares alike, implying that

$$\sum_{\alpha \in GF(q)} \chi(\alpha) = 0$$

Consider now the sum

$$\sum_{\alpha \in GF(q)} \chi(\alpha)\chi(\alpha + \beta)$$

for a fixed element $\beta \in GF(q)$. For any $\alpha \neq 0$ we can find an element $\gamma \in GF(q)$ such that $\alpha + \beta = \alpha\gamma$ and as α ranges through the nonzero elements of $GF(q)$ γ ranges through the nonunity elements, $\beta \neq 0$. Thus we can write

$$\sum_{\alpha \in GF(q)} \chi(\alpha)\chi(\alpha + \beta) = \sum_{\alpha \in GF(q)} \chi^2(\alpha)\chi(\gamma) = \sum_{\substack{\gamma \in GF(q) \\ \gamma \neq 1}} \chi(\gamma)$$

$$= \sum_{\gamma \in GF(q)} \chi(\gamma) - 1 = -1$$

since $\chi^2(\gamma) = 1$ for any nonzero γ. Applying these facts to the matrix S_q, we observe that the (i, j) element of $S_q S_q^T$ is the inner product of the ith and jth rows of S_q. Since each row of the $(q + 1) \times (q + 1)$ matrix has precisely one zero in it, the inner product of a row with itself is q (over $\mathbb{R}$), and since by assumption $q \equiv -1 \mod 3$, this is -1. The inner product of the first row with any other row is simply $\sum_{\alpha \in GF(q)} \chi(\alpha) = 0$. The inner product of the ith and jth rows is

$$\chi(-1)^2 + \sum_{k=0}^{q-1} \chi(a(k) - a(i))\chi(a(k) - a(j))$$

$$= 1 + \sum_{k=0}^{q-1} \chi(a(k) - a(i))\chi(a(k) - a(i) + (a(i) - a(j)))$$

$$= 1 - 1 = 0$$

2.7 Self-Dual and Quasicyclic Codes

by the previous result. Hence $S_q S_q^T = -I_{q+1}$, over $GF(3)$, and $S_q^{-1} = -S_q^T$. From the definition $\chi(-1)S_q = S_q^T$, implying that if $q \equiv 1 \mod 4$ (-1 is a square), then $S_q = S_q^T$, while if $q \equiv 3 \mod 4$ (-1 not a square), then $S_q = -S_q^T$. □

Theorem 7.2 Every symmetry code $C(q)$ is self-dual and the weight of every codeword in it is divisible by three.

Proof Consider the generator matrix $G = [I, S_q]$ of $C(q)$. Notice that since the elements of this matrix are either 0 or ± 1, the scalar product of a row with itself is simply the weight of that row. Thus, since every row of S_q has exactly one zero element, the weight of any row of G is $q + 1$, which is 0 mod 3 since, by assumption, $q \equiv -1 \mod 3$. Similarly, since $S_q S_q^T = -I$, the rows of S_q are orthogonal to each other and it follows that the rows of G are orthogonal to each other. Thus $C(q)$ is self-dual and, since every codeword is orthogonal to itself, its weight must be divisible by three. □

Corollary If $q \equiv 1 \mod 4$, then $G' = [-S_q, I_q]$ is also a basis of $C(q)$. If $q \equiv 3 \mod 4$, then $G'' = [S_q, I_q]$ is also a basis of $C(q)$.

Proof In general, the matrix $[-S_q^T, I]$ is a basis of $C(q)^\perp$ and hence of $C(q)$. The result follows from Theorem 7.1. □

The general weight enumerator of these codes is not as yet known. It is not difficult to show that the weight of any two rows of the generator matrix is $(q + 7)/2$ while the weight of any three rows is bounded below by this quantity. In fact for the first five possible values of q the code $C(q)$ has minimum distance exactly $(q + 7)/2$. For $C(47)$, however, the minimum weight is not of this form, being strictly less than the predicted value. The weight enumerators of these five codes are known and, by applying the theorem of Assmus and Mattson (Theorem 6.1 in Chapter 3), various new 5-designs have been determined (Table VII). Note that $d(C(q))$ denotes the minimum distance of $C(q)$ and A_i the number of codewords of weight i. If the codewords of weight r yield a t-design, then the number of blocks in the design is $A_r/2$ since the codes are over $GF(3)$. From this we can calculate

$$\lambda = \frac{A_r}{2} \frac{\binom{r}{t}}{\binom{n}{t}}$$

A great deal of information on the groups that leave these codes invariant is given by Pless (1972a).

TABLE VII

q	$d(C(q))$	λ	Design parameters
5	6	1	(5, 6, 12)
11	9	6	(5, 9, 24)
		576	(5, 12, 24)
		8,580	(5, 15, 24)
17	12	45	(5, 12, 36)
		5,577	(5, 15, 36)
		209,685	(5, 18, 36)
		2,438,973	(5, 21, 36)
23	15	364	(5, 15, 48)
		50,456	(5, 18, 48)
		2,957,388	(5, 21, 48)
		71,307,600	(5, 24, 48)
		749,999,640	(5, 27, 48)
29	18	3,060	(5, 18, 60)
		449,820	(5, 21, 60)
		34,337,160	(5, 24, 60)
		1,271,766,600	(5, 27, 60)
		24,140,500,956	(5, 30, 60)
		239,329,029,060	(5, 33, 60)

Clearly any code that has a generator matrix of the form

$$[I, S]$$

will be self-dual over $GF(q)$ iff $SS^T = I$, where the matrices I and S have the same dimension. If S is a circulant matrix (each row a cyclic shift of the previous row), then this is an example of a code equivalent to a quasicyclic code to be considered next [see Chen et al. (1969) and Townsend and Weldon (1967) but note that the term self-orthogonal in the title of this last paper does not mean self-dual]. Some interesting results on circulants and their application in binary coding are given by Karlin (1969). MacWilliams (1971) considers the problem of constructing orthogonal circulant matrices over a finite field.

A quasi-cyclic code is one in which every codeword shifted by n_0 digits is also a codeword. By permuting the column positions an (mn_0, mk_0) quasicyclic code of rate k_0/n_0 can be assumed to have a generator matrix of the form

$$G = \begin{bmatrix} C_{11} & C_{12} & \cdots & C_{1n_0} \\ \vdots & \vdots & & \vdots \\ C_{k_01} & C_{k_02} & \cdots & C_{k_0n_0} \end{bmatrix}$$

2.7 Self-Dual and Quasicyclic Codes

where C_{ij} is an $m \times m$ circulant matrix. In particular, for a rate $\frac{1}{2}$ quasi-cyclic code the generator matrix has the form

$$G = [C_{11}, C_{12}]$$

and if either C_{11} or C_{12} is nonsingular, this is equivalent to

$$G' = [I, C]$$

where C is again a circulant matrix. The case where C_{11} and C_{12} are both singular matrices is largely uninteresting since it leads to nonuniquely decodable codes (Tavares et al., 1974). Thus a rate $\frac{1}{2}$ quasi-cyclic code will be assumed in this systematic form.

Chen et al. (1969) are able to show that these codes have many interesting properties. The quadratic residue codes, considered in Section 5, with one digit removed are equivalent to rate $\frac{1}{2}$ quasi-cyclic codes. Karlin (1969) also investigates the quasi-cyclic structure of such codes. Chen et al. (1969) also show that there exist very long, but not arbitrarily long, quasi-cyclic codes that meet the Gilbert bound. Perhaps the class of quasi-cyclic codes deserves more attention.

Consider, for a moment, the set of all $n \times n$ circulant matrices over $GF(q)$. With the circulant matrix

$$A = \begin{bmatrix} a_0 & a_1 & \cdots & a_{n-1} \\ a_{n-1} & a_0 & \cdots & a_{n-2} \\ \vdots & \vdots & & \vdots \\ a_1 & a_2 & \cdots & a_0 \end{bmatrix}$$

we identify the polynomial

$$a(x) = \sum_{i=1}^{n} a_i x^i$$

Denote by P_n the polynomial algebra $GF(q)[x]/(x^n - 1)$. If C_n is the algebra of $n \times n$ circulant matrices over $GF(q)$, it is readily verified that the mapping

$$\eta: P_n \longrightarrow C_n$$
$$a(x) \longmapsto A$$

is an isomorphism. The transpose of the circulant matrix corresponding to $a(x) = \sum a_i x^i$ will correspond to the polynomial

$$a(x)^T = \sum_{i=1}^{n} a_{n-i} x^k$$

which we call the transpose polynomial. Of course $a(x)^T = a(x^{n-1})$ mod $(x^n - 1)$. If $a(x) = a(x)^T$, we say it is a symmetric polynomial since it implies $A = A^T$. Suppose B is the circulant matrix that is the inverse of A and the corresponding polynomials are $b(x)$ and $a(x)$, respectively. It is not difficult to show that if $AB = I$, then $a(x)b(x) \equiv 1 \mod x^n - 1$. We call $b(x)$ the inverse polynomial of $a(x)$ and write it as $a^{-1}(x)$. If $AA^T = I$, then A is an orthogonal matrix and the corresponding polynomial $a(x)^T$ is such that $a(x)a(x)^T \equiv 1 \mod x^n - 1$ and is said to be an orthogonal polynomial. An orthogonal polynomial is necessarily invertible. MacWilliams (1971) determines the orders and some of the structure of the groups G_n (invertible circulants), S_n (symmetric invertible), and O_n (orthogonal circulants). Berlekamp (1965) determines the number of $n \times n$ circulant matrices of a given rank.

We have previously observed that a code over $GF(2)$ with a generator matrix of the form

$$G = [I, A]$$

is self-dual if A is orthogonal and this is one reason for looking at techniques to construct orthogonal and orthogonal circulant matrices.

There are a number of operations on the polynomial of a circulant matrix which yield equivalent codes. Specifically, consider the binary quasi-cyclic codes with generator matrices

$$[I, C_1] \quad \text{and} \quad [I, C_2]$$

where C_1 and C_2 are circulant matrices with polynomials $C_1(x)$ and $C_2(x)$, respectively. Then Tavares et al. (1974) are able to show that the binary codes will be equivalent if any of the five following conditions hold: (i) $C_2(x) = x^i C_1(x) \mod x^m - 1$, $0 < i < m$; (ii) $C_2(x) = C_1^{-1}(x)$; (iii) $C_2(x) = C_1^*(x)$; (iv) $C_2(x) = C_1(x)^T$; (v) $C_2(x) = C_1(x)^{2^r}$, r an integer and m odd. The polynomial $C_1^*(x)$ is the reciprocal polynomial of $C_1(x)$ discussed in the previous chapter.

Some very significant advances in the weight enumeration of self-dual codes have recently been made. For the remainder of the section we review a few of these results.

Let $\mathscr{C}$ be a linear code of length n over $GF(q)$ and $\mathscr{C}^\perp$ its dual. If A_i is the number of codewords of weight i in $\mathscr{C}$, then we call the bivariate polynomial

$$W(x, y) = \sum_{i=0}^{n} A_i x^{n-i} y^i$$

the weight enumerator of $\mathscr{C}$. If the weight enumerator of the dual is given by

$$W(x, y) = \sum_{i=0}^{n} A_i^\perp x^{n-i} y^i$$

then the MacWilliams identities yield

$$\sum_{i=0}^{n} A_i x^{n-i} y^i = \frac{1}{|\mathscr{C}^\perp|} \sum_{i=0}^{n} A_i^\perp [x + (q-1)y]^{n-i} (x - y)^i$$

2.7 Self-Dual and Quasicyclic Codes

If the code is self-dual, then the right-hand side of this equation reduces to

$$\sum_{i=0}^{n} A_i \left[\frac{x + (q-1)y}{\sqrt{q}}\right]^{n-i} \left(\frac{x-y}{\sqrt{q}}\right)^i$$

since, in this case, $|\mathscr{C}^\perp| = q^{n/2}$. We conclude that for a self-dual code

$$W(x, y) = W\left(\frac{x + (q-1)y}{\sqrt{q}}, \frac{x-y}{\sqrt{q}}\right)$$

and call any homogeneous polynomial with complex coefficients that has this property formally self-dual. Clearly the weight enumerator of a self-dual code is formally self-dual but the converse to this statement is not true. For example, the polynomial $x^2y^2(x^2 - y^2)^2$ is formally self-dual but is not the weight enumerator of any code since it has a negative coefficient.

Theorem 7.3 (*Gleason*, 1971) Let

$$W(x, y) = \sum_{i=0}^{n} A_i x^{n-i} y^i$$

be a formally self-dual weight enumerator of length n over $GF(q)$ in which every weight is divisible by c.

(i) If $q = 2$ and $c = 2$, then $W(x, y) = W(y, x)$, n is even, and $A_{n-i} = A_i$. In this case define

$$f(x, y) = x^2 + y^2, \qquad g(x, y) = x^2 y^2 (x^2 - y^2)^2$$

and let $n = 2r + 8s$.

(ii) If $q = 2$ and $c = 4$, then n is divisible by eight. In this case define

$$f(x, y) = x^8 + 14x^4 y^4 + y^8, \qquad g(x, y) = x^4 y^4 (x^4 - y^4)^4$$

and let $n = 8r + 24s$.

(iii) If $q = 3$ and $c = 3$, then n is divisible by four and define

$$f(x, y) = x^4 + 8xy^3, \qquad g(x, y) = y^3 (x^3 - y^3)^3$$

and let $n = 4r + 12s$.

In each of these three cases the weight enumerator is given by

$$W(x, y) = \sum_{r, s} k_{rs} f(x, y)^r g(x, y)^s$$

where r and s are nonnegative integers satisfying the conditions given and k_{rs} are complex numbers.

Proofs of these statements are given by Berlekamp *et al.* (1972).

Example Consider the extended Golay codes, which, as we have already observed, are self-dual. The weight enumerator of the (24, 12) Golay code over $GF(2)$ is given by

$$W(x, y) = x^{24} + 759x^{16}y^8 + 2576x^{12}y^{12} + 759x^8y^{16} + y^{24}$$

Since $q = 2$ and $c = 4$, part (ii) of the theorem applies and we can express $W(x, y)$ as

$$W(x, y) = \alpha f(x, y)^3 + \beta g(x, y)$$

from which it is readily determined that $\alpha = 1$ and $\beta = -672$.

The (12,6) Golay code over $GF(3)$ has a weight enumerator

$$W(x, y) = x^{12} + 264x^6y^6 + 440x^3y^9 + 24y^{12}$$

and since part (iii) of the theorem applies, we can write this as

$$W(x, y) = \alpha f(x, y)^3 + \beta g(x, y)$$

A calculation reveals that $\alpha = 1$ and $\beta = -24$.

Using classical invariant theory, MacWilliams *et al.* (1972a) generalized the above theorem of Gleason to different weight enumerators. Mallows and Sloane (1973) show that if the minimum distance d of a self-dual code is maximized, then, for case (i) of Gleason's theorem $d \leq 2\lfloor n/8 \rfloor + 2$, for case (ii) $d \leq 4\lfloor n/24 \rfloor + 4$, and for case (iii) $d \leq 3\lfloor n/12 \rfloor + 3$. An explicit formula for the weight enumerator of such extremal codes is given and the existence of such codes is considered.

MacWilliams *et al.* (1972b) show that there exist binary self-dual codes with a distance that is asymptotically the same as that given by the Varshamov–Gilbert bound. Pless and Pierce (1973) extend the result to show that there exist self-dual codes over $GF(q)$, q an arbitrary power of a prime, that satisfy a modified Varshamov–Gilbert bound, which is asymptotically the same as the usual bound. Pless (1972b) catalogs a great deal of information on self-dual codes over $GF(2)$, including a complete listing of all $(n, n/2)$ self-dual codes, n even, $2 \leq n \leq 20$, and $(n, (n-1)/2)$, n odd, $3 \leq n \leq 19$. The number of codes in the equivalence class of each code, the complete group leaving the code invariant, and the weight enumeration of each code are given. Assmus and Mattson (1972a, b) also attempt to develop tools to investigate the weight structure and in particular the minimum weight of self-dual codes.

There seem to be at least four reasons for the recent interest shown in the class of self-dual codes. As mentioned previously, there exist codes in the class that asymptotically meet the Gilbert bound. The amount of information on the form of the weight enumerators has also been an encouraging development and will foster further work along these lines. It turns out that there are

2.8 Perfect Codes

some very important connections between some of the new simple groups found and automorphism groups of self-dual codes. Thus (Pless, 1972b) the Conway group (Conway, 1968b, 1969; Higman and Sims, 1968) is closely related to the (24, 12) extended Golay code. This group is, in turn, related to a remarkable lattice in 24-dimensional Euclidean space discovered by Leech (1967). Finally, MacWilliams *et al.* (1973) approach the problem of the existence of a projective plane of order ten by considering the information known about the weight distribution of the (111, 56) binary code that the incidence matrix of such a plane would yield. Clearly the study of self-dual codes is reaching into some deep and interesting areas of mathematics.

2.8 Perfect Codes

We have seen examples of a perfect linear code over a finite field. Specifically, we have:

(i) Hamming codes: single-error-correcting codes over $GF(q)$ with length $n = (q^m - 1)/(q - 1)$ and $k = [(q^m - 1)/(q - 1)] - m$. When $(n, q - 1) = 1$ a cyclic version of such a code will exist.

(ii) Binary repetition codes of odd length: codes with two codewords, the all-ones and all-zeros codewords.

(iii) The Golay codes: the (11, 6) code over $GF(3)$ of distance five and the (23, 12) code over $GF(2)$ of distance seven. As mentioned in Section 2.6, both of these are quadratic residue codes.

Golay (1949) described all these codes, except that he treated the Hamming codes only over prime alphabets, in a half-page article. It has taken a quarter of a century to prove that, with one exception, there are no others. In this section we will give the construction of the only other class of perfect codes known and state some of the results found along the way to the nonexistence result.

Suppose that C is a code consisting of M codewords of n-tuples over an arbitrary alphabet of q-symbols. If C is a perfect e-error-correcting code, then the usual sphere packing condition must hold, i.e.,

$$M\left[\sum_{i=0}^{e} \binom{n}{i}(q-1)^i\right] = q^n$$

If $e = 1$, the condition reduces to

$$[1 + n(q-1)] | q^n$$

If, in addition, q is a power of a prime, say p^r, then the length of the code n must be of the form $n = (q^m - 1)/(q - 1)$. For suppose

$$[1 + n(q-1)] = p^\alpha q^a, \qquad 0 \leq \alpha < r$$

then we must have that

$$n = \frac{p^\alpha q^a - 1}{q-1} = p^\alpha \frac{q^a - 1}{q-1} + \frac{p^\alpha - 1}{q-1}$$

and since the first term is an integer, the last must be also, implying $\alpha = 0$. Thus a perfect single-error-correcting code over an alphabet of q letters must have a length expressible in the form $(q^m - 1)/(q - 1)$ for some integer m. It follows immediately that the number of codewords in the code must be q^{n-m}.

There are examples of codes over alphabets of q symbols, q a power of a prime, where the alphabet is not a finite field (Lindström, 1969). There are also semilinear codes (Schönheim, 1969) and nonlinear codes (Vasil'ev, 1962; Schönheim, 1968) over finite fields, which are perfect. We will give the construction of these last codes by Schönheim shortly. It is not known whether perfect codes over nonprime power alphabets exist.

The approach of Golay in finding his nontrivial codes was simple. For the binary case he merely summed elements in the rows of the Pascal triangle and observed the parameters when he obtained a power of two. He found two cases in his search,

$$\sum_{i=0}^{3} \binom{23}{i} = 2^{11} \quad \text{and} \quad \sum_{i=0}^{2} \binom{90}{i} = 2^{12}$$

The first case corresponds to the (23, 12) Golay code.

As shown in the next chapter, it is a simple consequence of the t-design properties of perfect binary codes that no (90, 78) perfect code over $GF(2)$ with $d = 5$ can exist. The (11, 6) Golay code over $GF(3)$ was found in a similar manner.

We will consider the Golay codes further shortly. We now give Schönheim's generalization of Vasilev's construction of perfect, single-error-correcting, binary, nonlinear codes. We order the nonzero elements of $GF(q)$ in some arbitrary but fixed way as $\alpha_1, \alpha_2, \ldots, \alpha_{q-1}$ and let $v_i = (x_{i1}, x_{i2}, \ldots, x_{in})$, $i = 1, 2, \ldots, q - 1$, be an arbitrary set of vectors of $V_n(q)$. Define a parity check function on these $q - 1$ vectors as

$$p(v_i) = \sum_{i=1}^{q-1} \alpha_i \left(\sum_{j=1}^{n} x_{ij} \right)$$

Let $\mathscr{C}_n$ be a linear, single-error-correcting code of length $n = (q^M - 1)/(q - 1)$ and label the codewords in some fashion as c_i, $i = 0, 1, 2, \ldots, q^{n-M} - 1$. Define the code $\mathscr{C}_N$ as the set of vectors

$$\mathscr{C}_N = \{(v_1, v_2, \ldots, v_{q-1}, c + \sum_{i=1}^{q-1} v_i, p(v_i) + f(c)); \quad v_i \in V_n(q), \quad c \in \mathscr{C}_n\}$$

2.8 Perfect Codes

where $f: V_n(q) \to GF(q)$ is an arbitrary (but fixed) function such that $f(0) = 0$. Clearly the length of the code is $N = nq + 1 = (q^{M+1} - 1)/(q - 1)$ and $|\mathscr{C}_N| = q^{n(q-1)}q^{n-M} = q^{N-(M+1)}$. Thus, by induction, we can get codes of any length of the form $(q^m - 1)/(q - 1)$ with q^{n-m} vectors. From previous considerations, if we can show the code is single-error-correcting, then it must be perfect.

We break each codeword of $\mathscr{C}_N$ into three parts and denote the distances of corresponding parts of the two codewords

$$\mathbf{u} = (v_1, v_2, \ldots, v_{q-1}, c + \sum v_i, p(v_i) + f(c))$$

and

$$\mathbf{v} = (v_1', v_2', \ldots, v_{q-1}', c' + \sum v_i', p(v_i') + f(c'))$$

by

$$W_1 = d((v_1, v_2, \ldots, v_{q-1}), (v_1', v_2', \ldots, v_{q-1}'))$$
$$W_2 = d((c + \sum_{i=1}^{q-1} v_i), (c' + \sum_{i=1}^{q-1} v_i'))$$

and

$$W_3 = w(p(v_i) + f(c) - p(v_i') - f(c'))$$

To show that $W_1 + W_2 + W_3 \geq 3$, we consider the various possibilities. If $W_1 \geq 3$, we are finished. If $W_1 = 0$, then $v_i = v_i'$, $i = 1, \ldots, q - 1$, and if $u \neq v$, $W_2 \geq 3$. If $W_1 = 1$, then $\sum v_i$ and $\sum v_i'$ differ in precisely one place, and if $c \neq c'$, then $W_2 \geq 2$. Thus $W_1 + W_2 \geq 3$. If $W_1 = 1$ and $c = c'$, then $W_2 = 1$ and $w(p(v_i) - p(v_i')) = 1$ and thus $W_1 + W_2 + W_3 = 3$. If $W_1 = 2$, there are two ways this can happen; either $d(v_i, v_i') = 2$ for some i or $d(v_i, v_i') = 1$ for two values of i. In the first instance $W_2 \geq 1$ if $c \neq c'$, while $W_2 = 2$ for $c = c'$, and in either case $W_1 + W_2 + W_3 \geq 3$. In the second instance if $c \neq c'$, then $W_2 \geq 1$ and $W_1 + W_2 \geq 3$, while if $c = c'$, then we have to show either $W_2 \geq 1$ or $W_3 \geq 1$. Suppose that

$$w(v_i - v_i') = 1 \quad \text{and} \quad w(v_j - v_j') = 1 \quad \text{for two indices} \quad i, j, \quad i \neq j$$

This implies that $x_{i\beta} - x_{i\beta}' \neq 0$ and $x_{j\beta} - x_{j\beta}' \neq 0$. Now if $W_2 = W_3 = 0$ then

$$x_{i\beta} - x_{i\beta}' + x_{j\beta} - x_{j\beta}' = 0$$
$$\alpha_i(x_{i\beta} - x_{i\beta}') + \alpha_j(x_{j\beta} - x_{j\beta}') = 0$$

But these equations imply that

$$(\alpha_i - \alpha_j)(x_{i\beta} - x_{i\beta}') = 0$$

which implies that either $\alpha_i = \alpha_j$ or $x_{i\beta} = x_{i\beta}'$ contrary to assumption. Notice that the all-zeros vector is in the code and the code is linear or nonlinear according as $f(\cdot)$ is a linear functional on $V_n(q)$ or not.

Thus the result of Tietäväinen indicates that the only perfect codes over a finite field are the single-error-correcting codes, binary repetition codes, and two Golay codes. As has been mentioned, some of the results of finite fields can be extended to codes over other structures and in these cases the idea of a linear code is less meaningful. For example, as an Abelian group, $V_n(q)$ has the structure of $GF(q)^+ \times GF(q)^+ \times \cdots \times GF(q)^+$, where $GF(q)^+$ denotes the additive group of $GF(q)$. Herzog and Schönheim (1971) modify this structure to $G_1 \times G_2 \times \cdots \times G_n$, where G_i is an arbitrary Abelian group of order p^{α_i}, p prime, and the groups need not be of the same type. A linear code is then a subgroup of the product group and Herzog and Schönheim construct perfect linear and nonlinear codes for the Hamming metric.

Before the result of Tietäväinen great efforts were expended in proving the nonexistence of perfect codes for various sets of parameters and in finding necessary conditions for their existence. Among the latter conditions found are the following theorems of Lloyd (1957) and van Lint (1971), which we state without proof.

Theorem 8.1 (*Lloyd*) If a perfect e-error-correcting code of length n over $GF(q)$ exists, then the polynomial

$$P_e(x) = \sum_{i=0}^{e} (-1)^i \binom{n-x}{e-i}\binom{x-1}{i}(q-1)^{e-i}$$

has e distinct integral zeros among the integers $1, 2, \ldots, n-1$.

Lenstra (1972) generalized this result by showing that it holds for more general alphabets than $GF(q)$.

Theorem 8.2. (*van Lint*) The zeros of the polynomial $P_e(x)$, $\alpha_1, \alpha_2, \ldots, \alpha_e$, satisfy the equations

(a) $\displaystyle\sum_{i=1}^{e} \alpha_i = \frac{e(n-e)(q-1)}{q} + \frac{e(e+1)}{2}$

(b) $\displaystyle\prod_{i=1}^{e} \alpha_i = e!\, q^{k-e}$

where $\sum_{i=0}^{e} \binom{n}{i}(q-1)^i = q^k$.

It is appropriate to mention here some relationships between the Mathieu groups, certain Steiner systems, and the Golay codes, although the combinatorial aspects of these relationships will be considered in some detail in the next chapter. The Mathieu groups play such an important role that some information on them has been gathered as Appendix C. The Mathieu groups M_{12} and M_{24}, which are the only 5-transitive permutation groups known, are the automorphism groups of the $S(5, 6, 12)$ and $S(5, 8, 24)$ Steiner systems. The Mathieu groups M_{11}, M_{23} (4-transitive), and M_{22} (3-transitive) are the automorphism groups of the Steiner systems $S(4, 5, 11)$, $S(4, 7, 23)$, and $S(3, 6, 22)$, respectively. Witt (1938a, b) has shown that, up to isomorphism, these five Steiner systems are unique. Now the minimal weight codewords in a linear perfect code span the code [see, e.g., Assmus and Mattson (1969)]. Also, the minimal weight codewords in the extended (24, 12) and (12, 6) Golay codes form the Steiner systems $S(5, 8, 24)$ and $S(5, 6, 12)$, while those of the codes (23, 12) and (11, 6) form the Steiner systems $S(4, 7, 23)$ and $S(4, 5, 11)$, respectively (Pless, 1968). The following two interesting theorems, which we state without proof, are due to Pless (1968) and summarize the extent to which the Golay codes are unique.

Theorem 8.3 Let $\mathscr{C}$ be an $(11, 6)$ [resp. $(23, 12)$] code over $GF(3)$ [resp. $GF(2)$]. Then the following five statements are equivalent:

(i) $\mathscr{C}$ has the same weight distribution as the Golay code.
(ii) The nonzero coordinate indices of the minimum weight vectors of $\mathscr{C}$ form an $S(4, 5, 11)$ [resp. $S(4, 7, 23)$] Steiner system.
(iii) $\mathscr{C}$ is perfect.
(iv) $\mathscr{C}$ is self-dual and its minimum weight is five (resp. seven).
(v) $\mathscr{C}$ is equivalent to the Golay code.

The corresponding theorem for the extended codes is:

Theorem 8.4 Let $\mathscr{C}$ be a $(12, 6)$ [resp. $(24, 12)$] code over $GF(3)$ [resp. $GF(2)$]. Then the following five statements are equivalent:

(i) $\mathscr{C}$ has the same weight distribution as the extended Golay code.
(ii) The nonzero coordinate indices of the minimum weight vectors of $\mathscr{C}$ form an $S(5, 6, 12)$ [resp. $S(5, 8, 24)$] Steiner system.
(iii) The minimum weight of $\mathscr{C}$ is six (resp. eight).
(iv) $\mathscr{C}$ is self-dual and has minimum weight six (resp. eight).
(v) $\mathscr{C}$ is equivalent to an extended Golay code.

2.9 Comments

In this chapter an attempt has been made to present a few of the interesting and natural connections between the fields of combinatorics and coding. Many others have not been mentioned. The subject is further considered in the next chapter, where the connections of coding with t designs are treated. The books by Ryser (1963) and Hall (1967a) were used liberally and are the standard combinatorial references. An excellent source of material on finite geometries and their collineation groups is Carmichael (1956). All material relating to coding is referenced in the text.

Exercises

1 Let $g(x)$ be the generator polynomial of the dual of the rth-order projective geometry code of length $(p^{ms} - 1)/(p^s - 1)$. Show that the code of this length generated by $(x - 1)g(x)$ is $(m - r - 1)$-step majority logic decodable.

2 Let $g(x)$ be the generator polynomial of the dual of the rth-order Euclidean geometry code of length $p^{ms} - 1$ over $GF(p)$. Show that the code of this length generated by $(x - 1)g(x)$ is $(m - r - 1)$-step majority logic decodable.

3 Let d' be the minimum distance of the dual code of a linear (n, k) code. Show that the number of errors that can be corrected by one-step majority logic decoding is upper-bounded by the quantity $(n - 1)/[2(d' - 1)]$. Extend this result to the L-step majority-logic-decoding case assuming all codes are binary.

4 Show that the rth-order projective geometry code has a BCH bound on its minimum distance the same as the bound achieved by majority-logic-decoding arguments.

5 Show that if $r < (m + 1)/2$, an rth-order projective geometry code obtained from $PG(m, p^s)$ is two-step majority logic decodable. Similarly, show that if $r \leq m/2$, an rth-order Euclidean geometry code obtained from $EG(m, p^s)$ is two-step majority logic decodable.

6 (Reed–Muller Codes) Let G' be the generator matrix for the cyclic binary maximum length code with parameters $(2^m - 1, m)$ and distance 2^{m-1}. To G' we first add a column of all zeros and then a row of all ones to obtain

$$G = \begin{bmatrix} 1 & 1 & 1 & \cdots & 1 \\ \hline 0 & & & & \\ \vdots & & & G' & \\ 0 & & & & \end{bmatrix}$$

The codewords of the code with generator matrix G are those of the original code with a zero added in the first position, plus the complements of words in the original code with a one added in the first position. Label the rows of G by $v_0, v_1, \ldots, v_m$ and let $n = 2^m$. If $u = (u_1, u_2, \ldots, u_n)$ and $v = (v_1, v_2, \ldots, v_n)$ are two binary n-tuples, we define a componentwise product as

$$uv = (u_1 v_1, u_2 v_2, \ldots, u_n v_n)$$

It follows trivially that $u^2 = u$ for any binary vector u.

Exercises

Definition The rth-order Reed–Muller (RM) code is the subspace of $V_n(2)$ spanned by the set of vectors

$$v = v_0^{i_0} v_1^{i_1} \cdots v_m^{i_m}, \qquad i_j = 0 \text{ or } 1 \quad \text{and} \quad \sum_{j=0}^{m} i_j \leq r$$

Show that:

(i) The rth-order RM code of length 2^m has dimension $k = \sum_{j=0}^{r} \binom{m}{j}$ and distance 2^{m-r}.

(ii) The dual of the rth-order RM code of length 2^m is the $(m - r - 1)$th-order RM code.

(iii) The vector v_i, $i > 0$, may be interpreted as the incidence vector of a hyperplane in $EG(m, 2)$.

(iv) The vector $v_i + v_j$, $i,j > 0$, using the interpretation of (iii), is the incidence vector of the symmetric difference of the flats corresponding to v_i and v_j, i.e., if v_i and v_j are incidence vectors of the $m-1$ flats F_i and F_j, respectively, then $v_i + v_j$ is the incidence vector of the symmetric difference $(F_i \backslash (F_i \cap F_j) \cup F_j \backslash (F_i \cap F_j))$, where unions and intersections are in the set-theoretic sense. Show that this symmetric difference is also an $m-1$-flat.

(v) The vector $v_i v_j$ is the incidence vector of $F_i \cap F_j$, which is always an $m-2$ flat.

(vi) The complement of an $m-1$ flat is an $m-1$ flat.

(vii) The rth-order RM code of length 2^m contains all the t flats of $EG(m, 2)$, $t \geq m - r$. Conclude that the code is $(r + 1)$-step orthogonalizable.

7 (Bose and Bush, 1952) The solutions to the equation $\sum_{i=1}^{r} x_i = 0$ form an $r - 1$ flat in $PG(r - 1, 2)$ containing $2^{r-1} - 1$ points. Show that the set of 2^{r-1} points not in this flat consists of those elements of $V_r(2)$ containing an odd number of ones. Show that if we use these points as the row vectors for a $2^{r-1} \times r$ matrix $\mathbf{C}$, then the $2^{r-1} \times 2^r$ matrix $\mathbf{A}$ whose ith row is $\mathbf{C} x_i$, $x_i \in V_r(2)$, $i = 1, \ldots, 2^r$, is an $OA(2^r, 2^{r-1}, 2, 3)$ of strength three.

8 Show that if there exist k orthogonal Latin squares of orders n_1 and n_2, respectively, then there exists a set of k orthogonal Latin squares of order $n_1 n_2$.

9 (Hall, 1967a) Given two orthogonal arrays $OA(n_1^2, k, n_1, 2)$ and $OA(n_2^2, k, n_2, 2)$, both of index one, construct an $OA((n_1 n_2)^2, k, n_1 n_2, 2)$ of index one.

10 (Lin, 1969) It was shown in the previous chapter that a GRM code of length q^m over $GF(q)$ is invariant under the doubly transitive permutation group consisting of transformations

$$\mathbf{X} \to \mathbf{AX} + \mathbf{B}$$

where $\mathbf{X} \in V_m(q)$, $\mathbf{A}$ is an $m \times m$ nonsingular matrix, and $\mathbf{B} \in V_m(q)$. Each coordinate position is labeled with an element of $V_m(q)$ and the group acts on these elements. Show that when $q = 2$ this group is actually triply transitive. Conclude that the shortened code obtained by deleting the coordinate position labeled with the zero vector is invariant under a doubly transitive group and hence that its constant weight vectors yield a BIBD. The minimum weight vectors in the cyclic binary rth-order RM code correspond to the BIBD's formed from the $m - r$ flats in $EG(m, 2)$ through the origin, and those of the next highest weight correspond to the BIBD's formed from the $m - r$ flats not through the origin.

11 (Pless, 1972b) An (n, k) code $\mathscr{C}$ is said to be the direct sum of two codes $\mathscr{C}_1$ and $\mathscr{C}_2$, denoted by $\mathscr{C} = \mathscr{C}_1 \oplus \mathscr{C}_2$, if: (i) $\mathscr{C}_1$ and $\mathscr{C}_2$ are vector subspaces of $\mathscr{C}$; (ii) every vector $c \in \mathscr{C}$ can be expressed as $c = c_1 + c_2$, $c_i \in \mathscr{C}_i$; (iii) a projection of $\mathscr{C}_1$ onto n_1 coordinate places is an (n_1, k_1) subspace and a projection of $\mathscr{C}_2$ onto n_2 coordinate places is an (n_2, k_2) subspace, where $n = n_1 + n_2$ and $k = k_1 + k_2$. Show that if $\mathscr{C}_1$ and $\mathscr{C}_2$ are left invariant by the permutation groups G_1 and G_2 respectively, then the direct product group $G_1 \times G_2$ is in the group leaving $\mathscr{C}$ invariant. Show also that if there are A_i vectors of weight i in $\mathscr{C}_1$ and B_i in $\mathscr{C}_2$, then the number of vectors of weight k in $\mathscr{C}_1 \oplus \mathscr{C}_2$ is $\sum_{i+j=k} A_i B_j$.

12 (Hsiao et al., 1970) Recall that if we can form at least $d - 1$ check sums orthogonal on each digit, then the code has minimum distance at least d. Construct a binary parity check matrix:

$$H = \begin{bmatrix} M_1 \\ M_2 \\ \vdots \\ M_{2t} \end{bmatrix} \; I_{2tm} \;\;$$

where the $m \times m^2$ matrices M_1 and M_2 are given by

$$M_1 = \begin{bmatrix} \overbrace{1\,1\,\cdots\,1}^{m} & & & \\ & \overbrace{1\,1\,\cdots\,1}^{m} & & 0 \\ & & \ddots & \\ & 0 & & \overbrace{1\,1\,\cdots\,1}^{m} \end{bmatrix}$$

$$M_2 = [I_m \;\vdots\; I_m \;\vdots\; \cdots \;\vdots\; I_m]$$

and the M_i, $3 \leq i \leq 2t$, are constructed from a set $L_i = (l_{rs}^i)$, $3 \leq i \leq 2t$, of pols in the following manner: Define the incidence matrix Q_i^μ of the element μ in L_i in the usual fashion, i.e., $(q_i^\mu)_{rs} = 1$ if $l_{rs}^i = \mu$ and 0 otherwise. For a

Exercises

given L_i the rows of each of the m incidence matrices are concatenated to form an m^2-tuple, e.g.,

$$V_i^\mu = [(q_i^\mu)_{11}, (q_i^\mu)_{12}, \ldots, (q_i^\mu)_{1m}, (q_i^\mu)_{21}, \ldots, (q_i^\mu)_{2m}, \ldots, (q_i^\mu)_{mm}]$$

Finally, the matrix M_i is formed by using V_i^j as its jth row. Show that the resulting parity check matrix yields a code of length $m^2 + 2tm$, dimension m^2, and is capable of correcting t errors.

13 An $n \times n$ matrix whose ith row is the $(i - 1)$th row shifted cyclically to the left one position is called a back circulant. Show that such a matrix is symmetric. Show that the product of a back circulant matrix with a circulant matrix yields a symmetric matrix. Show that any two circulant matrices of the same order commute.

14 Show that -3 is a quadratic residue of primes of the form $6n + 1$ and a quadratic nonresidue of primes of the form $6n + 5$.

15 Show that the number of solutions to the equation

$$ax^2 + bx + c \equiv 0 \mod p$$

is given by $1 + [(b^2 - 4ac)/p]$.

16 (Berlekamp, 1968) Show that the cyclotomic polynomial of order 241 is irreducible over $GF(17)$. [*Hint*: It is sufficient to show that the multiplicative order of 17 mod 241 is 240 and this follows from the fact that $(17/241) = -1$. Use the law of reciprocity to establish this.]

3 Coding and Combinatorics

3.1 Introduction

Being concerned with problems of a finite nature, coding theory itself can be considered as a part of combinatorial theory. For example, certain coding problems themselves were treated under the title of packing problems before the concept of coding theory arose. [See, for example, Paige (1956).] In fact, the well-known Hamming–Golay codes were discussed by Zaremba (1950, 1952) before the results of Hamming and Golay appeared in print. We shall concern ourselves in this chapter, however, with the relationship between coding theory and certain aspects of experimental design and matroid theory.

3.2 General t Designs

Recall from the preceding chapter that a *t design* or λ-(t, k, v) *configuration* is an ordered pair (S, B), where S is a set of cardinality v, and B is a family of k-subsets (called blocks) of S with the property that each t-subset of S is contained in precisely λ blocks of B. For nondegeneracy, we shall always assume that $0 < t < k < v$. While not much is known about general t designs, much work has been done in certain special cases. For each triple t, k, v satisfying $0 < t < k < v$ there are many t designs that may be obtained

3.2 General t Designs

trivially as follows. Let S be any v-set. Form C, the set of all possible k-subsets of S. The result (S, C) is a t design that we call the full combinatorial design. In this design $\lambda = \binom{v-t}{k-t}$. Let B be the family of k-subsets of S that includes each member of C exactly n times. (The term family is used here to indicate that each k-subset of S may occur several times as a block of B.) The result is a λ-(t, k, v) configuration in which $\lambda = n\binom{v-t}{k-t}$. In fact, given any λ-(t, k, v) configuration, we can *replicate* it n times to get an $n\lambda$-(t, k, v) configuration by employing each of its blocks n times.

Nontrivial t designs have been known for some time for each t, $0 < t < 6$. However, it is only recently that it has been shown that t designs other than full combinatorial designs and their replications also exist for all $t \geqslant 6$.

Proposition 2.1 Every λ_t-(t, k, v) configuration is a λ_{t-1}-$(t-1, k, v)$ configuration in which $\lambda_{t-1} = \lambda_t(v - t + 1)/(k - t + 1)$.

Proof Let $D = (S, B)$ be a λ_t-(t, k, v) design. Let X be any $(t-1)$-subset of S, and $\lambda(X)$ be the number of blocks of D that contain X. Clearly X is contained in $v - t + 1$ t-subsets of S. Let $C(X)$ denote the collection of such subsets. Each of these t-subsets occurs in λ_t blocks of D, these being the $\lambda(X)$ blocks that contain X. Now each of these blocks contains $k - t + 1$ members of $C(X)$. Thus $\lambda(X)(k - t + 1) = \lambda_t(v - t + 1)$. Since $\lambda(X)$ does not depend on the particular $(t - 1)$-subset chosen, the result follows. □

Corollary 1 Let $\lambda_0 = b$ be the number of blocks (which contain the null subset), $\lambda_1 = r$ denote the number of blocks containing a given element, and λ_i be the number of blocks that contain a given i-subset, $0 \leqslant i \leqslant t$. Then $\lambda_i = \lambda_t\binom{v-i}{t-i}/\binom{k-i}{t-i}$.

Proof This follows from repeated application of the proposition. □

Corollary 2 Let u be an integer such that $0 \leqslant u \leqslant t$; then the number of subsets in B intersecting a given t-subset in u elements is independent of the t-subset chosen.

Proof This is equivalent to Corollary 1. □

Corollary 3 The complement of a t design is a t design.

Proof A straightforward application of the principle of inclusion-exclusion shows that the complementary configuration of a λ-(t, k, v) design is a λ'-$(t, v - k, v)$ design, where $\lambda' = \lambda\binom{v-k}{t}/\binom{k}{t}$. □

Proposition 2.2 The existence of a λ_t-(t, k, v) configuration implies the existence of a λ_t-$(t - i, k - i, v - i)$ configuration, $0 < i < t$.

Proof Let $C(x)$ be the set of blocks of $D = (S, B)$ that contain a given element of x of S. Every $(t - 1)$-subset of S-$\{x\}$ occurs with x in exactly λ_t blocks of D, these blocks being those of $C(x)$. Thus $(S - \{x\}, B')$, where B' is obtained from the blocks of $C(x)$ by removing x, is the required configuration for $i = 1$. Repeated application establishes the required result. □

Corollary The existence of a λ_t-(t, k, v) configuration implies the existence of a λ^t-$(t - 1, k, v - 1)$ design, where $\lambda^t = \lambda_t - \lambda_{t-1}$.

Proof This design consists of the blocks other than those containing a given variety x_1, that is, the set of blocks $B - C(x)$ in Proposition 2.2. □

Steiner Systems A 1-(t, k, v) design is called a *Steiner system*, which we denote by $S(t, k, v)$. The following is a brief catalogue of results on the existence of Steiner systems. For $t = 2$ (balanced incomplete block designs) various families have been found. Among the best-known families of such designs are:

(a) Steiner triple systems $S(2, 3, v)$, which exist for all $v \equiv 1$ or 3 mod 6.
(b) Hanani systems I, $S(2, 4, v)$, which exist for all $v \equiv 1$ or 4 mod 12.
(c) Hanani systems II, $S(2, 5, v)$, which exist for all $v \equiv 1$ or 5 mod 20.
(d) Projective and Euclidean systems, which exist for $n > 1$ and q a prime power: (i) $S(2, q, q^n)$ and (ii) $S(2, q + 1, (q^n - 1)/(q - 1))$.
(e) Hyperbolic systems $S(2, 2^n, 2^{2n+1} - 2^n)$ for n an integer > 1.
(f) Hermitian systems $S(2, q + 1, q^3 + 1)$, which exist for q a prime power.

In this regard we point out that it is known that for any given integer $k > 2$ there is a constant $c(k)$ such that $S(2, k, v)$ exists for $v > c(k)$ and $v \equiv k$ mod $k(k - 1)$.

For $t = 3$ the following systems are known:

(a) Quadruple systems $S(3, 4, v)$ exist for all positive $v \equiv 2$ or 4 mod 6.
(b) Inversive systems $S(3, q + 1, q^2 + 1)$ exist for q a prime power.

For $t = 4$ and $t = 5$ the only known Steiner systems are the Mathieu systems, $S(5, 8, 24)$, $S(5, 6, 12)$, $S(4, 7, 23)$, $S(4, 5, 11)$ [see Witt (1938b)].

Before investigating some of the connections between t designs and coding theory we digress as follows. With every linear code there is an associated combinatorial structure called a *matroid*. Many of the investigations concerning t designs and codes are in fact investigations of the properties of the matroids of linear codes, and we discuss briefly the concept of a matroid. Excellent sources of information on matroids are the publications by Tutte (1965, 1971). Matroids can be axiomatized in many ways; here we basically follow Tutte's (1965) work, which is ideally suited for our purposes.

3.3 Matroids

Definition A matroid M is a pair (S, F) where S is a finite set of elements called cells and F is a family of nonnull subsets of S such that (i) no member of F is a proper subset of another, and (ii) if a and b are two members of S, and X and Y are members of F such that $a \in X \cap Y$ and $b \in X - Y$, then there exists a member Z of F such that $a \notin Z$, $b \in Z$, and $Z \subseteq X \cup Y$.

The members of F are called the circuits of the matroid, and we refer to these axioms as the circuit axioms of the matroid. The *girth* $\alpha = \alpha(M)$ of the matroid is defined by the formula

$$\alpha(M) = \min_{X \in F} \{|X|\}$$

Definition The *weight of a circuit* X is its cardinality $|X|$.

Examples of Matroids We assume that the reader is familiar with the concept of a linear graph [see, for example, Tutte (1966)]. We denote the set of vertices of the graph by V or $V(G)$ and the edges by E or $E(G)$. A polygon of G is a connected subgraph of G in which each vertex is incident with exactly two edges. A bond in G is a nonnull subset B of $E(G)$ that satisfies the following condition: The graph H obtained from G by deleting the edges of B has two connected components C_1 and C_2 such that each edge of B has one end in each component.

Example 1 If F is the family of polygons of a graph G, then $(E(G), F)$ is a matroid, as is readily verified. This is called the polygon matroid of G.

Example 2 If F is the family of bonds of a graph G, then $(E(G), F)$ is a matroid, as is readily verified.

Definition A matroid is *graphic* if it is the bond matroid of a graph; it is *cographic* if it is the polygon matroid of a graph.

Proposition 3.1 Let F' be a family of nonnull subsets of a set S. If F' satisfies matroid axiom (ii), then the minimal members of F' form a matroid on S, where a minimal member is one which contains no other under set inclusion.

Proof We first show that if $a \in X$ where $X \in F'$, then there is a minimal member Y of F' such that $a \in Y \subseteq X$. Indeed, take Y as a member of F' with least cardinality, which satisfies $a \in Y \subseteq X$. If Y is not minimal, then there exists $Z \in F'$ such that $Z \subseteq Y - \{a\}$. Choose $b \in Z$; then there is a member Z' of F' such that $a \in Z' \subset Y - \{b\} \subset X$, by axiom (ii), which contradicts the choice of Y. Now let a and b be members of S, and X and Y be minimal members of F' such that $a \in X \cap Y$ and $b \in X - Y$. Then there is a member W of F' such that $a \notin W$, $b \in W$, and $W \subseteq X \cup Y$, and therefore there is a minimal member Z of F' such that $b \in Z \subseteq W$. Then $a \notin Z$, $b \in Z$, and $Z \subseteq X \cup Y$. □

Definition A *dendroid* of a matroid M is a subset D of S that meets every circuit of M and is minimal with respect to this property.

By definition, there is a circuit of M such that $X \cap D = \{a\}$. X is uniquely determined by this condition. Indeed, if Y is another circuit such that $Y \cap D = \{a\}$, there is by (ii) a circuit $Z \subseteq X \cup Y$ that does not meet D. The circuit X is denoted by $J(D, a)$.

Lemma 3.1 Let D be a dendroid of a matroid $M = (S, F)$. Let a and b be elements of S such that $a \in D$ and $b \notin D$. Then $D' = (D - \{a\}) \cup \{b\}$ is a dendroid if and only if $b \in J(D, a)$.

Proof If D' is also a dendroid of M, then, since it meets $J(D, a)$, it must do so in b. Conversely, if $b \in J(D, a)$, then D' meets every circuit of M, since $D - \{a\}$ meets every member of $F - \{J(D, a)\}$. Consider any element $c \in D' - \{b\}$. Then $I = D' \cap J(D, c)$ is either $\{c\}$ or $\{b, c\}$. If $I = \{b, c\}$, then by (ii) there is a circuit W such that $c \in W$, $b \notin W \subseteq J(D, a) \cup J(D, c)$, hence $D \cap W = \{c\}$. In either case there is a circuit that meets D' only in $\{c\}$, so that no proper subset of D' meets all circuits of M. □

Corollary All dendroids of M have the same cardinality.

Proof Let D_1 and D_2 be two distinct dendroids of M. Let D_3 be a dendroid of M such that $|D_3| = |D_1|$ and $|D_2 \cap D_3|$ is as large as possible. If $D_2 \not\subseteq D_3$, choose $c \in D_3 - D_2$. Then $J(D_3, a)$ meets D_2 in a cell b, which is not in D_3. Since $D_4 = (D_3 - \{a\}) \cup \{b\}$ is a dendroid of M, and $|D_4 \cap D_2| = |D_3 \cap D_2| + 1$, we have a contradiction of the definition of D_3 and therefore conclude that $D_2 \subseteq D_3$. By definition, no proper subset of a dendroid is a dendroid; thus $D_2 = D_3$ and the corollary is established. □

Definition The *rank* of a matroid M is the cardinality of any dendroid of M. This quantity is denoted by $r(M)$.

3.4 Chains and Chain Groups

Definition A subset C of the set S of a matroid $M = (S, F)$ is spanning if C contains a dendroid of M.

A matroidal property that has direct implication in coding is given in the following lemma.

Lemma 3.2 If M is a matroid of girth α defined on a set S of cardinality n, then every subset of cardinality $n - \alpha + 1$ is spanning and $r(M) \leq n - \alpha + 1$.

Proof Since every circuit has at least α elements, every subset S' of S which has cardinality of at least $n - \alpha + 1$ must meet every circuit, and any subset $T \subseteq S'$ that is minimal with respect to this latter property will form a dendroid. The lemma follows. □

To show the relationships between matroids and linear algebra, and thus coding theory, we turn our attention now to chain groups.

3.4 Chains and Chain Groups

Let S be a finite set and R a commutative ring with a unit element and no divisors of zero. A *chain* on S is a function f which maps S into R. If $a \in S$, we call the element $f(a)$ the *coordinate* of a in f. The *domain* dom f of the chain f is the set of all $a \in S$ such that $f(a) \neq 0$. A chain is a *zero* chain iff dom f is null. Clearly the zero chain is unique. We define a new chain on S as the sum of two chains f and g by the rule $(f + g)a = f(a) + g(a)$, $a \in S$.

The product λf of an element λ of R and a chain f on S is defined by $\lambda f(a) = \lambda(f(a))$, $a \in S$.

A *chain group* on S over R is defined as any subset of the set of all chains on S that is closed with respect to both addition and multiplication. Let G be a chain group on S. A chain f on G is *elementary* if it is nonzero and there is no nonzero chain $g \in G$ such that dom $g \subsetneq$ dom f.

With every chain group an S we can associate a matroid M on S as follows.

Lemma 4.1 Let N be a chain group on S over R. Then the family F of domains of the elementary chains of N is a matroid on S.

Proof Let F' be the family of domains of the nonzero chains of N. Let f and g be two such chains and a and b be elements of S such that $a \in$ dom f ∩ dom g and $b \in$ dom g − dom f. Multiply f by $g(a)$ and add the resulting chains to obtain the chain $h \in N$. Then $a \notin \text{dom } h$, $b \in \text{dom } h$, and dom $h \subseteq \text{dom } f \cup \text{dom } g$. Thus F' satisfies axiom (ii). Since the elementary chains have minimal domains, the result follows by Proposition 3.1. □

We call the above matroid the matroid of N and denote it by $M(N)$. For later reference we note the following definition.

Definition A chain group over $GF(2)$ is called *binary*.

The concept of a dendroid for matroids can be extended as follows to a chain group N on S over a commutative ring as above.

Definition A *dendroid* of a *chain group* N on a set S is a minimal subset of S that meets the domain of every nonzero chain of N.

Since each such domain contains that of an elementary chain, the dendroids of N are identical with those of $M(N)$.

If D is a dendroid of N, for each $a \in D$ there is a chain f_a of N such that dom f_a is the circuit $J(D, a)$ of $M(N)$.

Definition A set of chains f_a, one for each $a \in D$ as in the foregoing, is a *dendroid basis* of N.

Definition The weight of a dendroid basis $\{f_a\}$ is the product $\Pi_{a \in D} f_a(a)$, which is clearly nonzero.

Proposition 4.1 Let $B = \{f_a | a \in D\}$ be a dendroid basis of weight w of a chain group N over R. Let g be any nonzero chain of N. Then wg can be expressed as a linear combination of members of B, with coefficients in R.

Proof By adding suitable members of B to wg, one can reduce the coordinate of each $a \in D$ to zero. The resulting chain is zero, since its domain does not meet D. □

Corollary If dom g meets D in a single cell a, then dom g = dom f_a, and hence g is an elementary chain.

The rank of $M(N)$ in the sense of the theory of linear independence is therefore the rank of N.

In the case where R is a field the chains of the dendroid basis can be chosen so that $f_a(a) = 1$ for each $a \in D$. In this case a dendroid basis becomes a true basis for N.

3.4 Chains and Chain Groups

Proposition 4.2 Let $M = (S, F)$ be the matroid of a chain group N over a field K. Let L be a nonempty subset of F. Let T be a subset of S that meets every member of L. If T is minimal with respect to this property, then T can be extended to a dendroid of M.

Proof Let D be a dendroid of M such that $|T \cap D|$ is as large as possible. Let L' be the set of members of L that do not meet $T \cap D$. If L' is not empty, choose $x \in T$ such that x belongs to some member l of L'. Then $x \notin D$. Then $x \in J(D, a)$ for some $a \in T \cap D$; otherwise, since every chain on $l \in N$ can be written as a linear combination of chains on $J(D, a)$, $a \in [D-(T \cap D)]$, every chain on l would vanish on x, violating the choice of x. Then $D' = (D \cup \{x\}) - \{a\}$ is a dendroid meeting T in a set of cardinality $|D \cap T| + 1$, violating the choice of D. Therefore L' must be empty. Thus every member of L meets $T \cap D$. But T is minimal with respect to this property, thus $T \cap D = T$, that is, $T \subseteq D$. □

Corollary If L contains the domains of a basis of N, then T is a dendroid.

Proof If T is a proper subset of D, then the chains on $J(D, a)$, $a \in T$, generate a $|T|$-dimensional subspace that includes all chains whose domains lie in L, contradicting the fact that L contains the domains of a basis of N. □

Chain groups over S are studied because of the fact that structures on S have properties that are reflected in certain of the chain groups of S. For example, if there is a linear graph whose edge set is S, then its polygon matroid has certain properties that must be reflected in certain chain groups that share the same matroid, which allows one to determine whether or not a given matroid is *cographic*, that is, the polygon matroid of a linear graph.

Our main concern here will be the relationship between t designs and matroids, as reflected in the linear codes they generate. For our purposes, we require yet the following considerations.

Let N be a chain group on a set S over a commutative ring R having a unit element and no divisors of zero.

Definition If S' is a subset of S, then the *restriction* of the chain f of N to S' is the chain g on S' such that $g(a) = f(a)$ for each $a \in S$.

Definition The *reduction of a chain group* N to S' is the chain group consisting of the restrictions of the chains of N to S'. (It is evident that the set of such chains forms a chain group under the usual definitions of addition and scalar multiplication; we refer to this chain group as $N \cdot S'$.)

Similarly we have the following definition.

Definition The contraction of a chain group N to S' (denoted by $N \times S'$) is the chain group consisting of the restrictions to S' of those chains f of N such that $\text{dom } f \subseteq S'$.

It is evident that $N \times S' \subseteq N \cdot S'$.

Definition The *reduction of a matroid* M to a subset $S' \subset S$ is the matroid consisting of the minimal members of the class of nonnull intersections of S' with the circuits of M. (It is evident that these subsets form a matroid, which is referred to as $M \cdot S'$.)

Definition The contraction of M to S' (denoted by $M \times S'$) is the matroid of the class of all circuits X of M such that $X \subset S'$.

The reader can verify that $M(N \times S) = M(N) \times S$ and that $M(N \cdot S) = M(N) \cdot S$.

3.5 Dual Chain Groups

Definition Two chains f and g on S over R are orthogonal if
$$\sum_{a \in S} f(a) \cdot g(a) = 0$$
Let N^* be the class of all chains h on S over R such that h is orthogonal to every member of N. Then N^* is a chain group on S over R.

Definition The *dual chain group* N^* of the chain group N is the chain group of all chains orthogonal to the chains of N.

Clearly $N \subset N^{**}$, and if R is a field, then $N = N^{**}$.

Lemma 5.1 If N is a chain group over R, then $(N \cdot S')^* = N^* \times S'$ for any $S' \subseteq S$. Further, if R is a field, then $(N \times S')^* = N^* \cdot S'$.

Proof Let f be a chain on S. Then f belongs to $(N \cdot S')^*$ if and only if it is orthogonal to every chain of $N \cdot S'$, that is, if and only if the chain g on S that satisfies $\text{dom } g = \text{dom } f$ and has f as its restriction to S' is orthogonal to every member of N. This condition is valid if and only if f belongs to $N^* \times S'$. Thus $(N \cdot S')^* = N^* \times S'$. Now if R is a field, we write
$$(N \times S')^* = ((N^*)^* \times S')^* = ((N^* \cdot S')^*)^* = N^* \cdot S'. \quad \square$$

Before returning to coding theory, we remark that there is a corresponding theory of matroid duality, which is reflected in the theory of planar graphs. The theory of matroids is a rich and beautiful area of combinatorial mathematics, encompassing the area of finite geometries as well, but these considerations are beyond the scope of the present book. The reader is referred to Tutte (1971).

3.6 Matroids, Graphs, and Coding

Clearly every code C over a field K may be viewed as a set of chains defined on the set of coordinate positions in its concrete realization. For the remainder of this section we adopt such a vantage point. We refer to the chains of C as code chains or code vectors. We note that the Hamming weight of a chain f denoted by $w(f)$ is $|\text{dom } f|$ and the Hamming distance between two chains f and g [denoted by $d(f, g)$] is $w(f - g)$. A code over a field K is linear if and only if its sets of chains form a chain group.

Let us turn our attention for a moment to linear graphs.

Definition A *cycle* in a graph G is the edge set of a subgraph C of G such that each vertex of C is of even degree.

Definition By the mod 2 sum (or symmetric difference) of two sets A and B we mean the set $(A \cup B) - (A \cap B)$.

The cycles of G form a vector space $C(G)$ over GF(2) under mod 2 addition and scalar product $1 \cdot C = C$ for all cycles C and $0 \cdot C = \varnothing$, the subgraph with no edges.

Definition The *cycle space* of a graph G is the vector space of cycles of G under mod 2 addition. (Thus any linear graph yields a binary code.) Clearly the matroid of $C(G)$ is the polygon matroid of G.

The girth of a graph is the number of edges contained in the "smallest" polygon of the graph. Since the cycle space codes of graphs are linear, the distance d of such a code is the girth of the corresponding graph. Graphs of given girth and degree with as few vertices as possible are called *cages* by Tutte and have been investigated by Tutte (1966) and others. We do not pursue this interesting topic here.

Since by definition of girth we have the fact that in any linear (n, k) code the minimum mutual distance d of the code is the girth α of the matroid $M(C(G))$, Lemma 3.2, when interpreted for linear codes, is the well-known inequality $d \leqslant n - k + 1$ (Theorem 7.6 of Chapter 1).

Definition A linear code is maximum distance separable if $d = n - k + 1$.

Proposition 6.1 Every maximum-distance-separable (linear) binary code can be viewed as the cycle space of a linear graph.

Proof This follows from the fact that all maximum-distance-separable binary codes are of a trivial nature, as will be seen in Proposition 6.2. It will be seen that the graph in question either is a polygon or consists of a pair of vertices joined by several edges. □

In the following we refer to the circuits of least weight α of a matroid as the belts of the matroid.

Proposition 6.2 (*Assmus and Mattson* 1967a) An (n, k) code is maximum distance separable if and only if the belts of its matroid form a full combinatorial design.

Proof Let us assume that the belts of the matroid $M = (S, F)$ of an (n, k) code N form a full combinatorial design. Since in a linear code the minimum weight of the nonzero vectors is d, the design consists of the set of all d-subsets of the n-set S. By Lemma 3.2 every $(n - d + 1)$-subset of S is spanning. Moreover, each is a dendroid, since no subset of smaller size can meet all the belts of M; thus $k = r(M) = n - d + 1$.

Conversely, if $k = n - d + 1$, then $n - d = k - 1$. Now let us assume that some d-subset T of S is not a belt of the matroid M. Then, if T' is the complementary subset of T in S, T' meets all subsets of S with cardinality greater than or equal to d with the exception of T, and in particular all circuits of the matroid M. Thus T' is a dendroid and rank $r(M) < k$, a contradiction. □

Corollary Any binary maximum-distance-separable code is trivial.

Proof Let C be a binary optimal (n, k) code. If $k = 0$, the code is trivial. We now assume $k > 0$. Let $M = (S, F)$ be the matroid of C. Then the belts of C are the d-subsets of S. If $d \neq n$, then the mod 2 sum of any two d-subsets X and Y that intersect in a $(d - 1)$-set has weight two, and therefore $d \leq 2$. Hence $d = 1, 2,$ or n, and $k = n, n - 1,$ or 1, respectively. □

Let us say that a code C of distance d (over some alphabet that we may take to be a ring) is a matroid code if its set of minimal domains form a matroid M whose girth $\alpha(M) = d$. Then if the rank (or dimension) of the code is defined to be the rank of its matroid, we may say that a matroid code is optimal

3.6 Matroids, Graphs, and Coding

if and only if $r(M) = n - \alpha(M) + 1$. Then the above proposition is valid for matroid codes as well. A similar statement applies to many of the results that follow.

In the further study of the relationship between a code and its set of minimal domains the following concept is useful.

Definition A code C over a field K is *scalar complete to level l* if for every code chain f of weight l or less: (i) λf is also a code chain for each nonzero scalar λ of K, and (ii) for all $g \in C$ such that dom $g =$ dom f, the relation $g = \lambda f$ is valid for some scalar λ of K.

Definition A code C over a field K is scalar complete if it is scalar complete to level j, where j is the weight of the codeword of least nonzero weight in the code. Clearly, if a code is scalar complete to level $l > j$, it is scalar complete. Evidently every binary (not necessarily linear) code on an n-set is scalar complete to level n and every linear code is scalar complete. This result can be strengthened as follows.

Lemma 6.1 Every linear code C of distance d over $GF(q)$ is scalar complete to level $u = u(q, d)$, where u is the largest integer satisfying

$$u - \left\lceil \frac{u}{q-1} \right\rceil < d$$

where $\lceil x \rceil$ denotes the least integer that is greater than or equal to x. In particular, every linear code is scalar complete.

Proof It is evident that if $f \in C$, then $\lambda f \in C$ for all scalars $\lambda \in GF(q)$. Moreover, if f and g are any pair of weight w (>0) vectors of C such that dom $f =$ dom g, then there is a nonzero scalar λ of K such that f and $\lambda_0 g$ agree on at least $\lceil w/(q-1) \rceil$ members of dom f. Indeed, if we consider the average agreement $\bar{a}$ of f with the vectors $\{\lambda g : \lambda \in GF(q), \lambda \neq 0\}$, this average is $\lceil w/(q-1) \rceil$, and therefore the vector with greatest agreement agrees in at least $\lceil w/(q-1) \rceil$ places. Now, if $w \leq u(q, d)$, then $w(f - \lambda_0 g) < d$, which implies that $f - \lambda_0 g = 0$, that is, $f = \lambda_0 g$, which establishes the lemma. □

Theorem 6.1 (*Assmus and Mattson 1969*) Let A and B be linear dual (n, k) and $(n, n - k)$ codes over $GF(q)$ with minimum distances d and e, respectively, and which are scalar complete to levels $v_0 \geq d$ and $w_0 \geq e$, respectively. Let t be an integer less than d. Suppose that the number of nonzero weights of B that are less than or equal to $n - t$ is itself less than or equal to $d - t$. Then for each weight v with $d \leq v \leq v_0$ the domains of weight v of the code A form a t design, and for each weight w with $e \leq w \leq \{n - t, w_0\}$ the domains of weight w of code B form a t design.

Proof Let S be the common coordinate set of A and B. Choose a fixed value of t satisfying the conditions of the hypothesis. Let T be any t-subset of S. We consider the codes $A' = A \cdot (S - T) = A'(T)$, the reduction of A to $S - T$, and $B' = B \times (S - T) = B'(T)$, the contraction of B to $S - T$. By Lemma 5.1, A' and B' are dual codes. Moreover, by Lemma 3.2, every $(n - d + 1)$-subset of S is spanning; thus $S - T$ contains a dendroid of $M(A)$ that is also a dendroid of $M(A) \cdot (S - T) = M(A')$; therefore A' is an $(n - t, k)$ code and B' is an $(n - t, n - k - t)$ code. Let $0 < w_1 < w_2 < \cdots < w_{d-t} \leq n - t$ be the possible nonzero weights less than or equal to $n - t$ appearing on B. Let $W = \{w_1, w_2, \ldots, w_{d-t}\}$. Then the only nonzero weights of B' lie in W. The minimum weight in A is at least $d - t$. Employing the MacWilliams equations for B' and A' (cf. Section 1.5), the number x_j of vectors of weights v_j in B' is uniquely determined in terms of n, t, q, and k by the $d - t$ equations

$$\sum_{j \in W} \binom{n - t - j}{u} x_j = q^{n-t-k-u} \binom{n-t}{u} - \binom{n-t}{u}$$

$u = 0, 1, 2, \ldots, d - t - 1$, since it is readily verified that the determinant of the coefficient matrix is nonzero. Since the weight distribution alone of the code determines the distribution for the orthogonal code (MacWilliams, 1962; cf. Section 1.5) the weight distribution for A' is determined as well, and both are independent of the particular t-subset T chosen.

We use $D(C)$ to denote the set of domains of the code C. Now since B is scalar complete to level w_0, we see that the number of domains of weight $w \leq \min(n - t, w_0)$ in $D(B'(T))$ is independent of the particular subset chosen.

Let F_w be the set of domains of weight w in $D(B)$. Let $\bar{F}_w$ be the set of complements of the members of F_w in S. To show that F_w is a t design it is sufficient, by Proposition 2.1, Corollary 3, to show that $\bar{F}_w$ is a t design. But the number of members of $\bar{F}_w$ containing a given t-subset T of S is the number of members of F_w that exclude it, which is the number of domains of weight w in $D(B'(T))$, and this number is, as stated, independent of the choice of the t-subset T. This completes the part of the theorem relating to code B. The proof of the part of the theorem involving $D(A)$ is inductive. Since $d \leq v_0$ and d is the girth of $D(A)$, the number of domains of weight d in $D(A)$ that contain a given t-subset T of S is the number of domains in $D(A'(T))$ of weight $d - t$, which is independent of the choice of T since A is scalar complete to level d. Thus the domains of weight d in $D(A)$ form a t design. Proceeding by induction, we assume that for some v satisfying $d < v \leq v_0$, if v satisfies $d \leq v' < v$, then the domains of weight v' in $D(A)$ form a t design. Now for any t-subset T of S, the number of vectors of weight $v - t$ in $A'(T)$ is independent of T. Let F_v be the family of domains of weight v in $D(A)$. We need only show that the number of domains of weight $v - t$ in $D(A'(T))$ arising from members of F_v is independent of T. But all domains of weight $v - t$ in $D(A'(T))$ arise from domains of weight $\leq v$ in $D(A)$ and by Proposition 2.1, Corollary 2, and the induction hypothesis, the number arising from domains of weight $< v$ is independent of T. Since the number of vectors of weight $v - t$ in $A'(T)$ arising from members of F_v is the total number of vectors of weight $v - t$ in $A'(T)$ less those arising from vectors of weight $< v$ in A and this number is independent of T. By the scalar completeness condition, we see that the number of domains of weight $v - t$ in $D[A'(T)]$ arising from members of F_v is independent of T, which completes the theorem. □

Theorem 6.1 can be used to create new t designs by applying the theorem to codes for which the weight distribution is known. A catalog of several of these is given by Assmus and Mattson (1969), and the automorphism groups of some of the codes and designs discussed are given. This catalog gives nontrivial 5-designs that are not associated with the Mathieu groups, as well as an infinite family of 3-designs. See also Section 2.7 for the work of Pless (1972a).

3.7 Perfect Codes and t Designs

In this section we consider, without loss of generality, that every code is a set of functions from an n-set S to a ring R, since the alphabet A may be identified with a ring of order $|A|$, one of which, of course, exists for each finite cardinal A. In most cases R will be a finite field; however, this need not always be essential to the discussion. The set of all such functions we will refer to as the *entire module*.

Definition A code C over R of minimum distance $d = 2e + 1$ is *perfect* if every member of the entire module is within distance e of some member of the code.

Definition The set of members of the entire module that lie within distance r of a fixed member f is called a sphere of radius r about the center f.

We then see that a code of distance $2e + 1$ is perfect if and only if the set of disjoint spheres of radius e about the code functions exhausts the entire module.

If C is a code consisting of functions from an n-set into a ring of order q, then each sphere of radius r contains $\sum_{j=0}^{r} \binom{n}{j}(q - 1)^j$ members of the entire module. If the code is of distance $d = 2e + 1$, we immediately have the "sphere-packing bound"

$$|C| \leq q^n \Big/ \sum_{j=0}^{e} \binom{n}{j}(q-1)^j$$

with equality if and only if C is perfect.

If q is a prime power, it is now known (Tietäväinen, 1973) that the only perfect q-ary codes are the following, as shown in Chapter 2:

  (i) The binary repetition codes.
  (ii) The perfect q-ary codes with $d = 3$ and $n = (q^r - 1)/(q - 1)$ for some integer r.
  (iii) The perfect Golay binary code with $d = 7$ and $n = 23$.
  (iv) The ternary Golay code with $d = 5$ and $n = 11$.

For future reference we note that in any code C of distance $2e + 1$ containing zero, functions f and g of weight $2e + 1$ on a set S into a ring R cannot agree on a subset X of S where $|X| \geq e + 1$, since $d(f, g) \leq w(f) + w(g) - 2|X|$, whenever f and g agree on X.

Theorem 7.1 (*Assmus and Mattson, 1967a*) If a scalar complete code C on a set S over $GF(q)$ and of minimum distance $d = 2e + 1$ is perfect and contains the zero chain, then the set D of weight d domains of C is a $(q - 1)^e$-$(e + 1, 2e + 1, n)$ configuration, where $|S| = n$.

Proof Let V be the set of all chains on S over $GF(q)$. Let X be any $(e + 1)$-subset of S. Then X is the domain of $(q - 1)^{e+1}$ chains of V. Let $V(X)$ denote the set of all such chains.

Now every chain f of $V(X)$ is within distance e of some uniquely determined code chain $x(f)$. Since the code C contains the zero chain, each nonzero code chain is of weight $2e + 1$ or greater, and we see that in order to be within distance e of $x(f)$, we must have dom $f \subset$ dom $x(f)$ and further f and $x(f)$ must agree on dom f. Thus it is evident that x is a one-to-one map of $V(X)$ onto the set of code chains of weight $2e + 1$. Let $D(X) = \{$dom $x(f): f \in V(X)\}$. Clearly, for any $Y \in D$, $X \subseteq Y$ if and only if $Y \in D(X)$. But since the code is scalar complete,

$$|D(X)| = \frac{|V(X)|}{q - 1} = (q - 1)^e$$

independent of the choice of $(e + 1)$-set X, which establishes the theorem. □

Corollary If a binary perfect code of distance $d = 2e + 1$ exists, then $\binom{n-i}{e+1-i}/\binom{2e+1-i}{e+1-i}$ is an integer for $i = 0, 1, 2, \ldots, e$. In particular, $(n + 1)/(e + 1)$ is an integer.

3.7 Perfect Codes and t Designs

Proof The result is immediate from Corollary 1 of Proposition 2.1, noting especially the case $i = e$. □

As mentioned in the previous chapter, this result rules out the existence of a binary (90, 78) perfect code with $d = 5$.

The reader might observe that if the code C is defined over an arbitrary ring, an appropriate condition can be chosen to replace scalar completeness. At present such generality seems to be unwarranted in any practical sense.

The theorem also follows directly from Theorem 6.1 in the case of linear codes, after appropriate analysis of the weight distribution in a perfect linear code or, equivalently (and in fact), that of its dual.

When the above theorem is applied to the perfect Hamming–Golay codes of distance three, the associated $(q - 1)$-$(2, 3, (q^m - 1)/(q - 1))$ configuration consists of the set of all collinear triples in the projective geometry $PG(m - 1, q)$ (see Chapter 2). When applied to the nonlinear binary Vasil'ev codes (see Chapter 2) the results yield an abundance of nonisomorphic Steiner triple systems (Assmus and Mattson, 1966c). The perfect Golay codes with $d = 7$ and 5, respectively, yield the Mathieu systems, $S(4, 7, 23)$ and $S(4, 5, 11)$ (see Section 3.2).

Theorem 7.1 has a partial converse. This is given in the following theorem.

Theorem 7.2 (*Assmus and Mattson, 1967a*) Let C be linear code of weight $2e + 1$ on a set S over $GF(q)$. If D, the set of belts of $M(C)$, forms a $(q - 1)^e$-$(e + 1, 2e + 1, n)$ design, then C is perfect.

Proof Let us assume that the above hypotheses are valid, but that C is not perfect. Let v be a chain of least weight which is not within distance e of any code chain. Since the zero chain belongs to C, we have $w(v) \geq e + 1$. Let X be an $(e + 1)$-subset of dom v. Then X is in $(q - 1)^e$ members of D, which will constitute a subset $D(X)$. Since C is scalar complete, there are $(q - 1)^{e+1}$ code vectors whose domains are in $D(X)$. By linearity, these vectors must all be distinct on X. Thus one of these chains, say a, agrees with v on X. Thus $0 < w(a - v) \leq w(v) - 1$. Thus by choice of v, $a - v$ is within distance e of some code chain b. But $d(v - a, b) \leq e$ implies that $w(v - (a + b)) \leq e$. But $a + b \in C$, which contradicts the existence of v and establishes the theorem. □

Corollary A perfect linear code is spanned by its minimum weight vectors.

Proof Let V be the subspace spanned by the minimum weight vectors of C. Then the belts of $M(V)$ are the belts of $M(C)$. Thus V is perfect. In order to exhaust the entire module, we see that $|V| = |C|$; hence $V = C$. □

The interested reader can also verify that if one makes a simple parity check extension of a perfect binary code that contains the zero chain, then the set of minimal weight domains of the code yields a Steiner system $S(e + 2, d + 1, n + 1)$.

3.8 Nearly Perfect Codes and t Designs

It has been seen that one can obtain t designs from perfect codes, that is, codes that satisfy the equality of the Hamming sphere-packing bound. It is possible to obtain t designs from those codes called *nearly perfect* [by Goethals and Snover (1972), whose work is presented in this section] that satisfy a specialized version of the Johnson bound (see Section 1.11). The specialized version of the bound is proved here, using the following notation. Given the vector space $V_n(q)$, let $S_r(v)$ denote the sphere of radius r (in the Hamming metric) with center v. Given a nonperfect code C of distance $2e + 1$, there is at least one vector of the space that is at distance greater than e from every code vector. Let $T(v)$ denote the set of vectors at distance $e + 1$ from the particular code vector v. The set $T(v)$ can be partitioned into two classes, namely

$$T_\alpha(v) = \{x \in T(v) \mid \exists u \in C, x \in S_e(u)\}$$

and

$$T_\beta(v) = T(v) - T_\alpha(v)$$

Lemma 8.1 Let C be a binary code of distance $d = 2e + 1$. Then for each $v \in C$,

$$|T_\alpha(v)| \leq \left\lfloor \frac{n-e}{e+1} \right\rfloor \binom{n}{e}$$

Proof Choose $x \in T_\alpha(v)$. Then $x \in S_e(u)$ for some $u \in C$, and $d(x, v) = e + 1$, $d(x, u) \leq e$, and $d(u, v) \geq 2e + 1$, which, together with the triangle inequality, yields $d(u, v) = 2e + 1$. This implies

$$|T_\alpha(v) \cap S_e(u)| = \binom{2e+1}{e+1}$$

since each vector y of this set must agree with v in all coordinate positions except for those $2e + 1$ in which u and v differ; further, y must agree with v in all but $e + 1$ of these. Consequently,

$$|T_\alpha(v)| = \binom{2e+1}{e+1} |N_{2e+1}(v)|$$

3.8 Nearly Perfect Codes and t Designs

where

$$N_{2e+1}(v) = \{x \mid x \in C, d(v, x) = 2e + 1\}$$

Since any two vectors of $N_{2e+1}(v)$ are at least distance $2e + 1$ from one another, the $2e + 1$ sets of coordinate places in which both differ from v can agree on at most an e-subset. Since there are at most $[(n - e)/(e + 1)]$ $(2e + 1)$-subsets of an n-set intersecting in a given e-subset, then

$$|N_{2e+1}(v)| \leq \lfloor (n - e)/(e + 1) \rfloor \binom{n}{e} \bigg/ \binom{2e + 1}{e + 1}$$

and

$$|T_\alpha(v)| \leq \lfloor (n - e)/(e + 1) \rfloor \binom{n}{e} \quad \square$$

Corollary For each $v \in C$

$$|T_\beta(v)| \geq \binom{n}{e + 1} - \lfloor (n - e)/(e + 1) \rfloor \binom{n}{e}$$

Proof This is immediate from the fact that for given v

$$|T_\alpha(v)| + |T_\beta(v)| = \binom{n}{e + 1} \quad \square$$

Theorem 8.1 (*Specialized Johnson Bound*) For any binary code C of length n and distance $d = 2e + 1$

$$|C| \left\{ \left(\frac{1}{\lfloor n/(e + 1) \rfloor} \right) \binom{n}{e} \left(\frac{n - e}{e + 1} - \left\lfloor \frac{n - e}{e + 1} \right\rfloor \right) + \sum_{j=0}^{e} \binom{n}{j} \right\} \leq 2^n$$

Proof There are at least $|\bigcup_{v \in C} T_\beta(v)|$ vectors of the space not contained in any $S_e(v)$, $v \in C$. A given vector can belong to at most $[n/(e + 1)]$ distinct sets $T_\beta(v)$, $v \in C$, and therefore by the preceding corollary

$$\left| \bigcup_{v \in C} T_\beta(v) \right| \geq \frac{|C|}{\lfloor n/(e + 1) \rfloor} \left(\binom{n}{e + 1} - \left\lfloor \frac{n - e}{e + 1} \right\rfloor \binom{n}{e} \right)$$

which establishes the theorem. $\square$

Notice that this is a version of Theorem 11.3 of Chapter 1 in the form we require.

Definition A binary code that satisfies the equality of the specialized Johnson inequality is called nearly perfect.

Note that in a nearly e-error-correcting perfect code any vector is at most a distance $e + 1$ from a codeword, that is, nearly perfect codes are also quasi-perfect (see Section 1.5). Examining the requirements for equality in the overall proof of the specialized inequality shows that in any nearly perfect e-error-correcting binary code of length n any vector at a distance greater than e from every code vector is at distance $e + 1$ from exactly $\lfloor n/(e + 1) \rfloor$ code vectors; any vector at distance e from a given code vector is at distance $e + 1$ from exactly $\lfloor (n - e)/(e + 1) \rfloor$ other code vectors.

Theorem 8.2 In any nearly perfect e-error-correcting code C of length n the code vectors at distance $d = 2e + 1$ from a given code vector v determine a t design with parameters $\lfloor (n - e)/(e + 1) \rfloor$-$(e, d, n)$.

Proof Let S be the set of coordinate positions of the vector space of the code. Let $N_d(v)$ denote the set of code vectors at a distance d from v. Any vector u of $N_d(v)$ determines a d-subset of S, namely those coordinate positions in which u and v differ. But it has been noted that any e-subset of S is contained in precisely $\lfloor (n - e)/(e + 1) \rfloor$ such d subsets. □

Theorem 8.3 In any nearly perfect e-error-correcting code of length n the set $T_\beta(v)$ of vectors at a distance $e + 1$ from a code vector v and at a distance greater than e from every other code vector determine a t design.

Proof Let A denote the t design of Theorem 8.2. Let D denote the t design obtained from A by replacing each block β of A by the set of all $(e + 1)$-subsets of β. The design D has parameters λ^*-$(e, e + 1, n)$, where $\lambda^* = (e + 1) \lfloor (n - e)/(e + 1) \rfloor$.

Let C denote the trivial e design of all $(e + 1)$-subsets of S, the set of coordinate positions. It has parameters $(n - e)$-$(e, e + 1, n)$.

Now consider the set B of all $(e + 1)$-subsets of coordinate positions for which there exists an element of $T_\beta(v)$ that differs from v in this set of coordinate positions. These $(e + 1)$-subsets are precisely those that are not contained in the d-subsets of the design A; hence this set B of $(e + 1)$-subsets consists of the set of blocks of C with the blocks of D removed. Thus every e-subset occurs $(n - e) - (e + 1) \lfloor (n - e)/(e + 1) \rfloor$ times in the blocks of B, and B is the required design. □

Note that if $n - e \equiv 0 \mod(e + 1)$ in the preceding theorem, the specialized Johnson bound becomes the sphere-packing bound, and the nearly perfect code is perfect. If a is the least positive residue of $(n + 1) \mod(e + 1)$, any nearly perfect code with $n \equiv -1 \mod(e + 1)$ is perfect. However, it was shown in the corollary to Theorem 7.1 that in a perfect code n must be congruent to $-1 \mod(e + 1)$, so that this result is not surprising.

3.9 Balanced Codes and t Designs

Moreover, for $a = 0$ the design of Theorem 8.2 is an $e + 1$ design with $\lambda_{e+1} = 1$, namely the Steiner system of Theorem 7.2.

Again a simple parity check extension of a nearly perfect e-error-correcting code of length n gives rise to an $e + 1$ design on an $(n + 1)$-set with parameters $[(n - e)/(e + 1)]$-$(e + 1, 2e + 2, n + 1)$. (Consider the vectors at a distance $2e + 2$ from a given vector v, and the coordinates in which they differ.)

This in turn implies (cf. Proposition 2.2 and corollary) that in any nearly perfect e-error-correcting code of length n the vectors at a distance $2e + 2$ from a given vector v determine a t design with parameters λ^*-$(e, 2e + 2, n)$ with

$$\lambda^* = \left\lfloor \frac{n - e}{e + 1} \right\rfloor \frac{n - 2e - 1}{e + 2}$$

Nearly perfect codes were also studied by Semakov et al. (1971) (under the name uniformly packed codes) from a different point of view, but similar results were obtained.

3.9 Balanced Codes and t Designs

A binary code is *balanced* if each word has the same weight r, where $r < n$, the dimension of the code space. It is clear that the incidence matrix (see Chapter 2) of a t design can be interpreted as a balanced code in two ways: One can use either the rows or columns of the matrix as code vectors. If the incidence vectors corresponding to varieties are taken as codewords, then there is the advantage that the distance between codewords is constant and easily calculated. Indeed, given any two binary vectors of length n, then

$$d(u, v) = w(u) + w(v) - 2(u, v) \tag{9.1}$$

where (u, v) denotes the real dot product or *correlation* of u and v. If u and v are vectors of an incidence matrix corresponding to two distinct varieties of a t design, then $w(u) = w(v) = \lambda_1$ and $(u, v) = \lambda_2$ and $d(u, v) = 2(\lambda_1 - \lambda_2)$. Following standard practice, λ_1 will henceforth be denoted by r and λ_2 by λ, if there is no danger of ambiguity. A code is *equidistant* if the distance between any pair of distinct code vectors is constant. Thus the vectors corresponding to the varieties of the incidence matrix of a t design form a balanced equidistant code. This section examines certain conditions that guarantee that the code vectors form the incidence matrix of a t design.

Let $C(n, r, \lambda)$ denote a balanced binary code of length n in which every word has length r and the maximum correlation λ. The following theorems are given by Semakov and Zinov'ev (1969a, b).

Theorem 9.1 (*Semakov and Zinov'ev, 1969a, b*) The number a of words in the balanced code $C = C(n, r, \lambda)$ with $\lambda < r^2/n$ satisfies $a \leq n(r - \lambda)/(r^2 - n\lambda)$ with equality if and only if the vectors of C correspond to the incidence vectors of the varieties of a balanced incomplete block design (cf. Section 2.3) with parameters

$$\left(\frac{n(r - \lambda)}{r^2 - n\lambda}, n, r, \frac{r(r - \lambda)}{r^2 - n\lambda}, \lambda\right)$$

Proof Assume that such a balanced incomplete block design exists. (*Note*: the parameters satisfy basic relations on the parameters of a balanced incomplete block design.) Clearly the incidence vectors of its varieties form the required code.

Conversely, assume that such a code exists.

Let the code vectors be denoted by $v_1, v_2, \ldots, v_a$. By hypothesis $(v_i, v_j) \leq \lambda$ for $i \neq j$. Hence

$$\sum_{i \neq j} (v_i, v_j) \leq \lambda a(a - 1) \qquad (9.2)$$

Now consider the matrix

$$M = \begin{pmatrix} v_1 \\ v_2 \\ \vdots \\ v_a \end{pmatrix}$$

The sum $S = \sum_{i \neq j} (v_i, v_j)$ over the rows of M can in turn be computed along the columns. Let k_s denote the number of ones in the sth column of M. Then

$$S = \sum_{s=1}^{n} k_s(k_s - 1) = \sum_{s=1}^{n} k_s^2 - \sum_{s=1}^{n} k_s = \sum_{s=1}^{n} k_s^2 - ar$$

However,

$$\sum_{s=1}^{n} k_s^2 \geq \frac{1}{n}\left(\sum_{s=1}^{n} k_s\right)^2 = \frac{(ar)^2}{n}$$

with equality only if all k_s are equal. This yields

$$S \geq ar(ar - n)/n$$

This, with (9.2) and the fact that $\lambda < r^2/n$, yields

$$a \leq n(r - \lambda)/(r^2 - n\lambda)$$

But if $a = n(r - \lambda)/(r^2 - n\lambda)$, then all k_s must be equal and (v_i, v_j) must equal λ for all distinct subscripts i, j, $i, j = 1, 2, \ldots, a$. Thus the matrix M can be

3.9 Balanced Codes and t Designs

considered as an incidence matrix for a balanced incomplete block design with the parameters given. □

The case of $C(n, r, \lambda)$ codes with $\lambda = r^2/n$ is also of interest. Before dealing with this case a lemma is required.

Lemma 9.1 If in a balanced code $\lambda = r^2/n$, then $\lambda - 1 < (r - 1)^2/(n - 1)$.

Proof Consider $(n - \lambda)^2$. Since in a balanced code $n > \lambda$, we have

$$0 < (n - \lambda)^2 = n^2 + \lambda^2 - 2n\lambda = n^2 + \lambda^2 - 2r^2$$

then

$$4r^2 < n^2 + \lambda^2 + 2n\lambda$$

and thus

$$2r < n + \lambda$$

Hence

$$0 = r^2 - n\lambda > 2r - n - \lambda$$

and

$$(n - 1)(\lambda - 1) < (r - 1)^2 \quad \square$$

Theorem 9.2 (*Semakov and Zinov'ev, 1969a, b*) The number a of words in the balanced code $C = C(n, r, \lambda)$ with $\lambda = r^2/n$ satisfies $a \leq n(n - 1)/(n - r)$ with equality if and only if the code vectors of C correspond to the blocks of an affine-resolvable, balanced, incomplete block design with parameters

$$\left(n, \frac{n(n-1)}{n-r}, \frac{r(n-1)}{n-r}, r, \frac{r(r-1)}{n-r}\right)$$

Proof Assume that such a balanced incomplete block design exists. Since the design is resolvable and any pair of blocks intersects in either 0 or $\lambda = r^2/n$ varieties (see Chapter 2), the incidence vectors corresponding to the blocks of the design therefore have correlation either 0 or λ, and each such vector has weight r. This guarantees the existence of a code C with the required number of words. Conversely, let C be any code $C(n, r, \lambda)$ with a words. Let the codewords be $v_1, v_2, \ldots, v_a$. Consider the matrix

$$M = \begin{pmatrix} v_1 \\ v_2 \\ \vdots \\ v_a \end{pmatrix}$$

Then M has the property that no column of M contains more than $R = r(n-1)/(n-r)$ ones. Indeed, suppose that the sth column contains R_s ones. Consider the set S of all codewords with a one in the sth column. Deleting this coordinate position from S, we obtain a code $C_s(n-1, r-1, \lambda - 1)$. But by Lemma 9.1, $\lambda - 1 < (r-1)^2/(n-1)$. Hence by Theorem 9.1, this code has at most $(n-1)(r-\lambda)/[(r-1)^2 - (n-1)(\lambda-1)]$ code vectors. Simplification yields

$$R_s \leqslant (n-1)(r-\lambda)/(n+\lambda-2r) = (n-1)r/(n-r)$$

Now since the code is balanced,

$$a \leqslant nR/r = n(n-1)/(n-r)$$

with equality if and only if each column of M contains exactly $(n-1)r/(n-r)$ ones.

Now consider the case of equality. In this case the code $C_s(n-1, r-1, \lambda - 1)$ for each column s has vectors corresponding to the incidence vectors of varieties of a balanced incomplete block design, with blocks of size $r(r-1)/(n-r)$. In terms of M this states that if we consider the set of rows with ones in the sth column, then each of the remaining columns of this portion on M contains exactly $r(r-1)/(n-r)$ ones, that is, the scalar product of any two rows is $r(r-1)/(n-r)$. If M is viewed as the incidence matrix of a configuration whose blocks correspond to rows and whose varieties correspond to columns, every pair of varieties occurs in exactly $r(r-1)/(n-r)$ blocks.

Now since every row contains exactly r ones, the configuration is a balanced incomplete block design with the given parameters. To see that the design is affine resolvable, we note that by Theorem 9.1 the rows of $C_s(n-1, r-1, \lambda - 1)$ have correlation $\lambda - 1$. Hence any two blocks containing s intersect in exactly $\lambda = r^2/n$ varieties. Hence any pair of blocks is either disjoint or has intersection r^2/n, and by the results of Section 2.3 the design is affine resolvable. □

3.10 Equidistant Codes

As mentioned earlier, an equidistant code is a binary code in which the distance between any pair of distinct codewords is independent of the pair chosen. Equidistant codes are closely related to balanced codes, as the following lemma shows.

Lemma 10.1 Let A be an equidistant code of dimension n and distance d with at least two words. Then there exists a balanced equidistant code $C(n, d, d/2)$ with $|A| - 1$ words.

3.10 Equidistant Codes

Proof Let the code vectors be $v_1, v_2, \ldots, v_a$, where $|A| = a$. Consider the matrix

$$M = \begin{pmatrix} v_1 \\ v_2 \\ \vdots \\ v_a \end{pmatrix}$$

If in any column the roles of zero and one are interchanged, the distance between codewords remains unchanged. Thus by such an operation the matrix M can be transformed into another $a \times n$ matrix M^* whose first row is zero and which is such that the distance between any two rows of M^* is d. Let M_1^* be the matrix derived from M^* by removing the first row. Then every row of M_1^* has d ones. Moreover, if u and v are any pair of distinct columns of M_1^*, then since $d(u, v) = w(u) + w(v) - 2(u, v)$, we see that the correlation $\lambda = (u, v) = d/2$. □

Corollary In an equidistant code with three or more words d is always even.

Theorem 10.1 (*Bose and Shrikhande, 1959b*) Let A be a binary code of dimension $4t - 1$ and distance $2t$. Then $|A| \leq 4t$, with equality if and only if there exists a balanced incomplete block design with parameters

$$(4t - 1, 4t - 1, 2t, 2t, t).$$

Proof Let $\bar{d}$ denote the average distance between distinct words of A. Let $|A| = a$, and let the codewords be $v_1, v_2, \ldots, v_a$. Consider the matrix

$$M = \begin{pmatrix} v_1 \\ v_2 \\ \vdots \\ v_a \end{pmatrix}$$

Then

$$\bar{d} = 2 \sum_{i>j} d(v_i, v_j)/a(a - 1)$$

But $\bar{d} \geq d$ with equality if and only if the code is equidistant. Moreover, if x_s denotes the number of ones in the sth column of M,

$$\sum_{i>j} d(v_i, v_j) = \sum_{s=1}^{4t-1} x_s(a - x_s)$$

But $x_s(a - x_s) \leq a^2/4$, with equality if and only if $x_s = a/2$. Hence

$$2t = d \leq \bar{d} \leq 2\left(\sum_{s=1}^{4t-1} x_s(a - x_s)\right)/a(a - 1) \leq (4t - 1)a/2(a - 1)$$

whence $a \leq 4t$.

Now consider the case of equality. Since $\bar{d} = d$, the code is equidistant. Moreover, since each $x_s = a/2$, every column of M contains $2t$ ones. Applying the construction of Lemma 10.1 to the matrix M, one obtains a matrix M_1^* from M in which each of the columns contains exactly $2t$ ones. Moreover, the matrix M_1^* has correlation of t between its columns. Thus the columns of M_1^* are the incidence vectors of a balanced incomplete block design with the given parameters. □

Let C be an equidistant code of dimension n. Let $M = M(C)$ denote the $|C| \times n$ matrix whose rows are the vectors of C. Throughout this section let x_s, $s = 1, 2, \ldots, n$, denote the number of ones in the sth column of M. The code C is said to be trivial if, for $s = 1, 2, \ldots, n$, $x_s \in \{0, 1, |C|, |C| - 1\}$. Otherwise C is nontrivial.

Deza (1973) has shown that in a nontrivial equidistant code C of distance $2t$, $|C| \leq t^2 + t + 2$, with equality only if there exists a projective plane of order t. The following lemmas will be employed in the proof.

Lemma 10.2 Let α, β, α_1, and β_1 be any four real numbers, where $\alpha\beta \geq 0$. Then

$$F = \alpha_1(\beta - \beta_1) + \beta_1(\alpha - \alpha_1) - \frac{\alpha\beta_1(\beta - \beta_1)}{\beta} - \frac{\beta\alpha_1(\alpha - \alpha_1)}{\alpha} \geq 0$$

Proof The expression F simplifies to $\alpha\beta[(\alpha_1/\alpha) - (\beta_1/\beta)]^2$, which is clearly nonnegative. □

Lemma 10.3 Let C be a binary code of length n. Let E and F be nonempty subsets of C such that $E \cup F = X$ and $E \cap F = \emptyset$. Then

$$\sum_{\substack{x \in E \\ y \in F}} d(x, y) \geq \frac{|F|}{2|E|} \sum_{x, y \in E} d(x, y) + \frac{|E|}{2|F|} \sum_{x, y \in F} d(x, y)$$

Proof Consider the matrix $M = M(C)$. Since the Hamming distance is additive on the columns of M, it is sufficient to prove the result for a column of M. Let us assume without loss of generality that the vectors of E are the first e rows of M, and those of F the remaining $m - e = f$. Let us assume that column c contains e_1 ones in the first e rows and f_1 ones in the remaining f columns. Let $d^c(x, y)$ denote the Hamming distance between x and y in column c.

3.10 Equidistant Codes

Now

$$\sum_{\substack{x \in E \\ y \in F}} d^c(x, y) - \frac{|F|}{2|E|} \sum_{x, y \in F} d^c(x, y) - \frac{|E|}{2|F|} \sum_{x, y \in F} d^c(x, y)$$

$$= e_1(f - f_1) + f_1(e - e_1) - \frac{fe_1(e - e_1)}{e} - \frac{ef_1(f - f_1)}{f}$$

which by Lemma 10.2 is nonnegative. This is sufficient to establish the lemma. □

The following notation will be used in the next lemma. If C is a binary code of length n containing m words and $M = M(C)$, let x_s denote the number of ones in the sth column of M, and let $t_s = \min(x_s, m - x_s)$. Further, let $a = \min d(x, y)$ and $b = \max d(x, y)$, where (x, y) ranges over all pairs of distinct codewords, and T_s denotes the number of columns of M identical to the sth column.

Lemma 10.4 Let C be a binary code of length n containing m codewords. If the sth column of $M(C)$ is such that $t_s \neq 0$, then

$$T_s \leq b - a + \frac{am}{2t_s(m - t_s)}$$

Proof Let M^* denote the matrix derived from M by removing the T_s columns that are identical with the sth. Let E be the set of rows of M^* in which the sth column contains a one, and F the complementary set. Let v^* denote the row of M^* corresponding to the row v of M, and let d^* denote the Hamming metric defined on the rows of M^*. Note that if $x^* \in E$ and $y^* \in F$, then

$$d^*(x^*, y^*) = d(x, y) - T_s \leq b - T_s$$

Now if x^* and y^* are distinct members of E, then $d^*(x^*, y^*) = d(x, y) \geq a$. A similar statement holds in F. Applying Lemma 10.3, one obtains

$$t_s(m - t_s)(b - T_s) \geq \sum_{\substack{x^* \in E \\ y^* \in F}} d^*(x^*, y^*)$$

$$\geq \frac{|E|}{2|F|} \sum_{x^*, y^* \in F} d^*(x^*, y^*) + \frac{|F|}{2|E|} \sum_{x^*, y^* \in E} d^*(x^*, y^*)$$

$$\geq \tfrac{1}{2}|E|(|F| - 1)a + \tfrac{1}{2}|F|(|E| - 1)a$$

$$= t_s(m - t_s)a - \tfrac{1}{2}ma$$

which yields the lemma. □

Corollary 1 If $T_s > (b - a) + (a/2t_s)$ and $t_s \neq 0$, then

$$m \leq \frac{t_s^2}{[(t_s - a)/(2(T_s - b + a))]}$$

Proof By the theorem

$$2t_s(m - t_s)(T_s - b + a) \leq am$$

which reduces to the stated inequality. □

Corollary 2 Let C be an equidistant code of length n of distance $2k$ containing m words. Then $t_s(m - t_s) \leq mk$.

Proof The corollary is clearly true if $t_s = 0$. If $t_s > 0$, the result follows from the lemma since $T_s \geq 1$. □

Lemma 10.5 Let C be an equidistant code of length n of distance $2k$ with m words. If $t_s \leq [(m + 2k - 1)/(k + 1)] - 1$ for all s satisfying $1 \leq s \leq n$, then $t_s \leq 1$ for all such s.

Proof If $m = 1$, the result is trivial. If $m > 1$, apply Lemma 10.1 to obtain a new equidistant code C^* which contains the zero codeword but for which t_s remains unchanged. The remaining codewords form a balanced code $C(n, 2k, k)$. Let $[(m + 2k - 1)/(k + 1)] = t$. Then (i) $t_s < t$, for $s = 1, 2, \ldots, n$, and (ii) $m \geq k(t - 2) + t + 1$. Partition the columns of $M = M(C^*)$ into two types, those of type I containing $t - 1$ or fewer ones and those of type II containing $m - t + 1$ or more ones. Since $t_s \leq t$, every column is of type I or type II. Since $m \geq 2t - 1$, the two sets are disjoint. To prove the lemma, it is sufficient to demonstrate that (a) the number of columns of type II does not exceed k, and that every word other than the zero word has at least k ones in the columns of type II. (Recall that the correlation in the balanced part of the code is k.) Assume that there are at least $k + 1$ columns of type II. Each such column contains $t - 2$ or fewer zeros in the nonzero rows. By (ii) $(m - 1) - (k + 1)(t - 2) \geq 2$. Therefore there are at least two (nonzero) codewords that have no zeros in their columns of type II, and these two words have a correlation of at least $k + 1$, a contradiction; hence there are at most k columns of type II. Now let u be a nonzero codeword of C^*. Let q denote the number of ones of u that lie in the columns of type II. Now $2k - q$ columns of type I contain ones in u. Consider the submatrix M' of M obtained from M by removing the row u and all columns of M that contain a zero in the row u.

3.10 Equidistant Codes

The matrix M' contains $q(m-2)$ ones in the columns that were of type II and no more than $(2k-q)(t-2)$ ones in the columns that were of type I. Since the correlation between nonzero codewords is k, the matrix M' contains $k(m-2)$ ones. Hence

$$(2k-q)(t-2) + q(m-2) \geq k(m-2), \qquad q \geq k - \frac{k(t-2)}{m-t}$$

But by (ii), $k(t-2) \leq m - t$, and since q is an integer, $q \geq k$. □

Recall that an equidistant code is trivial if and only if $t_s \leq 1$, for $s = 1, 2, \ldots, n$. Such trivial codes are easily constructed. Let J_{ms} denote the $m \times s$ matrix of ones and 0_{ms} the $m \times s$ matrix of all zeros. Let I_m denote the identity matrix of order M_1 and $K_m = J_{mm} - I_m$. Then the rows of the matrix

$$J_{ms} I_m \cdots I_m K_m \cdots K_m 0_{mt}$$

will always form a trivial equidistant code. In particular given any pair of parameters m and $2k$, one can always form a trivial equidistant code with distance $2k$ and m words by forming the matrix

$$I_m I_m \cdots I_m$$

where I_m occurs k times.

Theorem 10.2 Let C be an equidistant code of distance $2k$ which contains m words. If $m \geq k^2 + k + 3$, then the code is trivial.

Proof Note that if $m \geq k^2 + k + 3$, then $t_s \leq k + 1$ for $s = 1, 2, \ldots, n$. Indeed, if $t_s \geq k + 2$ and $m \geq k^2 + k + 3$, then

$$t_s(m - t_s) - mk \geq (k+2)(k^2+1) - k(k^2+k+3) > 0$$

a contradiction of Corollary 2 of Lemma 10.4. Also

$$[(m + 2k - 1)/(k+1)] - 1 \geq k + 1 \qquad \text{for} \qquad m \geq k^2 + k + 3$$

Hence $t_s \leq 1$, and the code is trivial. □

Clearly, if there is a projective plane π of order k (cf. Chapter 2), then there exists an equidistant code of distance $2k$ with $k^2 + k + 2$ words. To construct such a code, one can proceed as follows. Let P be the incidence matrix of π. Form a matrix M by adding $k - 1$ columns of ones to P and adjoin a row of zeros to the resulting matrix. The rows of this matrix produce the required code.

Van Lint (1973) has proved the converse theorem, namely, if there exists an equidistant code of distance $2k$ with $k^2 + k + 2$ codewords ($k > 1$), then there is a projective plane of order k. Before proving this result, let us dispose of the case $k = 1$. The code consisting of the rows of

$$\begin{pmatrix} 0 & 0 & 0 \\ 1 & 1 & 0 \\ 1 & 0 & 1 \\ 0 & 1 & 1 \end{pmatrix}$$

forms a nontrivial code of distance two and with four words. Having disposed of this situation, henceforth it will be assumed that $k > 1$.

Theorem 10.3 For $k > 1$ there exists a nontrivial equidistant code of distance $2k$ with $k^2 + k + 2$ words if and only if there exists a projective plane of order k.

Proof In view of the preceding comments, it is only necessary to show that the existence of such a code guarantees the existence of a projective plane of order k. Let $M' = M(C)$. Without loss of generality we may assume that M' has no columns of zeros only or ones only since such columns contribute nothing to distances between words. Applying the transformation of Lemma 10.1 to M', one obtains a matrix M whose first row is zero. Considering the sth column of M, by Lemma 10.4, Corollary 2 one obtains

$$t_s(m - t_s) \leqslant mk \tag{10.1}$$

There are two cases to consider. If $k = 2$, then there exists the projective plane $PG(2, 2)$. Let A denote the incidence matrix of its complementary design, a block design with parameters $(7, 7, 4, 4, 2)$. By adjoining a row of zeros to A we obtain a matrix whose rows are an equidistant code of distance four with eight code vectors. Hence the theorem is true for $k = 2$.

For $k > 2$ note that since the left side of $t_s(m - t_s)$ is quadratic, and if $t_s \geqslant k + 2$, recalling that $t_s \leqslant m/2$, it follows that $t_s(m - t_s) \geqslant k^3 + 2k^2$. But $mk = k^3 + k^2 + 2k$. Since $k > 2$, then (10.1) is violated. Hence for $k > 2$ the inequality $t_s \leqslant k + 1 < k^2 + 1$ is satisfied.

Now split the columns of M into two classes, namely those columns with at most $k + 1$ ones (type I) and those with at least $k^2 + 1$ ones (type II). These two classes are disjoint. Assume that the columns of type II precede the columns of type I.

Case (a) Suppose there are at least $k + 1$ columns of type II. Since all rows of C except the first one have weight $2k$ and mutual distance $2k$, there can be at most one row which has ones in $k + 1$ fixed columns of type II. However, these $k + 1$ columns of type II contain a total of at least

3.10 Equidistant Codes

$(k + 1)(k^2 + 1)$ ones and this is possible only if, besides the zero row, there is indeed one row with $k + 1$ ones in these $k + 1$ columns of type II and furthermore all other rows have k ones in these $k + 1$ columns. This means that after a suitable permutation M has the following form:

$$M = \begin{pmatrix} 0 & 0 & \cdots & 0 & 0 & 0 & \cdots & 0 & 0 & 0 & \cdots & 0 \\ & E^{(1)}_{k,k+1} & & & F^{(1)}_{k,k} & F^{(2)}_{k,k} & \cdots & F^{(k)}_{k,k} & & & & \\ & E^{(2)}_{k,k+1} & & & & & & & & & & \\ & \vdots & & & & & M^* & & & 0_{k^2+k,\,k-1} & & \\ & E^{(k+1)}_{k,k+1} & & & & & & & & & & \\ 1 & 1 & \cdots & 1 & 0 & 0 & \cdots & 0 & 1 & 1 & \cdots & 1 \end{pmatrix}$$

where 0_{pq} and J_{pq} are as defined previously, $E^{(i)}_{pq}$ is the $p \times q$ matrix with zeros in column i and ones elsewhere, and $F^{(i)}_{pq}$ is the $p \times q$ matrix with ones in row i and zeros elsewhere.

We have the following information about the rows of M^*:

(i) Each row of M^* has k ones, one below each of the matrices $F^{(i)}_{k,k}$, $i = 1, \ldots, k$.

(ii) If two rows of M^* follow $E^{(i)}_{k,k+1}$, resp. $E^{(j)}_{k,k+1}$, $i \neq j$, then these rows have one one in common; if they follow the same $E^{(i)}_{k,k+1}$, then they have no one in common.

From (i) and (ii) we see that M^* is the incidence matrix of a *transversal system* $T_k(k, k)$ [cf. Hall (1967a, p. 224)]. The existence of such a transversal system is equivalent to the existence of an *orthogonal array* $OA(k, k + 1)$ (Hall, 1967a, p. 224), which implies the existence of a $PG(2, k)$ [cf. Hall 1967a, p. 191)].

Case (b) In the remaining part of the proof we may assume that in M there are at most k columns of type II. Now, consider any nonzero row of M without loss of generality the second row, and let this row have q ones in the columns of type II. Then M has the following form:

$$\begin{pmatrix} 0 & 0 & \cdots & 0 & 0 & 0 & \cdots & 0 & 0 & 0 & \cdots & 0 & 0 & 0 & \cdots & 0 \\ 0 & 0 & \cdots & 0 & 1 & 1 & \cdots & 1 & 1 & 1 & \cdots & 1 & 0 & 0 & \cdots & 0 \\ & C_1 & & & & C_2 & & & & C_3 & & & & C_4 & & \end{pmatrix}$$

$\longleftarrow$ type II $\longrightarrow$ $\longleftarrow$ type I $\longrightarrow$

where C_2 is $k^2 + k$ by q and C_3 is $k^2 + k$ by $2k - q$. We count the total number of ones in C_2 and C_3 in two ways, using the fact that mutual distances are $2k$ and the definitions of types I and II. This yields

$$k(k^2 + k) \leq q(k^2 + k) + (2k - q)k$$

i.e.,

$$q \geq k - 1 \tag{10.2}$$

Now assume there are k columns of type II. Now C must have the following form:

$$\begin{pmatrix} 0 & 0 & \cdots & 0 & 0 & 0 & \cdots & 0 & 0 & 0 & \cdots & 0 \\ \hline & E^{(1)}_{m_1,k} & & & & & & & & & & \\ & E^{(2)}_{m_2,k} & & & & & & & & & & \\ & \vdots & & & & & & & & & & \\ & E^{(k)}_{m_k,k} & & & & & & & & & & \\ \hline & J_{\overline{m},k} & & & F^{(1)}_{\overline{m},k} & F^{(2)}_{\overline{m},k} & \cdots & F^{(\overline{m})}_{\overline{m},k} & & & & \end{pmatrix}$$

Clearly $m_i \leq k$, $i = 1, \ldots, k$. If $m_1 = m_2 = \cdots = m_k = 0$, then the code is trivial. Hence $m_i \neq 0$ for some i. Each of the $m_1 + m_2 + \cdots + m_k$ rows that has a zero in a type II column must have exactly one one above each of the matrices $F^{(i)}_{\overline{m},k}$, $i = 1, \ldots, \overline{m}$. Hence $\overline{m} \leq k + 1$. This implies $m_1 = m_2 = \cdots = m_k = k$, $\overline{m} = k + 1$. We now count the number of ones in M that are below the ones of the second row in two ways and find

$$k(k^2 + k) \leq (k - 1)^2 + (k + 1)k$$

i.e., $k \leq 1$, a contradiction.

This contradiction combined with (10.2) shows that it remains to consider the possibility that M has the form

$$C = \begin{pmatrix} 0 & 0 & \cdots & 0 & 0 & 0 & \cdots & 0 \\ J_{k^2+k+1,k-1} & & & & & C_1 & & \end{pmatrix}$$

where the columns of C_1 are all of type I. We have the following information about C_1:

(i) Each row of C_1 has exactly $k + 1$ ones.
(ii) Two distinct rows of C_1 have exactly one one in common.
(iii) Every column of C_1 has at most $k + 1$ ones, hence exactly $k + 1$ ones.

These are precisely the conditions required for C to be the incidence matrix of a projective plane. □

Vanstone (1974) has shown that any nontrivial balanced equidistant code of weight $k + 1$ and mutual distance $2k$ has at most $k^2 + k + 1$ words. He has also found nontrivial equidistant codes for $k = 2$ with eight words, which do not have the form of those given for $k > 2$ in the preceding theorem.

Exercises

3.11 Comments

From the results of this chapter it is obvious that the ties between various combinatorial structures and coding theory are very close and deep. The arguments leading to the construction of certain designs often parallel those used to construct good codes. The matroidal approach to coding taken here was in keeping with our aim to provide as broad a mathematical background as was reasonable. Most of the results contained in this chapter were not originally derived with the use of matroids. However, their application to problems of coding is interesting and provides an alternative point of view.

Exercises

1 A regular t-wise balanced design is a generalization of a t design. Such a design consists of a finite set V of elements called varieties together with a family of subsets of V called blocks, which satisfies the following axiom:

For every $i \leqslant t$ every i-subset of V occurs in precisely λ_i blocks of the design where λ_i is independent of the i-subset chosen.

Show that if D is a regular $2t$-wise balanced design, then the design D' formed by taking the blocks of D together with their complements is a regular $(2t + 1)$-wise balanced design.

2 If there exists a λ_1-(t, x, v) design and a λ_2-(t, k, x) design, show that there exists a $\lambda_1 \lambda_2$-(t, k, v) design.

3 Show that $(m - 1)$-$(3, 2m, 4m)$ designs are invariant under complementation.

4 Let M be a matroid defined on a set E. A *separator* of M is a subset S of E such that each circuit of M is contained either in S or $E - S$.

(i) Show that the set of separators of a matroid M is closed with respect to union, intersection, and complementation.

(ii) Show that S is a separator of M if and only if $M \cdot S = M \times S$.

(iii) Let N be a chain group over the integers. A chain is *primitive* if it is elementary and its coefficients are restricted to the values 1, -1, and 0. N is regular if every elementary chain is an (integral) multiple of a primitive chain. Show that if N is regular, then a subset S of E is a separator of $M(N)$ if and only if each chain f of N can be written in the form $g + h$, where g and h are chains of N such that dom $g \subseteq S$ and dom $h \subseteq E - S$.

5 A kth-order Steiner system can be defined as follows: Let D_i be a collection of nonempty i-sets of S, $i = 3, 4, \ldots, k$; a free t-set of S is one not containing any member of $D_3 \cup D_4 \cup \cdots \cup D_t$; for $t = 2, 3, \ldots, k - 1$, every free t-set is contained in precisely one member of D_{t+1} and every proper subset of every element of D_{t+1} is free. The system is closed if and only if there are no free k-sets.

Show that if $n = 2^{k-1} - 1$, then there is a closed kth-order Steiner system on n points. Can this be generalized?

6 Let D be an affine-resolvable, balanced, incomplete block design (ARBIBD) (Shrikhande (1953)).

(i) Show that the parameters can always be written in the form

$$v = nk = n^2[(n-t)t + 1], \quad b = nr = n[n^2t + n + 1], \quad \lambda = nt + 1$$

(ii) Show that no ARBIBD with these parameters exists when n and t are odd and (a) k is not a perfect square or (b) k is a perfect square and $nt \equiv 1 \mod 4$ and the square-free part of n contains a prime $\equiv 3 \mod 4$.

(iii) Show that no ARBIBD with these parameters exists when n is odd and t is even and (a) $(n-1)t + 1$ is not a perfect square, or (b) $(n-1)t + 1$ is a perfect square and $n + t \equiv 1 \mod 4$ and the square-free part of n contains a prime $\equiv 3 \mod 4$.

(iv) Show that no ARBIBD with these parameters exists for any value of t if $n \equiv 2 \mod 4$ and the square-free part of n contains a prime congruent to $3 \mod 4$.

7 If $A_n(t)$ denotes an affine-resolvable design with parameters listed in Exercise 6, show that for n a prime power the existence of a design $A_n(t)$ implies the existence of a design $A_n(nt + 1)$.

8 A BIBD with parameters (v, b, r, k, λ) is said to be α-resolvable if the blocks can be grouped into t sets $S_1, S_2, \ldots, S_t$, each of β blocks such that in each group every variety is replicated α times. An α-resolvable design is affine α-resolvable if any pair of blocks of the same group intersects in q_1 varieties and any pair from different groups intersects in q_2 varieties. Show that in an α-resolvable design $v | k^2$ and $b = v + (b/\beta) - 1$.

9 Show that, in any nontrivial, balanced, equidistant code C of distance $2k$, $|C| \leq k^2 + k + 1$, with equality if and only if there exists a projective plane of order k.

10 Show that if C is a balanced equidistant code of distance $2k$ and correlation one, then if no projective plane of order k exists, and $k \neq 6$, that $|C| \leq k^2 - 2$.

Exercises

11 What is the size of the largest balanced equidistant code of correlation one and distance 12? (This problem is unsolved.)

12 Show that the binary linear code generated as the row space of the incidence matrix of a projective plane of order ten (should such exist) would have dimension 56. Generalize this result.

APPENDIX A
The Möbius Inversion Formula

The Möbius inversion function $\mu(n)$ defined on the positive integers is given by

$$\mu(1) = 1$$
$$\mu(p_1 p_2 \cdots p_k) = (-1)^k \quad \text{if } p_i \neq p_j, \ i \neq j, \ p_i \text{ prime}$$
$$\mu(n) = 0 \quad \text{if } p^2 | n \text{ for some prime } p$$

If $n = p_1^{e_1} p_2^{e_2} \cdots p_k^{e_k} > 1$, then the only nonzero terms in the summation

$$\sum_{d|n} \mu(d)$$

are those for which $d = p_{i_1} p_{i_2} \cdots p_{i_j}$, $p_{i_a} \neq p_{i_b}$, $a \neq b$. It follows that

$$\sum_{d|n} \mu(d) = \mu(1) + \sum_{i=1}^{k} \mu(p_i) + \sum_{i \neq j} \mu(p_i p_j) + \cdots$$
$$= 1 + (-1)k + (-1)^2 \binom{k}{2} + \cdots + (-1)^k \binom{k}{k}$$
$$= (1-1)^k = 0$$

When $n = 1$ then $\mu(n) = 1$. The Möbius inversion formula states that if

$$h(n) = \sum_{d|n} g(d)$$

then

$$g(n) = \sum_{d|n} \mu\left(\frac{n}{d}\right) h(d) = \sum_{d|n} \mu(d) h\left(\frac{n}{d}\right)$$

To show this, consider the sum

$$\sum_{d|n} \mu(d) h\left(\frac{n}{d}\right) = \sum_{d|n} \mu(d) \left[\sum_{b|n/d} h(b) \right] = \sum_{bd|n} \mu(d) h(b) = \sum_{b|n} h(b) \left[\sum_{d|n/b} \mu(d) \right]$$

and, by a previous expression, this last bracket is zero unless $n/b = 1$, in which case the last equality reduces to $h(n)$, as required.

APPENDIX B
Lucas's Theorem

Let m and n be positive integers, $m > n$, and p a prime. If
$$m = \sum_i m_i p^i, \qquad n = \sum_i n_i p^i$$
are the p-ary expansions of m and n, respectively, $0 \leq m_i < p$, $0 \leq n_i < p$, then
$$\binom{m}{n} \equiv \prod_i \binom{m_i}{n_i} \bmod p$$

The proof of this statement is by induction and we suppose $m = m'p + m_0$, $n = n'p + n_0$, and $0 \leq m_0, n_0 < p$. We have then that

$$(1 + x)^m = \sum_{k=0}^{m} \binom{m}{k} x^k = (1 + x)^{m'p + m_0} = (1 + x)^{m'p}(1 + x)^{m_0}$$
$$\equiv (1 + x^p)^{m'}(1 + x)^{m_0} \bmod p$$
$$\equiv \left[\sum_{j=0}^{m'} \binom{m'}{j} x^{jp} \right] \left[\sum_{l=0}^{m_0} \binom{m_0}{l} x^l \right] \bmod p$$

Comparing the coefficient of x^n in the first and last equations yields

$$\binom{m}{n} = \binom{m'}{n'}\binom{m_0}{n_0} \bmod p$$

Repeating the argument on m' and n' yields, inductively, the result. The proof used here is that of Berlekamp (1968).

APPENDIX C
The Mathieu Groups

The Mathieu groups have been mentioned in several places in the text, mainly in connection with combinatorial designs and perfect codes. In this appendix we gather some information of a general nature on these remarkable groups.

We recall first some definitions. Let G be a permutation group of degree n acting on $\Delta = \{1, \ldots, n\}$. We say that G is k-transitive if for any two ordered k subsets $\delta_1 = \{i_1, \ldots, i_k\}$ and $\delta_2 = \{j_i, \ldots, j_k\}$ of Δ there exists an element $\sigma \in G$ such that

$$\sigma(i_s) = j_s, \quad s = 1, \ldots, k$$

We say that G is sharply k-transitive if there exists only one such element. Equivalently, G is sharply k-transitive if it is k-transitive and only the identity fixes k points.

If G is k-transitive and of degree n then it can be shown that the order of G, $|G|$, is divisible by $n(n-1) \cdots (n-k+1)$, while if G is sharply k-transitive of degree n, then $|G| = n(n-1) \cdots (n-k+1)$. Denote by G_i the subgroup of G that leaves i invariant. Then if G is sharply k-transitive of degree n, then G_i is sharply $(k-1)$-transitive on $\Delta \setminus \{i\}$. Clearly the symmetric group on n letters, S_n, is sharply n-transitive of degree n. It is also sharply $(n-1)$-transitive. Also, if $n \geq 3$, then A_n, the alternating group on n letters, is sharply $(n-2)$-transitive and of degree n. Apart from these well-known examples, highly transitive groups are very sparse. Indeed, no k-transitive groups other than A_n and S_n are known when $k \geq 6$ and we shall discuss all 4- and 5-transitive groups known here. A theorem of Jordan (Passman, 1968, p. 283) states that if G is a nontrivial, sharply k-transitive group of degree n, then if $k \geq 4$, there are only two possible cases, namely $k = 4$ and $n = 11$ or $k = 5$ and $n = 12$. The Mathieu groups M_{11} and M_{12} are such groups. We

207

give the presentation of these groups due to Passman (1968, p. 290) and consider the elements

$$x_1 = (4\ 5\ 6)(7\ 8\ 9)(10\ 11\ 12)$$
$$x_2 = (4\ 7\ 10)(5\ 8\ 11)(6\ 9\ 12)$$
$$x_3 = (5\ 6\ 7\ 10)(8\ 9\ 12\ 11)$$
$$x_4 = (5\ 8\ 6\ 12)(7\ 11\ 10\ 9)$$
$$x_5 = (5\ 11\ 6\ 9)(7\ 12\ 10\ 8)$$
$$x_6 = (14)(7\ 8)(9\ 11)(10\ 12)$$
$$x_7 = (12)(7\ 10)(8\ 11)(9\ 12)$$
$$x_8 = (23)(7\ 12)(8\ 10)(9\ 11)$$

Then $M_{11} = \langle x_1, x_2, x_3, x_4, x_5, x_6, x_7 \rangle$ is a sharply 4-transitive group of degree 11 acting on $\{1, 2, 4, 5, 6, \ldots, 12\}$ and $|M_{11}| = 11 \cdot 10 \cdot 9 \cdot 8 = 7920$. The group $\langle M_{11}, x_8 \rangle = M_{12}$ is sharply 5-transitive of degree 12 and $|M_{12}| = 12 \cdot |M_{11}| = 95{,}040$.

The three other Mathieu groups, M_{22}, M_{23}, and M_{24}, which are not sharply transitive, are, respectively, 3-transitive, 4-transitive, and 5-transitive. Their orders are given by $|M_{22}| = 443{,}520$, $|M_{23}| = 10{,}200{,}960$, and $|M_{24}| = 244{,}823{,}040$. M_{23} is the stabilizer of an element on which M_{24} acts and M_{11} is the stabilizer of an element on which M_{12} acts. All five of the Mathieu groups are, furthermore, simple. While there are no other 4- or 5 transitive groups known and no 6-transitive groups known (apart from S_n and A_n), there are other 3-transitive groups known, as shown by the linear fractional groups constructed in Chapter 1. Until recently these Mathieu groups were the only finite simple groups known which did not fit into a known infinite family. However, this is no longer true, since several other finite groups are now known with this property.

The character tables of M_{11} through M_{24} are given in Tables C-1 to C-5 taken from the following sources: M_{11} and M_{22} from Burgoyne and Fong (1966), M_{12} from Whitelaw (1966), and M_{23} and M_{24} from Todd (1966). In each case we have standardized notation to coincide with that of Todd (1966). In this notation the first line of the table gives the type of element which is contained in the conjugacy class corresponding to that column. Thus 5^2 indicates the conjugacy class consisting of products of two five cycles, all other elements being fixed. In the second line of the table the order of the group divided by the order of the conjugacy class is given as a more convenient number than the order of the conjugacy class. The first column of the table gives, of course, the dimension of the irreducible representation whose characters are given in that row.

Some papers that consider further properties of the Mathieu groups and their relationship to coding and combinatorics are Assmus and Mattson (1966a, b, 1967b), Berlekamp (1971), Paige (1956), Garbe and Mennicke (1964), Coxeter (1958), Hall (1962), Stanton (1951), and Todd (1959, 1966) as well as the fundamental work of Witt (1938a, b).

TABLE C-1

$$M_{11}: z = (-1 \pm i\sqrt{11})/2$$

1^{11}	2^4	4^2	3^3	5^2	8·2	8·2	6.3.2	11	11
g	48	8	18	5	8	8	6	11	11
1	1	1	1	1	1	1	1	1	1
10	2	2	1	0	0	0	−1	−1	−1
11	3	−1	2	1	−1	−1	0	0	0
55	−1	−1	1	0	1	1	−1	0	0
45	−3	1	0	0	−1	−1	0	1	1
44	4	0	−1	−1	0	0	1	0	0
16	0	0	−2	1	0	0	0	z	$\bar{z}$
10	−2	0	1	0	$i\sqrt{2}$	$-i\sqrt{2}$	1	−1	−1
16	0	0	−2	1	0	0	0	$\bar{z}$	z
10	−2	0	1	0	$-i\sqrt{2}$	$i\sqrt{2}$	1	−1	−1

TABLE C-2

$M_{12}: z = (-1 \pm i\sqrt{11})/2$

1^{12}	2^4	4^2	3^3	5^2	$2\cdot 8$	$2\cdot 3\cdot 6$	11	11	2^6	$2\cdot 10$	$2^3 4^2$	3^4	6^2	$4\cdot 8$
g	192	32	54	10	8	6	11	11	240	10	32	36	12	8
1	1	1	1	1	1	1	1	1	1	1	1	1	1	1
11	3	3	2	1	1	0	0	0	−1	−1	−1	−1	−1	−1
11	3	−1	2	1	−1	0	0	0	−1	−1	3	−1	−1	−1
55	−1	3	−1	0	−1	−1	0	0	−5	0	−1	−1	−1	−1
55	−1	−1	1	0	−1	−1	0	0	−5	0	3	−1	−1	−1
55	7	−1	−1	0	1	1	0	0	−5	0	−1	−1	−1	−1
54	6	2	0	−1	0	0	−1	−1	6	1	2	0	0	0
66	2	−2	3	−1	−1	−1	0	0	6	−1	−2	3	0	−1
45	−3	1	0	0	1	0	1	1	5	0	1	3	1	−1
99	3	−1	0	0	−1	0	0	0	−1	1	−1	0	−1	1
120	−8	0	3	1	0	1	−1	−1	0	−1	0	0	0	0
144	0	0	0	−1	0	0	1	1	4	1	0	−3	1	0
176	0	0	−4	1	0	0	0	0	−4	1	0	−1	−1	0
16	0	0	−2	1	0	0	z	$\bar z$	4	−1	0	1	1	0
16	0	0	−2	1	0	0	$\bar z$	z	4	−1	0	1	1	0

The Mathieu Groups

TABLE C-3

M_{22}: $z_1 = (-1 \pm i\sqrt{7})/2$, $z_2 = (-1 \pm i\sqrt{11})/2$

	1^{22}	2^8	3^6	5^4	$4^4 2^2$	$4^4 2^2$	7^3	7^3	$8^2 \cdot 4 \cdot 2$	$6^2 \cdot 3^2 \cdot 2^2$	11^2	11^2
g	1	384	36	5	16	32	7	7	8	12	11	11
1	1	1	1	1	1	1	1	1	1	1	1	1
21	21	5	3	1	1	1	0	0	-1	-1	-1	-1
55	55	7	1	0	-1	3	-1	-1	-1	1	0	0
154	154	10	1	0	2	-2	0	0	0	1	0	0
210	210	2	3	0	-2	-2	0	0	0	-1	0	0
280	280	-8	1	0	0	0	0	0	0	1	-1	-1
231	231	7	-3	1	-1	-1	0	0	-1	-1	z_2	$\bar{z}_2$
385	385	1	-2	0	-1	1	0	0	1	-2	0	0
99	99	3	0	-1	-1	3	1	1	-1	0	0	0
45	45	-3	0	0	1	1	$\bar{z}_1$	z_1	-1	0	1	1
280	280	-8	1	0	0	0	0	0	0	1	$\bar{z}_2$	z_2
45	45	-3	0	0	1	1	z_1	$\bar{z}_1$	-1	0	1	1

TABLE C-4

M_{23}: $\alpha = \frac{1}{2}(-1 + i\sqrt{7})$, $\beta = \frac{1}{2}(-1 + i\sqrt{15})$, $\gamma = \frac{1}{2}(-1 + i\sqrt{23})$, $\delta = \frac{1}{2}(-1 + i\sqrt{11})$

1^{24}	1^82^8	1^63^6	1^45^4	$1^44^24^4$	1^37^3	1^37^3	1^28^242	$1^26^23^22^2$	1^211^2	1^211^2	$1 \cdot 15 \cdot 53$	$1 \cdot 15 \cdot 53$	$1 \cdot 14 \cdot 72$	$1 \cdot 14 \cdot 72$	$1 \cdot 23$	$1 \cdot 23$
g	2688	180	15	32	14	14	8	12	11	11	15	15	14	14	23	23
1	1	1	1	1	1	1	1	1	1	1	1	1	1	1	1	1
22	6	4	2	2	1	1	0	0	0	0	−1	−1	−1	−1	−1	−1
45	−3	0	0	1	α	$\bar{\alpha}$	−1	0	1	1	0	0	$-\bar{\alpha}$	$-\alpha$	1	1
45	−3	0	0	1	$\bar{\alpha}$	α	−1	0	1	1	0	0	$-\alpha$	$-\bar{\alpha}$	1	1
230	22	5	0	−2	−1	−1	0	−1	−1	−1	0	0	0	0	0	0
231	7	6	1	−1	0	0	−1	−2	0	0	$-\beta$	$-\bar{\beta}$	0	0	−1	−1
231	7	−3	1	−1	0	0	−1	1	0	0	$\bar{\beta}$	β	0	0	−1	−1
231	7	−3	−1	−1	0	0	−1	1	0	0	β	$\bar{\beta}$	0	0	−1	−1
253	13	1	−2	1	−1	−1	0	1	0	0	0	0	−1	−1	0	0
770	−14	5	0	−2	0	0	0	−1	0	0	0	0	0	0	$\bar{\gamma}$	γ
770	−14	5	0	−2	0	0	0	−1	0	0	0	0	0	0	γ	$\bar{\gamma}$
896	0	−4	−1	0	0	0	0	0	δ	$\bar{\delta}$	−1	−1	0	0	−1	−1
896	0	−4	1	0	0	0	0	0	$\bar{\delta}$	δ	−1	−1	0	0	−1	−1
990	−18	0	0	2	α	$\bar{\alpha}$	0	0	0	0	0	0	$\bar{\alpha}$	α	0	0
990	−18	0	0	2	$\bar{\alpha}$	α	0	0	0	0	0	0	α	$\bar{\alpha}$	0	0
1035	27	0	0	−1	−1	−1	−1	0	−1	−1	0	0	−1	−1	0	0
2024	8	−1	−1	0	1	1	0	−1	0	0	−1	−1	1	1	0	0

TABLE C-5

M_{24}: $\alpha = \frac{1}{2}(-1 + \pm i\sqrt{7})$, $\beta = \frac{1}{2}(-1 + i\sqrt{15})$, $\gamma = \frac{1}{2}(-1 + i\sqrt{23})$

1^{24}	$1^8 2^8$	$1^6 3^6$	$1^4 5^4$	$1^4 4^4 2^2$	$1^3 7^3$	$1^3 7^3$	$1^2 8^2 4^2$	$1^2 6^2 3^2 2^2$	$1^2 11^2$	$1 \cdot 15 \cdot 53$	$1 \cdot 15 \cdot 53$
g	21504	1080	60	128	42	42	16	24	11	15	15
1	1	1	1	1	1	1	1	1	1	1	1
23	7	5	3	3	2	2	1	1	1	0	0
45	−3	0	0	1	α	$\bar{\alpha}$	−1	0	1	0	0
45	−3	0	0	1	$\bar{\alpha}$	α	−1	0	1	0	0
231	7	−3	1	−1	0	0	−1	1	0	β	$\bar{\beta}$
231	7	−3	1	−1	0	0	−1	1	0	$\bar{\beta}$	β
252	28	9	2	4	0	0	0	1	−1	−1	−1
253	13	10	3	1	1	1	−1	−2	0	0	0
483	35	6	−2	3	0	0	−1	2	−1	1	1
770	−14	5	0	−2	0	0	0	1	0	0	0
770	−14	5	0	−2	0	0	0	1	0	0	0
990	−18	0	0	2	α	$\bar{\alpha}$	0	0	0	0	0
990	−18	0	0	2	$\bar{\alpha}$	α	0	0	0	0	0
1035	−21	0	0	3	2α	$2\bar{\alpha}$	−1	0	1	0	0
1035	−21	0	0	3	$2\bar{\alpha}$	2α	−1	0	1	0	0
1035	27	0	0	−1	−1	−1	1	0	1	0	0
1265	49	5	0	1	−2	−2	1	1	0	0	0
1771	−21	16	1	−5	0	0	−1	0	0	1	1
2024	8	−1	−1	0	1	1	0	−1	0	−1	−1
2277	21	0	−3	1	2	2	−1	0	0	0	0
3312	48	0	−3	0	1	1	0	0	1	0	0
3520	64	10	0	0	−1	−1	0	−2	0	0	0
5313	49	−15	3	−3	0	0	−1	1	0	0	0
5544	−56	9	−1	0	0	0	0	1	0	−1	−1
5796	−28	−9	1	4	0	0	0	−1	−1	1	1
10395	−21	0	0	−1	0	0	1	0	0	0	0

TABLE C-5—continued

1^{24}	$1 \cdot 14 \cdot 72$	$1 \cdot 14 \cdot 72$	$1 \cdot 23$	$1 \cdot 23$	12^2	6^4	4^6	3^8	2^{12}	$10^2 2^2$	$21 \cdot 3$	$21 \cdot 3$	$4^4 2^4$	$12 \cdot 6 \cdot 42$
g	14	14	23	23	12	24	96	504	7680	20	21	21	384	12
1	1	1	1	1	1	1	1	1	1	1	1	1	1	1
23	0	0	0	0	−1	−1	−1	−1	−1	−1	−1	−1	−1	−1
45	−α	−ᾱ	−1	−1	1	−1	1	3	5	0	ᾱ	α	−3	0
45	−ᾱ	−α	−1	−1	1	−1	1	3	5	0	α	ᾱ	−3	0
231	0	0	1	1	0	0	3	0	−9	1	0	0	−1	−1
231	0	0	1	1	0	0	3	0	−9	1	0	0	−1	−1
252	0	0	−1	−1	0	0	0	0	12	2	0	0	4	1
253	−1	−1	0	0	1	1	1	1	−11	−1	1	1	−3	0
483	0	0	0	0	0	0	3	0	3	−2	0	0	3	0
770	0	0	γ	γ̄	1	1	−2	−7	10	0	0	0	2	−1
770	0	0	γ̄	γ	1	1	−2	−7	10	0	0	0	2	−1
990	α	ᾱ	1	1	1	−1	−2	3	−10	0	ᾱ	α	6	0
990	ᾱ	α	1	1	1	−1	−2	3	−10	0	α	ᾱ	6	0
1035	0	0	0	0	−1	1	−1	−3	−5	0	−ᾱ	−α	3	0
1035	0	0	0	0	−1	1	−1	−3	−5	0	−α	−ᾱ	3	0
1035	−1	−1	0	0	0	2	3	6	35	0	−1	−1	3	0
1265	0	0	0	0	0	0	−3	8	−15	0	1	1	−7	−1
1771	0	0	0	0	−1	−1	−1	7	11	1	0	0	3	0
2024	1	1	0	0	0	0	0	8	24	−1	1	1	8	−1
2277	0	0	0	0	0	2	−3	6	−19	1	−1	−1	−3	0
3312	−1	−1	0	0	0	−2	0	−6	16	1	1	1	0	0
3520	1	1	1	1	0	0	0	−8	0	0	−1	−1	0	0
5313	0	0	0	0	0	0	−3	0	9	−1	0	0	1	1
5544	0	0	1	1	0	0	0	0	24	−1	0	0	−8	1
5796	0	0	0	0	0	0	0	0	36	1	0	0	−4	−1
10395	0	0	−1	−1	0	0	3	0	−45	0	0	0	3	0

References

Alanen, J. D., and Knuth, D. E. (1964). Tables of finite fields. *Sankhyā Ser. A* **26**, 305–328.
Albert, A. (1956). "Fundamental Concepts of Higher Algebra." Univ. of Chicago Press, Chicago, Illinois.
Alltop, W. O. (1969). An infinite class of 4-designs. *J. Combinatorial Theory* **6**, 320–322.
Alltop, W. O. (1971). Some 3-designs and a 4-design. *J. Combinatorial Theory Ser. A* **11**, 190–195.
Alltop, W. O. (1972). An infinite class of 5-designs. *J. Combinatorial Theory Ser. A* **12**, 390–395.
Anderson, D. R. (1968). A new class of cyclic codes. *SIAM J. Appl. Math.* **61**, 181–197.
Artin, E. (1957). "Geometric Algebra." Wiley (Interscience), New York.
Artin, E. (1959). "Galois Theory." Univ. of Notre Dame Press, Notre Dame, Indiana.
Assmus, E. F., Jr., and Mattson, H. F., Jr., (1966a). Perfect codes and the Mathieu groups. *Arch. Math. (Basel)* **17**, 121–135.
Assmus, E. F., Jr., and Mattson, H. F., Jr. (1966b). Disjoint Steiner systems associated with the Mathieu groups. *Bull. Amer. Math. Soc.* **72**, 843–845.
Assmus, E. F., Jr., and Mattson, H. F., Jr. (1966c). On the number of inequivalent Steiner triple systems. *J. Combinatorial Theory* **1**, 301–305.
Assmus, E. F., Jr., and Mattson, H. F., Jr. (1966d). Cyclic codes. Final Rep., AFCRL-66-348. Air Force Cambridge Res. Lab. April 28, Cambridge, Massachusetts.
Assmus, E. F., Jr., and Mattson, H. F., Jr. (1967a). On tactical configurations and error-correcting codes. *J. Combinatorial Theory* **2**, 243–257.
Assmus, E. F., Jr., and Mattson, H. F., Jr., (1967b). On the automorphism groups of Paley-Hadamard matrices. *Proc. Conf. Combinatorial Math. Its Appl. Univ. of North Carolina, April*, 1967, pp. 98–103, Univ. of North Carolina Press, Chapel Hill, North Carolina.
Assmus, E. F., Jr., and Mattson, H. F., Jr. (1969). New 5-designs. *J. Combinatorial Theory* **6**, 122–151.
Assmus, E. F., Jr., and Mattson, H. F., Jr. (1970). Algebraic theory of codes II Final Rep AFCRL-71-0013. Air Force Cambridge Res. Lab. October 15, Cambridge, Massachusetts.

Assmus, E. F., Jr., and Mattson, H. F., Jr. (1972a). Contractions of self-orthogonal codes. *Discrete Math.* **3**, 21–32.

Assmus, E. F., Jr., and Mattson, H. F., Jr. (1972b). On weights in quadratic-residue codes. *Discrete Math.* **3**, 1–20.

Berlekamp, E. R. (1965). Distribution of cyclic matrices in a finite field. *Duke Math. J.* **33**, 45–48.

Berlekamp, E. R. (1968). "Algebraic Coding Theory." McGraw-Hill, New York.

Berlekamp, E. R. (1971). Coding theory and the Mathieu groups. *Information and Control* **17**, 40–64.

Berlekamp, E. R., MacWilliams, F. J., and Sloane, N. J. A. (1972). Gleason's theorem on self-dual codes. *IEEE Trans. Information Theory*, **IT-18**, 409–414.

Biggs, N. (1971) "Finite Groups of Automorphisms." Cambridge Univ. Press, Cambridge, London and New York.

Bose, R. C. (1942). A note on the resolvability of balanced incomplete block designs. *Sankhyā* **6**, 105–110.

Bose, R. C. (1961). On some connections between the design of experiments and information theory. *Bull. Inst. Internat. Statist.* **38**, 257–271.

Bose, R. C., and Burton, R. C. (1966). A characterization of flat spaces in a finite geometry and the uniqueness of the Hamming and the MacDonald codes. *J. Combinatorial Theory* **1**, 96–104.

Bose, R. C., and Bush, K. A. (1952). Orthogonal arrays of strength two and three. *Ann. Math. Statist.* **23**, 508–524.

Bose, R. C., and Ray-Chaudhuri, D. K. (1960a). On a class of error correcting binary group codes. *Information and Control* **3**, 68–79.

Bose, R. C., and Ray-Chaudhuri, D. K. (1960b). Further results on error correcting binary group codes. *Information and Control* **3**, 279–290.

Bose, R. C., and Shrikhande, S. S. (1959a). On the falsity of Euler's conjecture about the non-existence of two orthogonal Latin squares of order $4t + 2$. *Proc. Nat. Acad. Sci. U.S.A:* **45**, 734–737.

Bose, R. C., and Shrikhande, S. S. (1959b). A note on a result in the theory of code construction. *Information and Control* **2**, 183–194.

Bose, R. C., Shrikhande, S. S., and Parker, E. T. (1960). Further results on the construction of mutually orthogonal Latin squares and the falsity of Euler's conjecture. *Canad. J. Math.* **12**, 189–203.

Burgoyne, N., and Fong, P. (1966). The Schur multipliers of the Mathieu groups. *Nagoya Math. J.* **27**, 733–745.

Carmichael, R. D. (1956). "Introduction to the Theory of Groups of Finite Order." Dover, New York.

Chen, C. L. (1971). On majority-logic decoding of finite geometry codes. *IEEE Trans. Information Theory* **IT-17**, 332–336.

Chen, C. L. (1972). Note on majority logic decoding of finite geometry codes. *IEEE Trans. Information Theory* **IT-18**, 539–541.

Chen, C. L., and Lin, S. (1969). Further results on polynomial codes. *Information and Control* **15**, 38–60.

Chen, C. L., Peterson, W. W., and Weldon, E. J., Jr. (1969). Some results on quasi-cyclic codes. *Information and Control* **15**, 407–423.

Conway, J. H. (1968a). Tabulation of some information concerning finite fields. In "Computers in Mathematical Research" (R. F. Churchhouse and J. C. Hertz, eds.). North-Holland Publ. Amsterdam.

Conway, J. H. (1968b). A perfect group of order 8,315,553,613,086,720,000 and the sporadic

simple groups. *Proc. Nat. Acad. Sci. U.S.A.* **61**, 398–400.
Conway, J. H. (1969). A group of order 8,315,533,613,086,720,000. *Bull. London Math. Soc.* **1**, 79–88.
Cooper, A. B., and Gore, W. C. (1970). A result concerning the dual of polynomial codes. *IEEE Trans. Information Theory* **IT-16**, 638–640.
Coxeter, H. S. M. (1958). Twelve points in PG(5, 3) with 95,040 selftransformations. *Phil. Trans. Roy. Soc. London Ser. A* **247**, 279–293.
Davenport, H. (1968). Bases for finite fields. *J. London Math. Soc.* **43**, 21–39.
Delsarte, P. (1969). A geometric approach to a class of cyclic codes. *J. Combinatorial Theory* **6**, 340–358.
Delsarte, P. (1970a). On cyclic codes that are invariant under the general linear group. *IEEE Trans. Information Theory* **IT-16**, 760–769.
Delsarte, P. (1970b). Automorphisms of Abelian codes. *Phillips Res. Rep.* **25**, 389–403.
Delsarte, P. (1971a). Majority logic decodable codes derived from finite inversive planes. *Information and Control* **18**, 319–325.
Delsarte, P. (1973a). An algebraic approach to the association schemes of coding theory. *Philips Research Repts. Supp.* No. 10.
Delsarte, P. (1973b). Four fundamental parameters of a code and their combinatorial significance. *Information and Control* **23**, 407–438.
Delsarte, P. Goethals, J. M., and MacWilliams, F. J. (1970). On generalized Reed-Muller codes and their relatives. *Information and Control* **16**, 403–442.
Dembowski, P. (1968). "Finite Geometries." Springer-Verlag, New York and Berlin.
Deza, M. (1973). Une propriete extremale des plans projectifs finis dans une classe de codes equidistants. *Discrete Math.* **6**, 343–352.
Dickson, L. E. (1958). "Linear Groups with an Exposition of the Galois Field Theory." Dover, New York.
Forney, G. D., Jr. (1966). "Concatenated Codes." MIT Press, Cambridge, Massachusetts.
Garbe, D., and Mennicke, J. L. (1964). Some remarks on the Mathieu groups. *Canad. Math. Bull.* **7**, 201–212.
Gilbert, E. N., (1952). A comparison of signaling alphabets. *Bell System Tech. J.* **31**, 504–522.
Gleason, A. M. (1971). Weight polynomials of self dual codes and the MacWilliams identities. *Act. Congr. Int. Math.* **3**, 211–215.
Goethals, J. M. (1969). A polynomial approach to linear codes. *Philips Research Repts.* **24**, 145–159.
Goethals, J. M. (1971). On the Golay perfect binary code. *J. Combinatorial Theory Ser. A* **11**, 178–186.
Goethals, J. M., and Delsarte, P. (1968). On a class of majority logic decodable cyclic codes. *IEEE Trans. Information Theory* **IT-14**, 182–188.
Goethals, J. M., and Snover, S. L. (1972). Nearly perfect binary codes. *Discrete Math.* **3**, 65–88.
Golay, M. J. E. (1949). Notes on digital coding. *Proc. IRE* **37**, 657.
Golay, M. J. E. (1958). Notes on the penny-weighing problem, lossless symbol coding with nonprimes, etc. *IRE Trans. Information Theory* **IT-4**, 103–109.
Goldman, J., and Rota, G. C. (1969). The number of subspaces of a vector space. In "Recent Progress in Combinatorics" (W. Tutte, ed.). Academic Press, New York.
Golomb, S. W., and Posner, E. C. (1964). Rook domains, Latin squares, affine planes and error-distributing codes. *IEEE Trans. Information Theory* **IT-10**, 196–208.
Goppa, V. D. (1971). Rational presentation of codes and (L, g) codes. *Probl. Peredachi Informatsii* **7**, 41–49.

Gore, W. C., and Cooper, A. B. (1970). Comments on polynomial codes. *IEEE Trans. Information Theory* **IT-16**, 635–638.

Gorenstein, D., and Zierler, N. (1961). A class of error correcting codes in p^m symbols. *SIAM J. Appl. Math* **9**, 207–214.

Graham, R. L., and MacWilliams, J. (1966). On the number of information symbols in difference-set cyclic codes. *Bell System Tech. J.* **45**, 1057–1070.

Griesmer, J. H. (1960). A bound for error-correcting codes. *IBM J. Res. Develop.* **4**, 532–542.

Hall, M. (1959). "The Theory of Groups." Macmillan, New York.

Hall, M. (1962). Note on the Mathieu group M_{12}. *Arch. Math. (Basel)* **13**, 334–340.

Hall, M. (1964). Block designs. In "Applied Combinatorial Mathematics" (E. F. Beckenbach, ed.) Chapter 13. Wiley, New York.

Hall, M. (1967a). "Combinatorial Theory." Ginn (Blaisdell), Boston, Massachusetts.

Hall, M. (1967b). Group theory and block designs. *Proc. Internat. Conf. Theory of Groups, Canberra, Australia, 1965*. Gordon & Breach, New York.

Hamada, N. (1968). The rank of the incidence matrix of points and d-flats in finite geometries *J. Sci. Hiroshima Univ. Ser. A*-1 **32**, 381–396.

Hamming, R. W. (1950). Error detecting and error correcting codes. *Bell System Tech. J.* **29**, 147–160.

Herstein, I. N. (1964). "Topics in Algebra." Ginn (Blaisdell), Boston, Massachusetts.

Herzog, M., and Schönheim, J. (1971). Linear and nonlinear single-error-correcting perfect mixed codes. *Information and Control* **18**, 364–368.

Higman, D. G., and Sims, C. C. (1968). A simple group of order 44, 353, 000. *Math. Z.* **105**, 110–113.

Hocquenghem, A. (1959). Codes correcteurs d'erreurs. *Chiffres* **2**, 147–156.

Hsiao, M. Y., Bossen, D. C., and Chien, R. T. (1970). Orthogonal Latin square codes. *IBM J. Res. Develop.* **18**, 390–394.

Hughes, D. R. (1965). On t-designs and groups. *Amer. J. Math.* **87**, 761–778.

Ireland, K., and Rosen, M. (1972). "Elements of Number Theory: Including an Introduction to Equations over Finite Fields." Bogden and Quigley, Tarrytown-on-Hudson, New York.

Johnson, S. M. (1962). A new upper bound for error-correcting codes. *IRE Trans. Information Theory* **IT-8**, 203–207.

Kaplansky, I. (1969a). "Linear Algebra and Geometry." Allyn & Bacon, Rockleigh, New Jersey.

Kaplansky, I. (1969b). "Fields and Rings." Univ. of Chicago Press, Chicago, Illinois.

Karlin, M. (1969). New binary coding results by circulants. *IEEE Trans. Information Theory* **IT-15**, 81–92.

Kasami, T., and Lin, S. (1966). Some codes which are invariant under doubly-transitive permutation groups and their connection with balanced incomplete block designs AFCRL-66-142, Sci. Rep. No. 6. Air Force Cambridge Res. Lab., Cambridge, Massachusetts.

Kasami, T., and Lin, S. (1971). On majority-logic decoding for duals of primitive polynomial codes. *IEEE Trans. Information Theory* **IT-17**, 322–331.

Kasami, T., Lin, S., and Peterson, W. (1968a). New generalizations of the Reed-Muller codes. Pt. 1. Primitive codes. *IEEE Trans. Information Theory* **IT-14**, 189–199.

Kasami, T., Lin, S., and Peterson, W. (1968b). Polynomial codes. *IEEE Trans. Information Theory* **IT-14**, 708–814.

Kasami, T., Lin, S., and Peterson, W. (1968c). Some results on cyclic codes which are invariant under the affine group and their applications. *Information and Control* **11**, 475–496.

References

Lang, S. (1971). "Algebra." Addison-Wesley, Reading, Massachusetts.
Lenstra, H. W. Jr. (1972). Two theorems on perfect codes. *Discrete Math.* **3**, 125–132.
Lin, S. (1968). On a class of cyclic codes. *In* "Error Correcting Codes" (H. B. Mann, ed.). Wiley, New York.
Lin, S. (1969). Some codes which are invariant under a transitive permutation group and their connection with balanced incomplete block designs. *In* "Combinatorial Mathematics and Its Applications" (R. C. Bose and T. A. Dowling, eds.), Chapter 24. Univ. of North Carolina Press, Chapel Hill.
Lin, S. (1972a). Shortened finite geometry codes. *IEEE Trans. Information Theory* **IT-18**, 692–696.
Lin, S. (1972b). On the number of information symbols in polynomial codes. *IEEE Trans. Information Theory* **IT-18**, 785–794.
Lindström, B. (1969). On group and nongroup perfect codes in q symbols. *Math. Scand.* **25**, 149–158.
Lloyd, S. P. (1957). Binary block coding. *Bell System Tech. J.* **36**, 517–535.
McEliece, R. J. (1969). Factorization of polynomials over finite fields. *Math. Comp.* **23**, 861–867.
MacWilliams, F. J. (1961). Error correcting codes for multiple level transmission. *Bell System Tech. J.* **40**, 281–308.
MacWilliams, F. J. (1962). A theorem on the distribution of weights in a systematic code. *Bell System Tech. J.*, **42**, 79–94.
MacWilliams, F. J. (1965). The structure and properties of binary cyclic alphabets. *Bell System Tech. J.* **44**, 303–332.
MacWilliams, F. J. (1969). Codes and ideals in group algebras. *In* "Combinatorial Mathematics and its Applications" (R. C. Bose and T. A. Dowling, eds.), Chapter 18. Univ. of North Carolina Press, Chapel Hill.
MacWilliams, F. J. (1970). Binary codes which are ideals in the group algebra of an Abelian group. *Bell System Tech. J.* **44**, 987–1011.
MacWilliams, F. J. (1971). Orthogonal circulant matrices over a finite field and how to find them. *J. Combinatorial Theory Ser. A* **10**, 1–17.
MacWilliams, F. J., and Mann, H. B. (1968). On the p-rank of the design matrix of a difference set, *Information and Control* **12**, 474–488.
MacWilliams, F. J., Mallows, C. J., and Sloane, N. J. A. (1972a). Generalizations of Gleason's theorem on weight enumerators of self-dual codes. *IEEE Trans. Information Theory* **IT-18**, 794–805.
MacWilliams, F. J., Sloane, N. J. A., and Thompson, J. G. (1972b). Good self dual codes exist. *Discrete Math.* **3**, 153–162.
MacWilliams, F. J., Sloane, N. J. A., and Goethals, J. M. (1972c). The MacWilliams identities for nonlinear codes. *Bell System Tech. J.* **51**, 803–819.
MacWilliams, F. J., Sloane, N. J. A. and Thompson, J. G. (1973), On the existence of a projective plane of order 10. *J. Combinatorial Theory Ser. A* **14**, 66–78 (1973).
Mallows, C. L., and Sloane, N. J. A. (1973). An upper bound for self-dual codes. *Information and Control* **22**, 188–200.
Mann, H. B. (1949). "Analysis and Design of Experiments." Dover, New York.
Massey, J. L. (1963). "Threshold Decoding." MIT Press, Cambridge, Massachusetts.
Mattson, H. F., and Solomon, G. (1961). A new treatment of Bose-Chaudhuri codes. *SIAM J. Appl. Math.* **9**, 654–669.
Mills, W. H., and Zierler, N. (1969). On a conjecture of Golomb. *Pacific J. Math.* **28**, 635–640.
Muller, D. E. (1954). Application of Boolean algebra to switching circuit design and to error detection. *IRE Trans. Elect. Comp.* **EC-3**, 6–12.

Paige, L. J. (1956). A note on the Mathieu groups. *Canad. J. Math* **9**, 15–18.
Passman, D. S. (1968). "Permutation Groups." Benjamin, New York.
Peterson, W. W. (1961). "Error Correcting Codes." MIT Press, Cambridge Massachusetts.
Peterson, W. W., and Weldon, E. J., Jr. (1972). "Error Correcting Codes," 2nd ed. MIT Press, Cambridge, Massachusetts.
Plackett, S. R. L., and Burman, J. P. (1946). The design of optimum multifactorial experiments. *Biometrika* **33**, 305–325.
Pless, V. (1963). Power moment identities on weight distributions in error correcting codes. *Information and Control* **6**, 147–152.
Pless, V. (1965). The number or isotropic subspaces in a finite geometry. *Acad. Naz. Lincei* [8], **34**, 418–421.
Pless, V. (1968). On the uniqueness of the Golay codes. *J. Combinatorial Theory* **5**, 215–228.
Pless, V. (1969). On a new family of symmetry codes and related new five designs. *Bull. Amer. Math. Soc.* **75**, 1339–1342.
Pless, V. (1970). The weight of the symmetry code for $p = 29$ and the 5-designs contained therein. *Ann. N.Y. Acad. Sci.* **175**, 310–313.
Pless, V. (1972a). Symmetry codes over GF(3) and new five-designs. *J. Combinatorial Theory Ser A* **12**, 119–142.
Pless, V. (1972b). A classification of self-orthogonal codes over GF(2). *Discrete Math.* **3**, 209–246.
Pless, V., and Pierce, J. N. (1973). Self-dual codes over over GF(q) satisfy a modified Varshamov-Gilbert bound. *Information and Control* **23**, 35–40.
Plotkin, M. (1960). Binary codes with specified minimum distance. *IRE Trans. Information Theory* **IT-6**, 445–450.
Reed, I. S. (1954). A class of multiple-error-correcting codes and the decoding scheme. *IRE Trans. Information Theory* **IT-4**, 38–49.
Reed, I. S., and Solomon, G. (1960). Polynomial codes over certain finite fields. *SIAM J. Appl. Math.* **8**, 300–304.
Riordan, J. (1958). "An Introduction to Combinatorial Analysis." Wiley, New York.
Riordan, J. (1968). "Combinatorial Identities." Wiley, New York.
Rudolph, L. (1964). Geometric configuration and majority logic decodable codes. M.E.E. Thesis, Univ. of Oklahoma, Norman.
Rudolph, L. (1967). A class of majority logic decodable codes. *IEEE Trans. Information Theory* **13**, 305–307.
Ryser, H. J. (1963). "Combinatorial Mathematics." Math. Assoc. of Amer., distributed by Wiley, New York.
Schönheim, J. (1968). On linear and nonlinear single-error-correcting q-nary perfect codes. *Information and Control* **12**, 23–26.
Schönheim, J. (1969). Semilinear codes and some combinatorial applications of them. *Information and Control* **15**, 61–66.
Semakov, N. V., and Zinov'ev, V. A. (1968). Equidistant q-ary codes with maximal distance and resolvable balanced incomplete block designs. *Problems of Information Transmission* **4**, 1–7.
Semakov, N. V., and Zinov'ev, V. A. (1969a). Complete and quasi-complete balanced codes. *Problems of Information Transmission* **5**, 11–13.
Semakov, N. V., and Zinov'ev, V. A. (1969b). Balanced codes and tactical configurations. *Problems of Information Transmission* **5**, 22–28.
Semakov, N. V., Zinov'ev, V. A., and Zaitsev, G. V. (1969). A class of maximum equidistant codes. *Problems of Information Transmission* **5**, 65–68.

References

Semakov, N. V., Zinov'ev, V. A., and Zaitsev, G. V. (1971) Uniformly packed codes. *Problems of Information Transmission* **7**, 30–39.
Shrikhande, S. S. (1953). The nonexistence of certain affine resolvable balanced incomplete block designs. *Canad. J. Math.* **5**, 413–420.
Shrikhande, S. S. (1964). Generalized Hadamard matrices and orthogonal arrays of strength two *Canad. J. Math.* **16**, 736–740.
Singer, J. (1938). A theorem in finite projective geometry and some applications to number theory. *Trans. Amer. Math. Soc.* **43**, 377–385.
Singleton, R. C. (1964). Maximum distance Q-nary codes. *IEEE Trans. Information Theory* **IT-10**, 116–118.
Slepian, D. (1956). A class of binary signalling alphabets. *Bell System Tech. J.* **35**, 203–234.
Slepian, D. (1960). Some further theory of group codes .*Bell System Tech. J.* **39**, 1219–1252.
Sloane, N. J. A. (1972). A survey of constructive coding theory and a table of binary codes of highest known rate. *Discrete Math.* **3**, 265–294.
Sloane, N. J. A., and Whitehead, D. S. (1970). New family of single error correcting codes, *IEEE Trans. Information Theory* **IT-16**, 717–719.
Smith, K. J. C. (1969). On the p-rank of the incidence matrix of points and hyperplanes in a finite projective geometry. *J. Combinatorial Theory* **7**, 122–129.
Stanton, R. G. (1951). The Mathieu groups. *Canad. J. Math.* **3**, 164–174.
Stiffler, J J. (1971). "Theory of Synchronous Communications." Prentice-Hall, Englewood Cliffs, New Jersey.
Swan, R. G. (1962). Factorization of polynomials over finite fields. *Pacific J. Math.* **12**, 1099–1106.
Tarry, G. (1900). Le Problème de 36 Officiers. *C. R. Acad. Sci. Paris.* **1**, 122–123.
Tarry, G. (1901). Le Problème de 36 Officiers. *C. R. Acad. Sci. Paris* **2**, 170–203.
Tavares, S., Bhargava, V. K., and Shiva, S. G. S. (1974). Some rate-$P/(P+1)$ quasi-cyclic codes. *IEEE Trans. Information Theory* **IT-20**, 133–135.
Tietäväinen, A. (1973). On the nonexistence of perfect codes over finite fields. *SIAM J. Appl. Math.* **24**, 88–96.
Tietäväinen, A., and Perko, A. (1971). There are no unknown perfect binary codes. *Ann. Univ. Turku., Ser. A* **148**, 3–10.
Todd, J. A. (1959). On representations of the Mathieu groups as collineation groups. *J. London Math. Soc.* **34**, 406–416.
Todd, J. A. (1966). A representation of the Mathieu group M_{24} as a collineation group. *Ann. Mat. Pura Appl. (IV)* **71**, 199–238.
Townsend, R. L., and Weldon, E. J., Jr. (1967). Self-orthogonal quasi-cyclic codes. *IEEE Trans. Information Theory* **IT-13**, 183–195.
Tutte, W. T. (1965). Lectures on matroids. *J. Res. Nat. Bur. Standards Sec B* **69**, 1–47.
Tutte, W. T. (1966). "Connectivity in Graphs." Univ. of Toronto Press, Toronto.
Tutte, W. T. (1971). "Introduction to the Theory of Matroids." Amer. Elsevier, New York.
van der Waerden, B. L. (1953). "Modern Algebra," Vol. 1. Ungar New York.
van der Waerden, B. L. (1970). "Algebra," Vol. 2. Ungar, New York.
Van Lint, J. H. (1971), "Coding Theory," Lecture Notes in Math., Vol. 201. Springer-Verlag, Berlin and New York.
Van Lint, J. H. (1973). A theorem on equidistant codes. *Discrete Math.* **6**, 353–358.
Vanstone, S. A. (1974). The structure of regular pairwise balanced designs. Ph.D. Thesis, Univ. of Waterloo, Ontario, Canada.
Varshamov, R. R. (1957). Estimate of the number of signals in error correcting codes. *Dokl. Akad. Nauk. SSR* **117**, 739 741.
Vasil'ev, Y. L. (1962). On non-group close-packed codes. *Prob. Cybernet.* **8**, 337–339.

Veblen, O., and Bussey, W. H. (1906). Finite projective geometries. *Trans. Amer. Math. Soc.* **7**, 241–259.

Wallis, W. D., Street, A. P., and Wallis, J. S. (1972). "Combinatorics: Room Squares, Sum-Free Sets, Hadamard Matrices," Lecture Notes in Mathematics Vol. 292. Springer-Verlag, Berlin and New York.

Weldon, E. J., Jr. (1966). Difference-set cyclic codes. *Bell System Tech. J.* **45**, 1045–1055.

Weldon, E. J., Jr.(1968). New generalizations of the Reed–Muller codes. Pt. II. Nonprimitive codes. *IEEE Trans. Information Theory* **IT-14**, 199–205.

Weldon, E. J., Jr. (1969). Euclidean geometry cyclic codes. *In* "Combinatorial Mathematics and its Applications" (R. C. Bose and T. A. Dowing, Univ. eds.), Chapter 23. Univ. of North Carolina Press, Chapel Hill.

Whitelaw, T. A. (1966). On the Mathieu group of degree twelve. *Proc. Cambridge Philos. Soc.* **62**, 351–364.

Witt, E. (1938a). Die 5-fach Transitiven Gruppen von Mathieu. *Abh. Math. Sem. Univ. Hamburg* **12**, 256–264.

Witt. E. (1938b). Über Steinersche Systeme. *Abh. Math. Sem. Univ. Hamburg* **12**, 265–275.

Zaremba, S. K. (1950). A covering theorem for Abelian groups. *J. London Math. Soc.* **26**, 71–72.

Zaremba, S. K. (1952). Covering problems concerning Abelian groups. *J. London Math. Soc.* **27**, 242–246.

Zierler, N. (1970). On $x^n + x + 1$ over $GF(2)$. *Information and Control* **16**, 502–505.

Zierler, N., and Brillhart, J. (1968). On primitive trinomials (Mod 2), *Information and Control* **13**, 541–554.

Index

A

Affine group, 62, 75, 93
Affine resolvable balanced incomplete block design, 125–132, 202
 and equidistant codes, 130–132
 parameters of, 202
Affine transformations, 60
Alanen, J. D., 89
Albert, A. A., 37, 40, 89, 90
Algebraic closure, 4
Anderson, D. R., 57–58
Artin, E., 89
Assmus, E. F., Jr., 44, 56, 144, 155, 160, 165, 180, 181, 183, 184, 185, 208

B

Balanced codes, 148
 and equidistant codes, 192–193
 and t-designs, 189–192
Balanced incomplete block designs, 119–132
 affine resolvable, 125–132, 202
 affine α-resolvable, 202
 and codes, 129–132
 complement of, 122
 derived, 123
 and finite geometries, 123
 incidence matrix, 121
 residual, 123
 resolvable, 125–132
 α-resolvable, 202
 symmetric, 121–122
BCH codes, 50–52
 design distance of, 51
 and Goppa codes, 52–53
 invariance under affine group, 65
 parity check matrix, 51
 and polynomial codes, 82
Berlekamp, E. R., 37, 38, 52, 89, 90, 109, 142, 143, 159, 169, 206, 208
Bilinear form, 10–12
Binary repetition codes, 55, 161
Binomial coefficient identities, 59
Binomial coefficients, Lucas's theorem on, 64
Bose, R. C., 50, 117, 125, 127, 128, 129, 136, 167, 193
Bounds on code dictionaries, 83–89
Brillhart, J., 38, 91
Bruck-Ryser theorem, 99
Burgoyne, N., 208
Burton, R.C., 117
Bush, K. A., 127, 128, 129, 167
Busscy, W. H., 96, 98

C

Carmichael, R. D., 89, 106, 166
Chain, 175–178
　domain of, 175
　primitive, 201
Chain group, 175
　contraction, 178
　dendroid, 176
　dendroid basis of, 176
　dual, 178
　reduction, 177
　regular, 201
Character table, *see* Group character table
Chen, C. L., 82, 83, 117, 156, 157
Circulant matrix, 147, 149
　algebra of, 157–158
Codeword polynomial, 41
Collineation group, 105–106
　and finite geometries, 104–106
Complement of balanced incomplete block design, 122
Conjugate roots, 4
Conway, J.H., 89, 161
Coset leaders, 20
Coxeter, H. S. M., 208
Cycle space of a graph, 179–180
Cyclic codes, 40–58
　equivalence of, 45
　and ideals, 41
Cyclotomic factorization of (x^n-1), 38

D

Delsarte, P., 27, 65, 66, 69, 73, 76, 89, 92, 111, 112, 114, 117
Dembowski, P., 117
Derived balanced incomplete block design, 123
Desargues's theorem, 98–99
Deza, M., 132, 194
Dickson, L. E., 37, 40, 89, 90
Difference sets, 149–152
　and circulant incidence matrices, 149
　Hadamard, 150
　multiplier, 152
　planar, 152
　and quadratic residues, 150–151
Difference set codes, 116, 152
Direct product of codes, *see* Kronecker product of codes

Direct sum of vector spaces, 11
Discriminant, 91
Distance of block code, 17
Dual basis, 13–15
Dual,
　of linear code, 18
　of a vector space, 6

E

Equidistant codes, 130–132, 189, 192–200
　and balanced codes, 192–193
　and affine resolvable balanced incomplete block designs, 130–132
　and projective planes, 194–200
Equivalence of codes, 19
Equivalence of cyclic codes, 45
Euclidean algorithm, 3
Euclidean geometry, 101–104
　flat, 99
Euclidean geometry codes, 112–116
　and majority logic decoding, 113–116
　and polynomial codes, 78–79, 112–116
　and projective geometry codes, 117–118
Euler totient function, 9
Expurgated code, 21
Extended code, 21

F

Factor space, 20
Fano geometry, 97, 106–107, 119, 137, 146, 151
Fermat's theorem, 139
Field, 2–6
　algebraically closed, 4
　perfect, 4
Field automorphism, 5
Field characteristic, 2
Field extension, 2
　algebraic, 4
　degree of, 2
　Galois group of, 5, 10
　normal, 4
　separable, 4
　simple, 4
　transcendental, 4
Field isomorphism, 5
Finite fields, 1–94

computations in, 15
fundamental properties of, 7–10
inclusion relations, 9
polynomials over, 29–40
primitive element of, 9
vector spaces over, 10–15
Finite geometries, 95–118
and balanced incomplete block designs, 123
collineation groups, 104–106
Fishers's inequality, 121–122, 125
Fong, P., 208

G

Galois field, *see* Finite field
Galois group of field extension, 5, 10
Garbe, D., 208
Gaussian coefficients, 59
Gauss's lemma, 141
General linear group, 60, 65, 104
and generalized Reed–Muller codes, 73
General linear nonhomogeneous group, 60, 62, 66
and generalized Reed–Muller codes, 72–73
Generalized Reed–Muller codes, 68–78
and the affine group, 75
and BCH codes, 75–76
and the general linear group, 73
and the general linear nonhomogeneous group, 72–73
generator matrix, 77
generator polynomial of cyclic, 74
nonprimitive, 77–78
and polynomial codes, 82–83
and Reed–Solomon codes, 76
Generator matrix, 18
of cyclic code, 42
Gilbert, E. N., 83
Gilbert bound, *see* Varshamov–Gilbert bound
Gleason, A. M., 159
Goethals, J. M., 54, 112, 117, 186
Golay, M. J. E., 138, 161, 162
Golay code,
characterizations, 165
and quadratic residue code, 143
weight enumerator of extended, 160
Goldman, J., 89
Golomb, S. W., 138
Goppa, V. D., 22

Goppa codes, 23
and BCH codes, 52–53
Gorenstein, D., 50
Graham, R. L., 116, 152
Greatest common divisor, 3
Griesmer, J. H., 94
GRM codes, *see* Generalized Reed–Muller codes
Groups,
affine, 62, 75, 93
collineation, 105–106
general linear, 60, 65, 104
general linear nonhomogeneous, 60, 62, 66
linear fractional, 61, 62
of linear transformations, 60–63
permutation, 62, 207
projective, 104–105
projective general linear, 61
projective special linear, 62
special linear, 61
Group character table, of Mathieu groups, 209–214

H

Hadamard difference set, 150
Hadamard matrices, 86, 144–148
and symmetric balanced incomplete block designs, 145–147
Hall, M., 123, 127, 135, 136, 137, 147, 165, 167, 199, 208
Hamada, N., 112
Hamming, R. W., 46, 85
Hamming codes, 46–50, 161
and maximum length codes, 49–50, 92
weight enumerator, 47–50
Hamming distance, 16
Herstein, I. N., 3, 89
Herzog, M., 164
Higman, D. G., 161
Hocquenghem, A., 50
Hsiao, M. Y., 168

I

Ideals and cyclic codes, 41

J

Johnson, S. M., 86
Johnson bound, 87
  specialized, 187

K

Kaplansky, I., 89, 91
Karlin, M., 156, 157
Kasami, T., 63, 64, 68, 75, 76, 78, 79, 80, 93, 94
Knuth, D. E., 89
Krawtchouk polynomial, 27, 92
Krawtchouk transform, 93
Kronecker product,
  of codes, 22

L

Lagrange interpolation formula, 36
Latin squares, 132–139
  and maximum distance separable codes, 138
  pairwise orthogonal, 133–136, 138
  and projective planes, 136
Lee metric, 16
Legendre symbol, 139
Lenstra, H. W., Jr., 164
Lin S., 82, 83, 113, 117, 167
Lindström, B., 162
Linear block codes, 15–29
Linear fractional group, 61, 62
Linear functional, 6
Linear transformation groups, 60–63
Linear transformations of vector spaces, 58–63
Lloyd, S. P., 164
Lucas's theorem, 64, 206

M

McEliece, R. J., 37
MacWilliams, F. J., 19, 24, 27, 28, 116, 117, 152, 153, 156, 158, 160, 161
MacWilliams identities, 24–27
Majority logic decoding, 107–117
  and Euclidean geometry codes, 113–116
  and projective geometry codes, 111–112
Mallows, C. L., 160
Mann, H. B., 117, 152
Massey, J. L., 108
Mathieu groups, 164–165
  character tables, 209–214
Matrix ring, 216
Matroid, 173–175
  cographic, 173
  dendroid of a, 174
  girth, 173
  graphic, 173
  rank, 174
  reduction, 178
  separator of, 201
  spanning subset of, 175
Matroid belts, 180
Matroid circuit, 173
  weight of, 173
Mattson, H. F., Jr., 44, 56, 66, 93, 142, 144, 155, 160, 165, 180, 181, 183–185, 208
Mattson–Solomon polynomial, 67, 76, 92
Maximum distance separable codes, 54–57
  and latin squares, 138
  and matroids, 180–181
  and Reed–Solomon codes, 56
  weight enumerator, 54–55
Maximum length code, 48–49
  distance of, 49
  and Hamming codes, 49–50, 92
  weight enumerator of, 48–50
Maximum likelihood decoding, 17, 20
Mennicke, J. L., 208
Mills, W. H., 91
Möbius function, 32
Möbius inversion formula, 32, 38, 205
Muller, D. E., 107

N

Nearly perfect codes, 186–189
Newton identities, 37
Norm of field element, 6
Normal basis, 13, 15

O

One-step orthogonalizable code, 108

Index

Optimal code, *see* Maximum distance separable code
Orthogonal arrays, 127–132, 167
 and projective planes, 128, 137
 and transversal systems, 199
Orthogonal latin squares, *see* Pairwise orthogonal latin squares
Orthogonal parity check sum, 108
Orthogonal vectors, 11

P

Paige, L. J., 170, 208
Pairwise orthogonal latin squares, 133–136, 138
 and maximum distance separable codes, 138
 and parity check matrices, 168–169
Pappus configuration, 98
Pappus property, 98, 99
Parity check code, 19
Parity check matrix, 19
 of cyclic code, 43
Parity check sum, 108
 orthogonal, 108
Pascal triangle, 162
Passman, D. S., 207
Perfect codes, 21, 161–165
 binary repetition codes, 55, 161
 Hamming codes, 47, 161
 and t designs, 183–186
 Vasil'ev codes, 162–163, 185
Permutation groups, 62, 207
 code invariance under, 63–66
 k-transitive, 207
 sharply k-transitive, 207
 transitivity of, 62
Peterson, W. W., 21, 52, 89
Pierce, J. N., 160
Planar difference set codes, 116
Pless, V., 24, 27, 153, 155, 160, 161, 165, 168, 183
Pless identities, 27–29
Plotkin, M., 84, 86, 147
Plotkin bound, 49, 84
 and Singleton bound, 53
Polygon matroid, 173
Polynomial
 codeword, 41
 cyclotomic, 38–40
 example of irreducible, 40
 exponent, 32, 39
 over finite field, 29–40
 Galois group of, 6
 irreducible, 2
 Krawtchouk, 27, 92
 minimal, 4, 30
 monic, 2
 number of monic irreducible, 33
 primitive, 32
 reciprocal, 42
 roots of irreducible, 3
Polynomial approach to coding, 66–83
Polynomial codes, 78–83
 and BCH codes, 82
 bound on distance of, 81
 and Euclidean geometry codes, 78–79, 112–116
 and generalized Reed–Muller codes, 82–83
 generator polynomial of, 79–80
 and projective geometry codes, 78–79, 109–111
 and Reed–Solomon codes, 82
Posner, E. C., 138
Prime subfield, 2
Primitive element, 9
Primitive root codes, 57–58
Projective general linear group, 61
Projective geometry, 96–101
 construction of, 97, 101
 Desarguesian, 99
 example of, 106–107
 flats, 99
 non-Desarguesian, 99
Projective geometry codes, 109–112
 and Euclidean geometry codes, 117–118
 and majority logic decoding, 111–112
 and polynomial codes, 78–79, 109–111
Projective group, 104–105
Projective plane, 96, 116
 and equidistant codes, 194–200
 and latin squares, 136
 and orthogonal arrays, 128, 137
Projective special linear group, 62

Q

Quadratic residue codes, 142–144
 and Golay codes, 143
Quadratic equations over a finite field, 90–91

Quadratic reciprocity, law of, 140
Quadratic residues, 139–144
  and difference sets, 150–151
Quasi-cyclic codes, 156–158
Quasi-perfect codes, 21
q-weight of an integer, 70

R

Ray-Chaudhuri, D. K., 50
Reed, I. S., 52, 107
Reed–Muller codes, 107, 116, 166–167
Reed–Solomon codes, 52–53, 76
  and maximum distance separable codes, 56
  and polynomial codes, 82
Residual balanced incomplete block design, 123
Resolvable balanced incomplete block design, 125–132
  and equidistant codes, 130–132
Riordan, J., 72
Rosen, K., 91
Rota, G. C., 89
Rudolph, L., 107, 112
Ryser, H. J., 122, 123, 125, 136, 165

S

Scalar complete code, 181
Schöneim, J., 162, 164
Self-dual code, 152–161
  weight enumeration, 158–161
Semakov, N. V., 130, 132, 148, 189, 190, 191
Shrikhande, S. S., 193, 202
Sims, C. C., 161
Singer, J., 152
Singleton, R. C., 56, 138
Singleton bound, 53,
  and Plotkin bound, 53
Slepian, D., 20
Sloane, N. J. A., 94, 160
Smith, K. J. C., 117, 152
Snover, S. L., 186
Solomon, G., 52, 66, 93, 142
Solvability by radicals, 5
Special linear group, 61
Sphere, 16

Sphere packing bound, 85, 184
Splitting field, 2
Standard array, 20
Stanton, R. G., 208
Steiner system, 136–137, 148, 172
  k th order, 202
  Mathieu, 165, 172, 185
Steiner triple systems, 136–137
Stiffler, J. J., 51
Stirling number of the second kind, 27
Subfield, 2
Subfield subcode, 83, 118
Subgeometry, 106–107
Swan, R. G., 37, 91
Symmetric balanced incomplete block design, 121–122
  and Hadamard matrices, 145–147
  incidence matrix, 123
  and projective geometries, 124
Symmetric function, 36
  elementary, 36
Symmetry codes, 153–156
  and t designs, 155–156
Syndrome, 21
Systematic code, 18

T

Tarry, G., 136, 139
Tavares, S., 157, 158
t Designs, 170–173
  and balanced codes, 189–192
  and nearly perfect codes, 186–189
  and perfect codes, 183–186
  regular, 201
  and symmetry codes, 155–156
Threshold decoding, 108
Tietäväinen, A., 18, 164, 184
Todd, J. A., 208
Townsend, R. L., 156
Trace of an element, 6
Trace function, 13
Transitive permutation group, 62, 207
Transversal system, 127–128
  and orthogonal array, 127, 199
Trinomial, 37, 91
Tutte, W. T., 173, 179

Index

U

Uniformly packed codes, *see* Nearly perfect codes
Unimodular group, *see* Special linear group

V

van der Monde matrix, 34, 51
van der Waerden, B. L., 89
van Lint, J. H., 27, 93, 132, 164, 198
Vanstone, S. A., 200
Varshamov, R. R., 84
Varshamov–Gilbert bound, 84
Vasil'ev, Y. L., 162
Vasil'ev codes, 162–163, 185
Veblen, O., 96, 98
Vector spaces, 10–15
 direct sum of, 11
 dual of, 6
 dual basis of, 13, 14
 linear transformations of, 58–63

W

Wallis, W. D., 147
Weight enumerator, 24–29
 of extended Golay codes, 160
 of Hamming codes, 47–50
 of maximum distance separable codes, 54–55
 of maximum length codes, 48–50
 of self-dual codes, 158–161
Weldon, E. J., Jr., 52, 107, 116, 117, 152, 156
Whitehead, D. S., 94
Whitelaw, T. A., 208
Wilson's theorem, 69, 140
Witt, E., 165, 172, 208

Z

Zaremba, S. K., 170
Zierler, N., 38, 50, 91
Zinov'ev, V. A., 130, 132, 148, 189, 190, 191